BOOKLOVER

BOOKLOVER

A One-Year Journal of
Reading, Reflecting & Remembering

BY
Timothy James Bazzett

TJ Bazzett

To Mark & Donna —
all best,
Tim
—
3/17/2013

RATHOLE BOOKS

BOOKLOVER

©2010 Timothy James Bazzett

Published by Rathole Books
Reed City, Michigan
www.ratholebooks.com

Publisher's Cataloging-in-Publication Data

    Bazzett, Timothy James.

        Booklover : a one-year journal of reading, reflecting & remembering /
        by Timothy James Bazzett. -- 1st ed. -- Reed City, Mich. : Rathole
        Books, c2010.

            p. ; cm.

            ISBN 13: 978-0-9771119-4-7
            Includes bibliography.

            1. Bazzett, Timothy James. 2. Bazzett, Timothy James--Books
        and reading. 3. Michigan--Social conditions--20th century. I. Title.
        II. Title: Book lover.

PS3602.A99 Z464 2010   2010929277
920--dc22   1008

Printed in the United States of America
10 9 8 7 6 5 4 3 2

Cover and interior design by Scott Bazzett
Photography by Benjamin Busch except dog photos by Tim Bazzett
First Edition: August 2010
First Paperback Edition: August 2010

To order additional copies send check or money order made payable to TJ Bazzett to:

TJ Bazzett
330 West Todd Avenue
Reed City, MI 49677

For more information, visit us online at:

www.ratholebooks.com

To my grandchildren –
Taylor & Brooke,
Nicholas & Zachary,
and Adam

ALSO BY TIMOTHY JAMES BAZZETT –

Reed City Boy (2004)

"Beautifully written, with an easy grace, by a guy who obviously knows the craft and has a fine ear for the rhythm of the language. Not a false or insincere or self-serving note anywhere, which is oh so rare in memoirs. The easy and intimate voice of a friend, telling his story, laughing at himself from time to time. That's the writing voice here. And it's just perfect."

~ MOLLY GLOSS
award-winning author of the bestselling novel, *The Hearts of Horses*

Soldier Boy: At Play in the ASA (2005)

"Bazzett's story is anything but dry military history. I was so impressed by the sheer degree of his recall and the graphic quality of his memories as he recreates the experience of army life essentially through the eyes of the boy he was in the 60s. But this is far more than just a story about the US Army. It's simply a helluva good story!"

~ HAROLD SHUKMAN
Emeritus Fellow St. Antony's College, Oxford; author of *War or Revolution* and co-author of *Secret Classrooms*

Pinhead: A Love Story (2006)

"Part *American Graffiti*, part coming-home tale, *Pinhead* is a barrelling road-trip into a long-ago America — not a simpler time, just funnier. Tim Bazzett has done it again — he's told a story of a small town with poignance, yet with bravado and unfailing honesty -- the guy's a hoot!"

~ DOUG STANTON
author of the NY Times bestsellers, *In Harm's Way* and *Horse Soldiers*

Love, War & Polio: The Life and Times of Young Bill Porteous (2007)

"This life story of a remarkable man who lives with honor, courage, and love is also a slice of history, filled with authentic details ... *Love, War & Polio* transported me to the 1940s ... A remarkable re-creation not only of one man's life, but of a simpler time, with its references to ten cent milk shakes and listening to the Hit Parade ... Bill Porteous's letters to Mable shine with youthful optimism and, most of all, love ... A pleasure to read."

~ PEG KEHRET
author of the award-winning memoir, *Small Steps: The Year I Got Polio*

"We should write out our own thoughts in as nearly as possible the language we thought them in, as though in a letter to an intimate friend. We should not disguise them in any way ..."

William Butler Yeats

"When we allow ourselves to be most open to others, I believe that is a moment with God."

Rabbi Albert Lewis

"Outside of a dog, a book is man's best friend. Inside of a dog it's too dark to read."

Groucho Marx

Introduction

I'm having a difficult time trying to figure out just what to say here, how to begin. I was excited about reading the manuscript for my dad's newest book a few months ago. I think I enjoyed *Booklover* more than any of my dad's previous books, probably because this time I have memories of my own that coincide with some of the things he writes about here. I loved *all* of the book. But parts of it had me pulling away and crying for minutes at a time. Reading about my parents' separation in 1992, for example, was very hard for me. *Horribly* hard, as I'm sure it was for my dad to write it. It was so strange, *surreal* even, to read about events that played such a painful and pivotal part in my growing up, only this time it was all from my father's perspective. That time and those events changed who I was in a way that I had never let myself think about until I read about it again here, in my father's words. I read *his* story, and I remembered *my* story, and I cried when I realized how very different our versions were; and I kept reading, and I felt so, so much better. I wanted to thank my dad for writing about that time, thank him for letting me read it, and for making me remember, and *think*, and feel better. An adult perspective, my *own*, makes such a difference.

Like my father, I love books. But I think of myself more as a reader than a writer, so I was thrilled when he asked if I would write an introduction for this book. I've already waited too long to honor this request, but Dad sends home stacks of books for me to read every time I visit, so I will blame him, at least in part, for my procrastination.

My father's love of books has been a positive influence and ongoing motif throughout my life - during my childhood, my adolescence, my young adulthood, and even now, as a parent to my own son. As a little girl, reading was what I did with my dad after dinner every night. I don't remember ever *not* knowing how to read. I guess I was reading fairly early; family lore said I was reading children's books completely by myself by the time I turned three. I can still clearly remember my disappointment during my first week of kindergarten, and coming home every day near tears because they wouldn't let me *read* there. Later I had no patience for our school "readers,"

i

those anthologies with stories that were supposed to appeal to children that I never got over my disdain for. But I took comfort in knowing that I could read whatever I wanted to when I got home.

I made regular trips to the library with my dad pretty much weekly, or maybe bi-weekly, during my early elementary school years. By the summer before third grade I'd read all the Beverly Cleary books two or three times each (I *loved* Ramona Quimby). And I think I may have read Judy Blume's *Superfudge* at least a dozen times.

My childhood best friends (still my adult best friends, actually), Missy and Andrea, were also avid readers, all three of us bright and precocious, probably to the point of being quite annoying at times. When Missy moved about an hour away when I was in the second grade, my parents would let me go visit her for weekends now and then. I still can remember being in fourth grade, spending a whole weekend holed up in her massive bedroom in Burkittsville, each of us with a stack of young adult paperbacks (mine *Sweet Valley High*, hers *The New Adventures of Nancy Drew*), reading an entire book in about two hours, and making stacks for each other. I believe "You'll love it" and "Nah" were the categories we wrote on the post-it notes. And at the end of the weekend when I had to go home, we traded those piles of books. I had more fun on that weekend than I did on the one when her mom took us to Busch Gardens. I also remember being in fourth or fifth grade and spending many afternoons at the Odenton Library with my other best friend, Andrea, collecting stacks of books to check out, doing homework, and then scouring the magazine section for teen magazines, where we'd find pictures and posters of cute teen stars (Kirk Cameron, Richard Greico, Johnny Depp), and then scrounge around in our denim purses for dimes so we could photocopy them and put them up in our lockers at school and on our walls at home. So many of my very best childhood memories revolve around reading; and, growing up in the Bazzett home with my dad as a role model, I guess that's not really so surprising.

My dad's love of books was immediately apparent when you walked into our home, where I remember being the only kid I knew who actually had full, double-stacked bookcases not only in our living room and bedrooms and hall, but in our bathrooms as well. My brothers and I can still remember titles and authors of books we have never even read from our time spent sitting on the toilet. I never read any of the books by one of my dad's favorite authors, John Updike, but I can still picture many of his titles, just because they were right there staring back at me every time I pooped, until I moved out of my parents' house.

My father definitely passed down his love of reading to his children, and of the three of us, I've probably remained the most voracious reader. That legacy has been a gift to me. Reading has always been more than just a hobby or pastime for me. It has been my academic savior, my relief when I'm stressed, my solace when I'm lonely, my connection to the students I've taught throughout the years, and now my favorite activity to share with my two year-old son.

When my father started writing his memoirs several years ago, he started to change. I had always seen my father as a sort of authoritarian-type, very set in his ways, with a quick temper when he became frustrated (yes, believe it or not, Tim Bazzett has a fiery Irish temper—don't let his "aw shucks" writing-style fool you!). But somehow his writing has made him ... well, *mellow* - an adjective I would never have used to describe my dad for the first 26 years of my life. Some of that personality shift may have occurred naturally, as a by-product of age and retirement and being back in his hometown, but I've always thought that his writing was the real catalyst. He's been a happier man since he began writing, and with each book, he seems to be a little happier, a little more relaxed - a little *mellow*-er. It seems that telling his stories, finally getting them down on paper, knowing that his family (and other readers too, I suppose) are going to get a chance to understand his life experiences from his point of view has made him lighter in his walk, more able to grin broadly, laugh heartily, and cry unashamedly.

We have never been a family inclined to big serious talks or discussions. I don't think that's necessarily a bad thing; it's just an undeniable characteristic of our odd brood. One of the magical things about Dad's writing, especially with this book, is that finally having something in print about some of our more difficult times as a family, like my parents' separation and the deaths of my grandparents, allows us to individually revisit those times, and deal with them in our own ways as adults, with an understanding and breadth of experience much greater than what we had as children. His writing, his books, make our lack of communication as a family in those years when we were growing up kind of a non-issue for us. His books afford us another chance to reflect on those times and reevaluate our own perceptions of the events. When we were old enough to understand, he let us in through his books, and, as Bazzetts, I think most of us have always learned best by reading and ruminating individually. And why should learning about our family history, even the hard parts, be any different?

My dad's memoirs have all allowed his children to have the unique experience of getting to know their father better. First we met the *Reed City Boy* - the thoughtful, movie cowboy-loving, accommodating brother and son. Then we met the *Soldier Boy* - the young man who learned about discipline, friendship and inner strength, and who loved rock and roll and good books. We have been lucky (if somewhat embarrassed at times) to read the sweet and honest love story between our then-young parents that he gave us in *Pinhead*. And now with this most recent volume of memories, we are privileged to read his recollections of becoming a father, of *being* a father to us. And we are given the opportunity to learn more about the man he became and is now, and often in the role we all remember best - a *Booklover*.

My dad's love of books was come by honestly, from his mother - my grandmother, Daisy. And now I can see that chain continuing, because my son, Adam, has never been the kind of kid who attached himself to a special stuffed toy or blanket. Many nights my husband and I watch him on the small screen of our baby monitor as he slowly falls asleep, clutching tightly in his tiny hand - a book.

Susan Bazzett-Griffith
St. Clair Shores
May 21, 2010

Timeline

For the benefit of those readers who are more chronologically inclined, I thought perhaps I should include a more ordered timeline of how my life has gone thus far. I hope it helps.

1944-1962 See my first book, *Reed City Boy*.

1962-1965 See my second book, *Soldier Boy*.

1965-1967 See my third book, *Pinhead*.

My story continues from 1967 to the present in the book which follows, but here is that more ordered timeline of the sequence of events –

1967-1970 We lived in Mount Pleasant, Michigan, while I completed college and graduate school at CMU. Our first son was born during this time.

1970-1975 We lived in Monroe, Michigan, where I taught English at Monroe County Community College. Our second son was born in Monroe.

1976-1981 I reenlisted in the US Army in January of 1976. For the next five years our lives were filled with frequent moves and upheaval, as we were subject to the orders and whims of the military. Some of the time we lived together. At other times Treve and the boys lived with her parents in Belleville, Michigan, while I was posted to distant military posts on temporary duty (TDY) for additional training. We were separated for most of the first five months of my enlistment while I completed an abbreviated basic training in Missouri, then sat in administrative limbo for a time, awaiting orders and a promotion. After that we spent more than a year together in Monterey, California, where I studied Russian at the Defense Language Institute Foreign Language Center (DLIFLC). Upon my completion of that program, we were separated again from August 1977 through February 1978, during which time I was TDY for more training in Texas and Maryland. In March of 1978 we traveled together to Germany, where we spent three years in Augsburg. Our daughter was born in the Augsburg Army Hospital.

1981-2001 In February of 1981, I was separated from the US Army in Augsburg, taking two months of terminal leave.

In April of that year I began work at the National Security Agency at Fort Meade, Maryland. We lived in Maryland for the next twenty years.

2001-Present I retired from NSA in November 2001. That December we moved to Reed City, where we continue to reside. We are now – so far, so good – living "happily ever after."

January 16, 2009

A book in a month. Can it be done? I don't know. But here goes.

Why would I want to try to write a book in just a month? It's a little hard to explain ... Well, no, it isn't, but I get lazy sometimes, and everything just seems like too much trouble to even try. In fact laziness is probably the main reason. Why I'd try. To write a book in a month, I mean. Because I wasn't always quite so lazy. I've accused myself of laziness for most of my life, but that's really just a goad I use to keep myself going, to work hard and meet deadlines. To get things done *ahead* of deadlines even.

Here's the thing. I published four books in four years, which is pretty unheard of in the publishing industry, unless you're Joyce Carol Oates or Stephen King, when he was younger. Oates is a real writer, of course, while King is a hack who writes what I call potato-chip books. Those are books that you can read while you're eating your way through a giant bag of Frito-Lays. And, also like potato chips, you can't eat just one. King's books, in other words, are the salty, unhealthy stuff of bestseller-dom that leave you feeling fat and faintly unsatisfied. Oates books, on the other hand, are the health food of literature. They make you feel a little better about yourself, and perhaps a bit wiser. Oats are always better for you than chips.

But no matter. As you can see I get easily distracted and am prone to digressions. That was obvious in my first four books, and I admitted it, but I don't have an editor to get on my case about it, and to tell the truth, my readers – and there are several – don't seem to mind. But what happened, see, after I finished my fourth book, was that I seemed to kinda run outa steam. I just stopped writing. I've had a lot of ideas in the past year or so about what I could write next, but I just couldn't seem to make myself get started. And anyone who's ever written a book – or tried to – will know what I mean when I say that almost anything can distract you and keep you from the business – or the *discipline* – of writing. Because that's what writing is – a discipline. If you're not disciplined, you'll never write anything. And that's what happened to me in the past year and a half or so. I lost my sense of discipline. And I do know about discipline. You can't spend eight years in the army without learning something about discipline. And I did. Do eight years in the army, that is. And I'll try to work some of that in here somewhere along the line. I already wrote a book about my first hitch, from 1962 to 1965. It was my infamous, or notorious, second book. What the locals whisperingly call "that dirty book." There was another army hitch though, one that was a *to*tally, I mean a com*plete*ly different kind of experience, that came along later, after I was married. And I want to tell you something about that time.

Yes, I'm married. For a long time now, and so I guess I'm also old. Although old is relative, if you know what I mean. For instance, I just finished reading these really good books, memoirs. Two of them were written by this woman, this really interesting and book-ish kind of woman named Doris Grumbach. The first memoir, called *Coming into the End Zone*, she wrote because she was turning seventy, and was feeling kinda glum about it, figuring the end was near and all that, I suppose, so she did a lot of reflecting and musing about her life, which has been a tremendously interesting one. At least I thought so, because, in case you haven't guessed it, I'm a book-ish kinda guy myself. I mean Doris has been married and has four daughters, she's been a teacher and a novelist and a book critic for some pretty prestigious magazines and newspapers. She got divorced and has had a woman "partner" now for around thirty years or more. I'm not sure why I put the word partner in quotes. Maybe I'm just too aware of the fact that some people are not comfortable with that kind of thing. I'm not one of those people, or at least I like to *think* I'm not. But I was raised Catholic, so ya never know what kinda stupid crap might still be lurking in the dark recesses of my subconscious. Because growing up Catholic back in the fifties involved a lot of surreptitious brainwashing, if you know what I mean. Come to think of it, most of it wasn't "surreptitious" at all. It was right out there in the open – all that rote memorization from the Baltimore Catechism and all.

But no matter. You might see this phrase a lot – if you decide to keep reading this, I mean. It acts as my own special segue from an uncontrolled digression, like the one(s) above, to the next matter. Or maybe even as a not-so-subtle transition between one or more digressions before I get back to the next matter. Kinda like the late Kurt Vonnegut's "hi-ho" and "so it goes." But don't get me started on Vonnegut. Loved that guy.

Where was I? Oh yeah, I was digressing about Doris Grumbach. See, the thing was, after Doris wrote down all these somewhat morose thoughts about aging and edging towards death – but it's a really *great* book, *honest*, just chock full of very profound stuff and information about all kinds of people, some famous and some not – she didn't *die*. So what she did was, five years later, when she turned seventy-five, she wrote this *other* book, called *Extra Innings*. I know, I know. She's mixing her metaphors here. I mean, after *End Zone* shouldn't the next book have been called "Extra Point" or "Sudden Death Overtime." I mean going from football to baseball just kinda drove me crazy, and I'm not even a sports fan. Doris does mention, too, that these two books have often been mistakenly shelved in the sports section of bookstores, so maybe she shoulda just called them "Getting Old" and "Getting Older" just to avoid that kinda confusion. In any case, these books were both a while back. Doris is ninety now and she's still writing, and I'm really happy about that, because I love her stuff. It's the kind of writing that makes you sit there nodding your head in recognition and sometimes chuckling or laughing right out loud (although that doesn't happen too often with Doris, who does tend just a bit toward the serious side), or wincing at her description of unpleasant experiences you might have had yourself, like a sick child, an unexpected injury or some sort of impending surgery. And of course those latter things do happen more often as you get older.

But no matter. I was talking about how old is relative. The other writer, Roger Angell, is another old guy whose work I admire tremendously, although I've only read this one book of his. It's called *Let Me Finish*. It's a memoir too. I read mostly memoirs now; I think it's part of getting old(er). You become more curious about other people's lives. And with me, the more I read about other people's lives and experiences, the more I want to write more about my own life. It presents a kind of delicious dilemma though. You can't read and write all at the same time. So when I stop and take the time to write, like I am right now, I can't help thinking about all those books waiting on my bookcase shelves – or stacked in that precariously teetering pile by my bed – crying out to me, "Hey, what about *me*? *Read me!*" Kinda like that cake and bottle in *Alice in Wonderland* – "Eat me" and "Drink me" – when she got real big and then shrank real small. How do I remember all this crap?

Anyway (I won't use "but no matter" this time; I don't wanna wear it out), Roger's book – Roger Angell, I mean (I don't want you to get Roger's book confused with John Updike's book, *Roger's Version*. I love Updike too) – is not just about getting old. It's a pretty straightforward autobiography, pretty upbeat for the most part, although there have been sad things and tragedies in his life. Angell was a writer and editor with *The New Yorker* for over fifty years, and still writes for them on occasion, I think. But Angell is eighty-eight years old. He doesn't "write old" though, if you know what I mean. He's a guy who knows just who he is and isn't afraid to laugh at himself. He may be "coming into the end zone," but he's not morose about it. I've got this other writer friend, Sam Hynes, who is also in his eighties. Sam, who is a really talented writer and scholar – and that proverbial "gentleman" too – once told me that one of the most important ingredients you can have in a book, whether it's fiction or non-fiction, is a *likeable* protagonist, or main character. Good advice, I think. And I like Doris Grumbach and Roger Angell. And I liked Sam Hynes too, when I read his two wonderful memoirs: *The Growing Seasons* and *Flights of Passage*.

So, take a look at these folks I've been reading and enjoying so immensely lately. Doris is ninety. Roger and Sam are in their eighties. Am I old? Of course not. I'll be sixty-five next week, of course, but it's all relative.

And yes, as I said earlier, I've been married for a long time – to a really wonderful, loving, and pretty patient and understanding woman. Although we would probably both agree that the understanding part comes with time – on both sides – and not always easily, and not without some pain.

Here's why I'm trying to write a-book-in-a-month. My wife left yesterday and she won't be back for a month. I drove her down to Gerald R. Ford Airport in Grand Rapids yesterday, where she was flying out, via Detroit, to BWI in Baltimore, on her way to see the kids and grandkids, the ones who live in Maryland and Pennsylvania. We have a daughter who lives with her family down by Detroit, but I'll get to her later – I hope. Our newest grandchild, a girl named Brooke, was one month old yesterday, and Treve (that's my wife), just can't wait to meet her. She's the main reason for this trip, which we wouldn't normally make in these "dead of winter" days, the roads and airline flight schedules often being so iffy. Yesterday the high temperature here, and also in the Grand Rapids area, only reached nine or ten degrees. And on the trip down yesterday morning, just north of Big Rapids, we were passing a small farm on the west side of 131 and we saw this black steer standing in the barnyard, his head hanging down, nose to the ground. There was no cloud of breath and it never moved as we sped by, both of us watching him. Our dashboard thermometer showed an outside temperature of minus fourteen. We both had the same thought: that Angus steer was frozen in place, either "deader than a doornail," as we used to say as kids, or perhaps in suspended animation, to thaw out good as new once the temperature rose a bit.

That's the kind of weather we have in mid-January here in western Michigan. Which is why we both hate to travel this time of year, and usually don't. But that new baby was calling out to Treve, in a manner of speaking. And this could well be our last grandchild, so off she went, apprehensive but determined to be that "good grammy" most women want to be once they've reached a certain stage of life. Tiny Brooke is our fifth grandchild, and so far Treve has been one helluva good grammy, especially considering we are separated from our children by so many hours and miles. I can't claim the same kind of devotion and dedication I'm afraid. I'm not sure that men in general have quite as strong an instinct for Grampa-ing. The biological imperative for that sort of thing is simply not as strong. I mean I guess I love kids, but by now, I've been there, done that, and have learned to love my peace and quiet. Babies are fine in small doses, but it's great to be able to hand them back to their parents and then go home, ya know?

But no matter. I *do* love my kids, and I love their kids too. God bless 'em all. But I'm perfectly happy to just deliver

Grammy to the airport, wave good-bye and come back home to my dogs. Well, not perfectly happy, because I already miss my wife. Especially, I miss her when I go to bed at night.

In fact, this is where I meant to start this book-in-a-month, and I've finally gotten there, to my perfect starting point. Sex. I wanted to start right out with sex, because people are always interested in sex, and sex sells.

But that's not why I miss my wife in bed. Not anymore. I'm gonna be brutally honest here, okay? I already told you I'm almost sixty-five. Well, sex at sixty-four or –five ain't exactly the same as it was when you were *twenty*-four or –five. I mean it's not that it's worse – or better. It's *different* though. It's richer somehow, suffused with all that history that you share – the joy and the pain, the anger, the misunderstandings, the sorrow, the making-up. All that *living* you've done. Treve and I have been together for over forty-one years now, so that is a lot of living, you have to admit. Remember that song, "I've Got a Lot of Living to Do"? Well, we've already done a lot of that living. I hope we've got a lot more left, and I don't want to get all glum about what's left or how much, like Doris did, but getting older ain't no piece of cake, as we all know. Nevertheless (isn't that a great word – *nevertheless*?), we want as many more years together as we can get. My mom is still around; she's ninety-two, so I'm hoping I've got her genes. And Treve's mom lived well into her eighties, so maybe, if we're lucky, we still *do* have a lot of living to do. (I'm not allowed to say how old my wife is, so don't try to figure it out. She'd appreciate it if you didn't.)

But back to sex. One of the last things my wife asked me yesterday before we left for the airport was, "Do you think you can get along without sex for a month?" I didn't really answer, except for this kind of embarrassed shrug. Because, to tell the truth, sex has become less frequent for us in the past few years. And I'm not complaining, really. When it *does* happen – and it's not *that* infrequent – it's beautiful. Not at all like it was forty years ago, of course, but beautiful all the same.

Forty years ago, wow! How can that be? But true.

Isn't it strange how clearly some things remain in our memories despite the passage of time, even such a *long* time?

Let me tell you about the bed in our first apartment. It was what was called a furnished apartment back then, but only if you interpret "furnished" in the very loosest sense. I'll get to that bed, but first maybe I oughta tell you a bit about our first home. I described it a little in my third memoir, *Pinhead*, but there's more.

Our first home was the back upstairs apartment of an old Victorian house that had been rather clumsily cobbled into an apartment house situated on the northern edge of campus at Central Michigan University. There were four apartments, divided by some very thin and not very adequate partitions. And the furnishings were pretty old too. I picked ours out of a collection of dusty, holey and thoroughly defeated-looking stuff that was stored in the garage behind the house. Actually, I think perhaps it was a carriage house before it was a garage. That's how old the whole place was. I picked out the most presentable looking piece of a two-piece sectional couch so impregnated with dust and the filth of the ages that you couldn't really even tell what color it had once been. After attempting unsuccessfully to beat the dust out of it, I finally gave up and covered it with a throw, an old Indian blanket I'd brought from my folks' basement when I moved into the place. There was a rickety end table, a couple of lamps, an old and well-scarred single pedestal wooden desk and a heavy Formica and wrought iron dinette set of a table and four chairs. The iron feet of this table jutted out at angles which resulted in many stubbed toes and plenty of rather colorful and creative curses on my part. Even so, that dinette set was probably the newest stuff in the apartment. I'd bought it from the previous tenants for just ten bucks. They'd probably suffered their own toe jams from the set and were glad to see the last of it. Perhaps its primary appeal for us, since we had nothing, was its four chairs. We only needed two for eating, so one was used at the desk, or for extra seating in the event of company, and the fourth chair usually stayed in the bedroom to pile our clothes and other junk on.

That bedroom was pretty crowded, since there was also a chest of drawers and a vanity with a huge oval mirror crammed in there. Those pieces were already in the apartment when we moved in, so I assume they were part of the advertised furnishings. I don't think there was a stool with the vanity, because there wouldn't have been room for one between it and the bed. If I remember correctly, when Treve did use the vanity to put on her makeup, she just sat on the edge of the bed.

So now we're back to the bed. And we'll be getting to that twenty-something kind of sex soon, so just hold your horses, okay? The bed, which was also already in the apartment when we moved in, was kind of a sad affair. There was no headboard, or anything fancy about it, and it only had three legs. They were those little wooden kinds that screw into the corners of the box spring. At the corner where the leg was missing, there were three bricks, which usually served us just fine, unless the sex got a little too vigorous, which might cause them to slide apart, collapsing that corner of the bed, causing the celebrants – us – to slide toward that corner. But what we both remember the most about that old bed is the way it sagged in the middle like a tired old swaybacked nag. For me, *good* memories. For Treve, not so good, or at least that's what she always tells me now. I *liked* the way this malformed mattress made us collapse up against each other in the middle. Because I've always been a very tactile person, particularly when it comes to sex. I like to feel things, touch 'em, smell 'em, *taste* 'em even. And you guys probably know right away what those "things" and "'em" are. Yeah, I'm a very feeling kinda guy. It probably comes from watching my dad and mom in the kitchen when I was a kid. Dad was always trying to cop a feel. He used to sneak up behind Mom when she was cooking and slip a hand over her shoulder and down into the front of her housedress while he moved in behind her. He didn't know us kids were watching, or maybe he did, and just didn't care, but we all remember it, I'm pretty sure. And there were six of us eventually. We all grew up thinking then, that sex starts in the kitchen. It's just the beginning of a whole natural progression.

But yeah, I remember that bedroom, that ol' bed. It was great. It was the best, really. I don't care what Treve says. Some of my best memories were made in that bed.

Here's one. (Sorry, Treve, but this is *my* book, okay?) It must have been the summer of '68, because that was our only summer in that apartment, and it was really hot and sticky that night. So much so that we were both stark naked, trying to catch even a little of the humid air currents coming in the bedroom window off from Bellows Avenue. I should probably tell you that even back then Treve didn't usually like to sleep naked. She told me then, and still does, "What if there was a *fire* and we had to get out right away?"

Well, hell. What are the odds of *that*? And naked is so great, especially when you're only twenty-something years old and still *look* so damn good naked. And at not quite twenty-one, she certainly was fine to behold that summer.

But it was really godawful hot that night, and we'd both shed everything. There we were, slumped together in the middle of that bed's valley, shiny sweaty flesh on flesh. Naturally, I had an "idea." You don't have to be a genius to know what my idea was, of course. It was actually my one-eyed friend's idea.

Treve didn't want any part of it though. Hot, irritable and uncomfortable, she rolled away, or tried to, telling me, "We already *did* that. What is *wrong* with you? It's too *hot*! Get *away* from me!"

You know, the usual kinda words of love, pillow talk and all that. Nothing to get alarmed about, so ol' one-eye and I pressed on.

Pulling herself away from me with that sucking sound made by two sweaty bodies suddenly disengaging, Treve grabbed the edge of the mattress on her side and yanked herself up and – quite unexpectedly – *over* the precipice that marked the end of the bed. I should point out here that the room was so small that there was only about a ten- or twelve-inch gap between the side of the bed and the wall. So when she went precipitously over the edge, face down into that small space, she suddenly found herself wedged between the bed and the wall, hands and knees pinned, ass in the air, unable to move.

"Oh *shit! … Help* me!" she hollered. "I'm *stuck!*"

Picture this perfect bottom, its heart-shaped whiteness winking palely in the half-light cast by the streetlight in front of Barnard Hall across the way. It was like a vision. I was initially struck dumb by its beauty. I mean *really*. My bride was such a *babe*. But then I started to laugh. I couldn't help it. Erotic yes, but also hilarious. This at first made Treve simply furious, and she began to scream (sotto voce, of course – the window was open, after all) and splutter at me, but as I continued to laugh, completely helpless, she too began to see the humor of the situation and started to giggle. Finally I pulled myself together enough to get up on my knees and rescue her from the crack and pull her back to safety, into the damply sheeted lifeboat that was the middle of our bed.

And yes, we did. Again. Damn the torpedoes. Full speed ahead.

How can you ever forget a moment like that? Of *course* I loved that bed.

The truth is, sex was central to those early days of our marriage. It probably is to most young marrieds. It's like having a new toy. You want to play with it all the time, and find out how many things you can do with it. And, because I was a student and we never had very much money, I suppose I thought of it as a kind of free entertainment too. Which is probably why I suggested stupid stuff – like, let's try it on this dining room chair, until we'd eventually "tried" all four of them. In fact, I don't think any piece of furniture in our tiny apartment escaped our "experiments." (Bet you'll think twice before ever coming to eat at *our* house again, huh? Just kidding, we're not really like that anymore.) Fortunately for me, Treve was almost always pretty agreeable to whatever I wanted to try. She tells me now that she was so young and naïve, she just figured she was *supposed* to do whatever I wanted. I mean, I was the *hus*band. She was just the wife. Wow! Remember *those* days?

She always claims that she can't remember much about the early days of our marriage, but, strangely, she does recall that before we got married, one of her sisters-in-law told her she should take along some Vaseline for the honeymoon. She asked why, and thinks she was told she'd need it for her knees and elbows. Hmm …

The honeymoon itself is another embarrassing story – for me. Because we stayed at the Pontchartrain Hotel, at the time one of the newest and most luxurious lodgings in all of downtown Detroit. It boasted a fine restaurant with music and dancing on the top floor. We never saw it. In fact, I don't think Treve ever left the room, and the only time I did was to hike a few blocks over to the bus station where I got some day-old egg salad sandwiches (the only kind left) from a vending machine. I took this fine cuisine back to our room where, ravenous, we consumed them with some by then not-very-cold complimentary champagne, which came with the room. (To this day Treve is not very fond of egg-salad sandwiches and hates champagne.) When we got to the hotel, I had hung out the Do Not Disturb sign, and never took it down.

The closest we came to "entertainment" that weekend was watching Doris Day and James Garner in a movie on the color TV in our room. We both remember it of course. It was called *The Thrill of It All*. Indeed.

Maybe that's enough sex for a while. It's time we moved on to other things. But I'll try to slip a little sex in every now and then, just to make sure you're paying attention, like those awful army training films they used to show us, with a pinup stuck somewhere in the middle. 'Cause remember? I *did* say I went back into the army again. I'll tell you about that tomorrow.

I didn't tell you about the bathroom in that first apartment at Fancher & Bellows. Maybe I shouldn't call it a bathroom though. A powder room? A toilet with attached sink and shower, maybe. Because it was an extremely tiny WC – a water closet, that's it! It was pretty small, okay? It was small enough that you could sit on the can and, leaning forward only slightly, you could brush your teeth over the sink. And the shower, which boasted multiple coats of various-colored paints over its rust-pocked, clanging tin walls was wedged right up against the sink. The door into the bathroom from our main room was also small, both short and narrow, probably about six feet high. I'm six feet four, but back then I was still six feet five, so I had to duck my head just to enter the WC. Occasionally I would forget, only to be promptly and painfully reminded. I remember going to class a few times with an angry red crease across my forehead. It was embarrassing to have to use that old line, "I ran into a door." Well, a door*frame*, actually.

The one good thing we got out of that diminutive and dingy room was our first set of friends at Central as young marrieds. Because someone else lived on the other side of the paper thin wall that separated our shower from the one in the front upstairs apartment.

Dave and Joyce Roof were pretty new at marriage too. They'd married that summer of 1967, only a few months before we did. They were from North Carolina. Dave was a recent Clemson graduate whose major was chemistry and he'd snared a job as a chemist with Dow Chemical in Midland, so he commuted there five days a week. Joyce was finishing up her undergraduate degree, getting her teaching credentials at Central.

Dave and I met in the shower one morning. I can't remember what it was I might have been singing, but suddenly the water came on beyond the tin wall and someone started singing along with me. It was Dave. We met in person soon after that. Treve and Joyce were only briefly uncomfortable with the unusual circumstances of our meeting, but soon learned to roll their eyes whenever it came up, like *Guys!*

The four of us became friends though, and it was a good thing, especially for Treve, who felt quite isolated for the first couple months of our marriage. She wasn't a student and she didn't have a job. And she was missing her friends and her family. She was only twenty, after all. She doesn't like me reminding her of this, but on an early shopping trip to the Yankee department store over on Mission I bought her a coloring book and crayons. It was supposed to be a gentle sort of joke, but she actually began using it, and would show me what she'd colored when I got home from class. She stayed inside the lines very well.

So she was glad to find a friend, even a part-time one, in Joyce. We went to each other's place for pot luck dinners, and when spring arrived we picnicked on a rickety old picnic table out on our lawn. Since he was already employed by a major corporation, Dave was undoubtedly making more money than we were, but he never flaunted it. Our rent was seventy-five dollars a month. Their apartment was a little bigger than ours, but I assume their rent was comparable. But Dave may have been making car payments too, since he was driving a sporty new yellow Chevy Malibu. I think I remember that car mostly because he wrecked it that first spring we knew the Roofs. He was on his way to work in Midland one morning, driving in a dense fog. As he described it, two horses suddenly materialized like giant ghosts out of the fog, galloping straight at him. He swerved to miss one, but hit the other one head-on, so to speak. The horse went over the hood and onto the roof of the Malibu, pancaking it nearly flat down to the doors. Fortunately, Dave reacted the only way he could. He flopped sideways onto the seat toward the passenger side. Luckily, he wasn't wearing a seat belt or he wouldn't have been able to perform this quick-thinking maneuver. Hell, I can't remember if cars *had* seatbelts in 1968. In any case, Dave walked away from the accident without a scratch. The Chevy was totaled, and the horse had to be destroyed. Talk about luck. Dave and Joyce Roof. Our first friends at CMU. I found them again not too long ago. They're back in North Carolina now, semi-retired, but they remember that first place too. And like us, they have grown kids and grandkids now too. Time flies, huh?

A whole little story for my maybe book-in-a-month just from that crummy li'l john. Go figure.

January 17, 2009

The army redux. *Ree-ducks*. I've always wanted to use that word, probably ever since Updike did, which was when I first heard it, or *read* it, actually. I didn't know, when *Rabbit Redux* was published, what the word meant at all. I had to go look it up. I figured it was probably just me that had to go to a good dictionary or an old Latin grammar. But now, thinking about it, I'll bet even all those erudite reviewers with the major newspapers might have done the same thing, did a quick sneaky check on the word, without telling anyone, and then wrote their reviews, acting like it was the most natural word in the world to use. It means something like "brought back," "revisited," or maybe, in my case, *ree-in-duck-ted*. Because I was, re-inducted into the service again, after more than ten years out of it. It was voluntary on my part though; make no mistake about that. I'm not sure if I ever did completely figure out exactly why I did it.

I celebrated my thirty-second birthday in a mess hall of the Minuteman Training Company at Fort Leonard Wood, Missouri. And it really was a celebration. There was a party. It went completely against all my memories of the army and basic training from my first time around. Because back then, at eighteen, I had pretty much lived in a constant state of quaking terror.

This time around though, it was so very different.

In the first week of January 1976, I kissed my wife and boys (yes, there were two little kids by then, and I'll get back around to all that eventually) good-bye and left home to go back into the army. I had signed the re-enlistment papers back in November, after several talks with the local army recruiter in Monroe. I wasn't the same naïve, gullible (is that a redundancy?) kid I'd been in 1962 the first time I joined the army. But I can't positively say I was in my right mind when I re-upped either. A lot of people probably didn't think so, and I can understand that. Because here's the thing. By the end of 1975 I was set, career-wise. And I mean for *life*, if I'd wanted to be. I had this job – this *profession*, I suppose, if you wanna call it that, because I was an assistant *professor* of English at Monroe County Community College, down in the southeast corner of Michigan, kinda between Detroit and Toledo. (The students at MCCC called it "MC cubed" or MC3, and thought of it as just a couple more years of high school). I'd been there for five years by that time, and I'd really kept my nose to the grindstone, so to speak, toiling my way up the promotional ladder. Not only had I been teaching a full load of classes every semester, but I'd also been taking a graduate class or two evenings and Saturdays from the University of Michigan or Eastern Michigan. They were both only about forty minutes away from Monroe. See, the salary scale at MCCC promised a considerable pay raise after you'd earned another thirty hours of graduate credit beyond your Master's degree, which you had to have just to get the job. I had come to Monroe right after earning my MA at Central. There were two reasons we'd settled in Monroe in the fall of 1970. One, it was the first college to offer me a job; and two, it was only about a half hour away from Treve's folks in Belleville. And, well, maybe the third reason was we already had a baby, so I was pretty desperate to be gainfully employed, as I was feeling a pretty heavy sense of responsibility by then.

So, like I started to say earlier, by the fall of 1975 I'd been at Monroe for five years already. I'd worked hard, gained tenure, gotten as far up the salary scale as I could, short of earning a Ph.D., which wasn't gonna happen. We had bought our first house, a little rancher on a slab in a pretty nice subdivision; we had the station wagon, two kids and two dogs. It seemed like we had settled in for the duration, if you know what I mean.

Maybe that's why I bolted back to the army. Maybe I was just plain terrified. Remember that Peggy Lee song, "Is That All There Is?" I actually do remember thinking that; wondering, even after I'd painstakingly earned that extra thirty credits and got the "assistant professor" title tacked onto my shingle, "Is this it then? Forty more years of *this*?" Of teaching Freshman Composition to a bunch of bored kids who could care less if they could write a complete sentence?

I wonder now, looking back, if every guy at some time in his life experiences this crisis of the spirit, this what? This foreboding sense of a lifetime of being this ant, this worker bee, this beast of burden. I mean, was it just me? I also wonder sometimes if I might have been clinically depressed that dark November of 1975. Not quite in my right mind. But what the hell! Why dwell on it now, more than thirty years after the fact? The point here is that I did it. I reenlisted.

Here's another funny thing I need to mention though. For several years before I did this strange deed I had recurring dreams about being back in the army. They weren't nightmares exactly, but like most dreams are, they were strange jumbles of past and present. I mean my old army roommate, Joe Capozzi, was often there in the dream, but then Treve was there too, and sometimes Jeff and Scotty, our little boys. After having these dreams, I would often wake up sweating and anxious, and then be suddenly relieved and overwhelmingly glad to find Treve sleeping safely in bed beside me. I would even get up and go take a look at the boys, sleeping in their beds. Then I'd go take a long leak. Maybe it was just a full bladder causing those weird dreams.

Is there such a thing as a self-fulfilling dream? Maybe.

Lemme tell you about Minuteman training. First of all, it came as a big surprise to me. Because my recruiter had told me that since I was enlisting specifically to go to language school, which would be at DLIFLC – that's the Defense Language Institute Foreign Language Center – in Monterey, then I would take my basic training at Fort Ord, which was just a few miles away, near Seaside, California. It was a part of the Army's then-current push to sort of centralize training and cut down on unnecessary travel expenses for new recruits. I was not very enthused, of course, about having to go through basic training again. But if I had to do it, I rationalized that California in January would certainly be better than Missouri, which was where I'd endured basic the first time around, and was the home of Minuteman.

The Monroe recruiter had told me about Minuteman right away, the first time I visited his office. When he heard I was prior service, that was the first thing he began talking about. Because Minuteman was a training program designed especially for guys who were coming back after a break in service. And the best part about it was that basic training had been compressed from the traditional eight weeks to just *two* weeks. Which sounded great to me. But then, after getting more information from me about my first enlistment and then consulting his regulation manuals, the sergeant reluctantly informed me that because it had been more than ten years since I'd left active duty I would have to repeat the normal basic training cycle – the whole eight weeks of it.

Well, shit. Bummer. But I thought about it some more over a week or two and decided I could do it. Maybe I didn't mention that I made several visits to the recruiter's office over a period of a month or more before I actually made the decision to reenlist. And I talked it all over with Treve, who was, I confess, a bit unhappy about this new turn of events in our lives, if not outright angry and even a bit terrified. After all, she was pretty happy with our life in Monroe. She was only about a half hour from her parents, and she'd made several pretty close friends in the neighborhood – Shirley and Claire, Joyce and Priscilla. And she had this new little house that she loved. She didn't want to leave all this. And on top of it all, she couldn't even *drive*. She'd never gotten her license. And I was just going to *leave* her, in the dead of winter no less?!

Well, yup. In fact that's just what I was going to do. Years later we would joke about this. I would tell people I tried my best to leave her when I reenlisted. But she refused to be left. She bit the bullet and she got her driver's license and she sold the house and she followed me all the way to California. My wife claims to be a timid soul, but in truth she is anything but. She may not know it, but she is made of the same stuff that pioneer women were over a hundred years ago. And I love her for it. In fact I'm always telling her, "You're one helluva woman, Treva Jean."

So my family managed to make the changes necessary to accommodate this crazy, early mid-life crisis of mine, and on January 6, I kissed them all good-bye and caught a ride with my recruiter to the AFEES station in Detroit. I was just three weeks short of turning thirty-two.

Although this was all my own doing, my own selfish decision, I was feeling pretty low that day, leaving my loved ones behind. However, after spending a few hours standing around in the usual long lines or sitting in waiting areas at the AFEES, I got some news which considerably brightened my day. The army, in its infinite wisdom, had screwed up. I would not be going through the standard eight weeks of basic at Fort Ord. Incredibly, I was issued orders to report to the Minuteman Training Company at Fort Leonard Wood, Missouri. I stood there and read the freshly cut orders several times, very carefully; from beginning to end I read and reread the Army-ese gobbledygook. There was no mistake. I was going to Minuteman. Should I tell someone there'd been a mistake? Hmm ... Eight weeks of hell, or just two weeks? Hmm ... I kept my mouth shut, of course, except to call Treve and tell her – very quietly. Inside I was cheering, but on the outside I continued to do my best impression of a glum new recruit. I had taken the pledge and signed the papers. The army owned me again.

I have been reading Donald Hall this week. Once the Poet Laureate of the U.S., Hall has been a practicing poet for most of his life. He began writing poetry as a teenager; he is eighty now. In addition to his numerous books of poetry, Hall has also written some wonderful books of prose and a few volumes of memoirs. His newest, a slim book called *Unpacking the Boxes*, is a study in spareness. Poetry is a kind of science of finding the exact word, so years of writing poetry has honed Hall's prose to something equally spare and exact. It's not something you can just whip on through. Nearly every sentence causes you to stop and consider its content, and usually I can find something parallel to Hall's experiences in my own life. In other words, Donald Hall's work as a wordsmith makes me pause and consider. It makes me want to remember, and to write about my own life. Which is what I'm doing here, or working at it anyway.

And then there's that other book I already mentioned, the memoir by Roger Angell. I liked his book so much that I sent him a copy of one of my books yesterday. I sent him *Love, War & Polio*, the biography I wrote about Bill Porteous. I thought Roger might relate, since he and Bill are the same age, both born in 1920. The thing about Angell's book is that it kind of skips around in his life, it's not a strict chronological look at stuff. And I found I really liked that method of telling your life. So I'm going to try it here, partly because my wife keeps telling me to just *finish* telling my story. She doesn't see the necessity for telling every single bit of what happened to me – to *us* – and dragging it out over several more *volumes* of memories. And she's probably right.

So I'm gonna use the Angell method. But I'll get back to the Army Redux stuff eventually, or at least parts of it, okay? Bear with me, 'cause right now I'm making one of those non-chronological jumps.

Our son Jeff was born in 1969, just a few months before our astronauts first set foot on the moon. I remember that first moon landing, of course, but I remember the birth of my first son a lot better. In my own small universe, Jeff's arrival was a lot more important than any space ship stuff, which never seemed quite real to me somehow. In fact, I vaguely remember sitting out on the lawn at Washington Courts one July night a day or two after that moon landing, having a beer with Tom Derda and Dave Bluem. They were a couple of our neighbors there in the CMU married housing complex. Tom lived downstairs underneath us with his wife, Sharon, and little girl, Debbie. Dave and his wife, Mary Ellen, lived down at the end of the building. We'd been talking about this moon landing stuff and were looking up at the moon, swigging our Blue Ribbons in a manly manner. It came up in our discussion that maybe this whole thing was just a fake; that it had all been filmed on some giant sound stage, with phony space suits and Styrofoam lunar surfaces and just plain old sand instead of moon dust, and lots of special effects, just to reassure the taxpaying public that all that money spent on the space program hadn't been in vain, that by golly we'd beaten the Soviets to the moon. Of course we were probably about half drunk as we made these speculations, so they seemed pretty plausible at the time. In retrospect, maybe they still do. I mean, have you ever seen that film, *Wag the Dog*?

But back to Jeff, born the same year as *Sesame Street*. Jeff was not a surprise to us. Well, hang on a minute. He *was* a surprise, I guess you could say, but certainly a *wel*come one. The way we found out he was coming was a little strange, at least it was for me. See, Treve had had been having problems with recurrent sore throats and low grade fevers for most of the first year we were married. It was tonsillitis, actually, and we knew it, but she resisted having her tonsils out for quite a while. Which was understandable. No one ever gets too excited about surgery, no matter how minor. And a tonsillectomy was considered pretty routine, even way back in 1968. Instead of opting to eliminate the problem, she tried other stuff, like gargling with warm salt water, to alleviate the symptoms. And we both remember the time she bought this new stuff at the drugstore to try. It was called Chloraseptic, I think, and it was supposed to kinda numb your throat when it was sore. And it did, actually. But I must have misread the directions on the label, because the first time she used it, I told her she was supposed to gargle with it and then swallow it. Well, I was the husband, so she did. She damn near threw up. You weren't supposed to swallow it. It was not long after that unhappy experience that she finally agreed to have the tonsillectomy. It was the fall of '68 and we had just moved into our second "home," a one-bedroom apartment at Washington Court, which was right on the CMU campus. This apartment was also a "furnished" one, but this time the furniture was really nice – a genuine "pleather" couch, for example, a practically new Maytag washer and dryer right in the kitchen, and a decent double bed that didn't sag in the middle and had a bookcase headboard and all four legs. What *lux*ury. I remember that we were so pleased with our new home that we spent the first few weeks sort of "playing house," buying some little frilly kitchen curtains to hang and other small knick-knacks to put our own stamp of ownership on the place. But what I remember most is the morning she cooked breakfast for us wearing only an apron. It was like having a real live *Playboy* centerfold right there in the kitchen. I mean, I'm tellin' ya. It was all I could do to choke down the bacon before we quickly adjourned to the bedroom. Home really *was* a *sweet* home.

But no matter. Back to how we first heard about Jeff. Our doctor in Mount Pleasant was a pleasant, middle-aged general practitioner, Dr. Chamberlain. His office was in his house and he had several kids of his own and a nurse named "Hank," whom Treve was very fond of. Anyway, he did the surgery for Treve. Since outpatient surgery was rare back then, she had to be admitted to the hospital the night before the operation, and then spent one more night there after it was over. So she was two nights in the hospital. She can still remember her two roommates. One was a real pretty young brunette who was having some spidery varicose veins removed or something like that. She and Treve got along fine. The other was this skanky stringy-haired girl who was there because she'd slashed her wrists, an attempted suicide. We think she was a little nuts, actually. She was obviously pretty poor, so Treve felt a little sorry for her, partly because she had this greasy-looking low-life boy friend who came to see her a couple times and tried to crawl right into bed with her. Anyway this girl thought the hospital food was great and didn't want to leave. So when she was due to be discharged, she swallowed a razor blade or some opened paper clips. I can't really remember, but it must have been something that was sharp enough that they had to keep her for another day or so, to x-ray her or wait until the foreign body had passed, as they put it. This nutcase was happy again then. She'd get a few more days in a clean bed with free meals.

Treve, on the other hand, wasn't at all fond of the bland hospital diet, so as soon as they discharged her, with special instructions to take only bland clear broths for the next day or two, she came right back to our new apartment and scrambled herself up some eggs. She was *hungry*, dammit, and no bossy nurse was gonna tell *her* what she could or couldn't eat, swollen throat or not. Those eggs may have hurt a bit going down, but she was not about to admit it, to me or anyone else.

So why am I talking about Treve's tonsillectomy if I was gonna tell you about Jeff's origins? I'm almost there; just be patient, okay?

This was, I think, probably around October, and a week or so after the surgery, Treve had to go back to Dr. Chamberlain for a post-op checkup. It seemed kinda pointless to me, since she seemed perfectly fine again within just a couple of days. But she seemed fine about going back to the doctor again, even a bit eager perhaps. So I sat in the waiting room, leafing thru the old torn magazines you find in every doctor's anteroom. When Treve came out of the exam room she had this big smile on her face.

"Everything okay?" I asked.

"Yup. Everything's fine," she replied. "Let's go."

As soon as we'd gotten back into the VW, she turned to me and blurted out, "I'm pregnant!" Her whole face just glowed.

"Wha- *What?*" I said, totally confused and taken by surprise.

"I'm *preg*nant!" she repeated excitedly.

Still trying to figure out the logistics and sequence of events here, I responded stupidly, "But I thought he was checking your *ton*sils. You mean he looked down your throat and ...?"

"*No*, silly! I missed my last two periods, so I brought in a urine sample and they checked it and I'm *preg*nant!" The words all came out in a sudden rush, her long-kept secret finally revealed.

"Oh," I said. "*OH!*" I repeated, as the impact of it all suddenly hit me. "You mean we're gonna have a *baby*?" (Well, *du-uh!*)

I know, really stupid. But that's how confused – and excited – I felt at the moment I first learned I was actually going to be a father, that I had reproduced. That we had procreated. It had all just seemed like a lot of fun when we were doing it. Now, suddenly, there was this awful – I mean *awe-full* - feeling of responsibility. I mean I was happy, don't get me wrong. We wanted kids and had talked about it a lot. But I think I was probably a little scared too. After all, wasn't I still practically a kid myself? Okay, I was twenty-four, but was I really a *man* now? Was I ready to be (GULP!) a *father*? Well, ready or not ...

When I decided to try to write all this down, I tried idly to determine exactly when Jeff might have been conceived, a pretty impossible task, actually, when I consider how much whoopee was going on between Treve and me that first year we were married. In fact we both remember with some embarrassment the time I took her in to see an OB-GYN specialist because of some "discomfort" she'd been having. After examining her, this doctor, an old stern-looking gray-haired guy (I think his name was Junker, of all things), looked at Treve and said, "Are you married, young lady?"

Too shocked to be insulted, Treve simply stammered, "Y-yes."

"Well, that's a damn good thing. But just the same, you'd better give it a rest!" the doctor stated flatly. Then he called me in, and told me pretty much the same thing, to give this "poor girl" some rest.

So okay, maybe we were overdoing things a bit. That "new toy" syndrome I mentioned earlier. All my fault, I admit it. Mea culpa, and all that other Catholic guilt stuff.

But no matter.

When I do think back about those few months just before we learned of Treve's pregnancy though, one occasion does stand out. Not because we *did* it that night. Hell, what night *didn't* we? No, it was because of where we spent the afternoon and part of the evening, and what became sort of an historical event in the annals of sports. It was towards the end of August on a Saturday. I wasn't going to school that summer. I'd found a job working on the maintenance crew of a natural gas pipeline over at Lake George, about twenty-some miles northwest of Mount Pleasant. It was kind of a dumb, numbnuts sort of job, cleaning up around the pumping station, along with digging holes and painting and planting cedar posts as line markers. I actually enjoyed the job; it was a pleasant break from the past few years of studying. For once I had no homework or term papers to worry about. I could read whatever I wanted and had more time to spend with Treve.

Treve had a job that year too. She had gotten her cosmetologist's license back in January after successfully taking the state board examinations in Lansing. Then she found a job almost immediately, at a little shop called Wanda's, inside the lobby of the Hotel Chieftain. She liked her job too, it seemed a perfect fit for her. Her boss, Wanda Garber, reminded her of her mom (also named Wanda, quite coincidentally), only younger. Wanda sensed immediately that Treve felt a bit out of her element and a bit homesick here in this college town where she was neither town nor gown. So she kind of adopted Treve, became her surrogate big sister/young mom. And Treve loved Wanda from the start. She made her feel finally at home in Mount Pleasant. She was finally able to put away her coloring book and crayons and join the adult world, where her new toys were hair colors, perms, combs and brushes.

And there was another girl working in the shop with her, Susie Dunn. Her parents, the Dunns, owned the hotel, so the atmosphere in the hotel and shop was kind of a family one in many ways.

That summer of 1968 the Chieftain was almost the only game in town when it came to hotels. It wasn't until a few years later that the big chains moved into town. The chieftain had maybe a couple dozen rooms, including the ones in a long annex built out back. It also had a bar and dining room and a pool. It's that pool that I'm working toward here.

Wanda closed the shop on Saturday afternoons. That August was a hot one. Since Wanda and her "girls" were like hotel employees – like family, actually, since Susie *was* family – they were given free access to the hotel pool. Wanda and her husband, Bob, who worked at the Leonard oil refinery in Alma, decided that Saturday to come cool off in the pool, and she called Treve and told us to come on over too if we wanted. So we did. It was late August and hotter than hell that day, probably in the eighties, so the pool felt just wonderful to all of us. The bar was handily nearby too, and offered "employee discounts," so we were availing ourselves of all the perks – sunning, swimming, soaking and getting a little sloshed. Bob and I made periodic bar runs to replenish our drinks. The Tigers were playing a double-header with the Yankees that day, and we had the game going on the radio, poolside.

I got fairly drunk that afternoon, what with the cheap liquor and the sun. We probably all did. I remember I kept trying to pin Treve up against the far end of the pool – Bob and Wanda were down by the other end – to engage in a little furtive water sex. Crude, I know. I *said* I was drunk. But Treve was not – or at least not drunk enough for *that!*

So there was the ball game on the radio and this lingering sexual tension through the afternoon. The Tigers lost the first game, and the second one got underway. After nine innings the Tigers and Yanks were tied, 3-3, and the game went into extra innings. The sun was going down and the heat lessened somewhat. We and the Garbers still sat around and in the pool, thinking, perhaps, we'll go home as soon as the game is over. The game went on and on, a pitchers' duel, with lots of foul balls and batters adjusting their cups and stepping in and out of the batter's box. The pitchers stepping on and off the rubber, adjusting their caps (and cups), shaking off signs. Finally, around 10:00, we figured this game was never going to end, gave up and went home. And even lax with the liquor and beer and sun, after all those hours of wanting her, I know I must have nailed Treve when we got home.

So, when I try to trace back to when Jeff got started, I often remember that long hot summer day, the Garbers, the pool, the beer and the booze, and the baseball game that wouldn't end, and I wonder idly if that might have been the time.

And that game actually did *not* end that night. The teams stayed locked in that same tie until the game was called, I think because of a curfew law, after nineteen long innings which lasted around five hours, perhaps one of the longest single games in major league history. They finished the game a day or two later, but I can't remember who won. It was an historic year for the Tigers anyway. Denny McClain won 31 games and also the Cy Young award, and the Tigers won the pennant and the World Series.

But no matter. And I can say that easily since I'm not really much of a sports fan. Never have been. Water sports, maybe.

The day Jeff was born - May 3, 1969, a Saturday – Treve was supposed to be working at the shop. And it was going to be a very busy day, as it was the weekend of all the big spring formals at Central. Lotsa hair to be done. But she went into labor instead. I was as nervous and jittery as a first-time father could be, so I rushed her post haste to the hospital, where she was examined and told it was too early. She should go home and put her feet up. But Treve had already decided this was going to be the day, so instead of putting her feet up, she went home and scrubbed the kitchen floor. Then she stood in the kitchen doing some ironing, until the pains started coming closer together. Meanwhile I kept getting more and more nervous.

I kept watching her as she periodically doubled over, trying to get her breath. "Hadn't we better go?" I kept asking.

"Not yet," she'd say, gasping. "They're not gonna send me home again!"

And so we would wait a little longer, until *she* decided it was time to go to the hospital. But then, she asked me to stop in town at a department store. She wanted to buy a new nightgown to have to wear in the hospital. I didn't want to, of course, but she insisted, so we went into the store and I paced back and forth while she deliberated over the ladies nightwear on the rack. Finally she picked one out and we took it over to the counter. The saleslady, trying to be helpful, asked if she'd like it wrapped.

"Wrapped? Hell, No! She's having a baby!" I screamed at this poor woman. *"We have to GO!"*

Treve apologized for me, smiling sweetly, as I grabbed the sack with the nighty and headed for the door. Even then, Treve lingered a moment longer to look quickly through a rack of women's swimwear.

"JEEZUZ!" I hollered. "You're looking at *bathing* suits?! *Look at you, ferChrisesakes! Bathing suits?!"* I was nearly dancing with fright, terrified that she would deliver right there on the floor in swimwear. *"Let's GO, Dammit!"*

Treve shot one more sweetly apologetic look at the by-now nearly cowering saleslady, and we finally left the store. She still likes to tell this story, about how *funny* Daddy was on the day Jeff was born.

As it turned out, I really didn't need to be so worried. It was several hours before Jeff finally made his entrance. We'd had time for several games of Yahtzee in the labor room while we were waiting, in between extended walks up and down the hospital hallways, trying to move things along. We remember seeing another expectant mother, very young, making the same walk. Her stomach was grossly distended, much more so than Treve's. Twins, we learned, and she'd been there for eighteen hours.

It was right around 9 PM when Jeff was born. He was long and skinny and a funny kind of gray color. I don't think he'd enjoyed the day much, and immediately expressed his displeasure. Of course I wasn't actually there at the birth. I was in the waiting room, which was considered the proper place for fathers back in 1969. And I still kinda think that. I would not see my second son born either. I had to wait for my daughter to come along, in 1978, to be present at a birth. That will be another story, included in here somewhere, I hope.

This baby, our firstborn son, was always Jeffrey Thomas. Had always been Jeffrey Thomas, even before he was born, and this was in a time when the baby's sex remained a mystery until he arrived. The name, however, was a given. I'm not sure why. It was a name Treve had picked out years before she even met me, just because she liked the sound of it. And it was okay with me. The name was not so important as the fact that our family had begun. We were parents. I was both proud and petrified all at the same time. I was twenty-five years old. Treve was twenty-one. And together we had made this whole other small human being. Imagine that!

January 18, 2009

By 1978 we figured we'd pretty much perfected this new skill, making other human beings, I mean. That was the year our daughter, Suzie, was born. I'd prefer to spell it Susie-with-an-s, since her name is Susan, but Suzie-with-a-z prefers the z, so ... The thing is though, when Suzie was born, we thought she was just about perfect, probably because she was just what we wanted. A girl, I mean. See, we already had two boys by then, and whenever Treve tells our whole-life-story-in-five-minutes-or-less, it's usually in there somewhere that "...eversinceI-wasalittlegirlIalwayswantedtohavetwoboysandagirlandthe-firstboywasgonnabenamedJefffreyThomas." You have to listen really fast if you get our life story from Treve because that's how fast she tells it. She still can't figure out why it's taking me so long to tell my life story. She can't believe I've already written three whole books about my life and only got up to the age of twenty-three. And I'm not sure how to explain it to her, except maybe it's just that I write a lot slower than she talks.

But no matter, I guess. I'm trying to go a little faster in this book. Anyway, like I said, Suzie really did seem pretty perfect by the time she finally came along. So perfect, I guess, that Treve decided that it was enough. I mean *we* decided. We had that perfect family she'd planned since she was a little girl. I guess she figured – I mean *we* figured – why take a chance on screwing things up? So she had me fixed. I mean, *we* ... hmm ... Ah! A *va-sec-tomy! That's* the word I couldn't think of. I had a vasectomy.

There's a backstory to this. Suzie was born in an army hospital in Augsburg, Germany. You'll remember I said I went back into the army in 1976. I was actually in a training status for more than two years, and I'll try to get back to that. We got to Germany in March of 1978 though, and Suzie was born in August.

The reason I decided to write about Suzie today, jumping from Jeff's birth in 1969 all the way to Suzie in '78, was that I turned on the kitchen TV this afternoon, just to have a little company with my fried eggs and toast supper. It seems weird to be able to watch whatever I want while I eat, because Treve usually has Rachael Ray or some other funky Food Network show on while we're eating. But she's gone now, so I've got the remote. I took a quick look at MSNBC and CNN for a few minutes. Lotsa stuff on about Obama's inauguration coming up on Tuesday, and it looks there's a continuous party going on in DC until then. All that's fine, of course. Barack was my man. Treve and I even got political this year for the first time in our lives and did some door-knocking and phoning on his behalf.

But no matter. I switched over then to TCM, and there was Warren Beatty, who'd just died. It was this movie, *Heaven Can Wait*, and it had just started. It's a pretty good film, with Julie Christy and Charles Grodin in it too, but I'm not gonna tell you all about it. You can look it up in Leonard Maltin's movie book, or you can rent it. So I watched this movie for about fifteen minutes while I ate. When you're all by yourself that's about as long as it takes to eat. It almost takes longer to fry the eggs and make the toast than it does to eat it. And all the time I was watching it I was thinking about Suzie – and Treve and the boys too.

Here's why. I think it was in July of 1978 when I saw this film the first time. Because Treve was about eight months pregnant at the time and big as a house. That's what *she* says about herself then, understand, not me. *I* didn't think so. I thought she was just beautiful. Anyway, she had gone in for her regular monthly – or bi-weekly or whatever – checkup with her doctor at the Augsburg army hospital over on Flak Kaserne. Kaserne, I think that's German for camp or barracks, or something. I used to know a little German, but it's pretty much gone now. Her doctor was this huge black guy, Major Lockett. He must have been almost as tall as me, but he outweighed me by at least fifty pounds. The first time we met him, he shook my hand and my hand almost disappeared in his. I remember thinking – and this is no shit, I really *did* think this – *Wow, this guy's got hands like catcher's mitts. Great hands for catching babies.*

Anyway, that July day he looked at Treve and saw how her feet and ankles were all swollen up. "This is not good," he said. "This is serious. We're going to have to admit you and keep you until we get this fluid retention under control."

Or something to that effect, because that was it. He wouldn't even let her go home. He called someone up and got her a room right then and there. Treve was all upset, but between me and the Doc we got her sort of semi-calmed down, and the boys and I went back to our apartment and got her some stuff, some underwear and toothbrush and nighty and stuff, you know. It was a Saturday afternoon, so I was off. After we brought Treve's stuff back to the hospital and got her kind of settled in for the evening, I wasn't quite sure what to do with the boys. But right there on the same block with the hospital was the Flak theater. And it was hotter than hell that day, and the theater was air conditioned. Our third-floor apartment was not. So I took 'em to the movies. Yup, you got it - *Heaven Can Wait*, starring Warren Beatty. I wonder if the kids remember that. Jeff and Scott, I mean. Suzie wouldn't remember it, of course. We had popcorn for supper. We usually had popcorn on Sunday nights at home, but this was kind of a special occasion, I mean the movies and all. And Treve in the hospital, of course.

They only kept her a couple days, I think, and she came home with much trimmer feet and ankles, which was what Doc Lockett wanted, since that swelling indicated something that could be a pretty serious complication, only I can't remember any more what it was called.

Treve actually liked that hospital stay better than the next one, because she was on strict bed rest and had to keep her feet up. So she got waited on and had her meals brought, and didn't have to make her bed and mop the floor like she did the next time she was there, which was when Suzie was born.

I know. You women are probably thinking I got that wrong. New mothers don't have to make their beds and mop floors. If you're thinking that, then you've never been in a military hospital. Because, yes, you *do* have to do that stuff there, if you're able, I mean. And the army didn't believe in spoiling anyone. Treve still remembers that: "AndafterSuziewasborntheyhadmeupthatsamedayandIhadtomakemyownbedandeve nmopthefloor!Canyoubelievethat?!"

Believe it, Ladies.

But no matter. Like I said, we all thought Suzie was pretty perfect – except maybe for Scotty, who was nearly seven by then, but had gotten pretty used to being the baby, and wasn't quite sure about this new one. The night before I brought Treve and Suzie home from the hospital, I made this little sign with a magic marker to pin to the top of her bassinet. It read: **Bee-YOO-ti-ful!** And, except maybe for this really stubborn cowlick that wouldn't stay down no matter how much you spit on it, she was.

Maybe I should explain a little more about that vasectomy thing. It wasn't really Treve's idea, and it sure wasn't mine. It was the army's. The army is a very regimented organization, as everyone knows. They like to have all their ducks in a row, and they hate surprises. I mean they don't hate *babies*, per se. But babies can come along at the most inconvenient times, and they can get expensive too, over the years. Because one of the best benefits for servicemen is free health care. Or at least it was still free back then, in the seventies. I'm not sure if it still is today. Anyway, the army kinda thought three kids was plenty for a serviceman. Or two. Or one. There used to be this saying in the old army, "If the army'd wanted you to have a wife (or family), they'da issued you one."

Every so often then, probably once a month or so, there was a mandatory "health class" held at the hospital for all the couples who'd recently had babies. At this health class they talked about various birth control methods, but mostly they were looking for vasectomy victims. I mean, the fewer rugrats there were, the cheaper it was gonna be for the army. But they also made a pretty good case for vasectomy as the most foolproof method of birth control, and how it would relieve "you young parents" of the worry of an "unexpected pregnancy." I mean, they didn't really pressure us to do it; they just laid out all the facts and let us make up our own minds. And I think they might have showed us a slide show or something about how very simple and virtually painless the operation was, and explained how it was much less complicated than a tubal ligation would be, and how it could be a husband's "gift" to his wife.

To tell the truth, it was a pretty good presentation. Well, Treve and I went home and talked it over for a few days. She didn't pressure me either, but, like I said, she already had that perfect family she'd always wanted, so *she* was okay with it.

So I got the vasectomy. And it really was a pretty simple procedure, although I have a funny story to go with it. There's always a funny story to go with anything that has to do with your balls. Every guy knows that. So here's mine. The day I had my "procedure," the doctor who was doing the surgery had a medical corpsman doing a little OJT. That's On-the-Job-Training, of course, which I'm all in favor of, but I didn't feel too good about this guy practicing on me. And I was *awake*, because they do this thing under a local anesthetic, see. My problem was, I was the first one to get the big V that day. Because there was a whole *roomful* of guys waiting to go under the knife that day. There was no roster or anything though; this nurse came out and just asked, "Who wants to be first?"

Well, it was about 10:00 by this time and I'd had to fast from the night before – don't ask me why; it was a local, like I said – and I was *hungry*. I wanted to go get some *break*fast, so I volunteered. Hell, I didn't know they had this OJT-er in there waiting to practice on me.

So I was on the table, in one of those stupid gowns and had already gotten the shot – and yeah, in the *scrotum*, ferChrisesakes. And that wasn't much fun either. And here are these two guys in surgical scrubs and masks and gloves and all, hovering there over my poor, wrinkly ol' balls, with their heads together. And I hear the older, grey-haired guy say, "Okay. Go ahead, make the incision, right there."

And I'm numbed up, so all I feel is a little bit of pressure.

"Good. Now see that white thing. That's the vas."

And I'm trying not to pay too close attention, but I can see them monkeying around down there with some little tongs or tweezers or something and muttering a bit.

And the old guy says, "And then you just snip it"

And the younger guy leans in with some instrument and starts to do something – snip it, I suppose.

"*No, NO!*" The old guy says, raising his voice just a little, and reaches over real quick and grabs the other guy's hand. "Not *that* one!"

Well, I sat right up straight on that table. It took them and the OR nurse a couple minutes to talk me back down. And I would only lie down after I'd made it perfectly clear that I wanted the old guy to finish this thing up. And he did. Let the new guy practice on all them other poor fuckers, I thought.

And that's my funny story about my vasectomy. I won't bore you with the details about how you have got to bring a few "samples" in – usually holding the container under your arm to keep it warm – over the next couple months or so, just to make sure the operation took. It may have been the only time in my life I jerked off knowing it was all for a good cause. And it did – take, I mean.

Remember how I wondered about exactly when we might have conceived Jeff? Well, Suzie is the only one of our kids that we know exactly when she was made. On the floor of Treve's childhood bedroom in her parents' house in Belleville. And we were on the floor because the springs of her bed squeaked way too loud. I was home on leave from Fort Meade, Maryland, for Thanksgiving break and we hadn't seen each other in nearly three months because I had been at temporary duty stations in Texas and Maryland since we left California in August. She and the boys had been living in Belleville. So even though her folks were sleeping in the next room and the boys were right upstairs, it couldn't wait another minute. Well after three months, it sure didn't take long, so we didn't make much noise. A few days later I went back to Fort Meade, and nine months later along came Suzie.

And I was there when she arrived. I mean right in the delivery room with Treve and the doctor and nurses and everybody. It was the first time I'd ever seen a baby born. With Jeff and Scott, I was just a "waiting room dad," like pretty much all of us were back then. But with Suzie I was right there, grunting and pushing right along with Treve. I guess I was really empathizing with her because I had bad hemorrhoids for weeks afterwards. No shit, I *did!*

The funny thing about it was we didn't plan for me to be there. It just happened. I had figured I'd do the standard waiting room thing just like I had before. Because they offered those natural childbirth Lamaze classes at the hospital for expectant parents, which was actually pretty progressive for an army hospital in 1978, or at least I think it was. But we'd decided not to participate, mostly because I was working a rotating shift schedule, and it would have been a real hassle for me to try to get time off for the classes. And Treve wasn't really all that anxious to have a baby by natural methods. She was all in favor of drugs and as little pain as possible. And I could certainly understand that.

Suzie was born on a Sunday morning, but we went to the hospital on Saturday afternoon, because Treve was having some bad labor pains. I must have been on break that weekend, because I was there. We'd been in Augsburg nearly six months by then and were pretty good friends with our neighbors across the hall from us. We lived on the third floor of the army's Cramerton married housing complex, and John and Carol Olivas lived right across the landing from us. Their two boys, Anthony and Damien, played with our boys all the time. I went over and got Carol, and she came right over to stay with our boys so we could hightail it to the hospital over on Flak. We needn't have hurried so, because we were there all afternoon and all night. It was a long hard labor for Treve, and I was feeling really bad for her. I guess maybe it's not quite as easy to have a baby at thirty as it is at twenty-something. I can't remember what we did for all those hours. I probably had a book, and she might have played solitaire, and probably kept telling me too where all the food was in the cupboards and fridge and what I should feed the boys and where their clothes were and stuff, 'cause she was always worried I wouldn't know how to look after the kids without her there. Because Treve is a super mom, and always has been. And even when she was hurting and about to give birth she was still thinking about her boys, and even missing them a little already, even after just a few hours. Of course they were probably having a good time playing with Anthony and Damian and eating cookies or something, but I couldn't tell *her* that. I just kept nodding my head and acting like I would remember all these instructions she was giving me, and telling her not to worry, we'd all be fine. And we were, of course.

It was nearly five AM when the nurse finally decided Treve was whaddayacallit, *dilated* enough, and they got ready to wheel her into delivery from the labor room where we'd been camped all this time.

So this nurse, she looked at me and said, "Are you coming?"

"Huh?" I said. (A really clever comeback, right?)

"Aren't you coming too?" she asked.

"Whaddayamean?" I asked. (More cleverness.)

"Aren't you the father?" she asked.

"Yeah."

"Well, don't you want to go with her?"

"Okay, sure." I replied.

This was, of course, a completely unexpected development to us, but Treve was looking at me expectantly too by this time, so what else could I say? I think I was beginning to shake just a little, as a medical orderly brought me some surgical scrubs to put on over my clothes, and even some little paper booty kinda things to put on my feet, but I managed to get everything on, and then the orderly led me into the delivery room where it was really bright and Treve was already up on a delivery table, and she was crying about how it hurt and she wanted some drugs.

"You'll have to wait for the doctor, dear," the nurse told her.

The thing was, we'd been there for about fifteen hours by then and hadn't seen the doctor once, although the nurse assured us she had called him and he was on his way. And sure enough, he showed up just a few minutes later, big Doc Lockett, strolling into the delivery room, freshly shaved and dressed in crisp, starched fatigues and gleaming, spit-shined boots.

"So how's Mom doing?" he asks in this jovial friendly manner.

"I want some *drugs!*" Treve shouted.

The ol' doc, he peeps in there under the drape between the stirrups, and he says, "I don't think so, Honey. You waited too long."

"*I* waited too long!" Treve screams. "I was *here!* Where were *you?!*"

"That baby is gonna be comin' along any minute now," the doc says, smiling this big toothy grin. "They ain't gonna be no time for no drugs, I'm afraid." And just then Treve's water broke and came splashing out off the end of the table all over those spit-shined boots.

"Well, shee-it!" the Doc muttered, looking down at his boots, his smile gone.

"What? What happened?" Treve asked, a frightened look on her face.

"Nothing, nothing. Everything's okay, Honey. You just take it easy. I'll be right back," Major Lockett said, and left the room, still looking down at his boots and shaking his head disgustedly. The nurse and the orderly were looking at each other and they were both smirking behind their masks; you could see it in their eyes.

January 19, 2009

Me, I wasn't smirking. I was too traumatized just from being there. I was torn between wishing there were something I could do to make Treve feel better, to take away her pain, and wishing I were in the fathers' waiting room where I belonged. But it was too late for the latter wish, and all I could do about the former was to hold on to Treve's hand, and when another wave of pain would overtake her, she would squeeze my hand so hard I was afraid she was going to crush all my knuckles.

But the tardy doctor returned a few minutes later, properly attired in sterile scrubs and rubber gloves this time. He did a quick check of things and told her it wouldn't be long now, and to go ahead and push. The OB nurse gave us a ten-second tutorial on the Lamaze breathing method, so both Treve and I started doing this funny little puffing stuff, which probably didn't help at all, since we had absolutely no idea what we were doing. But every time Treve bore down and pushed so did I, in empathy, I guess. I wanted so badly to help somehow. It's a wonder I didn't shit myself right there in the delivery room. I did, however, end up with those hemorrhoids I mentioned earlier.

But no matter. Within several minutes Suzie finally arrived, slipping easy as pie it seemed right into those enormous catcher's mitt hands of Doc Lockett. I'd been right about those hands. He was a natural. Suzie arrived squalling and pink-faced, and with a full head of dark hair. Nine years after our first boy and nearly seven after our second, we finally had our girl. Treve's family plan was complete.

By the time Suzie was born we were practically old hands at parenting. Our first baby, Jeff, was our "practice baby." We knew practically nothing about babies when he came along. Fortunately, Treve's mom, Wanda, came to stay with us for a week or so when Jeff was born, and provided us with some much-needed training. Wanda had raised four kids, after all, and had done a pretty damn good job too, all things considered.

So it was her mom Treve turned to with a lot of the early questions about the proper care and feeding of an infant. We still remember a few things from those days. For example, when we first brought Jeff home from the hospital he was still a little on the long and skinny side. He'd weighed six pounds and something when he was born, but had lost several ounces of that by the time he came home a few days later, which I guess is not unusual. The first time Treve put him on our new changing stand to change him, she was frightened when she got a good look at Jeff's bottom. And it was a little unusual-looking. There was a crease from near his oversized baby balls (and what is *that* all about, with baby's balls, I mean?), and then there was a smooth flat area before another slightly rounded crease near his tailbone.

"Oh, my *God*, Mommy! What's wrong with his *butt*? It looks all flat and squashed!" Treve cried in horror.

"Oh, my goodness, Honey," Wanda replied, wiping off Jeff's flat little tush and then sprinkling a bit of baby powder over it. "Calm down. There's nothing wrong with him. He just needs some fattening up, that's all. He's just fine." And pinning a clean cloth diaper onto the baby, she bent over and blew on his tummy, causing Jeff's face to crease into what may have been one of his earliest smiles.

The case of the flattened baby butt solved.

We were very fortunate to have Treve's mom around for a week or so. There were so many questions Treve had, so many things to learn all at once. And they were mostly her questions, I'll admit. I was like a lot of new fathers forty years ago. My primary function was to help make the baby, and then to make the money to support the baby. One of my perks was that I got to hold the baby and give him his bottle on occasion. And another major perk, after a decent interval, of course, was I got to boff the baby's mother again, whenever there was time, and the baby was sleeping. You know, normal daddy kinda stuff.

I think Treve's mom only stayed about a week, and then her dad, Chet, came up from Belleville for the baptism, which was held in the campus chapel of St. Mary's. Back then the Church still believed that babies should be baptized as soon as possible. Remember back then how the nuns taught us that unbaptized babies could never go to heaven? They didn't go to hell or purgatory either, but to this in-between eternal place called Limbo. I wonder who made *that* crap up. But we believed it or perhaps were afraid not to – so Jeff was just a week old when he was baptized. None of this "Limbo waiting room" just outside the gates of heaven for *this* kid if anything should happen to him, God forbid. I even said something to that effect out loud right after the baptism. We were all coming back to the apartment from church and I was carrying the baby up the stairs at HH8 Washington Court. Wanda cautioned me to be careful going up the concrete steps.

"Not to worry," I shot back at her cockily. "This kid's all baptized and sanctified now. If I drop him, he'll go straight to heaven."

My mother-in-law was horrified. She told that story to everyone who would listen for the next thirty years.

Treve's folks left shortly after the baptism and then we were on our own. Or maybe I should say *she* was, since I'm the first to admit I probably wasn't much help, other than perhaps as moral support.

When Jeff was born I was in the last month of my senior year at Central, and was finishing up my semester of student teaching just across town at Mount Pleasant High School, under the watchful eye of Mrs. Edna Wright, a lovely lady. I'm pretty sure I worked pretty hard at preparing lesson plans and lectures for that, but I sure can't remember much about it at this stage of my life. Only a couple memories remain. I was teaching senior level English, and that spring one of the kids in one of my classes – I think his name was Bob – got suspended from school for a short time. He was a very popular student athlete and he was riding the players' bus home after a game, feeling his oats a bit, obviously, and he mooned some people in a car following the bus. Well, somehow he got reported for this, and he wasn't in class for a week. I've often wondered who ever decided that making a kid that age stay home from school for a week was a punishment. It always seemed like a reward to me. I remember too that Bob got treated like a hero by all the other kids when he came back to school. And I think I did a unit on haiku poetry with the kids. Haiku was a very cool thing for high school English classes back then. Now I can't remember much about it. Something about counting the syllables in the lines and being very vague and ethereal. I could look it up, but you probably don't care anyway. I know I sure don't.

Besides that moon landing, the other important thing that happened the year Jeff was born was that *Sesame Street* debuted on PBS. I had actually seen a pilot film of *Sesame Street* the previous fall while taking an Education course called TV in the Classroom. That pilot film is just about the only thing I remember from that class now, because it was little different from most of the education classes I was required to take if I wanted to get my provisional secondary teaching certificate. And they all seemed like a lot of garbage. Anyway, we got to see this really neat film, featuring Big Bird, Oscar the Grouch, Bert and Ernie, as well as Gordon and Susan and Mister Hooper. These were all brand-new, original characters at the time, not like they are today, practically household words. After we saw the film, we all had to fill out a survey form about how we liked it, why we did or didn't like it. And the form even asked for suggestions. As I remember it, the show got rave reviews from just about all the students. I guess the pilot film was circulated to teachers' colleges all over the country before it finally actually debuted on TV in November of 1969, nearly a year after I saw it. The rest is history, as they say.

I remember how excited I was when I found out it was coming on TV as a regular show that fall. Jeff was only about six months old, but we sat him up in our rocking chair right in front of the television with a big pillow on each side of him and another one across his lap to prop him in place. My folks bought us that rocker right after Jeff was born; it was green with soft cushions on the seat and back. We gave Jeff one of those teething biscuits he really liked, to munch on while the show was on. I think maybe he took just one gnaw on that biscuit when we first gave it to him, but then, from the opening strains of "Sunny Day" to the closing credits he mostly just sat there staring at the tube, eyes wide and drool running down his chin. I mean, he was just *mesmerized* by that show from the very first episode. Jeff literally grew up on *Sesame Street*, and so did our other two kids.

It just occurred to me that Treve might not be too happy with me slipping this stuff in here, because it kinda demonstrates that our first baby is gonna be forty this year. Which would make her …

But no matter. She always tells people she was only twelve when we married.

I can't tell you how much joy we got from Jeff when he was a baby. I mean we were really amateurs as parents, I know, but we sure had fun learning how to be better at it. Treve even dropped him on his head once. It's not really as bad as it sounds. It was an accident. She had him up on the changing stand when he was about six months old and she only turned her back for a split second or so, to get a diaper or some powder or something, and all of a sudden he was on the floor. So we don't really know if he actually fell on his *head*, or some other part, but lemme tell ya, he cried blue murder and it scared the hell outa Treve. So much so that she actually called me at work, which she hardly ever did, probably because I'd told her not to unless it was an emergency.

I was in graduate school by then and had landed a teaching assistantship, which means I taught a couple sections of Freshman Comp while taking a full load of classes too. I think it paid some princely sum like twelve hundred dollars a year or thereabouts. So I had a desk in an office with three or four other grad students and teachers over in Anspach Hall, which was only about three or four blocks from our apartment. When I got this phone call from Treve, she was crying so hard I could barely understand her, and I could hear the baby crying too. When I finally figured out that she was saying she'd dropped Jeff, and *may*be on his head and she couldn't get him to stop crying, I got pretty worried too and told her I'd be right home. I mean I didn't even pick up my books or papers or coat or anything, I just flew out of that office and down the stairs and ran as fast as I could all the way home. I must have looked like a crazy man, because everybody I passed was turning around and looking at me. But at six foot five I was never a very graceful runner, so maybe it was just this loony-looking Ichabod Crane apparition flapping down the sidewalk that made 'em gawk.

Well, by the time I came tearing into the apartment, all sweaty and panting and wild-eyed, Jeff had stopped crying and so had Treve. The crisis seemed to have passed, but we were both pretty worried and kept thinking awful things like what if there were brain damage and stuff? So we called Dr. Chamberlain and told him what happened. This was back when if you called your doctor's office you actually got to talk with your doctor. He told us not to worry, but that we should try to keep the baby awake for a few hours, not to let him go to sleep. I guess that was just in case he might slip into a coma or something, or at least that's what *we* were worried about. So I stayed home with Treve and we played with Jeff and kept him awake and he was laughing and gurgling like babies do normally, so gradually we got a little less nervous about the whole thing and decided he was okay.

But now that I think of it, that's probably not a very good example of all the fun we had learning to be better parents. But we did have fun with him, really. One of the funniest things that happened when Jeff was still brand new, I think it was around the second week, was when Tom and Sharon Derda came up from downstairs to see the new baby, and they brought their little girl, Debbie, who was just a toddler. And Tom had this tiny little football he'd brought as a present for the baby, and we were all standing around the changing stand while Treve was changing Jeff's diaper and Tom was holding this little football up to show Jeff, who was looking at it and cooing and gurgling and stuff and just then he peed straight up into the air and this stream of piddle just went up and over in this perfect arc and went in Tom's shoe. And I think they were new loafers too. Treve got all red in the face and was trying to apologize for this little mishap, but Sharon was just cracking up, she thought it was so funny. For Tom, of course, it was one of those "well, shee-it" kinda moments, but he got over it right away, probably mostly because his wife was laughing so hard, and little Debbie, she didn't really see what happened, I guess, cause she kept asking her mommy what was so funny. Not exactly a Kodak moment, but we still remember it.

And speaking of baby pee, Jeff trotted out that trick one other memorable time for company. And this is a really good memory, because it involves this wonderful woman we got to know there at Central. Catherine O'Connell was a reference librarian over at the CMU library. I got to know her pretty well because my last year at Central, when I was in grad school, I had all these damn term papers to do. Just about every class I took required either one major term paper or several small ones every semester. Well, the truth is I was really hurrying through grad school as fast as I could, so I always had a full load of classes. I finished my BA in June of 1969 and about a week or two later I began grad school, taking two or three accelerated summer terms before regular fall semester classes started. By doing this I was able to finish my MA by the following June. I doubt if you can get an MA in one year anymore, but it was just barely doable back then, and only if you were willing to work your ass off, which I was, and which I did.

But no matter. So since I was in the library doing research for these papers all the time, Miss O'Connell got to know me pretty well, and she was just so darn helpful, always finding me obscure journals and articles and even ordering stuff for me from other libraries. I was really grateful to her, believe me. Without her help I might not have been able to get through grad school as quickly as I did. She was just the sweetest lady you could ever meet. She was probably fifty-ish or so. And yes, she was a "Miss," a spinster, or what we used to call an "old maid" as kids. Yeah, like the card game. The truth was Catherine O'Connell was perhaps one of the homeliest women you were ever likely to meet. The kindest thing you could say about her was that she was "rather plain." And she had a bit of a hump too, probably scoliosis or maybe osteoporosis. But she was so nice to me, and such a kind and helpful person that after I'd known her a while I didn't even notice much how she looked. And what was perhaps even more important was that she loved art and literature and books even more than I – and that's saying something.

So after I'd known Miss O'Connell for a while I invited her to dinner at our place. Of course I cleared it with Treve first. And she was a little nervous about it at first, I'll admit, because she didn't think she was much of a cook. Well, maybe she didn't cook anything really fancy, but I sure never went hungry. The fact of the matter is, when we first got married Treve could barely boil water without burning it, but she got better. For the first month or so we were married, our big meal was Banquet pot pies with a green salad. Remember back when you could get those little pies – chicken, turkey beef or tuna – so cheap, usually on sale, four or five for a dollar? Well we both liked them and ate a lot of them in our early days. Hell, I was having so much fun in the sack I didn't really care what we ate. Glorious days those – pot pies and sex, sometimes several times a week. We were so new to each other that it took us a couple weeks to admit that one pie with a salad didn't really fill us up. Finally we confessed to each other. Then we baked three pies and would split one. But when we reached the four-pie threshold we were both finally a lot happier. We both still remember one night when I got home from working in the Ronan food commons where I washed dishes and mopped up. I was really hungry, but more than a little horny too – and maybe she was too. So we put four pies in the oven and went to bed while they baked. We woke up at about two am to this kinda burning smell. We had to throw those pies out, but we didn't care.

But no matter. By the time we invited Miss O'Connell to dinner, Treve's culinary skills had come along some. She progressed from scratch-made macaroni and cheese to more complicated stuff like pot roast with potatoes and gravy and vegetables – whole deluxe meals like that. In fact we might have had a pot roast the night Miss O'Connell came to dinner. And it must have been a success because she sure didn't complain any. In fact she showered Treve with praise about her cooking. And I think maybe we had a chocolate cake for dessert. Anyway, after dinner we were sitting around talking about books and stuff and Treve excused herself, saying she had to give Jeff his bath in the kitchen sink. And Miss O'Connell, she asked if she could watch. As far as we know, Miss O'Connell's only relative was a brother in Chicago, so she didn't get much chance to see babies or little kids, and she thought Jeff was just darling. So she came over and watched Treve get Jeff into the sink, where he was just as happy as pie, of course, patting the water and splashing and playing with his rubber duck, just like Ernie's. (Did you know that Ernie's song from *Sesame Street*, "Rubber Ducky," was a Top 40 tune when it was first released around 1970? No kidding, it *was*; and it was even on the juke box over in the student union.) She was standing right beside Treve, watching, when Treve leaned Jeff back to wash and rinse his hair, and that's when Jeff decided to let loose with another one of those arcing streams of piddle, up and over, right on Miss O'Connell's dress. I think he got her on the shoulder and sleeve or thereabouts.

Treve was horrified, of course, that Jeff had so defiled our dinner guest, but Catherine's first comment was one of absolute delight.

"Oh, isn't that *love*-ly," she exclaimed. "Just like a *Roman fountain!*"

This from a woman who had traveled to Rome and Athens and all over Europe and Mexico. So I guess she knew what she was talking about.

We knew she'd been to all those places because during our last year at Central Miss O'Connell became a dear friend of ours, who visited our apartment several more times and invited us to her tiny two-bedroom rancher over on the west side of town, a house that was filled to the gills with books, paintings, pottery, pieces of sculpture and other objets d' art from all over the world. She was a collector of lovely things and had surrounded herself with beauty. So if she said our kid pissing on her dress was lovely, then, by God, I guess it was. *Like a Roman fountain!*

Miss O'Connell also was a lover of music, and one of the things in her crammed little house was a state-of-the-art stereo system that I might have sacrificed my left nut to possess. It was an AM-FM radio and record player with changer encased in a beautiful round wood grain cabinet, and the best part of it was that a very cushy reclining chair was connected to it with wings that came out of the back on both sides of your head and these wings were fitted with speakers. So when you turned on the set and sank back into this chair you were surrounded with sound, just like being in a concert hall. Her collection was mostly classical. I didn't know much about classical music then (still don't, actually), but whenever she put me down in that chair – and she did it almost every time we visited – it was like heaven.

We stayed in touch with Catherine (it wasn't until after I'd graduated and we had moved away that we finally became comfortable calling her by her first name) for many years after we left Central. She gave me a graduation present of a silver CMU letter opener, and she also gave us a small boxed set of Christmas ornaments to hang on our tree. She has been gone for many years now, but every Christmas we think of her, and whenever I use the letter opener I remember her too. It's like she's still here for us. Wise gifts, and a warm and wonderful woman.

I won't say no matter this time. Because she did.

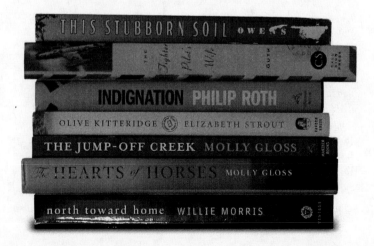

January 21, 2009

I missed a whole day in there, no writing. I was watching Barack Obama's inauguration stuff on TV off and on all day yesterday. But mostly it was just laziness. I read the latest issue of *The New Yorker* and a few of Donald Hall's poems from his *White Apples* book. And then last night I made some popcorn and started reading this memoir called *Chosen by a Horse*, which is pretty darn good, so ... no writing yesterday.

But no matter.

I've been trying to remember specific things about my stint in Minuteman, but not much is surfacing, only small fragments. Once I got my orders for Leonard Wood there was more of that waiting and hanging around at the Detroit AFEES, of course, but finally a bunch of us were given a lift to the airport in an army van. There were about a dozen of us in the group for Leonard Wood, and I think I was even "in charge," probably because I was the oldest. But all the guys were retreads like me, so it's not like I had to be "responsible" for them or anything. I mean if I lost one of them on the way to Missouri what were they gonna do, fire me?

There were a lot of those déjà vu moments those first few days, but the fact that we flew instead of taking a train kinda sped things up from the very beginning. And the fact that our BCT – that's Basic Combat Training – was squeezed into just two weeks made it all a lot faster. In fact it was kind of a blur. Maybe that's why I can't remember all that much. What I remember most though is that this time around I wasn't afraid like I'd been back in 1962. Because back then, when I was only eighteen, those drill sergeants had just scared the living shit out of me nearly every day. BCT back then had been, without a doubt, the most miserable and frightening time of my young life. Not this time. It was different from the time we got off the bus at the reception camp.

The DI's were right there in your face, of course, but this time they just didn't faze me. I gave the right responses, the "Yes, Drill Sergeant" or "No, Drill Sergeant," and managed to keep a straight face, but inside I was just kind of smiling, because this was all so familiar. I looked at these guys in their Smoky hats and their fatigues that were starched into these knife-edge creases and boots spit-shined to hell-and-back and I thought, *Why, these guys are younger than I am*. Because they were. So yeah, everything felt different this time around, like that old song, "Love's more *comfortable*, the second time around …"

Well, it wasn't exactly *love*, but it was familiar, you know? Reception Camp hadn't changed much in the past ten years. The food was still awful, and we were left kind of on our own for a few days other than having to fall out for formations a couple times a day. And we all marched to the quartermaster and got our clothing issue and got it all into our duffel bags and marched back again. And we probably got haircuts and all our shots and dental checks and stuff like that. Déjà vu, like I said.

I'd brought along a little bound book with blank pages, because I thought maybe I'd have time to keep a journal this time around. I remember this book I'd read some years back by an army reservist, *The Sunshine Soldiers*, which had really been funny, so I thought maybe I could do something similar. It didn't work out though. I did make a few entries, but once we left the reception camp I never really had time to use it again.

Well, shit. I thought I'd look up that book I just mentioned, and found out that the author, Peter Tauber, died about 5 years ago. He dropped dead of a heart attack while he was on a ski trip to Utah. He'd been a freelance writer and reporter in New York for most of his life. He was only fifty-six. Sometimes the stuff you find on the internet isn't exactly what you'd hoped for. R.I.P., Pete. It was a damn good book. You absolutely nailed just what BCT was like forty years ago.

I still remember the first morning at Minuteman when our platoon fell out in front of the barracks, all decked out in our brand-new fatigues and boots. I think we were all pretty much ready to get started with this accelerated version of BCT, or maybe, more accurately, to just get it over with, so we could head on out to our next duty station for the training we'd actually signed up for.

So we were all out there milling around in the early morning darkness and shootin' the shit, most of the guys smoking. I don't smoke. I did my first time around in the army, but I'd quit when I got out. Anyway, here comes this DI in his Smoky hat, a short stocky guy, and he finds his mark out there under the streetlight and he hollers out in this stentorian authoritarian voice.

"Awright, mins (that's DI for 'men'), gimme four ranks!"

And all these guys – all of us prior service, you have to keep in mind; we've already been through all this crap before, and most of the guys were Vietnam vets, so they'd been through a lot worse – they kinda glance over at the DI for a second, then they go right back to their smoking and talking and milling around.

"I said I want four *ranks* over here, an' I mean *NOW!*" The DI is getting a bit upset now.

Most of the guys turned toward the DI and regarded him seriously, but nobody put out their cigarettes and none of us made any move towards forming up. Me, I would have, but I was kinda going with the flow here, waiting to see what would happen. This was all brand-new to me; nothing like the basic I remembered from my first time around. It was very interesting, actually.

Well, the DI, he was getting really pissed off here. He got himself all puffed up like a little banty rooster and he starts *screaming* at us, I mean he was losin' it.

"What the fuck's a *matter* wit'chu guys?! Can'tchu *hear*? I said gimme four *ranks* over here! *Fall in*, dammit!"

This time he had our attention, but what happened was all of us just turned around enough so we were facing the drill sergeant. Otherwise nobody moved. We'd quit talking and we were all just staring at this little foul-mouthed prick and some of these guys were pretty big and menacing-looking. The DI stood there looking back at us. It was his move. Suddenly his whole demeanor changed. It was like someone had let the air out of him.

"*C'mon* you guys. We got a lotta stuff to do today. So let's fall in so we can get started, okay?"

It wasn't a whine so much as a kind of wheedling tone this time, but so obviously no longer an order. It was a request, between equals. The face-off was over. The tension dissolved almost immediately. There was a little quiet laughter and last-minute muttering as the guys put out their smokes and field-stripped the butts, and then we all started moving into place, getting quickly into a formation of four ranks and spacing ourselves properly, left arms extended, an exercise easily recalled from our previous military lives.

And that's kind of the way it went for the next two weeks. We were all there because we'd volunteered, but we weren't about to be bullied and terrorized the way we had been as kids that first time around. There was, from that moment on, a kind of tacit agreement between the men and that DI – and the others we encountered too – that we were there to do a job and that was all.

The training went very quickly. That DI was right. We did have a lot to do and not very much time to do it in. And I think the army realized that if you had a whole unit of prior service types it would be a different atmosphere, and it certainly was. It was a "you-don't-fuck-with-us" and we'll do what we need to do kind of atmosphere, and it pretty much worked most of the time. I will make that qualification, because I think the whole Minuteman concept was abolished not too long after I went through it.

We did a lot of classroom refresher training, on the UCMJ (Uniform Code of Military Justice) and the Geneva Convention and general orders. And there was some cursory field training on first aid, map reading, gas masks, and PT (Physical Training) and so on. But there was no week-long bivouac, no extended time at the rifle ranges, and none of the horrible physical and mental harassment that had marked my first basic training. I never felt any particular pressure during Minuteman. In fact, after more than five years of teaching, with all the preparation and paperwork that went with it, I felt a kind of freedom from responsibility that I hadn't felt in years. Minuteman training, although it was physically demanding and left me exhausted at the end of each day, was actually kind of fun, like a summer camp kinda vacation (although it was winter time). In fact I can still remember feeling somewhat guilty about it all, because I knew Treve was back home with the boys trying to hold it all together. We had been married for over eight years by this time, but I had always been there to help. Suddenly she was doing a solo act in what had been a duo, coping with bills and household problems, still nervous about being a new driver, and also facing the prospect of selling the first home we'd ever owned and moving across the country. I mean she had all this stuff on her plate. And all I had to do was get up each morning and go play army, just like I'd done when I was seven and eight years old, digging foxholes in the nearby sandpit in Holdenville with my brothers and the neighbor kids – Kenny Roggow, Dave Coon, Lessel Lofgren and Roger Stager – and throwing crabapple grenades and creating mock explosions.

I was nearly thirty-two years old and I was out playing in the sandpit again. Only I got to use real grenades and a genuine M16 rifle this time. What fun it all was! So sure I felt a little guilty. It was, I suppose, a kind of regression for me.

That M16 was quite a surprise to me. I'm not a firearms sort of guy at all. I've always been a little leery of weapons of all kinds. My first basic training I'd been issued an M-1, a weapon much admired by real rifle enthusiasts, but one I had never really mastered, and didn't learn to love. I only barely qualified as a marksman with the M-1, and I always suspected that the range cadre had taken pity on me at that, and fudged in a couple extra targets for me.

The M16 was a completely different story. For some reason I took to it right away. I wasn't afraid of it the way I had been with the M-1. Maybe it was just the added maturity on my part, but I think there was more to it than that. First of all, the M16 weighed about three or four pounds less than the M-1. It was smaller all around, and had parts made of high-impact plastic. It fact it reminded just a little bit of a toy Tommy gun my little brother had played with years ago. Remember the one when you pulled the trigger it made this plasticky but satisfying rat-tat-tat sound? Apparently I wasn't the only one who felt that way and remembered those toy guns, because we joked among ourselves about it being a "swell" rifle, because "If it's Mattel, it's swell."

But I think that sort of casual attitude toward the M16 only held sway among the non-combat vets like me. The guys in the unit who'd been to Vietnam and had relied every day on their M16, just to stay alive, would have none of that. They respected the weapon, and told us some real horror stories about their experiences. So I learned right away not to make any jokes about the M16, out of respect for these vets – and I did, and still do, respect those guys tremendously for all they went through.

Just in case you hadn't done the math about when I reenlisted, by 1976 we were out of Vietnam. After more than a dozen years there, our involvement was over. All the troops had been pulled out, the embassy abandoned – we were gone. And just in case you don't know your history – *psst*, we *lost*. Not because of what the military did or didn't do, but because of the jerks in Washington at the time. At least that's the way I saw it then, and still do.

But, strangely enough, one of the things I remember most about Minuteman was meeting the M16 and learning to break it down and maintain it and then to fire it. It was fun. I wasn't afraid this time. In fact I qualified as an expert with the M16, which is the highest level of marksmanship badge, and I was pretty proud of that.

When I'd decided to reenlist, I had been a little worried about the physical part of things. Here I was an old man of thirty-one who hadn't done much of anything to stay in shape for the past several years, so I was a little afraid I wouldn't be up for the physical challenges that BCT would present. I knew I'd have to pass a timed two-mile run as part of the PT test, so for a month or two before I left for the army, I started running. I marked out a two-mile course around Riverside Manor, our Monroe subdivision, and up Custer road and back; and every morning (well, al*most* every morning – I wasn't *that* disciplined yet), I'd put on my sneakers and old clothes and I'd run that course, and time myself. And after just a few weeks I was running the distance in the time allotted by the army for someone in my age group, over thirty.

So when it came time for the PT test in minuteman, the two-mile run was really a piece of cake. I managed to run it in well under the time allowed. I maxed out on sit-ups and even managed to do okay on pushups. Another part of the PT test was not so easy. The horizontal ladder event, or "the bars," was no easier for me at thirty-one than it had been at eighteen. Tall guys just don't do well on that event. I did get to a point where I could almost do the minimum number of rungs. The NCO who scored me took pity on me. I was a couple rungs short of the minimum required when I fell off on my last try. He shook his head, but then he smiled and said, "Close enough, Bazzett." And went ahead and marked the minimum score on my card.

That was sort of typical of the Minuteman attitude though. The cadre seemed to appreciate the fact that we were all veterans here and were doing the best we could, so small allowances were occasionally made. It was never an adversarial kind of atmosphere between the trainees and the DI's, and that short two-week window to get in all that training was a real challenge in itself. It all went by so fast and we were always so busy or tired that there wasn't even much time to get to know your fellow trainees, let alone the DI's and other permanent party cadre in the Minuteman company.

But in spite of that, Minuteman actually threw a party for me the night of my birthday. I can't remember anyone's name from those weeks, but I still remember the cake and all the good will that surrounded me that night. It came as a complete surprise to me too. One night our DI came into the barracks and ordered the whole platoon over to the mess hall where we were to stand by for some special training. So we all marched over to the mess hall, grumbling and wondering what the hell *this* was all about. So we all got inside and were standing around between the tables, and out come the cooks, our platoon sergeant and two or three of our DI's from the kitchen, and they're all singing Happy Birthday. The mess sergeant was carrying this enormous sheet cake with a few candles burning on it. And he brought it over and put it down on the table right in front of me. And on the cake was written in frosting, "Happy Birthday, Tim." And then all the rest of the platoon got it, and they joined in the singing. I was thirty-two years old that day, and, as it turned out, the oldest guy in my platoon – maybe in the company.

Well, I was simply flabbergasted, I was so surprised. And I damn near cried. Wouldn't *that* have been embarrassing? But

I managed not to; instead I thanked the cooks and everybody. I was really kind of overwhelmed, and I think they could tell. I made my wish and blew out the candles. There was a lot of laughing and talking and everybody was shaking my hand and slapping me on the back and joking about my being such an "old man." It's just hard to describe what I was feeling. The cake got cut and milk materialized and we had a sit-down party. I was a celebrity for a half-hour or so – the "old guy" of the company. It was surreal, but in a nice kind of way, and I have never forgotten it.

So those are my memories of Minuteman. A lot of it was cold and muddy and uncomfortable – it was January, after all. But I got through it, and, unlike my first time around in basic, I even have some warm and fuzzy memories from it.

And then, just as the training cycle came to an end, I got some bad news and some good news. The bad news was that my orders for DLI in Monterey hadn't come through. Our training was over and practically everyone in the company had gotten their orders to their next training or permanent duty station, as well as travel and leave papers. That last day of training I kept checking the company bulletin board and going into the company orderly room trying to find out what had happened to *my* orders. But no one seemed to know anything. By that evening, a Friday, practically everyone was gone and the company area had nearly emptied out. I felt sick. I wandered over to the mess hall and had dinner with the cooks and a few other permanent party, who all sympathized with me, and tried to reassure me it would probably all get straightened out by *Monday!* I thought. Shit-fire, everyone had pulled out and left for home and here I was, all by myself in an empty company area. Some things never change, I thought angrily. The army is just as fucked up as it ever was. What the hell was I thinking anyway, reenlisting?!

I was just finishing up my supper, feeling extremely sorry for myself, when a short, grey-haired Master Sergeant in dress greens came into the mess hall and looked around. He looked familiar.

"Is PFC Bazzett here?" he asked the cooks.

"That's Bazzett," said the mess sergeant, pointing my way.

I got up as the man made his way over to me. And then I remembered where I'd seen him before. He was the NCO in charge of the ASA Processing Detachment where I'd spent part of an afternoon the previous week filling out papers to have my AIT orders confirmed. (That's Advanced Individual Training, for you non-military types.)

"Bazzett, I don't know if you remember me; I'm Sergeant Booth from the ASA Det. I imagine you're a little worried about not getting your orders, and I'm afraid I don't have any real good news," the sergeant said, shaking his head. "The fact is your assignment to language school was never verified by your recruiter. I just found out a few days ago that you don't have a slot for a February Russian class at DLI. I've been working ever since to try to get you one, but the best I could do was get you started in the middle of March."

The middle of *March?* I thought. But that's almost *six weeks* away! I was stunned. I sat back down. My disappointment must have shown, because Sergeant Booth sat down too.

He reached over and put a hand on my shoulder. "I know you were probably figurin' on going home today, but I'm afraid that ain't gonna happen."

All I could think of right then was Treve and the boys, who had indeed been expecting me home in the next twenty-four hours. I looked down at my shoes, trying to come to grips with this shitty mess.

"I can't get you home this week," Sergeant Booth continued sympathetically. "But maybe we can work something out for you soon."

I looked up, feeling a glimmer of hope.

"For right now though, let's go get your gear and see about getting' you checked into my personal hotel for holdovers. It ain't much, but it's a hell of a lot better than what you've had these past few weeks. Whaddaya say? You ready to go?" And he got up and smiled at me.

And that was the good news, such as it was. I was finished with the less-than-sterling accommodations of the Minuteman Training Company, which had been the normal open bay setup with rows of double bunks kind of thing. I was about to get something I had never before had in the army: my own private room. Of course, I'd have much preferred to go home, but if I couldn't do that, then this was certainly better than nothing.

Master Sergeant Earl Booth was a good man. And that is my highest form of praise. I got to know him a little over the next several weeks. He loved his job and he loved the army, and loving the army is not always an easy thing to do. Sometimes it is damn near impossible. But apparently Sergeant Booth had not always loved the army, because he had been discharged from it twice. The second time he reenlisted, he must have found his niche, because he was a happy man who now had more than twenty years of service, so he could retire whenever he wanted, but, like I said, he loved his job. He was probably ten or twelve years older than I was at the time I met him and explained that he'd gotten out of the service twice and then come back again, so he had kind of a soft spot for prior service guys.

"Hell, a soft spot in my *head*, more than likely," he laughed, as he told me this, driving me in his car from Minuteman to the 'Booth Hotel.' "But I figure I know what it's like to be gone for a while and then come back again, and all the doubts you have about it. But let me tell you right now, young man. You did *not* make a mistake. The army may screw up now and then, but the army looks after its own, and that's what I'm doing right now."

I can't remember for sure at this late date, but I think Sergeant Booth had been in the Infantry for most of his off-and-on career. He had served in Korea and Vietnam and had the medals to prove it. He had only transferred over to the Army Security Agency a few years before I encountered him at Leonard Wood, where he was in charge of a detachment of five or six low-ranking clerk-typists at the ASA PP&T Det (Procurement, Processing & Training Detachment). It was a pretty cushy assignment. He could have just put in his time and coasted, but he was always looking for other things he could do – helpful things; things that would make the army a better place for its people.

Hence, the Booth Hotel.

The PP&T Det occupied the bottom floor of an old wooden WWII-era barracks building. The same kind I had just left behind at Minuteman, and the same kind I'd lived in for regular BCT back in 1962. These old barracks had been upgraded some by the 70s though, mostly by adding much need insulation and installing gas or oil furnaces to replace the old coal burners of the past. The ASA offices on the ground floor was comprised of a couple rows of about six or eight desks where the clerks did their work, and Sergeant Booth had a small private office at one end of the building. At the other end was the normal barracks style latrine. But the toilets were enclosed by stalls with doors here, a much more civilized arrangement that the BCT barracks, where the commodes had neither partitions or doors. There were also sinks, urinals and a shower room with several shower heads.

When Sergeant Booth had taken over the PP&T Det a year or two before, the upstairs floor had been standing empty, a large open bay room used only for storage. With a little ingenuity and some raw materials he appropriated from supply or from other barracks that were being torn down around post, he had transformed the upper floor into living quarters with four large semi-private rooms (two single bunks in each room with foot lockers and wall lockers too). There was also a sizable common area at one end – a dayroom with a few comfortable chairs, a couch, with end tables, lamps and coffee table, a full-size pool table, and – the piece de resistance – a large console color TV.

It's true that the rooms were quite bare. The drywall that enclosed them had yet to be primed and painted, but my *God!* I was *amazed* when I saw the place. After the Spartan living conditions of Minuteman, the place seemed positively palatial. And right at the top of the stairs there was also a small makeshift kitchen off the common area which held a refrigerator, a two burner hotplate on a table (with two chairs), and an electric popcorn popper, as well as a small collection of pots, pans and dishes. Sergeant Booth had even stocked a shelf with a few cans of soup and other canned goods.

It was already dark when he brought me and my duffel bag up to my new digs, so, without wasting a lot of time, he went down the hall to the empty end room and got me some linens and pillows and a couple of blankets out of a locker and brought them out and threw them on the couch.

"You can pick either one of the rooms on this end," he said. "One of my clerks is officially living in the room on the far left, but he's got himself a honey in town, so he's almost never here. For right now, you're my only tenant, so make yourself at home. Bathroom and shower's downstairs, as you know." Then he fished around in his pocket and found me a key. "This here's the key to the front door," he added. "Be sure to lock it whenever you go out."

I was just standing there with my mouth hanging open, still trying to get my mind around this sudden and drastic change in my circumstances. So Sergeant Booth, he reached out and took my hand and dropped the key into it.

"I guess you're all set then," he said, smiling. "I'll see ya Monday morning and then we'll see what we can do about gettin' you some leave, okay?"

"Okay," I nodded, suddenly remembering my manners. "Thanks for everything, Sergeant. This is really great."

"No problem. Okay then. Oh, our mess hall's next door and breakfast starts at 7 on Saturday, but they're usually open 'til around 9, so you don't have to hurry. The chow's pretty good, and I told the cook you'd be here. You have a good weekend now, hear? And try not to worry. We'll get them orders straightened out for ya."

Then he went down the stairs, out the door and was gone. And I was all alone for the first time in nearly four weeks. The quiet was deafening. I looked around me, at the soft couch and chairs, the color TV. This was all so very *un*-army, it was almost a little unnerving. It was Friday night at Fort Leonard Wood. I had the weekend off. Un-fucking-be-*LIEV*-able, as we used to say my first time around. I wasn't going home yet, but I had definitely come up in the world.

I spent the rest of February and a little of March there at Booth's Hotel. And Sergeant Booth made good on his promise to get me home. On Presidents' Day weekend, he cut me loose on a Thursday morning and asked if I could be back by the next Wednesday night. I'm not kidding. He *asked* me if that would be long enough. This was supposed to be a three-day weekend, understand, and he gave me a whole week off. And here's how he did it.

"Now this is just between you and me, Bazzett," he told me one day in his office the week before the holiday. "Here's what I'm gonna do. I'm gonna write you up leave papers for the whole week, and I'm gonna keep a couple copies here just to make it look official. And if any MPs or police or anybody needs to see your leave papers, you'll have 'em to show. But when you get back from leave, you come back here to me and we'll just tear these leave papers up; that way you won't get charged for any time off. How's that sound to you?"

"Sounds great, Sergeant. I can't tell you how much this means to me," I replied. What I was *think*ing was more along the lines of, *Holy* crap! *Is this great or what?*

If all this sounds just too good to be true, I understand. But I lived this strange shadow existence at Sergeant Booth's holdover hotel for the next several weeks. It was almost like I had ceased to exist, as far as the army was concerned. I had no formations to fall out for, no schedule, no duties. I couldn't really handle it. Usually every morning during the week I'd come down and kind of "report" to Sergeant Booth and ask if there was anything he had for me to do. Usually he'd say no, almost apologizing.

"I thought maybe I'd have some typing or filing you could do if you really wanted to do something, Bazzett, but as it is I don't even have enough work to keep my own people busy."

So I was set free each day, to wander around post, to the PX or snack bar, or maybe just to go back upstairs and watch TV, read or play a solitary game of pool. At night sometimes I'd go to a cheap movie at the nearest post theater. It was all so free and easy that it was almost surreal, but gradually I settled into this strange routine and learned not to feel too guilty about it all.

And on top of all this, Sergeant Booth also allowed me to use the phone in his office to call home whenever I wanted. I tried not to abuse this privilege and usually only called Treve on weekends, which could be especially lonely.

When it wasn't too cold, I would often wander about the post, trying to find the barracks, service clubs and theaters I had spent time in back in 1962, but there was such a sameness to the architecture and layout of the various buildings and unit areas that I never was able to find anything for certain.

It's hard to remember now how else I occupied those long days, how I got through them. I read a lot. There were a bunch of paperbacks in the dayroom that I went through. I remember reading William Goldman's thriller, *Marathon Man*, and wincing at the dental torture inflicted by the despicable villain therein. I found and read a copy of T.H. White's *The Once and Future King* with its wonderful and fanciful tales of King Arthur. I reread *The Last Detail* and *Cinderella Liberty* and then wrote to their author, Darryl Ponicsan. Ponicsan was a navy veteran whose novels I had admired for some time. I wrote to him about where I was and about my mid-life crisis reenlistment blues. Much to my surprise, he actually wrote back, commiserated with me over the strangeness of life, particularly the military life, and wished me well. I've still got that letter, and I re-established contact with Darryl a couple years ago. I sent him a copy of my book, *Soldier Boy*; he liked it enough to write me a little blurb for it. Cool. Well, come to think of it maybe it was just kinda tit for tat thirty years later. Because back in 1975 when I was still teaching I reviewed his novel, *Tom Mix Died for Your Sins*, for *Best Sellers* magazine.

When the work day was over downstairs at the PP&T and everyone had left for the day, I would go down and clean the place up. It was something I'd volunteered to do, just to feel like I was earning my keep, I guess. Sergeant Booth had at first told me I didn't need to do anything, but that just didn't feel right for me. So I would go through the office and empty the ashtrays and waste baskets, and then I would sweep the floor and do any necessary mopping. I'd finish up by getting out the buffer and polishing the floor. The whole thing never took me more than an hour or two at the most. I think my doing this stuff was just part of what my dad had taught me: do your work *first*; then you can play. So I felt a little better about going upstairs to read or watch TV then for the night.

I have one rather vivid memory of a Saturday night alone in the barracks in early March. I'd made popcorn and was sitting and watching *The Sound of Music* on TV, and the wind was gusting and howling outside the windows. It was like, "the hills are alive," ya know? I'd never seen this Julie Andrews classic and quite enjoyed it. Probably if there'd been other guys around we would all have been too embarrassed to watch such a film. Not manly and all that. But what the hell, I was all by myself, so I watched it. Popcorn always helps, of course. Then I went to bed and slept soundly. On my way to chapel the next morning for Mass, I walked by a building just a block away with its roof torn completely off. I had slept through a tornado.

My AIT dates were finally confirmed and orders cut. I left Fort Leonard Wood and the homely delights of Booth's Hotel sometime around the first or second week of March, I believe. After a week's leave back home with Treve and family, I flew from Detroit to Los Angeles, and then to Monterey. My days as a Monterey Mary were about to begin.

January 22, 2009

There is another son I need to talk about, our second son, Scott. My wife still calls him Scotty, or, even more accurately, "my Scotty." With that ubiquitous possessive pronoun that she also often tacks onto the TV shows she watches on a regular basis, shows like *Oprah, Rachael Ray's 30-Minute Meals, ER,* or *The Bachelor.*

Whichever one it might be, she announces it simply by saying, "It's time for 'my show'."

I wonder if that kind of possessiveness about how one views the media comes with a certain age. I remember my Grandma Whalen, who used to come to live with us for a few months at a time, years after Grandpa died, having certain favorite shows she needed to watch every weekday afternoon. In her case it was a couple of soap operas, shows that no one usually watched at our house otherwise. But Grandma watched these two shows regularly enough that she knew who all the characters were and their whole histories. So when it was time for these shows – I think they were *Search for Tomorrow* and *The Edge of Night* – Grandma would hustle into the living room, turn on the television and settle into her favorite chair with her knitting or crocheting.

"Time for my shows," she'd say. And the rest of us knew that for the next hour or two, we'd better be quiet, because "her shows" were a lot more important than anything we might have to say.

My Grandma Bazzett, who lived next door, had her own shows too, but the only one I know she really hated to miss was *The Lawrence Welk Show*, with her favorite Irish tenor, Joe Feeney.

Maybe it's a Grandma thing. Did Treve only start calling them "my shows" after she became Grammy B? I'll have to think about that.

But no matter. Our son Scott is still "my Scotty" to her, and probably always will be. But he's my son too, and here's what I remember about how things were when – and where – he was born.

At the time of Scott's birth we lived on the wrong side of the tracks. And I mean on the *far* wrong side of the tracks, in Monroe, Michigan. But let me back up just a little here, to provide some background.

When I completed my Master's degree in English in the spring of 1970 the job picture for teachers in the humanities was pretty bleak. Teaching positions for English majors at the college level were especially scarce. There were almost none listed on the job board at CMU's placement office, and the few colleges that were hiring could pick and choose among candidates who already had Ph.D.'s, so they weren't really very interested in freshly minted MA's. But I had a wife and a year-old son to support by this time, so I set to with a vengeance, typing up resumes and cover letters. I started sending them out several months before I'd even earned the degree, qualifying those letters by specifying my graduation date. I was pretty nervous about looking for a job like this when I wasn't even certain I would *have* my degree by June. But I was even more scared that if I waited too long there would be no jobs at all.

So, starting in January, while I was still on semester break, I got out the Sears Selectric typewriter that my older brother, Rich, had loaned me nearly two years before – and which had seen yeoman service ever since – I began cranking out letters. I had gotten a list of colleges, junior colleges and community colleges from the library. Each day Treve and I would run down the list looking at the possibilities. And we didn't really rule any place out. We sent letters to schools in nearly all of the lower forty-eight. It didn't matter that they weren't advertising openings. I was desperate, and I was hoping against hope to just get lucky. The resume part was easy. I got one clean copy typed up and then ran off copies at the library. But the cover letter I typed fresh for every letter. I didn't think a fill-in-the-blank form letter would look very serious. And I was serious. Hell, I wasn't just serious. I was terrified. I simply couldn't imagine ending up unemployed after five hard years of nearly continuous study. Especially with two additional mouths to feed.

Treve helped. She wasn't the best of typists, but during the next five months or so she got that cover letter down pretty well, and typed plenty of them herself while I was in class or teaching. We sent out over one hundred letters and resumes that winter and spring. Most of the colleges never responded at all. The few that did, perhaps a dozen or so, were not very encouraging, but often enclosed an employment application that they would "keep on file." Each time we got one of those I had it filled out and back in the mail the very next day. It was, to say the least, a rather discouraging process. But we kept at it. We felt we didn't really have any other option. We were grownups now, and parents, and this was serious business. I think we were both a little scared about all this responsibility stuff.

Finally, I think it was in mid-April, I got some good news. Monroe County Community College had an opening for an English teacher and I was invited down for an interview. We hardly dared to hope for anything at this stage, but Treve was nearly ecstatic, because Monroe was only about thirty minutes away from her hometown of Belleville.

"I'd be close to my *mom*," she exclaimed when we read the letter. "And we'd get to take Jeffy and go visit whenever we *wan*ted!"

I tried to calm her down and told her it was just an interview, not a job offer.

I made the appointment and traveled downstate to Monroe the following week, talked in a pretty relaxed informal setting with the Humanities Department Chairman, John Weber, and a few other faculty members, then went back to Central to wait. There had been several other applicants being interviewed for the same position, so I didn't dare to hope too hard. Two days later I got a call. I hadn't gotten the job. It had gone instead to Bill Baldwin, an applicant from Villanova, which was, of course, a much more prestigious place than Central. So I understood, sort of. At least I told Dr. Weber I did. Inside I was completely crushed. Four months of typing and stuffing letters and this had been my first and only interview. And I'd come up short. Dr. Weber told me that if it made me feel any better I was the unanimous second choice of the selection committee. It didn't make me feel any better, but I thanked him just the same. I hung up feeling utterly defeated.

But Treve wouldn't let me give up. She told me we just had to have faith, and she kept right on typing those letters and would have them ready for me to sign each night when I got home. It was beginning to seem useless – if not hopeless – to me.

Then about two weeks later – it was May by now, only a few more weeks until graduation – I got another call from Monroe. It was John Weber again. He had wonderful news for me. One of his English teachers had just resigned to take a better-paying job in public relations at Ford. Was I still interested in coming to Monroe?

Is a bear Catholic? Does the Pope shit in the woods? Was I still *interested?* Holy crap! Holy Mary Mother of *God!* Thank you, *JE-sus!*

I didn't say any of that on the phone of course. He said since I'd already been there and everyone had met me – and *liked* me – the job was mine if I wanted it, and that he would send a contract in the mail. I was stunned. Treve had been right. We just had to have faith. When I told her, I'm pretty sure we did our own little dance of joy right there in the kitchen. I felt – we *both* felt, I'm sure – like a tremendous weight had been lifted. We felt saved. Maybe we could manage this being-grownups thing after all.

So that's how we got the job in Monroe. It was a damn good thing too. During the last few weeks of school I got only two more invitations to come for a job interview. One was from Harrisburg Community College in Pennsylvania, and the other one was from a community college in Hazard, Kentucky. I'd already signed the Monroe contract, so I called those two places and conveyed my regrets. But I had no regrets. I had a job. Treve remembers those other eleventh-hour offers and likes to remind me from time to time that we *could* have ended up in Hazard, Kentucky. Well, I don't really know much about Hazard, except that it's coal-mining country, and what if *they'd* been our only chance? Nope, I'm not gonna knock 'em, not even this many years later.

Our first home in Monroe was a brand new apartment complex, John Anderson Court, just off North Telegraph Road behind the Nortel Lanes bowling alley. It was really too expensive for us, but we didn't have much time to look, so we took it. It was two bedrooms and we were on the second floor of a three-story building. I think our rent was around a hundred seventy-five dollars a month. That was a lot back then. Our first home in Mount Pleasant had only been seventy-five a month. But we were nearer Detroit now, so prices were high. We had to sign a year's lease, and that's how long we stayed. We had no furniture other than Jeff's crib and a small chest of drawers and changing stand. We had promised ourselves, since we'd gotten married, that our first major purchase would be a king-size bed. So we bit the bullet and bought one – a super firm Stearns and Foster set on sale just down the road at the Lazy-Boy furniture store on Telegraph. So we had a place to sleep but nothing else in the house.

Treve's folks did us a huge favor. Her mom said they needed new living room furniture anyway. So they brought us their old overstuffed couch and chair. Treve's mother's sister, Aunt Mart, brought us two old end tables and lamps. Then Aunt Mart, who lived in Monroe and worked at the Ace Paper plant, took us back over to the Lazy-Boy store and bought us a dinette set with four chairs. Treve and I found the Red Seal second-hand store downtown and bought a big heavy chest of drawers for our bedroom. Within just a week or so of moving in, we had a full complement of furniture, thanks to the Zimmers, Lazy-Boy, and Red Seal. And thank God, too, of course.

I look at all this every-day kind of stuff now and I think: *this* isn't relevant; *this* isn't interesting. Well, maybe not. But yet it is; because when I think back on it now, I can still remember how *excited* we were every time another thing was added, every time we found a new bargain of some sort. It was that feeling, when you're just starting out, that can never really be duplicated again once you're doing better and have become more comfortable financially and professionally. You know what I mean? Everything was still so *new* to us. And Treve was so beautiful and Jeffy was so sweet and perfect. It was all just so …. *Help* me here! Oh well, you know what I mean, I think.

The best thing about that first too-expensive apartment was that Treve found an instant friend there, the very first day we moved in. Priscilla Weaver lived right upstairs in the top-floor apartment, with her husband, Teakus, and their son, Little Teke. Their boy was nearly the same age as Jeff, so that was a natural fit. And although I think Priscilla was a few years older than Treve, they acted right from the start as if they'd known each other all their lives. It must have been the shared bond of new motherhood. The Weavers were recent "immigrants" up from West Monroe, Louisiana. They had met in college there where Priscilla was in the teaching program and Teakus was playing football. Now the town we were living in was pronounced Mon-ROE, just like the president's name. But the town in "Looziana" was properly pronounced MUN-roe. It was one of the first things Priscilla taught us. Both the Weavers had this syrupy southern kinda drawl that just kinda tickled us. Priscilla was this tall, very attractive bottle blonde who reminded me of the country singer, Lynn Anderson, who had recently scored a Top 40 crossover hit with "I Never Promised You a Rose Garden." Teakus was a pipe-fitter who was working on the construction of the new Detroit Edison plant in Monroe. He worked hard and long hours and wasn't around all that much. Priscilla had her teaching degree, but had followed her man up north where the work was. I don't think they'd been there very long, so Priscilla seemed just overjoyed to have Treve there. And the feeling was mutual. I should probably mention here that Treve has always had this knack for making friends quickly, and that was probably a good thing, considering we moved something like fifteen times over the years.

Now I know I said this part of the story was gonna be about Scott, and I'm getting there, because Scott was a made-in-Monroe baby, and I've at least got us in Monroe.

It's hard for me to remember much about our first year in Monroe, probably because it was my first year of teaching and I was really concentrating on trying to do everything right. I had lots of course outlines and lesson plans to do and class preparations and papers to correct, so I guess I was just busy all the time. But I don't think Treve minded all that much, mostly because she had Priscilla – and vice versa. They spent a lot of time together, comparing parenting methods and stuff, I suppose. The only story she likes to tell that comes to mind is that Jeff and Little Teke were both working on toilet training around the same time and both had gotten their first pair of "big-boy pants" to wear. And the way Treve tells it, one day she and Priscilla were sitting at the table chatting and the boys were playing with their blocks or something in the living room and all of a sudden Teke, he stood up and looked around, and then this stream of pee came rushing right out through the front of his brand-new big-boy pants. Well, before either Treve or Priscilla could even get up, Jeff, he stood up and looked at Teke, and then *he* let loose right through the front of *his* pants – twin golden showers right there on the living room carpet. Apparently the two moms got quite a laugh out of that, once they'd overcome their initial surprise. And it was only a minor lapse in the potty training; they were both completely housebroken by the time they turned two.

Like I already said, that place was too expensive for our budget. I think I grossed just over nine thousand dollars that first year at Monroe, which I know sounds pretty measly by today's standards, but it was actually considered a pretty decent teacher's salary back in 1970. In fact, I remember when I first got the job and told some of my professors at Central about it, they wanted to know right away what my starting salary was. Well at the time it was something just over eight grand, but when I reported for work that fall, the faculty was already starting to picket. It was a year to negotiate a new contract, and the faculty association and the administration were at odds. I didn't feel real comfortable about going out to picket, since I hadn't even started work yet, but I did. It seemed the thing to do. So we did finally get a small increase for our efforts – although those negotiation years always did seem to stir up a lot of hard feelings around campus and in the community, which was one of the things about teaching I never felt very good about. But even when I told my professors at Central eight grand they were pretty impressed. In fact one of my teachers, a brand-new Ph.D. who'd just started teaching at Central was a little angry, I think, that I would be starting out with just a Master's making almost as much as he did with his Ph.D.

But no matter. What I started to say was that we couldn't really afford John Anderson Court, so when our lease was up we looked around some and we found this duplex over on the east side of Monroe. The *far* east side of Monroe. In order to get to this neighborhood, which wasn't a very good one, you had to cross several sets of railroad tracks, if I remember correctly, and I think I do. And this was back when the rails were still in use too – by trains, I mean. This neighborhood was so far out on the edge of town that it was nearly under the I-75 Expressway, which ran by us between Detroit and Toledo, emitting its near constant thunder of heavy traffic.

I can't remember anymore how we found out about the vacant duplex on Fernwood Drive. It was owned by a couple who lived over on the south side of town, Joe and Pat Griesek. They owned several rental properties around town, and I think they were also actively involved in church activities and fostering children who needed a safe haven. Joe was a very nice man and also very handy at fixing and installing things.

The price was right for the place, but Treve and I were a little worried about the neighborhood. It was, without question, the kind of place Johnny Rivers was singing about in his hit tune, "The Poor Side of Town." The outside of the house was covered in the old-fashioned type gray and white speckled asphalt shingle siding which had seen better days. There was a front door and back, and both had decent storm doors on them. The back door opened into a small kitchen which was big enough to accommodate only a very small kitchen table and chairs. The kitchen floor was covered in linoleum with a large red and yellow squares pattern. The countertop was a matching red linoleum and had a good-sized stainless steel sink in it. There was an empty space at the counter end inside the door, where a clothes dryer would fit. But there was no refrigerator and no stove. The living room was a fairly good size, maybe nine by twelve or so, with a non-descript badly-worn linoleum floor. But there was a built-in wall bookcase on one end, which caught my eye immediately, something only a booklover would count as an asset. There were two small bedrooms, perhaps eight by ten each, and a narrow bathroom with a tin shower stall. It wasn't much, we could see that immediately, but the rent was only eighty dollars a month, nearly a hundred dollar savings from what we'd been paying over on "the good side" of town.

When Joe showed us the place, he granted that the place could use some TLC, and immediately offered to supply the paint if I wanted to redo the walls in the living room and bedrooms (the kitchen had a fairly fresh coat of yellow paint and didn't look too bad), and said he'd waive any security deposit if I did the painting. It was starting to sound better, but I went ahead and noted the terrible condition of the living room floor. Joe said he knew a carpet installer who often had some used carpet remnants he took up from other homes that were in mint condition and he could put me in touch with him about getting a piece, probably with padding thrown in. It was sounding even better, but I kept pushing, and asked what about the lack of kitchen appliances. Joe said to give him a few days, and maybe he could find me something. Treve and I thanked him for showing us the place and said we'd call him.

We drove back west on Oak Street slowly, looking even more closely at the neighborhood. There was a small mom-pop grocery store on the corner of Clark that looked to be on its last legs, its sign fading and window filthy. We turned right up Conant and left on Third Street, and drove slowly past the Traffic Jam bar, where a few black guys were lounging around out on the sidewalk and giving us the eye, and you could hear the bass thud of a jukebox from inside. Bumping over more railroad tracks, we passed Mignano's Grocery, which looked a lot more prosperous than the Clark Street place.

We talked it over pretty seriously for the next couple of days. We both agreed that Fernwood was a bit off the beaten track, being one of the easternmost streets in town. It seemed a bit isolated and perhaps even frightening. I wasn't sure it was the right place for us, even if the price was right. After all, I was usually at school all day, which was way out past the other side of town, and Treve would be there alone with Jeff all day. But the more we thought about that big savings, the more we thought it might be a smart move, at least economically. And Treve pointed out that there was a family living in the other apartment of the duplex. She'd seen a woman and a couple kids there when we were coming out. So she wouldn't really be alone there, she reasoned. I asked if she was sure she'd be all right with this place. It sure wasn't what we'd gotten used to. She said she'd be fine.

So we called Joe Griesek told him we'd take the place. He made good on his promises. He got us the paint and we painted the interior walls a pale green. The carpet guy found us a nearly-new piece of dark blue-green carpet and gave us a new pad and installed it for us, all dirt cheap. We found a GE kitchen range and refrigerator in the want ads that sounded like a steal and borrowed a pickup to go over near Sterling State park to pick them up. To our horror, the set was a bright *pink*. We had never *seen* appliances that color before. The seller must have seen the look on our faces, and when we sputtered something about the color and how that hadn't been in the advertisement, he barely missed a beat knocking another twenty bucks off the already reasonable price. We loaded 'em up. Treve rationalized that she'd always wanted a refrigerator with a bottom freezer, which this one had. As you can imagine, those hot pinks didn't exactly match the red and yellow kitchen color scheme, but we learned to live with it, and even to joke about it. At least we now had kitchen appliances, and they *worked*; that's what was important.

It was August 1971 when we moved into the duplex on Fernwood and it didn't take long for it to feel like home. We brought along the portable Hoover washing machine that we'd bought for the other place. It was one of those tiny washers on casters that you could roll right up to the kitchen sink to use. We could only wash one king-size sheet at a time in it, but we used it mostly for diapers and smaller things. The washer came with a faux wood-grain top, so when we weren't using it, it served as an end table in the living room. And we also splurged on a new Sears gas dryer which Joe installed for us at the end of the kitchen counter. Treve's mom swapped her smaller kitchen table and chairs for the dinette set Aunt Mart had bought us. So everything fit. Well, just barely, when it came to the bedrooms. Our king-size bed, along with the second-hand bureau, was a pretty tight squeeze. But barely was good enough. We were home again. We had been married less than four years, and this was our fourth move.

I'll get around to some of the bad stuff about living in that duplex, but first I want to tell about the best part of our time there: our neighbors. Because Treve's talent for quickly making friends was as strong as ever.

Dale and Sheryl Walls were a few years younger than I was, but they'd been married nearly twice as long as we had. They had two kids, Kevin and Tammy, who were around eight and five, I think. Dale worked for the railroad as a track foreman, and I think Sheryl was at home, like Treve was, and they got along well from the start. And that was important, because Treve was already about five months pregnant when we moved to Fernwood. That new bed had turned out to be a pretty fertile playground.

Being pregnant, one of the things Treve missed the most when we moved over to Fernwood was a bathtub. We both liked showers okay, but sometimes there's nothing like a good long soak, and that may be even more true for pregnant women. I felt kinda bad about that, so I tried to at least half-remedy the situation. I went out to a hardware store and bought her one of those big round galvanized steel washtubs, which just barely fit on the floor of the shower stall. What I wished I could have got was one of those big oval shaped ones, which would have been nicer, but it wouldn't fit in the shower, and there was really no place else to put it. But Treve, she made a big fuss over it anyway when I brought it home, acting like it was such a *great* idea. She's that kind of person, my wife. She always tries to make *you* feel good, even when you know your ideas aren't all that swift.

But she *used* that tub. She'd fill it up with hot water and suds and climb on in, with the water sloshing out over the top, and she'd sit there with her knees drawn up against her swelling belly and she'd soap up and wash and sometimes just sit there, all doubled up and soak for a little while. But by that fall, into October and later, she got so big the only way she could get in the tub was to set her butt real carefully down into it with her legs out over the side. And the last time she did this, it was probably almost November by then, what happened was she got stuck in there and couldn't get back up by herself and had to call me to help. She'd created kind of a suction and sealed herself in there, so it took us some doing to finally hoist her out of there. I think I told her I might have to go next door and get Dale to help me. I was kinda half-joking, but she sure splashed herself up out of there in a hurry then. That was the last time she used our "bathtub." Until after Scott was born, that is.

Remember? That's where all this was going, to tell about where we lived when Scott was born. Well, we're almost there. I mean we *are* there, I guess. But there's still more to tell.

January 25, 2009

I missed a whole day – or was it *two*? – of writing in there. Once again a book was the culprit. I started reading this memoir by Marge Piercy called *Sleeping with Cats*, and I just didn't want to stop. I've been reading Piercy's novels off and on for over thirty years now. She grew up poor in Detroit – on "the mean streets" of Detroit, in fact – but she managed to escape to the University of Michigan and a subsequent life in poetry, fiction and feminist and civil rights activism. What a *life* this woman has lived! But now, as they say, "back to our story."

Scott was born on a Saturday, just like Jeff. Another Saturday's child – who "works hard for his living." And they both do too. Both of Treve's parents came over that morning, because she knew the baby was coming soon and she wanted her hair bleached again. She was a blonde then and she hated to have her dark roots showing. So she enlisted her mom, the senior beautician in the family, to come do the job. I think today this would probably be considered highly unhealthy for both the mom and the baby, putting all those harsh chemicals onto the scalp, which could somehow leach into the bloodstream and wreak havoc with the unborn child. But who knows how accurate all this new information is. All Treve knew at the time was that she wanted to be the best-looking mom in the maternity ward. (And she was.)

So the in-laws were there that Saturday, November 14, and not only did Treve get her hair done, she also did some laundry and fixed a pot roast dinner for all of us before she decided it might be time to go to the hospital. I was plenty relieved when she finally said let's go, because I was worried about all those railroad tracks we had to get across and hoping like hell that there wouldn't be any trains. Fortunately for us, there weren't. And she wasn't worried at all about Jeff, because her parents were at the house to look after him.

In fact, this birth was a considerably less stressful one for both of us. I think we were only at the hospital for a few hours this time before Scott Brandon made his much-anticipated entrance, around 11PM. So I was able to go home that night and get some sleep. I think Treve's folks went back home to

Belleville that night, then came back to the hospital the next day to see Treve and the new baby. My parents drove down from Reed City that day and both saw the new baby and our new place for the first time too. Dad went back home, but Mom stayed for about a week, to help out while Treve healed.

Scotty was a much prettier baby that Jeff had been, but Treve always thought of him as her "round-headed" baby. We both learned the word episiotomy when Scott came along. He did seem to have a big round head, very unlike Jeff's rather misshapen little noggin – a direct result of that long labor and difficult delivery. With Scott, the doctor just made the cut, so to speak, and out he popped.

Back then, a new mother was generally kept in the hospital for three or four days. This was quite a difference from when Treve and I were born, when the normal hospitalization time was ten days. But even the four days that Treve was hospitalized were very difficult for her; not because she didn't heal quickly, but because she missed Jeff so badly. Even today she remembers how, when they brought Scotty in to her to nurse, she had a hard time warming up to this new little stranger, because he was keeping her from her other baby, the one she already knew and loved so fiercely. So she seemed a bit blue during her hospital stay this time.

It's possible, of course, that this may have been a minor case of post-partum depression, but I don't really think so. Because she had acted this way once before – and it was all my fault, as she is quick to remind me when we talk about that time. It had been in October of 1969. The English Department at Central organized a trip for faculty and students to travel to Stratford, Ontario, for the annual Shakespeare Festival there. I was a teaching assistant, in graduate school at the time, and the deeply discounted tickets to a couple plays there just seemed too great an opportunity to pass up. It never occurred to me when I bought the tickets for the four-day excursion how difficult it would be to leave our new baby behind, even for a few days. And this was that early stage of our marriage when Treve pretty much went along with whatever I wanted to do. (Not so anymore; we have a much more democratic arrangement now, and her vote is usually the tie-breaker.) So off we went to Ontario, after having deposited Jeff with my folks in Reed City. He was just barely six months old.

My mom and dad both had a great time playing Grandma and Grandpa that long weekend, but Treve was not a happy camper, being without her baby. We had a beautiful, unseasonably warm weekend in the picturesque Stratford-on-Avon, which capitalized on its name and the Shakespeare Fest. We saw two plays that weekend, *Hamlet* and Moliere's *Tartuffe*, and both were excellent. We stayed in a very quaint bed-and-breakfast, where our only complaint was that the bed was too short. It had high headboard and footboard which made it impossible for me to stretch out. So I was sleeping diagonally, leaving Treve a small corner to curl up in, unless she woke me up and moved me over, causing *me* to curl up. But we ate well, took in the sights, and strolled along the banks of the Avon which was populated by groups of graceful swans. I bought my first pair of bell bottom pants, which were coming into vogue, and a pair of sandals. Treve didn't buy much of anything, which was very unlike her, and picked at her food, also not at all typical. She was homesick. Not for our Washington Court apartment, but for her *baby*. And she has never let me forget what a terrible thing I did by forcing her to *abandon* her baby that way. And I have to agree. I was indeed a thoughtless cad.

So when Scott was born, I wasn't too surprised at her blue mood in the hospital. This new baby, while a very beautiful child, had, through no fault of his own, come between Treve and "her Jeffy."

My mom still remembers that week at our duplex in Monroe. The one kind of embarrassing thing she likes to tell is how she and I "slept together" for a couple of nights while Treve was in the hospital. Which is true, but she stayed way over on her side of the king-size bed and I on mine. The only other choice would have been for one of us to sleep on that prickly, lumpy old couch inherited from the Zimmers. I think that week we bought a twin bed for Jeff, which Mom then slept in for the rest of her stay. Jeff was still able to sleep in his crib, which he would soon cede to Scotty, who slept in a bassinet for the first few months. I'm not sure why I feel compelled to tell you all this except perhaps to avoid any possible intimations of incest in the Bazzett family.

We were happy to have Mom around for that first week at home, because she helped with the cooking and diapers and both babies immensely. And Mom is the kind of person who always seems to find pleasure in very small things. She was always exclaiming about what a "pretty little kitchen" we had, with its big sink and "bright colors." Yeah, Mom – hot pink appliances with a bright red and yellow color scheme on floor, walls and counters. Very pretty. But we knew what she meant, and we appreciated everything she did for us.

It's a time-worn tradition, of course, that custom of a mother or mother-in-law coming to help when a new baby is born. It goes way back and is still going on. As I write this, my wife is in Maryland helping out at Jeff's house with the newest baby, the second of two girls. She'll stay there for two weeks, then will travel to Pennsylvania to see Scott's family, - two grandsons there. Last year during the holidays she was gone for seven weeks – yes, *seven!* That was right after Scott and Kathy's second boy, Zachary, was born. She had a great time, mostly bonding with Zach's older brother, Nick, but finally admitted, just this year, that she might be getting a little too old for such long stays anymore. She missed her naps and my bringing her coffee every morning. (I missed doing that too; and I'm missing it again this year.) But Treve feels this is important, this helping out. She knows the grandkids probably won't remember any of it – they're still too young – but she still wants to do it, and I'm happy to let her. I'm a lousy traveler these days, and it kinda lets me off the hook. We'll both drive back east in the spring and I'll see the new baby and everyone else again then. The older I become, the more I believe that flying is an unnatural act.

Finally then, our son, Scott, has entered the picture. But there aren't many, pictures that is. And that has come to be a very embarrassing thing for us, for me mostly. I was twenty-seven when Scott was born, and into my second year of college teaching. I guess I was feeling pretty pleased with myself at the time, probably because I had accomplished a lot of the things I'd set out to do when I got out of the army that first time. I'd hurried through college and graduate school, worrying the whole time that I might run out of money, or might not be smart enough or talented enough to do this thing, to become a teacher of English at the college level. But somehow I'd managed it. That first year of college I had also nearly despaired that I would ever find someone to love me and share my life and my dreams with me. Then I'd met Treve and was smitten from day one; and the most amazing part of that was to find out that she loved *me* too! Then marriage and a baby, all in just a couple of years. It was like I was finally living this grown-up life I'd always imagined. While it was true we were living in kind of a *shack* when Scott was born, we both knew that this was only temporary, to save money for a real house. Everything seemed to be coming along according to plan, or *Vsyo po planu*, as the Russians say.

So yes, I was feeling distinctly cocky by the time Scotty came along. I can remember telling Treve how, Hell, he looks pretty much like Jeff did. All babies look pretty much alike. What do we need a lot of pictures for? We've got enough of Jeff as a baby. We'll just show him some of *those* when he gets older.

I know, I know. What a *horrible* attitude to have about your own baby! I was an asshole. I admit it. The upshot of all this is that we have almost no baby pictures of our second son. This is a very sore point with Scott, and he has never let us forget it. This probably explains – at least in part – why Scott has taken literally *thousands* of photos of his two boys, Nick and Zach. They are also both extremely photogenic children. But *thousands?*

Mea culpa, my beloved second son. You were just as beautiful as your own boys are. I was just a negligent jerk.

One of the very few extant photos of Scott as a new baby is one he's not in at all. It's a photo of Jeff standing next to the bassinet, peering down with a look of wonder. You can't see Scott in the bassinet, but he was in there. Another photo, probably from that same roll of film, is a little better. In it, Jeff is sitting on our gold slip-covered old couch. That harvest gold Hoover washer was there too, just outside the frame, modestly masquerading as a tall end-table. Jeff, two and a half, is holding

Scott, a enormously pleased smile on his little face. Scott's expression, half hidden behind a pacifier, is quite inscrutable; he was still pretty new.

Not too long after Scott was born, we moved. We got tired of hearing the rats scritching around inside the walls when we were sitting in the bathroom or living room or reading in bed, and one night we had a window peeper, which was kind of a last straw. We found a little house we could almost afford over on the west side of town and bought it.

While I only ended up staying at Monroe County Community College for five years, both Terri and I have good memories of our Monroe years. Her memories center primarily around home and the friends she made in the neighborhood. She and Shirley Nation still keep in touch, over thirty years since we left the area. Shirley and her husband Richard lived right across the street from us on John Rolfe Drive in Riverside Manor. That was the Monroe subdivision we moved to from Fernwood, when we bought our first house, a small three-bedroom, one-bath rancher. (Just in case you don't remember your American history, John Rolfe was the guy who married Pocahontas.)

Richard Nation was a fireman with the Monroe Fire Department. He and Shirley had married right out of high school, just before he shipped out to Vietnam, and they had a couple kids, both older than ours. Just as she'd quickly made friends with neighbors at Central and then at John Anderson Court and Fernwood, she found Shirley almost as soon as we moved into our house. Shirley probably brought over cookies or something; she was that kind of neighbor. Whatever it was, she and Treve have been friends ever since. Terri and I both remember about how during tornado season in the spring and fall, we would sometimes decamp to the Nations house to take shelter, because our house was built on a concrete slab, with no basement. The Nations' house was a split-level, so technically it didn't have a basement either, but the first floor was kind of half underground. So when the tornado warning sirens went off and the sky turned that strange shade of yellow and the winds were gusting, we'd take our boys and dog over to Shirley and Richard's, where the wives would put the kids under the table with coloring books and crayons and they'd sit at the table and snack and smoke and chat. (Yes, they smoked. Nearly everyone did back in the seventies. Once they baked a chocolate cake, and, before the storm alert had been lifted, we ate the whole thing.) Meanwhile Richard and I would stand out in the street and survey the sky for funnel clouds or other suspicious shapes or weather anomalies. I know we'd already heard the sirens and been warned to take cover, but it seemed more manly to stand outside. Most of the men in the neighborhood did the same thing. Tornado weather was kinda like snowstorms in that respect. It gave the neighborhood men an excuse to talk and socialize a bit, whether it was while watching the sky or shoveling snow. Because men are never really very good at establishing relationships or making friends. That's usually left to the wives. Hell, if men of a certain age – the "competitive years" – didn't have wives they probably wouldn't have any friends at all.

So Treve had Shirley as her best friend. And just down the street she had some pretty good backups too, in Claire Strini and Joyce Anspach. Claire's husband, Dave, was a teacher and coach at Monroe High; and Joyce's husband, Dick, worked for the local Social Security office. Dick's Uncle Charley had been a president of CMU, and most of my classes my last two years at Central had been held in Anspach Hall, a new building on campus. I mention what all these guys did for a living, because we weren't really close, and that's pretty much how we "defined" ourselves back in those unenlightened times. And most of the women were still at home taking care of the kids back then, so they had time to visit and form friendships. Guys never really talk about anything important. It's probably because we're so territorial and competitive. With guys everything is like some kinda dick-measuring contest, you know? But fortunately I think we do outgrow that when we get older, once that testosterone level has gone down some.

Just in case you're interested, one of the things I enjoy most about writing down all this stuff is that it motivates me to find out where all these people we knew so long ago might have ended up. So I get on-line and try to find them. You'd be surprised how often I *do* find them too, even thirty or more years later. The internet can be a handy thing sometimes. The

Nations are still in Monroe, and so are Dale and Sheryl Walls. Strinis are in Texas now, and the Anspachs are in Livonia. We're all grandparents now and mostly retired, so it's usually kinda fun catching up on everything.

Most of my memories from Monroe go back to the college and the people I worked with there. And most of those memories are pretty good, actually. The only bad ones I seem to remember are the ones associated with the collective bargaining process. I was in the teacher's union, but I was never completely comfortable with it. In fact if I had to give you one concrete reason for why I left, it might be the fallout from those years we had to renegotiate a contract. Because it made everyone tense, and people who were normally kind and courteous to each other, and even *friends*, would suddenly become adversaries. The school would be divided between the administrators and the teachers and employees. It was just so … well, *tense*, like I said. And I hated it.

The other reason I guess I left, if I'm gonna be completely honest about it, was just all those really horrible Freshman Comp papers I had to face and grade every semester. Because those composition classes are the bread-and-butter English classes of any community college. They are "required" courses for nearly every program, so the kids *have* to take them; they don't have a choice. And whether you know it or not, people like me who *like* to write – and read – are in the minority. So the majority of the kids I taught every semester – or *tried* to teach – were there against their will, some of them under extreme duress. Writing for most of them was an onerous chore. And it showed in the themes I got. I mean they were simply *awful*. It's not that I didn't understand what these kids were going through. I did. Because I remember back when I was in high school and yes, in college too, when I was "assigned" a certain topic to write on, and I didn't want to, and I resisted it mightily, and how I used to write a sentence or two and then count how many more words I had written, and then figure out how many more I still had to write to get the required five hundred words, which is the standard length of a paper for most composition classes. Yeah, I understood. But that didn't make it any easier to get through a tall stack of some of the shittiest writing you've ever read several times a week.

There were bright spots, of course. And I could usually identify those early each semester. There were usually a few graduates of St. Mary's Academy, an all-girls Catholic school in Monroe, who were exceptional writers, and sometimes a few boys from Catholic Central too. There's something about a Catholic education. Those Sisters and Brothers usually do a good job of drilling in the fundamentals of grammar and sound sentence construction in a way that sticks. But the bright spots were rare, to tell the truth. The comp classes that were often the best were the evening classes, which tended to fill up with older students – veterans, housewives or people who were working during the day. Those people usually had some real stories to tell; they'd lived a little longer and were actually interested in learning how to best tell their tales. Those folks were a pleasure to work with.

But in addition to all those comp classes, I also got to teach a literature class now and then too. Those were the bones the department threw us from time to time to keep us in line. I got to teach the usual Intro to Lit classes, either the novel and short story or poetry and drama. I've never been a great lover of poetry, and Shakespeare was never my cup of tea either (despite that trip to Stratford), so I preferred to teach the fiction side. But let me be honest here; I have no idea whether I was ever a very effective teacher. I was like a lot of English teachers back then. I'd just been a kid who loved books all his life. Loving books doesn't automatically mean you'll make a great teacher. And I'm not sure if I was ever any good at it or not.

Let me give you an example here. I had been a fan of John Updike's fiction since my junior year of college when I first "discovered" Updike by reading *Rabbit, Run* – which was *not*, by the way, required reading for any course I was taking. It was just a book I found one day in the Student Book Exchange at Central, browsing books when I should have been studying, probably. That book clicked for me at once and I was hooked. I went right out and found more of his books and read them all. But that first one I read stayed with me, remained a favorite. So when I got a chance to choose a novel for my compositions class to read, I chose *Rabbit, Run*. And I have always remembered a comment I got from one of my students that first year I taught. I just could hardly wait to learn what my students thought of this book, one of my favorite novels at the time. So I didn't wait for voluntary reactions, I asked this one kid, who seemed a fairly intelligent person what he thought, based on what he'd read so far. The kid looked a little uncomfortable and said he hadn't really read very far yet, but I pressed him for an opinion anyway.

"Well, Mr. Bazzett," he said, looking around the class nervously. "You know how sometimes when you start reading a book you just don't want to put it down?"

"Yes, yes?" I replied eagerly.

"Well, this book, this *Rabbit, Run* ..." He hesitated. "Well, *it's* the kind of book that once you put it down you just don't wanna pick it up again."

The class erupted in laughter. I think I probably blushed. I guess I could have gotten angry at this remark, but I figured right then and there, what would be the point? So I moved on to other things. But I've always remembered that moment. Now, years later, now that my own tastes have changed, I recognize that Updike's stories certainly are not for everyone. They often tend to examine the dark underside of man's nature. The man is a master wordsmith, which is why I have always loved his writing, but his stories are not very happy. And *Rabbit, Run* was not a happily-ever-after kind of tale either. So I understand now what that kid was reacting to, or at least I *think* I do. Because it's possible he just hadn't read his assignment and that was his wiseass way of weaseling out from under my question. But I don't really care anymore; the truth is, *I* don't read Updike much anymore either. He's just too dark – still. And I guess I've changed. I'd prefer to read something a bit more happily-ever-after myself these days.

That's a sample of how doubt could creep in though, back in my teaching days. I often wondered, during those five years, *Do I want to do this for the next forty years or so?* And the answer to that was, finally and simply, no. And I don't believe the academic world suffered any when I left.

My best memories from MCCC though are from the people, and the friends I made, some of whom I still keep in touch with.

I'll tell you about some of them tomorrow. Right now it's time to let my dogs out and then I'm looking forward to more of Marge Piercy's memoir. It's the kind of book you hate to put down.

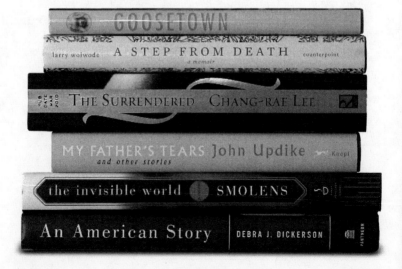

January 26, 2009

In my continued reading of *Sleeping with Cats* last night and again this morning, I was struck by a comment Piercy made about her life in the early sixties during her second marriage while living in Brookline, Massachusetts. Her second husband was a computer scientist who liked order and comfort in his life, so Marge was trying her best to be "the good wife," although she was also struggling to be a good writer too. But she found she enjoyed cooking, which gave her a small measure of comfort. She said, "Our social life as a couple was typical of the times. Wives made elaborate dinners, husbands mixed and poured drinks and talked shop."

Not much had changed on the bourgeois middle class scene by the early seventies when I was teaching in Monroe. The wives still made dinners – although I can't attest to their *elaborateness* – and the husbands still made drinks and talked shop. Some of these dinners were more fun than others. It depended mostly on who was giving them and how many people were there. I vaguely remember attending quite an elaborate dinner at our department chairman's house that included everyone in the department, which meant there was quite a large number of people milling around and making small talk at the Webers' big old farmhouse out west of town. Our chairman, John Weber, was a likeable sort of guy, but he was not a very good mixer. I was never sure if he was trying to maintain the proper "distance" required by his position as chairman, or if he just wasn't very good with people. I suspect it was a combination of the two, because in spite of his advanced degrees and educational accomplishments, I always thought John seemed like a very shy person. I liked him, but I never felt completely at ease around him. John's wife, Nola, was just the opposite. She was a very warm and outgoing person, very down-to-earth and easy to talk with. Although she was probably as educated as most of us, she never flaunted it. Her style was the perfect complement to John's shy introvert, making her a tremendous asset to his career – the perfect faculty wife.

I can only remember one female faculty member in the Humanities at the time, although there may have been more.

A very beautiful and cultured woman, Irma Cowell was not someone you were likely to forget. She taught speech and foreign languages – French and Spanish. Her smooth olive complexion suggested a Hispanic heritage. I never knew Irma well, but she was always gracious to me and seemed a perfect lady.

The fact that she was the one female faculty member was reflective of the times.

John Holladay, who may have been one of the college's earliest hires in the late sixties, became a close friend during my tenure there. John had his doctorate in education and always struck me as the stereotypical sort of absent-minded professor in his outward demeanor, but he was one of the few guys on the faculty that I could actually talk books with. He had a very inquiring and analytical approach to things, which may have come from his study of philosophy, a subject he taught, along with literature and writing courses. John was from Marine City, and I think so was his wife, Linda (who was also a teacher, retired now). I *think* that because, if I remember correctly, John and Linda had known each other since childhood, and they were as perfectly natural and at ease with each other as any married couple I've ever known. Terri and I had dinner at their home in town more than once, and we always enjoyed ourselves there. After we left, many years ago now, the Holladays built a new house right across the street from the campus on Raisinville Road. John is the only person I knew well in my Monroe years who is still teaching at the college as I write this. He has only to walk across the road to get to work. He's been there for over forty years now. When I look now at his photo on the college website, he reminds me of *Mister Peepers*, once played by Wally Cox on television in the fifties. And that's a compliment, John. I loved that show as a kid. John and I still keep in touch.

Perhaps two of our closest friends from our Monroe years were the Deans. Maury taught English too, but what he really wanted to be was a rock star. I could relate to that, so we clicked almost instantly over our shared love of Buddy Holly and all things rock and roll. Maury came from Detroit and had actually already enjoyed some small successes in music when I met him. In 1967 his garage band, The Woolies, put a cover of Bo Diddley's 1956 tune "Who Do You Love" into Detroit's top ten radio play list, but nationally the record only managed to bubble briefly into the top 100. Maury also claimed to have worked very briefly as a songwriter for Motown Records, although I kinda doubt you'd find his name in any definitive Motown history. Maury's elfin-sized wife, Toni, grew up in west Michigan's farm country near the tiny town of Fountain, northeast of Ludington. The two met in college at Michigan State and were near immediate soul mates. Maury can be a bit scattered in his enthusiasms and interests, while Toni is a more settled, "earth-mother" sort – an anchor to Maury's kite-like flights of fancy. In short, a perfect match. When we met the Deans they already had one child and another one on the way, an odd-looking but lovable dog named Snarf, and maybe a cat or two. There may have been a garden in the back yard of the huge, creaking old house they'd bought near downtown Monroe. Toni liked getting her hands into the dirt and growing things. There was a vintage rusting Cadillac parked in the driveway, one of a long line of old Detroit dinosaurs that Maury rescued on its way to the junkyard. He had a theory back then that you should never pay more than a hundred dollars or so for a car, and he was skilled at finding "bargains" well within his price range. He figured if it ran for a year then he'd gotten his money's worth; if it lasted longer, then his buying it had been an absolute stroke of genius.

Besides being an as-yet undiscovered rock star, Maury was also a great and uninhibited teller of stories. He told us once about how he was walking in downtown Detroit back in the days of the race riots and stubbed his toe on a crack in the sidewalk. In trying to break his fall, he threw both hands out in front of him. In doing so he managed to save damage to his face, but broke both his wrists, which necessitated plaster casts on both arms for the next several weeks.

"Man, you find out in a hurry just how much your wife really loves you when you can't even wipe your own butt," Maury told us, laughing and glancing fondly in his wife's direction.

"Oh, Maury!" Toni responded, blushing only slightly, as she was obviously used to this story by then.

Isn't it true though, that faithful and loving women like Toni are the butt-wipers of the world, from babies to disabled spouses to aging parents. What would we do without them?

One of my own favorite memories of our friendship with the Deans was the time I took both Terri and Toni to an afternoon showing of the new movie, *Love Story*. Both women were hugely pregnant at the time, and, standing in line, we got a lot of strange looks and double takes from the other filmgoers, perhaps wondering if I'd been enjoying too many "matinees." I made the most of it, smiling hugely and putting my arms around both of them as we went into the theater. And this was probably at least five years before the song "Afternoon Delight" hit the charts.

But Maury had many stories to tell, making him a delight to be around. He reminded me at times of that old vaudeville-era comedian we used to see on Ed Sullivan, with his trademark tag line, "I got a million of 'em."

Sometimes Maury's stories got written down. He had already written and published what may have been one of the first rock and roll history books, *The Rock Revolution*. And he was pursuing an advanced degree in those years at the University of Michigan where he managed to win a Hopwood prize in fiction for an excerpt from a novel he was writing. I don't think the novel ever got published, but Maury did earn his degree, a Doctor of Arts, which was a relatively new degree at the time, offered as an alternative to the traditional Ph.D. I often wondered if Maury chose that program because its successful completion would give him a D.A., which, as any child of the fifties and sixties knows, stands for Duck's Ass – the standard Elvis-type hair style of all respectable rock-and-rollers. Alas, the actual acronym for the Doctor of Arts turned out to be the more Latinate A.D. For Maury, however, an exception needs to be made. Because if anyone ever earned a lasting D.A. in this life, it is Dr. Maury Dean.

One of the most popular elective courses at MCCC during the Dean years was a History of Rock class that Maury taught. It was always full to capacity, and those kids got their money's worth. Not only did they learn all about rock music's origins, they also got to be part of a special project that culminated in cutting a record. Maury trucked a bunch of the kids up to a recording studio in Lansing and made an album one of those last years. I still have a copy, which has to be a real collector's item, filled with original songs. (I wrote the lyrics to one myself.) It's called *The 2nd Time Around*, by Transition – or maybe it's the other way around, I can't remember, and I'm not gonna go dig it out right now.

Maury left Monroe a year or so before I did, and spent a year or two at a college in Florida trying to teach English to classes made up primarily of Caribbean immigrants, which I imagine posed quite a challenge. Eventually, however, he landed on Long Island where he has been teaching at a branch of SUNY for over thirty years now, as well as running and participating in marathons. He's still writing too. He has self-produced one original CD of his own with eleven original tunes called *Far from Every Day*, and has penned one of the most mammoth histories of pop music I've ever seen, a coffee-table sized book filled with photos and facts that weighs several pounds and runs nearly seven hundred pages – *Rock 'N' Roll Gold Rush*. (More recently he's written an equally huge bio of Buddy Holly called *This'll Be the Day*.) And yes, Dr. Dean's history of rock class, transplanted now to New York, is still one of the most popular courses on the Suffolk County campus.

January 29, 2009

It's been over thirty years now since we left Monroe, so some of those memories have grown dim, but we still recall isolated names and events from those years. The academic dean during our years at Monroe was Bob Kollin, who, with his wife, Lois, was unfailingly kind to us, and one summer even invited us up to their cottage on Lake Bellaire, northeast of Traverse city, where their son, Carl, took me for a sail on a tiny two-man boat, called, I want to say, a Sunfish? We remember attending a small birthday party for Bob that summer, who, smiling, told me it was a "big one" and playfully asked me how old I thought he was.

I guessed, stupidly, "Fifty?"

Bob's face fell; he was crushed. He was forty.

Treve berated me about that stupid gaffe all the way home. "How could you have *said* that?" she ranted at me.

I cringed appropriately. But geeze, Bob; you had all that prematurely *gray* hair! I had apologized profusely to Bob – *and* Lois – but the psychic damage was done. Not that they held it against me. The Kollins were not the kind of people who took themselves that seriously.

And there were Art and Beth Kidd. We didn't know them that well, but Art, a math teacher at the college, was a very environmentally conscious guy, far ahead of his time, who designed and built a windmill with tower and set it up out on the corner of the campus's parking lots. It was an experiment in harnessing the wind to charge a storage battery to generate electricity – a successful one, I might add. When the Kidds left Monroe (also before we did), it was to relocate to the northern wilderness of Minnesota, near Grand Marais, where they planned to live as naturally as possible. Art dismantled the windmill and took it with him, to be used as their only source of electricity (at least initially) in the tiny house he had constructed on their remote wooded property.

The faces of so many other Monroe friends and colleagues can still be conjured up as I sit here: Bob and Carolyn Merkel, Bill and Karen Baldwin, Don and Sandy Emerson, Grant Strickland, Dave and Donna McKay, President Ron Campbell,

Paul Ross, Frank Green, Dave Moore and Carol Kish, Noel and Libby Dentner, Larry Wilson, Audrey Warrick and Joanie Woodruff.

My own office at the college was located in the Science building, separated from the library and learning center building where most of the English and Humanities teachers were housed. There were only a few of us in that building. Maury was across the hall from me, sharing an office with Art Kidd, I think. And Don Emerson, the drama teacher, had his office down at the end of the hall from me. I kind of enjoyed being "separate but equal" in the Science building. For the first year or so, there was an empty office directly across from mine. My son Jeff still remembers the time I brought him with me to work one summer day while I was tending to some paper work. We went over to the audio-visual center and checked out a video version (VCRs were still relatively new then) of the 1933 black-and-white film, *King Kong*. I wheeled a TV and VCR into that empty office and put it on for Jeff to watch, leaving the doors between the two offices ajar so he wouldn't be afraid. Which he might well have been, watching a film like that at the tender age of five. Maybe he was traumatized and that's why he still remembers it. He scarcely made a sound for two hours as he sat there in the flickering semi-dark, mesmerized by jungle drums, the giant ape and Fay Wray.

One other memory stands out from Monroe, the night we fed and entertained a "famous writer," in our tiny apartment on the east end of Monroe. John Beecher, who was probably moderately well-known in the literary world of the 1970s, had been raised in the deep south, where his father was a US Steel executive. He had developed a social conscience as a young man and later became active in the civil rights movements. His poetry, which he began writing in the 1920s, reflected the turbulence of those times, as well as his youthful experiences in Alabama and his time as a naval officer on a troop transport ship with a racially mixed crew during World War II. During the McCarthy era Beecher was blacklisted from teaching in 1950 after refusing to sign a loyalty oath. In short, John Beecher, who was also a descendant of *Uncle Tom's Cabin* author, Harriet Beecher Stowe, led a very eventful and colorful life.

I'll be honest. In 1971, when Beecher was booked by the Humanities Department as a guest speaker, I had never heard of him. But our department chair, John Weber, circulated flyers and information on Beecher, so, having been an English major, and now a teacher, I was suitably impressed by the man's credentials. He had published several books of poetry by then, had taught at the university level and also worked as a journalist. I wasn't really a big fan of poetry, but I did look up a few of his poems before he arrived, and liked what I read.

What happened was Beecher was slated to speak and read his poetry at an evening event in the college cafeteria. He came in on a plane the afternoon before and a driver from the college picked him up at Detroit Metro and deposited him at the local Holiday Inn. I remember asking John Weber what Beecher was doing that afternoon. John shot me a kind of blank look and said he wasn't scheduled to do anything until the next day, when he would be visiting some classes and then presenting his talk that night. Well, I had seen this guy's picture. Beecher sported a full and flowing white beard and a mane of white hair. I was thinking, this poor *old* guy. He's just got to sit around the hotel for four or five hours all alone tonight. So I phoned Treve and told her about it, and asked if we could invite him to supper. She was kind of apprehensive about having somebody famous over to eat in our cramped crummy little duplex with its hot pink appliances and clashing red and yellow color scheme, but I guess I talked her into it, once I'd told her I would pick up some steaks on the way home.

So I called Beecher at his room at the hotel and he was absolutely delighted at the invitation, saying he hadn't really looked forward to dining alone. So I picked up a few rib-eye steaks (which was about all we could afford) and headed for the Holiday Inn to pick up the poet. I can still remember wondering what Beecher might have been thinking as we neared our apartment, bumping over all those sets of railroad tracks and going deeper and deeper into what was probably, by its looks, the poorest part of Monroe. It was March, and there were still dirty snow banks here and there, making the neighborhood seem even seedier than it was. But he never commented on it. Treve welcomed him warmly into our color-clashed kitchen, took the steaks from me and put them immediately under the broiler. I took Mr. Beecher ("Call me, John, please!" so I did) into our tiny living room where Jeff was playing with some toys. I think I put some soft music on the stereo, some odd instrumental mix, perhaps Wynton Kelly and Chet Atkins, which would provide background music for dinner. I can't remember any more what we might have talked about while we waited for our steaks to cook, probably books and writers. Jeff, who was two, was fascinated by Beecher's white beard, and stood big-eyed, staring at this snowy-haired stranger. I must have told him not to stare, that it wasn't polite.

Beecher, leaning forward, thrust his face gently toward Jeff and said, "Do I look like Santa Claus?" To which Jeff nodded solemnly. Beecher chuckled and asked if Jeff would like to feel his beard. Another solemn nod. "Well go ahead, I don't mind," Beecher said.

Jeff looked at me and I nodded my head. Jeff very carefully stroked the poet's whiskers. "Soft," he whispered.

Treve put together a delicious meal of steak, baked potato and salad that night. Over dinner Beecher talked a bit of his life, where he'd grown up, and asked about ours. Normal kind of dinner conversation, even if he *was* famous. The details are lost now, but the specialness of the occasion has remained. And we will always remember the night the poet came to dinner.

Beecher visited the campus the next day and his reading went well that night with a pretty respectable – and respectful – crowd on hand. And the next morning he flew back to wherever he had come from – California, I think. But at some point he must have mentioned our dinner together to my department chair, because about a week later I received an inter-office memo from John Weber, which read:

Tim, thanks for taking John Beecher "under your wing" the day before his program. The situation was awkward, and your and Terri's human concern for an old man in a lonely motel speaks well for you both. Personally and on behalf of the college, my sincere appreciation. - John

I just found that note again. Obviously John regarded Beecher as an "old man" too. And yet, looking back now and doing the math – Beecher was born in 1904 – I realize, somewhat to my dismay, that Beecher was only a couple of years older then than I am right now. And I might say to myself, *Why he wasn't old at all!* Except I just went and looked in the mirror – at my white hair. Time has a way of kinda sneakin' up on ya, doesn't it?

Beecher's allotted "fifteen minutes of fame" was probably long over by the time we met him. I never saw – or even heard much about – John Beecher again. But that night after dinner he gave us a copy of his book, *Hear the Wind Blow! Poems of Protest & Prophecy.* It is inscribed: *For Treva & Tim Bazzett, in friendship, John Beecher.*

John Beecher died in 1980. I treasure his gift, and his friendship.

Two days ago – one of those days I wrote nothing here – I turned sixty-five. A milestone birthday of sorts, I suppose. I'm officially on the rolls of Medicare now. And one of the things I have learned from this new vantage point of advanced age is the importance of friendships. So I'm going back to Central here, in one of those non-chronological time jumps, because I want to talk about some of our friends from those long-ago college days.

Donnie Dobson, or "Dawnie" as his wife, Mary Ellen, calls him in her still-noticeable northern Maine accent, has been my friend now for over forty years.

January 31, 2009

Damn! I missed *another* day of writing. I was distracted by a book I had picked up and started reading – and finished today. Debra Dickerson's *An American Story* is a memoir that bears very little resemblance to my story. She's black and came from a very poor background in East St. Louis, but through her own determination put together her own success story – twelve years in the Air Force, two or three college degrees and Harvard Law School. But I think the part that most intrigued me was her description of her year at DLI in Monterey, where she studied Korean. It brought back some memories of my own, which I'll be getting to soon – unless another good book gets in the way; and I still have Piercy's book to finish.

But back to Don Dobson. I met Don, and his still-new bride, Mary Ellen, a year or so before I met Treve. He and I met on the first day of school at Ferris, back in the fall of 1967. He and I were both freshly discharged from the service, he from the navy and I from the army. Since we shared a common "fuck the army/navy" mindset, we became friends almost immediately. This nastiness is better explained, and in more detail, in my book, *Soldier Boy*. And the circumstances of how Don and I met can be found in my other book, *Pinhead*. I'm not trying to plug my other books here, honest. It's just that I hate to repeat myself; and now that I'm sixty-five I know I probably do it all the time. It comes with the territory, but I'm trying my best not to. Repeat myself, I mean.

So here are some stories about our dear friends, the Dobsons. Some Central stories, because Don and I both transferred from Ferris to Central at the same time, in 1967. I've already told a few Ferris stories in that other book. Although I forgot to tell the one about how Don and I stole a Christmas tree from some tree farm near Paris. Don couldn't afford to buy a tree, but he didn't want to deprive Mary of a proper Christmas, so … I don't think it was exactly grand theft. And he damn near tore the transmission out of that old Pontiac, bumping around out in that field over stumps and brush, weaving between rows of evergreens, looking for just the right one. Meanwhile, I kept looking fearfully around and over my shoulder, watching for the owner – or the police. Because we had open containers in the car too, A&P's awful but affordable barely-beer Tudor Ale. There was no functioning heater in that car and we needed to keep warm somehow. Alcohol seemed the answer. Somehow we managed to locate that perfect tree, hack it off and cram it into the back seat (well, there wasn't really any back seat, just a lot of trash rolling and sliding around back there) and get it back to their apartment.

But no matter. I'm not gonna tell that story. It's a forgotten Ferris tale. And I'm not sure if Mary ever knew that tree was hot. Is there a statute of limitations on Christmas tree theft?

Here's a Central story – about our first New Year's Eve together. Donnie and Mary are in it. They hosted the party in their elegant new digs at Northwest Apartments. They had only been in the place for about a month, having moved there from their rented upstairs rooms in Shepherd, where they'd camped for a couple of months upon returning from Maine, where Don had spent the summer painting houses and Mary gestating Dougie, their first baby, who was born in August of 1967.

Donnie had been smart enough to get their names on a waiting list for campus housing before they'd gone back to Maine, but the Northwest Apartment complex, brand-spanking new when they moved in, had been slightly behind schedule in its opening. In fact, when the Dobsons moved into the place in November, part of the quadrangle of apartments was still under construction and it was kind of a muddy mess around there. I think they got in early because Don had been hired as a resident student supervisor, to handle any minor maintenance or repair problems at the complex. Major stuff he simply referred to the housing office.

By the end of December, however, mud was no longer a problem. Deep snow and freezing temperatures were. Undeterred, Donnie & Mary decided to have a combination housewarming and New Year's Eve party, and we were invited. We had only been married a little over a month, so it was our first party as a married couple and Treve and I were both kind of excited about it. We were living, newly installed, in that back upstairs apartment on the corner of Bellows and Fancher.

It was bone-chillingly cold on that last night of the year, well below zero. The snow was nearly a foot deep and covered by a shiny hard crust.

I still remember thinking that Treve had spent what I considered an inordinately long time laying out and trying on several different outfits before finally choosing one. Then she took even more time with her hair and makeup. I was pretty new to all this kinda stuff, you have to remember, I mean to actually *witnessing* all that went into putting a woman together. Guys, of course, just shave, shower and dress. Which I'd done; and then stood around looking at my watch and jingling the car keys and stuff. I wasn't fully housebroken, so to speak, on the ways of women and didn't quite understand why it took so long for her to get ready. The party was to start at seven, and it was already a little past that when she finally pronounced herself ready.

It was very dark and very cold when we came outside. A bright half moon hung in a cloudless sky, causing that crusted snow to fairly glisten as we crunched up to our locked car. When I put my key into the door lock of the VW it wouldn't turn. The lock was frozen solid. I cursed softly. Terri shot me a worried look.

"Gimme your lighter," I said.

Fumbling a moment in her purse, she located the lighter and handed it over. Ratcheting up a tall flame, I passed the car key carefully back and forth through it, warming the metal thoroughly, and then tried the door again. This time the lock turned, but the door remained frozen shut. With a hard emphatic jerk, I pulled it open and climbed in onto the icy vinyl bucket seat. Leaning across, I attempted to open the passenger door. The handle turned, but the door stuck, until I battered it sharply open with the flat of my hand. Treve climbed quickly in, already shivering and rubbing her hands briskly on her nyloned knees.

But it was all for naught. When I put the key in the ignition and turned it – nothing. Not an "rrrr." Not a click. Not even a groan. Not a sound. The battery was dead, defeated by the bitter cold.

"Well, shit," I muttered softly. Then shouted, *"SHIT!"* beating the heels of my hands on the icy steering wheel as I stared at the frosted windshield.

Treve sat there, looking over at me, teeth chattering and a worried expression on her face. "Wh- what're we gonna d-do?" she asked.

Still fuming, I looked back at her, noting her teased and backcombed blonde hair and carefully chosen party clothes, but, most of all, the expectant look in her brown eyes. And I knew I was not going to disappoint this girl, who deserved some fun and had been so looking forward to this party. I heaved an enormous sigh.

"I guess we'll have to walk," I replied. "But we better go up and put on some warmer clothes."

So we went back upstairs and took off our party clothes and shoes and placed them carefully into a shopping bag to carry. Then we put on long johns and warmer clothes and boots, our winter coats, scarves, gloves and wool stocking caps. Treve balked at this last, not wanting to ruin her hair. But when I mentioned the possibility of frostbitten ears, she grimaced and gave in, adding brush, comb and hairspray to the clothes bag. Finally, suitably attired for the weather, we set off down Bellows, heading west to Northwest Apartments about seven blocks away, our boots crunching loudly in the silence as we trekked across the top edge of the deserted campus. Treve carried the clothes bag and I carried another bag holding a six-pack of beer and a macaroni and cheese casserole. Every party we attended at college was always pot luck and BYOB. We were all poor and we all knew it, but that was no obstacle to having some fun now and then.

And we *did*, by God – have fun, I mean. Don and Mary Ellen greeted us warmly at the door, exclaiming about the cold as we stomped the snow off our boots and took them off just inside. Don took the beer to put on ice, and Mary whisked away the food to reheat while Treve and I repaired to an upstairs bedroom to put on our party clothes and re-comb our hair. It was between terms, of course, so it wasn't a big party. There were probably four or five couples there that night, and a few babies too, including four month-old Dougie. The Tillotsons were there, friends from Ferris, where Sandy had been a Delta Zeta sorority sister of Treve's and John had been in the pharmacy program. He had graduated the previous year and was working at the Walgreen's out on Mission.

We ate, we drank, smoked, talked and laughed a lot that night. We swapped stories and passed babies around and marveled over the newness of the apartment and its furnishings and appliances, since we were all still pretty new at this marriage thing and were making do with mostly second-hand stuff. And we danced – the Twist, the Mashed Potatoes, and the Shing-a-ling, a brand new simple little dance that involved a two steps left, kick-and-clap; two steps back, kick-and-clap – and repeat as necessary. The song we did it to was "Nobody But Me" by The Human Beinz. Most of the dances we did back then were accompanied by our own personal styles of hunching our shoulders, pursing our lips, winking and other kinds of white boy shuckin' and jivin' – rhythmic or not-so-rhythmic stuff that now make me cringe to remember. Treve and I can still do them, although not without some embarrassment. But our memories of that first New Year's Eve together at the Dobsons are the best.

The Dobsons gave us some of our first OJT for parenting too, or rather little Dougie did.

February 3, 2009

A couple days missed here for the sake of eye health. My eyes had become red, itchy and weepy and I noticed that when I turned on the TV later in the day to watch the news, things looked blurry. Too much time staring at a computer screen. So I took a couple days off, even trying to read a bit more sparingly. It is, I suppose, a sign of the times, or my own lifestyle, that I felt extremely frustrated in not being able to work at the computer, watch TV or even read. Well, I cheated a bit on that last. It seems that reading and writing are the two major activities in my life that I am loath to give up. I hope I don't have to.

I didn't mention here that we lost John Updike last week, on my birthday. He was only seventy-six and died of lung cancer. I was shocked to read of his death. A very private person for most of his life, I don't think many people even knew he was ill. He played such an important role in my love of good writing for so many years. I immediately felt guilty that I have not read his more recent work – the last ten years worth, probably. In his fifty-plus years of writing he produced nearly a book a year, and all quality stuff too. I will miss reading his essays and reviews in *The New Yorker* and hearing of his latest book. I had finally written him a letter just five or six weeks ago. In the past few years I have begun the practice of writing or e-mailing letters to many authors I admire, so it occurred to me a letter to Updike was long overdue. I also sent him a copy of *Reed City Boy* and told him what an inspiration his work had been to me, how much he had mattered. Now he and his work belong to the ages. Thank you for all of it, John.

But I need to finish my story of Dougie Dobson. It must have been in the early spring of 1969, when we lived upstairs at HH8 Washington Court. I should probably mention that we lived in two apartments there. The first one was HH5, a one-bedroom unit just downstairs and across the landing. We had moved there in the fall of 1968 when school started. A lot of things happened in our lives in the next few months, during my senior year at Central. First, we learned that Treve was pregnant (the tonsillitis story I told you earlier), and shortly after that we also learned that our upstairs neighbors across the hall, Dick and Linda Napolitano (I *think* that was the name), were moving across campus to the new Northwest Apartments. If I remember correctly, it was so Dick could take a building supe job there, like Don Dobson had. Well, as soon as we learned this, I went directly to the campus housing office and told them we were expecting a baby and asked if we could move upstairs. The people at the housing office were just super about it. They told me if I would just bring them a note from Treve's doctor verifying the pregnancy then we could have the upstairs apartment as soon as it was vacated. The timing could not have been better. I think the Napolitanos moved out one day in November, and we moved in just a couple days later. The move was pretty simple, since there was virtually no furniture involved. All the apartments were furnished with same stuff. So it was just a matter of carrying our clothes upstairs and putting them back into the drawers and closets up there, along with boxes of books and records and kitchen stuff. It probably didn't take us more than a couple of hours.

So in the course of two months we moved twice. Treve was so very happy with our new larger quarters and we immediately bought some bright yellow paint and painted the second bedroom walls. Yellow was a popular color for nurseries back in the sixties, when the baby's sex was a mystery until he (or she) was born.

The other thing I remember about that fall semester was a good news-bad news kinda thing. The bad news was that there was a virulent flu epidemic that swept across campus and community, emptying out classrooms and offices, indiscriminately striking down students and teachers alike. By the second week of December, nearly a thousand cases had been reported, so on December 14 President Boyd officially closed the school. The *good* news was that all final exams were canceled. I was one of the lucky ones who had not caught the flu, so I was, needless to say, extremely happy to hear there would be no final exams. I mean I was a *student* – of *course* I was happy. *Whoopee! School's out! No more tests! Let's go play in the snow!* And I think we did. And we probably drove home to Belleville early for Christmas too.

I'll get back to the baby Dougie Dobson story, honest! I'm just kinda filling in a few gaps here first about our living arrangements.

I say we went to Belleville for Christmas because we'd gone to Reed City to *my* folks for Thanksgiving. We were trying to be fair about alternating our holidays between sets of parents. I'm pretty sure we must have spent our first married Christmas at Zimmers, although, strangely enough, I have no memories of that first big holiday as a married couple at all. Anyway, I had been quickly reminded, during the 1968 Thanksgiving holiday, just how young my bride of a year still was. She may have been twenty-one by then, but she missed her family badly on that first big holiday without them. We both remember her retreating to a back bedroom to cry. I tried not very successfully to comfort her, rationalizing male-fashion that, "Hell, you'll see 'em at Christmas in just another month! What's the big deal?"

Of course that didn't work very well, and finally my mom went in and talked with her, and must have offered some sort of comfort I hadn't learned to give yet, or being a man, might never learn. But we somehow got through the holiday.

So Terri was happy too about the fall semester being cut short and an early vacation in the offing. She was nearly five months pregnant, but we did go out in the yard in the apartment quadrangle and build a snowman the day we heard school was canceled. And a few days later we packed up and headed for Belleville, where she quickly got involved in all the holiday cooking and preparations – making pierogies and baking cookies and pies and shopping with her mom. Christmas was a big deal at the Zimmers back then. Her brothers Don and Bob usually came home with their wives and kids and her other brother Dick was there too, sometimes with his girlfriend of the moment. There would be expensive cigars and brandies and liqueurs being passed around with dishes of mixed nuts and candies and other snacks sitting out for easy consumption. On Christmas Eve they feasted on pierogies and ham, and on Christmas day a standing rib roast with all the trimmings was de rigueur, an edible sign of prosperity, preferably medium rare. The television was on constantly and the house was awash in good cheer, charged with lively conversation and redolent with the scent of cigar, cigarette and pipe smoke. I realize that the smoke part doesn't sound very appetizing now, but back then it was simply part of the pervading atmosphere and no one thought much about it.

The major things I remember buying Treve for Christmas that year were two maternity outfits I'd found at a store downtown. They were wool, and both in shades of green, I think. One was a plaid and the other in small checks. She just loved both of them, and although she didn't quite need them yet, she wore them anyway. I probably got books and records. Reading and music have always been my gifts of choice and still are.

What I remember even more than Christmas that year, however, was the trip back and its aftermath. The flu had finally caught up with me while we were in Belleville and I was feeling thoroughly miserable. Treve had wanted us to stay a little longer, but I wanted to get back home where I could be sick in our own bed, so we set off under lowering skies a few days after Christmas. We ran into a snowstorm of rather frightening force and volume north of Lansing, somewhere around St. Johns, which we ever after labeled as the "bad weather belt," which it invariably was. Highway 27 (since redesignated 127) was completely covered at some points and we were breaking trail in our trusty Volkswagen. I still think that rear-mounted engine may have been the only thing that got us through some of the heavier drifts across the road, with the extra traction the engine weight added. We were so happy to see the Mount Pleasant exit sign that day, but when we got back onto the CMU campus we found that the roads had not been plowed yet, so our belabored Bug continued to plow its way through deep snow and drifts until we finally made it back to our apartment complex. By this time I had a raging fever and chills, but I couldn't rest yet. Not only was the road behind our apartment not sufficiently plowed, but our parking places were all filled with snow. We seemed to be the first residents back, as there were no other cars in sight. So we struggled through the drifts with our luggage to our entrance on the other side of the building. After depositing our stuff inside, I came back out with a shovel and proceeded to dig out a parking place for my Beetle, so I could get it off the road. Meanwhile, Treve discovered we had very little food in the house, so she made a short list of groceries we needed. Plunging back out into the storm, glassy eyes weeping and nose running, I headed to the grocery over on Mission to get in supplies before I collapsed completely.

When I returned, I found, much to my dismay, that our downstairs neighbors, the Derdas, had returned in my absence and Tom had parked in the place I had so laboriously dug out just a half hour before. Near utter collapse by this time, I parked behind him in the street and carried our bags of groceries upstairs and told Treve what had happened. She was outraged. She took the groceries from me and put them on the counter and told me to go to bed. Then she took my car keys and grabbed our snow shovel off the landing and marched downstairs and banged on the Derdas door. I didn't hear the exchange, I was too exhausted. But from what Tom told me days later, my girl just lit into him with a fury for taking *our* parking place. She told him that I was *sick*; and then thrust our car keys and shovel at him and told him to get the hell out there and dig out another parking place of his own and then park our car, *dammit!* And by God, he did.

In the meantime, I got into bed and practically passed out from exhaustion and fever. A few hours later, Treve awakened me to give me aspirin and hot Campbell's chicken noodle soup. Still feverish, but feeling better, I asked her if she'd come to bed with me. So she did. Then I asked her if she'd put on that new rabbit fur winter hat I'd bought her downtown at Grant's, the one with the strings that tied, with little bunny tails at the end of each string that hung down just so over her chest. So she did. And would she please take off that flannel nightgown? She would, and she did. I may have been sick, but I wasn't *that* sick. It was better than the soup. And I still remember.

February 4, 2009

This was all just prefatory information, to let you know that that's where we lived – at HH8 Washington Court – when we got an object and practical lesson in child care from little Dougie Dobson in April of 1969, about a month before our first son, Jeff, was born. Don and Mary Ellen had something to do that day and we had agreed to babysit for Dougie, so they dropped him off at our place so we could get in a little practice parenting. Don't get *too* excited, because this is a pretty short story, when you come right down to it. About all I remember from that long-ago afternoon is what amounts to the punch line. I think it must have been a Saturday, since I was home. I had just taken a shower and put on a clean shirt and my favorite pair of tan jeans, washed so many times they were nearly white. Mary handed the baby off to Treve at the door and told us to have fun; they'd be back in a couple hours.

Treve was doing some laundry at the time, so she gave little Dougie to me. I have always been fine with babies. I fondly remember helping to take care of my younger brother and sister, seven and nine years younger than me, and once spending a pleasant afternoon playing with my little cousin, Tim Whalen, when he was a baby. So I'd been looking forward to playing with Dougie that day.

I had no sooner seated myself on our tan institutional pleather couch with Dougie on my lap than he began pooting, which I found hilarious.

"Didja hear that, Treve?" I asked, laughing "Dougie farts just like his father!"

Then, without any warning (well actually I suppose I *had* been warned), it happened. The baby's butt literally seemed to just blow up, and this runny greenish shit suddenly squirted explosively out of both leg holes of his diaper, running all over my aforementioned "favorite" jeans.

"Holy *SHIT!*" I shouted, jumping to my feet and holding the baby out at arm's length as I looked down in horror at my babyshit-splattered pants. "Aw, cripes! Aw, *FUCK!* Aww … *Look* at this! Look what he *did!* Look at my *pants!* Aw, *shit.*"

Shit indeed. I was going to say "in one fell swoop" my pants were ruined. But I'm not gonna say that. Let's be subject appropriate here. In "one swell poop" my pants were irredeemably ruined forever, at least for me. Because, while Treve was able to remove much of the stain, there was always a faint shadow there to remind me of the day Dougie Dobson blindsided me with that unexpected explosion of excrement.

Treve came running, of course, but her reaction was more one of mirth than sympathy. She was laughing so hard it was all she could do to take the baby from me as I still stood there wide-eyed in horror at what had happened to my once-favorite pants.

Is there a lesson here? Like maybe, "Never wear good clothes while handling a strange baby, because you never know what that baby might have recently eaten or what effect it might have on his plumbing."

Doug was probably about a year and a half old at the time and now there's a forty-one or –two year-old man out there somewhere who still owes me for those jeans. Because his father's only reaction when we told him what had happened was his usual high-pitched cackle of delight, and probably a "That's my boy!"

I got no satisfaction and no sympathy. Like poor Rodney Dangerfield, "I got no respect." But, hey, I got a story from it, and just inflicted it on you, dear reader. Maybe *you'll* know what the moral is here, because *I* sure as hell don't.

I just took a break to field a call from Treve, now encamped comfortably at Scott's in Pennsylvania. I told her my magnum opus continues to grow; and she once again asked me why I felt this need to keep writing all this stuff down, and "who cares?" And once again, I thought about this after I'd hung up. Perhaps it's because in the last few years I have finally come to think of myself as a writer. It was an uncomfortable fit for me at first, when I would hear that people around town refer to me as "the writer," or that "author fella." But now – four books later – I find that I'm finally okay with it.

Last night I finished reading *Sleeping with Cats*. Marge Piercy is several years my senior and grew up very poor in

Detroit, her mother Jewish and her father from a family of anti-Semites, which didn't make for the healthiest of a home life in her early years. I first discovered Piercy back in the seventies when I was putting together a course at Monroe called Modern Michigan Authors and I found her early novel, *Small Changes*, with its many autobiographical touches about Detroit and Ann Arbor (where Piercy attended the U of M). Since then I've read several of her other books, the best of which is perhaps the WWII-era novel, *Gone to Soldiers*. Or if it's not her best, it's certainly one of my favorites. Somewhere towards the end of *Sleeping with Cats* she says this about writing and writers –

> *Writing is a futile attempt to preserve what disappears moment by moment ... Writing sometimes feels frivolous and sometimes sacred, but memory is one of my strongest muses. I serve her with my words. So long as people read, those we loved survive however evanescently. As do we writers, saying with our life's work, Remember. Remember us. Remember me.*

I got goose bumps when I read this last night. Because that's how I feel about writing too. I know I'll never be famous, but the words I put down here are my own perhaps futile desperate attempts at a kind of immortality, not just for me, but for my wife, my parents, my kids and all those people who have had a hand in making me who I am. Writing is, for me, a kind of open love letter to the world and the people I've known and loved – "Remember us. Remember me." Thank you, Marge.

That's why I keep writing, Treve.

About a month or so after the shit-stained pants episode, our son Jeff was born. And my friend Don Dobson was there for me again, helping me assemble a crib in our bright yellow second bedroom. I had never put together a crib before, but maybe Donnie had, since he felt that the printed instructions were unnecessary. I had picked out a yellow crib at the big Yankee department store on Mission. It matched the new paint job Treve and I had so lovingly applied in the excitement of anticipation to the cinder block walls of what would now be the baby's room, the nursery. We had put off getting the crib out of superstition of queering the deal somehow. Because what if something happened – an unspoken fear for most parents perhaps. But Jeff was finally here, was healthy with all his fingers and toes, and would be home in just a day or two, thank God. (And I did; we both did.)

So I had enlisted the help of my friend, vastly more experienced in these things than I. Mary was pregnant with their second child at the time, I think. As with all of our joint projects, I had sweetened the deal with a couple six-packs of beer. And none of that Tudor Ale shit this time either. This was a special occasion that called for the *good* stuff – Hamm's beer, my brand of choice in those years. As we got deeper into the construction of the crib, our alcohol-addled little minds got a bit confused, so we did finally consult the assembly construction sheet to attach some of the seemingly "extra" hardware parts to the crib. I think we were probably down to our last two beers by the time we'd finally finished and stood back to admire our handiwork, with its shining yellow-painted wooden bars, headboard and footboard, its gleaming steel link springs and the plastic casters on each of the four legs.

Handing Donnie his last beer, I popped mine open and belched with a long satisfying sonorousness, smiling hugely at my accomplishment – the burp, not the crib. Donnie saluted me with his raised bottle, replying in kind.

"What's that metal bar underneath the side for?" I asked, pointing with my bottle.

"I dunno," Don replied. "But it was supposed to go there. The directions said so. (*Bu-urrrp!*)"

"Huh." I said, burping again myself.

"Hmmf," Don muttered, and softly kicked the metal mystery bar, causing the side of the crib to drop smoothly down. "*Shit!*" he exclaimed, and quickly pulled the side of the crib back up, causing it to click smoothly back into place.

"*Ah!*" I said, the little light bulb in the balloon over my head nearly visible. And I kicked the bar myself, causing the crib side to drop again. I then raised it back up, clicking it into its raised position.

"*Ah!*" responded Don. Mystery solved. Mechanical genius in action. We drained our last beers and both belched loudly.

The nursery was ready.

About a month after Jeff was born I finished my senior year and graduated with a B.A. in teaching and a major in English. A week after graduation I began summer school, getting an early start on earning an M.A. in English.

I thought of that final grinding year of college this week when I took my mom out to lunch up in Cadillac. Afterwards we indulged our mutually favorite pastime, book-browsing. We went to The Book Nook, a cavernous used books store up on Pine Street that might have once housed a grocery store or something similar, but we learned the books have been at this location for over twenty years now. Mom was delighted to find several books by her favorite author, a British writer of historical romances. (I have never read Catherine Cookson, but I know that she was, and perhaps still is, one of the most widely read writers in the United Kingdom, having authored nearly a hundred books. So Mom has plenty of company in her enthusiasm for this author, who died in 1998 at the age of 91.) I found a memoir by Reynolds Price, a southern author first introduced to me in grad school at Central, by Dr. John Hepler. That book by Price, his first novel, was called *A Long and Happy Life*. I'm not even sure it was on the assigned reading list for the American Lit seminar Dr. Hepler taught, but I know he was a Price fan himself, so I read it. Like John Updike, Price was and still is a masterful storyteller and wordsmith. Since grad school days I have read several of his other books.

My graduate school days at Central were a mixture of heaven and hell. Heaven was represented by all the books I enjoyed. *Finally*, having completed all those damn compulsory, "required" courses from my undergrad curriculum, I was free to graze freely in the green pastures of great literature, nearly to my heart's content. The hell part came not just in all the research papers I was required to write, sometimes spending whole days in the library (where I met Miss O'Connell), but also from some of the great world literature I still had to read, works by Sophocles, Euripides and Aeschylus, for example. The Greeks were a mixed bag; some I liked and some I did not. I remember a whole semester spent mostly on Euripides, whom I came to know quite well, although I wasn't that crazy about him. Somehow, however, I managed to throw together a twenty- or thirty-page term paper on him in one frenzied flurry of activity over a single weekend. Poor time management. And also too much time spent reading other things – more contemporary stuff – that I enjoyed a lot more than all those dead Greeks. I still remember those long days in the library when I was supposed to be making notes and preparing those term papers, and how I would occasionally take a break and get up and wander through the fiction shelves. That was how I found Vance Bourjaily and his wonderful then-new book, *Brill among the Ruins*. Bourjaily was one of those returning WWII vets trying to make a name for himself in literature, who never quite achieved the stature of James Jones or Norman Mailer, but was, all the same, one hell of a good writer.

Another now nearly forgotten writer I discovered that year was Edward Hannibal, and his very enjoyable novel, *Chocolate Days, Popsicle Weeks* – a love story I discovered in the book rack at Walgreen's and read when I should have been reading Aeschylus or Euripides, or perhaps translating passages from the Old English story of *Beowulf*. (And yes, you had to "translate" Old English – another required grad course – which was oddly Germanic in its foreignness.)

Another tantalizing offering from Dr. Hepler was a book called *Tike and Five Stories*, by a very young novelist called Jonathan Strong. Hepler brought this book into class one day to offer as an example of the current crop of authors who were still emulating the terse, short-sentence style of Hemingway, dead for nearly ten years by then. The book circulated among the several students in our seminar and we discussed it in class. I much preferred Strong to some of the more staid traditional authors we were reading, people like Stephen Crane, Theodore Dreiser, Frank Norris, William Dean Howells, William Faulkner, and of course Hemingway. I mean I didn't dislike these guys, so-called "modern" writers, but I was hungry for books about the time I was living in – the "right now" – and people like Updike, Bourjaily and Strong were writing about those things. I watched for *Tike* to come out in paperback and got my own copy later that year. I kept that book for nearly thirty years, carting it around halfway around the world and back. I think I gave it to my daughter, Suzie, some years back when she was offered a slot at the prestigious writer's school at Breadloaf, because I learned that Jonathan Strong was one of the regular faculty members there. Unfortunately, Suzie was unable to attend Breadloaf for various reasons, and I never got the book back either.

Books. How important they can become; how important they have always been in my life. Every now and then I will recall a book I once owned and wish I could lay my hands on it again. Not necessarily to *read* it, but just to hold, to open, to read the jacket notes, to sample a random passage. Like looking fondly through an old photo album. A few years ago I divested myself of over a thousand books. It was painful, but they were threatening to crowd us out of our small house. Most of them went to the Chase Public Library several miles west of Reed City, where they were carefully catalogued and shelved and I was given an itemized receipt. I miss many of those books, but at least I know they found a good home, even though many of them may never be read again. And I can still go visit them if I want.

This past year when Barack Obama was waging his unprecedented and ultimately successful campaign for president, perhaps because of the historical novelty of a mixed-race African-American running for this high office, I was reminded of an obscure novel I read many years ago called *The Last Western*. Its author, Thomas S. Klise, published the book himself, much as I now publish my own books, I suppose. It was, if I remember correctly, a futuristic story of a mixed-race boy who grew up orphaned and became a star major-league sports figure and ultimately went on to become the Pope in times of intense turmoil, intrigue and terrorism. I can't be sure if I've got that right, but I know that it was an utterly absorbing novel that Obama's own story brought back. (And yes, I *have* read *Dreams from My Father*, a wonderful book about and by a remarkable young man, now our president. How odd, and even a bit unsettling, to have reached an age where I think of our *president* as "young.")

In spite of all that extra-curricular reading during the 1969-1970 year, I somehow managed to emerge with an M.A. in one year. Our friends the Dobsons had gone by then; Don found a job in sales with Johnson & Johnson. Some years later I remember asking Don what a major in Sociology had to do with selling baby and health care products.

In typical Donnie fashion he responded breezily, "Sociology, sales – it's all bullshit, and I've always been good at that." And then laughed his trademark high-pitched cackle.

Amen, Don. I talked with both Don and Mary Ellen last year when I was trying to get this book started. They were wending their way slowly up the intra-coastal waterway on their sailboat, Solace, when we finally made contact. I hadn't talked with Don in a couple years and found his old telephone number from where they'd lived for years down in the Florida Keys was no longer in service. I finally managed, through the convenience of the on-line white pages, to locate their son Doug. (Yes, the same one who shit all over me at Central.) Doug gave me a cell phone number for his mother.

"I'm not sure if Dad has a new cell phone yet, 'cause he dropped his in the canal last week," Doug informed me, then erupted in a cackle that sounded just like his father's. It was positively eerie.

Yes, the Dobsons are semi-retired now, plying the inland waterways and the Caribbean whenever they can get enough money and supplies together to go exploring. They made a voyage to the Tortugas a few years back. And last summer they sailed up from the Keys to the Chesapeake Bay and back. They don't own a home; they have lived on their small boat for years now. Their life, like Don, is simple, and they make the most of it.

Probably our closest friends during my year of grad school were the ones nearby, either my classmates or our neighbors at Washington Court. Luther Hanson was my closest classmate. He was a US Navy veteran and we took many of the same classes that year. He and his wife, Sandy, a willowy blonde, had no children, but came to our place often to share potluck dinners, visit and play with Jeff. Another mutual friend that year was Larry Leffel, a married Air Force vet with a young child. He was taking his Master's degree in Creative Writing, so was only in some of the classes with Luther and me. The three of us sometimes made clandestine trips to the Main

Bar on Mission in the afternoon between seminars, when we should have been studying, to discuss the prosecution of the war in Vietnam or the current political situation. I still remember the three of us sitting at the bar one afternoon when we heard breaking news on the TV about US forces going into Cambodia – or was it Laos? – and the pundits of the day discussing how the action might shorten or lengthen the war. The jukebox was blasting out the fuzz-bass-heavy notes of Norman Greenbaum's "Spirit in the Sky" while the bombers delivered their deadly payloads and we sipped our draught beers and collectively thanked our lucky stars that we had already done our time in the service of Uncle Sam. I had received my final discharge papers from the army by mail in 1968, my inactive reserve time completed.

Like other college campuses around the nation at that time, CMU was awash with student protests and demonstrations for most of the time I was a student there. I can vaguely remember the ROTC building being taken over for a few days by student protesters, and also a candlelight protest march snaking across campus and through town one night involving several hundred students and faculty. I knew about all this stuff, but I think that by this time I was simply too overwhelmed by a sense of responsibility, by the gnawing need to take care of my own family to get involved. Usually I was working when this kind of stuff was going on, at my various part-time jobs in the food commons or unloading trucks at UPS, and, later, correcting papers as a graduate teaching assistant.

There wasn't a lot of socializing for us during that last busy year at Central either, but we did get out from time to time. Treve and I both remember one movie we attended with the Leffels and maybe the Hansons too at a downtown theater. I had read John Nichols' novel, *The Sterile Cuckoo*, that year in paperback, so I was eager to see the film version, which starred a young Liza Minnelli as the irrepressible and yes, slightly cuckoo character of Pookie Adams. It was about college students in the sixties, so of course we could all relate. The theme song for the film was the hauntingly beautiful "Come Saturday Morning" by the Sandpipers, which made the Top 40 that year.

We also attended a party at the Hansons' small apartment over near the high school that year. The Leffels were there, as was, I think, Ben Mocini, another classmate who'd gotten his undergrad degree at Grand Valley, which was a brand-new college back then. Ben was a little "different," in that he tried to follow the current fashions, unlike we vets, who tended to show up in mismatched old khakis, field jackets or pea coats. I think Ben may have been one of the first people I knew personally who actually wore a Nehru jacket, and maybe a gold chain or two as an accessory. The main attraction at the Hansons party was, I believe, a fondue pot, the latest thing for small parties and gatherings. Remember those little pots you filled with oil and placed over a candle or flame of some sort to heat the oil, then you had long skewers or forks to dip small chunks of meat or bread into it? Or sometimes maybe you'd put cheese in the pot, for cheese fondue.

Treve's friends at Central were mostly the other wives who lived nearby. Nancy Powell was probably one of her best friends at Washington Courts. Richard, her husband, was about my age, and was working on his Master's in history, trying to finish a troublesome thesis. They had two boys, around six and four, I think, named Jeff and Darin. Treve and I both remember waking up early in the summertime that year, or on Saturday mornings when the Powell boys were both at home. The swings in the playground out in the apartment complex quadrangle would begin to creak noisily as soon as the sun was out. And we would hear Jeff and Darin singing as they swung. Their favorite tune that year was "Michael (Row the Boat Ashore)," delivered at full-throated top volume.

Nancy was already an accomplished homemaker and cook when we met them and gave Treve a lot of help in those areas. Any time Treve had a question on the proper way to do something around the house or kitchen, she'd call Nancy.

Another couple who became fairly close friends there were Tom and Teri Bell, who had a little girl named Missy. After Tom graduated with his degree in teaching and found a job in Vestaburg, then it was Teri's turn to be the student and get her degree. They were still there when we left.

And there were Dave and Mary Ellen Bluem, who lived down at the end of our building. Dave and I both worked part-time for most of a year at the UPS warehouse and transshipment point on the north end of town, where we unloaded and loaded trucks and pulled and sorted packages from numerous fast-moving conveyor belts, learning by heart dozens of Michigan zip codes in the process. UPS was the best-paying part-time job in town back then and a real plum for a hard-working student trying to earn his way through school. It was hard, sometimes back-breaking work, especially when we would get in a shipment of heavy steel trailer hitches from the Draw-Tite company, located in Treve's hometown of Belleville, less than a half-mile from her house right on Martinsville Road. It was a nightmare trying to untangle a bunch of those hitches of various shapes and sizes that had all been thrown in a jumble on the floor of the truck. But probably the worst part of that job was its hours. We started work about ten at night, and often worked until two or three in the morning. That really played hell with your sleep patterns, especially if you had an eight o'clock class the next morning, which I often did.

I contacted Dave Bluem last year in Saginaw. Like me, he is now retired and back in his hometown. We talked of those days and laughed about them too. We both remembered the night we came back from work around two AM and were stopped and questioned by the campus police, because someone in our building had just phoned in a report of a peeping Tom. Dave left CMU later that year and went into the army, where he endured training in the swamps of Fort Polk, Louisiana, and then did a tour in Vietnam, where he admitted to being one of those REMF types. That's a "rear echelon motherfucker" for the uninitiated, an epithet which implied a much safer job that the poor grunt bastards out humping the boonies in that long, sorry, ill-fated misadventure.

Still another couple down the block from us in married housing was the Plouffs. I don't think we knew it at the time, but for the first year or so we were there, Billie was living there alone with their little boy and going to school. Harry was in the army, I think in Vietnam. But he came home our last year there and began taking classes himself. They were from

Ludington and had married right out of high school. I talked with Harry and Billie on the phone last year. They still live in Mount Pleasant and both have spent thirty-plus years as teachers there.

Some of our friends from those years in married housing are no longer together, which makes us a bit sad, but at the same time makes us grateful we've stuck it out and are still together. Because we too have had our rough patches. No one is immune from marital problems no matter how well- or ill-matched they might be. Talking of this makes me remember the little limerick we once heard, perhaps even back in our Central days.

Friends may come and friends may go
But some friends peter out, you know
But we'll be friends through thick and thin
Peter out or peter in.

February 5, 2009

I've been thinking about DLI this morning, so California here we come.

I arrived in Monterey in March of 1976 after a brief leave back in Monroe with Treve and the boys, during which time we squeezed in trips to both Belleville and Reed City. Under the terms of my enlistment contract I had re-entered the army as a PFC/E-3 and would be promoted to Specialist 4th Class (SP4), or pay grade E-4, upon successful completion of four months active duty. The promotion was, of course, contingent on the fact that I didn't screw up in some major way during those first four months. I mention this because I knew that we would not be eligible for government housing until I got that first promotion. So I was determined to do my absolute best. I wanted to get my family out to join me in California as soon as possible.

Since I was alone, or "unaccompanied," when I arrived at DLI, I was assigned to a two-man room in one of the barracks. The two and a half months I spent there were not the best, but I managed to keep busy and not think too much about the continued separation from my family.

My roommate and I were not a very good match. I was thirty-two with a couple college degrees and a family. This many years later I can't even remember my roommate's name, which is perhaps for the best. Our relationship was a little rocky. I'll call him Ron (Roommate). Ron was just nineteen and had been through basic and AIT to become a military policeman (MP). He was slated for a tour in Germany and had been lucky enough to get this assignment to DLI to learn German. Ron didn't see it this way. He thought learning another language was "stoopid." He just wanted to hurry up and get to Germany where he'd heard the beer was better and cheaper and the girls were easy. He already knew how to be an MP and he was anxious to start "bustin' heads" and doing his job. Ron was a gun freak and had a subscription to *Guns & Ammo* magazine which he studied a lot more faithfully than he did his German homework. In fact, I'm not sure if Ron ever did graduate, since during the two months we spent together I rarely saw him study. Instead he was out drinking at the Enlisted Men's (EM) Club with his buddies (also newly-minted MP's) at least three or four nights a week. I tried not to be too judgmental, remembering my own drinking days in the ASA my first time around. But it was hard to think kindly about this kid when he would come staggering in around midnight or one AM – whenever it was that the EM Club closed – stinking of beer and crashing about in the dark, mumbling and cursing. And sometimes – even more endearing – he would lean out of his bunk later and throw up into his wastebasket, or, if the basket wasn't there, onto the floor and himself, and then fall back asleep, leaving an overwhelming stench of vomit that filled the room. Anyway, you get the picture, and probably understand now why I can't remember his name.

The only good thing about Ron was that he was rarely in the room, so I did have some privacy and plenty of quiet time to read and study. And there was plenty to study. My class at DLI that year was one of several cycles that were part of an experiment to change the way Russian was taught to military linguists. Since our primary job would be monitoring Russian communications, or "listening," the powers that be at DLI decided to try to fashion a course that would de-emphasize speaking skills and put special emphasis on listening and comprehension. In other words, they didn't care if we learned to speak Russian well, or become fluent in the language. They just wanted us to be able to understand what we heard. Almost all of the day-to-day teachers we had were native speakers of Russian, emigrants from the Soviet Union. One of the senior professors there was named Valery Postovsky, a man I can't remember if we ever met. But he had designed a shortened course of instruction for beginners. The standard course of Beginning Russian had involved plenty of practice speaking the language and memorizing dialogues to parrot back in class. That course ran a full year, fifty-two weeks of training. The new experimental course, using what came to be called "the Postovsky method," or the Aural Comprehension Course, was shortened to just thirty-nine weeks, a feature which would also save money for the Department of Defense (DoD), no doubt a primary consideration when the decision was made to modify the course.

The new course worked and it didn't. I say it worked because I felt it gave me a pretty good base for beginning to understand the Russian language and I was able to do my job adequately once I got to the field. I say it didn't work because, as projected, I never did learn to speak Russian very fluently. And there must have been other ways it didn't work too, because not long after I left DLI the Postovsky method was scrapped and the military went back to the old fifty-two week course. I think Professor Postovsky may have died either while we were still in training, or shortly thereafter. I do remember that he was honored with a special award for his contributions while we were there. This is, of course, pretty standard procedure, the way the federal government does business. Give someone an award and make speeches about him, then junk his program a few months later and try something else. Believe me, I know. After all, I ended up working for the feds in one capacity or another for the next twenty-six years.

In any case, my classmates and I were guinea pigs for the Postovsky method. I can still remember my first few days of class, where we watched videotaped instruction, beginning with very simple vocabulary lessons. The screen would show a simple line drawing of a table and a voice would say, "Ehto stol," meaning "This [is a] table." Then it would show a pencil, and say, "Ehto karandash" – "This [is a] pencil." I know this may sound dirt simple, and it was. But it worked. And we were almost immediately loaded down with lengthy vocab lists to memorize and practice saying, starting with just a few dozen words perhaps, but eventually, as the days and weeks progressed, our vocabulary was soon reaching into the hundreds and even thousands of words. And grammar was being taught all at the same time. The most unique part of all this was that our classes were conducted almost completely in Russian. Many of our native speaker instructors spoke only broken English themselves, so it was sink or swim in those classrooms. Although we did have an hour or so each day with a *non*-native instructor who would answer our questions on grammar and usage. He was a young man, very casually fey in his mannerisms, named "Misha," who hailed, I think, from Fort Smith, Arkansas – a place he spoke of with undisguised scorn. Misha was a welcome relief from our mostly dour old-country primary instructors. He made us laugh and we all liked him. For the first several weeks, however, there was no shortage of frustration and despair that we would ever learn this strange language, but eventually we settled in for the long haul and the words and rules began to make sense and stick. Oh, I forgot to mention, just in case you didn't know, that one of the other first things we had to learn was a whole new set of letters, the Cyrillic alphabet. That was quickly done during the first week or so. And I should probably confess that I had bought a Berlitz Russian book even before I'd left home for Fort Leonard Wood and taught myself that alphabet and a few other simple rules of grammar. So I had a bit of a head start, I suppose, although it didn't last long with the rapid pace the instruction took right from the get-go. If you didn't keep up on a daily basis, you would just sink. And quite a few people did. The general rule, as I remember it, was you only got one more chance after you'd fallen too far behind to catch up. You got re-cycled, but only once. Re-cycling simply met you joined a newer class, one that had started after your original one – and there was usually a new class starting every two to four weeks. If you failed to keep up your second time around, then you simply disappeared from DLI, assigned to another post, to another military occupational specialty (MOS). Because learning a new language requires a lot of discipline and time management skills, the attrition rate at DLI was high. I was determined not to become a casualty. I had way too much riding on this – a whole new life for me and my family.

Those ten or twelve weeks I spent in the barracks went fairly quickly for me, particularly during the week, when I would study frantically to keep up, as I kept telling myself, *You've got to do this, Bazzett. You no longer have a choice. You owe it to your family.* I actually did give myself these little pep talks; they kept me going, focused on the future and a better, more meaningful life.

The weekends, however, were harder. I tried to do some extra studying, but study-burnout would often defeat me. So I did a lot of walking around the area, and wished I could get a bit farther afield to see more. One weekend I met a young lieutenant after Sunday mass at the chapel, He was there studying Arabic, I think. Officers and enlisted aren't really supposed to mix socially. But like me, he was lonely. And he had a car, so he invited me along to drive down the coast and look around a bit. That day I got my first look at Point Lobos and the Big Sur area as we drove down Highway 1 gawking at the spectacular ocean views and the cliffs and rocks along the way. A few months later, I would retrace that route in our own car with Treve and the boys along.

That afternoon convinced me, stupidly, that I needed a car. I really didn't, but I *thought* I did. So I bought an old Chevy Impala for just a few hundred bucks from a guy in the barracks who was shipping out. The price tag should have tipped me off, but I was anxious to get some wheels under me again. My very first jaunt down the highway the following weekend, the car died on the highway near Seaside, giving me barely enough time to steer it onto the shoulder. I walked back into town and called a wrecker and had it towed to a garage, where I found out it needed a new alternator, and also that all the emission controls equipment had been removed from the engine, something quite illegal in California. I ended up trading the car in at a local Mazda dealer. This time I got a Mazda RX3 that was only a few years old. I had to have Treve send me a check to help me purchase this one. I somehow managed to convince her that it would be handy to have a second car, since she was driving now too. The Mazda with its Wankel rotary engine was a very zippy little car, a five-speed with lots of pickup that I really enjoyed driving. Unfortunately, the gas mileage was very poor. And about six months later, with Treve and the boys in the car with me coming back from the beach in Pacific Grove, the clutch began to go out. We barely made it home. To shorten the story, buying those cars was a stupid and costly mistake. I ended up selling the Mazda back to the dealer at a considerable loss just to get it off our hands. We didn't need a second car. I don't think Treve ever drove in California. She was terrified of all the traffic.

I also bought a small nine-inch black-and-white GE television while I was still living in the barracks. I must have watched it, but I can't remember anymore exactly *what* I watched, so it was probably another stupid, ill-advised purchase. What I do remember is reading a lot on weekends. I discovered John Irving that spring when I read *The Water Method Man,* which remains my favorite of all his books. I also started reading Kurt Vonnegut there, beginning with *Slaughterhouse-Five.* And, since I was studying Russian, I tried again reading Anthony

Burgess's *A Clockwork Orange*, with its mix of Brit and Russian vernacular scattered throughout the story. It meant much more to me this time than it had a few years before. Its violence and dark humor mixed with irreverent pidgin Russian slang often made me wince and laugh out loud, sometimes on the same page, with its references to "devochki with bol'shie grudy," which simply means "girls with big tits." I also read and very much enjoyed a translated Russian classic, *And Quiet Flows the Don*, by Mikhail Sholokhov.

One of the culture shocks of the new army for me upon my arrival at DLI in 1976 was the number of women now in the ranks. Language school, a big enlistment draw for women, was filled with female soldiers, airmen and sailors, and even a few women marines. And some of these women were quite strikingly pretty – often a distraction in the very competitive atmosphere of the classroom. I tried not to be distracted. I was a married man, after all. But a lot of these women were very friendly to me, probably because I was ten or twelve years older and had that wedding band on. They figured they would be "safe" with me. And they were. I enjoyed their company, although I would often feel guilty about hanging out with these pretty girls, thinking of Treve back home trying to keep everything together, taking care of the boys and selling the house and dealing with movers. Many of the girls at DLI were top students, highly motivated to succeed.

I didn't know much about the backgrounds of these female classmates, but thought of them again just last week while reading that memoir called *An American Story*. Its author, Debra J. Dickerson, arrived at DLI as a young airman just a few years after I left. I didn't buy the book because Dickerson was, like me, a former "Monterey Mary." I found that out only while reading it. What drew me to the book was its sense of being a unique American success story. Dickinson, who is black, came from a very poor working class background in East St. Louis. After enduring a very tough childhood and youth, she finally enlisted in the Air Force, which she credits in many ways with saving her life. In fact, part of her dedication reads: "For the United States Air Force – it aimed me high and let me go." The Air Force gave Dickinson a sense of her true worth as a person, but it wasn't all roses. While stationed in Korea, she was raped by another airman. It took her years to fully recover from this. Dickinson went to Officer Training School (OTS) and became an officer. Altogether she spent twelve years in the Air Force. Later she attended Harvard Law School and went on to become a journalist.

But what caught my attention early in her story of life in Monterey was her description of how, after the rigors of basic training, things seemed much laxer at DLI, where "... mostly, the Air Force left us alone to learn our languages and to be initiated into the time-honored military traditions of binge drinking and promiscuous heterosexuality. Life was good." She goes on to tell that there were some rapes during her time at DLI which made many of the women students fearful. And unreported "date rape" was not uncommon among the enlisted ranks; often heavy drinking was involved.

One of the things I remember about a few of the prettier enlisted women at DLI was how they were constantly being "hit on" by the men in countless subtle and sometimes not at all subtle ways. It must have become tiresome and perhaps for some, even a bit frightening. Two of the women in my class married classmates within a month or two after their arrival at DLI. Their new husbands were, for the most part, strangers to them, and I was just amazed at how quickly and casually these matches seemed to have been made. I wondered then, and still do, if perhaps these marriages were simply ones of convenience, or represented a kind of safety from the predatory attentions of all the on-the-prowl males who had been bird-dogging them unmercifully.

Dickerson says this about those quickie GI marriages at DLI: "Given the volatility of military life and the mawkish sentimentality and immature notions of romantic love the lower classes are weaned on, GIs, especially young GIs, often marry hastily, to people they barely know." She tells of one young and inexperienced classmate who married hurriedly to a classmate she'd known only a month and got pregnant almost immediately.

> *... by her second trimester she was reporting for duty*
> *red-eyed and compulsively chugging Listerine. She hated*
> *her new husband now that she knew him. He was forcing*

her to send him off to work each morning with a kitchen
table blow job, since her increasing girth "made sex suck and
[you] owe me."

Shocking stuff, but I believe it, since I saw how one of the two girls from my Russian class that married during my time at DLI changed soon after her marriage. Her former bubbly personality was gone, replaced by a guarded wariness, a haunted look. It could very well have been an earlier version of the same story Dickerson tells.

There were other kinds of GI marriages at DLI too – marriages of convenience. Many of these young GIs wanted to get out of the barracks and the discipline that goes with living on post. If they got married then they were entitled to quarters allowance and could afford (just barely) to move off post to an apartment. An attractive woman I worked with nearly twenty years later at NSA, also a Russian linguist who had trained at DLI, told me her first marriage was one of those monetary marriages of convenience. She liked the guy, she told me, but they certainly weren't in *love*. They arranged some kind of a divorce-by-mail after they left DLI. Given my Catholic background, I guess I seemed a little shocked that marriage could be that casual an arrangement, but she assured me it was pretty common during her time at DLI, which was in the late eighties.

One of the disadvantages of living in the barracks were things like weekly room inspections and morning formations, things which I was looking forward to leaving behind once my family joined me and we were assigned family quarters. My platoon sergeant at DLI was a short stocky Marine, who was always looking for something to gig me for, even though I tried my best to keep my hair cut and my uniform sharp. I remember vividly one particular item he gigged me on, but I got him for it later. Since he was only about five foot eight and I was six foot five, he had to look up at me when he inspected me, something I'm sure he hated. On this particular morning, having carefully checked out my shoes, creases, brass and hairline, he must have been desperate to find something to get me for.

Peering up at me that Friday morning, he narrowed his eyes and then grinned evilly. "Nose hairs. You need to trim those nose hairs, Bazzett."

His assistant platoon sergeant, rolling his eyes at me sympathetically as he passed by, duly noted this egregious infraction of military neatness on his clipboard as I responded dutifully, "Yes, Sergeant. I'll take care of it right away, Sergeant," thinking to myself, *You measly little sawed-off prick! Why don't you get a life?*

Not too long after that, my family finally arrived to join me. It was the end of May by this time. In fact I'm pretty sure it was Memorial Day when I went to pick them up at the Monterey airport. Treve flew in with Scotty, who was not quite five, and our dog, Heidi. As a new and very timid driver, she had never even considered driving our car all the way from Michigan. Her father, Chet, had volunteered to do that, and when my brother, Bill, heard about it, he decided he'd like to make the trip too, and help Chet with the driving. Bill was still single at the time, and liked to travel, although he didn't get much opportunity for it. So this was a perfect chance for him to see some of the country and do us a favor at the same time. Chet could easily pick him up in Chicago on his way west in our 1975 AMC Hornet wagon. And our older boy, Jeff, made the cross-country trip with Grandpa Zimmer and his uncle Bill. Jeff and Bill have two different versions of the same story from that trip.

One of the reasons Jeff wanted to go in the car was that he'd met Uncle Bill a year or two before when we'd visited him in his bachelor rancher in Schaumburg. To entertain Jeff during our visit, Bill showed him how to make a couple different kinds of hats by folding newspapers just so. Maybe some of you remember how we used to make paper hats and boats out of old newspapers when we were kids back in the forties and fifties. That's basically what Bill showed Jeff, who was just five at the time. Jeff got to wear the end products and was very impressed with the process too. For years after that, whenever Uncle Bill came up in a conversation, he would usually say, "I remember Uncle Bill. He makes *hats!*" I always found this rather amusing, since Bill majored in physics in college and was in fact a technical writer who was writing manuals for guided missiles at the time. Not exactly a rocket scientist, but close. And on top of all that, *he made hats!*

In any case, Jeff was happy for an opportunity to spend some more time with his talented uncle, and was also hoping they would stay in motels along the way that had swimming pools. I can't remember if it took them two days or three to make the journey from Belleville to Monterey, but at one of the stops further west they did indeed stay at a motel with a pool. Jeff was very excited that he was finally going to get to go swimming. While Bill and Chet were busy getting settled in the room and looking at the menu for dinner that night, Jeff got himself into his bathing suit and asked if he could go swimming. Uncle Bill said sure, pretty soon. A few minutes later Bill and Chet looked around and Jeff was gone.

I still remember Bill telling me how he just panicked, thinking, *Oh my* God! *He's in the* pool! *If anything happens to that kid, Tim and Treve will* kill *me!* And he went on a dead run for the pool. Sure enough, there was Jeff, fortunately in the shallow end and upright, playing with some little rubber toys he'd packed with his swim suit. There was no one else in sight. Bill was too scared to leave him there by himself, so he just shucked his clothes, down to his jockeys, and got in the pool with Jeff to keep an eye on him, breathing a huge sigh of relief.

Jeff's version of the story is shorter, something to the effect that *Uncle Bill was* funny, *Daddy. He went swimming in his* underpants!

The important thing was they all arrived in Monterey with our car, everyone safe and sound, and a day or two later Bill and Chet flew back home.

When Treve and the kids – and the dog – arrived in Monterey, we didn't have quarters assigned yet. I was on the list at housing, but there was nothing yet available, so we moved into temporary housing on Fort Ord, which was several miles from the Presidio, where DLI was. It was not at all convenient, because I had to drive to class every day, leaving Treve to cope with the kids and dog in a strange place. The temporary housing was simply a couple of old WWII-era wooden barracks that had been partitioned off to make several separate bedrooms for families awaiting permanent quarters. There were communal bathrooms and a common area, as well as a kitchen for cooking. It was not too terribly different from the arrangement Master Sergeant Booth had created above the PP&T Det where I had stayed for several weeks. It had worked fine for me, but for a family it was pretty awful. I think we only lived there for about a week, but it seemed a lot longer.

To make matters worse, our furniture and household goods arrived in Monterey in a moving van before we'd been assigned an apartment. The moving company had to put everything into storage, which added to our moving expenses – which were all coming out of our own pocket this time. (Future moves and storage expenses would be paid for by the army.)

I would go to the base housing office at Fort Ord every day to check our status on the waiting list. The civilian whom I saw there each day, a heavy, probably overworked woman, wasn't very sympathetic, so about the fifth time around I went and got Treve and the boys and took them with me to the housing office. I instructed them all to try to look sad, which probably wasn't really necessary by that time. This time I asked how far down the list I was. She consulted a document on her desk and told me I was sixth. I asked if I could see the list. Reluctantly she turned it around so I could read it. What I noticed was that the four of the five names were followed by unit designators for the infantry. Fort Ord was mostly an infantry base then. The other name, lo and behold, was that of a Marine, the same one who had objected to the length of my nose hairs at the Friday morning in-ranks inspection just a week or two before. Wheels began spinning in my brain.

"Umm, you know I'm at DLI, right?" I asked the woman.

"Yes," she replied.

"Well, um, I think the only other DLI guy on this list is this Marine sergeant here, right?"

The woman peered again at the list and said, "That's right, and there'll be an apartment opening up on DLI this Friday, so he'll probably get that. Then you'll be first on the DLI housing list, since these other names will all want Fort Ord."

"Well, that's the thing, see," I said. "I know this Marine. He's my platoon sergeant, and I know he's been hoping to get assigned to Fort Ord, 'cause that's where all his buddies are living."

As I delivered this blatant and outright lie, I did my best to look earnest and helpful. It must have worked, because after thinking a moment and then glancing over at Treve and the boys, who were all looking especially tired and hopeful, this woman clerk suddenly remembered she had a heart – and probably a family of her own – and made a "command decision."

"*Well*, then," she said decisively. "I'll just put you down for that apartment that's opening up on DLI. You can move in on Friday." And she quickly pulled out a fresh DoD form and rolled it into her typewriter and began typing up our housing papers. That weekend we moved into a first-floor bright and spacious three-bedroom two-bath apartment right on the Presidio. I have no idea where that Marine sergeant ended up living, and I didn't care in the least. *Nose hairs!*

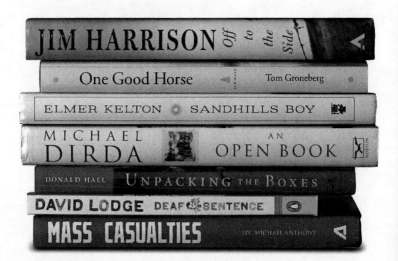

February 6, 2009

For the most part, our memories of life on the Presidio are extremely fond ones. Monterey is, first of all, simply a beautiful place, and our apartment couldn't have been more strategically located to take in that beauty. We lived in a bright spacious three-bedroom two-bath apartment at 559C Bellegarde Way. It was a short street, just a block long, which ran along one wing of a quadrangle of two-story brick apartment buildings. We were right across the street from the Tin Barn, a large auditorium used for special events and graduation ceremonies. These apartments represented the only family housing for enlisted personnel on the base. I found out after we had moved in that getting assigned there was not an easy thing, and we thanked our lucky stars for the next fourteen months that we had gotten in, because off-base apartments in the Monterey area were extremely expensive. Living in government quarters only cost you whatever your quarters allowance were at the time, and I think all our utilities were included. Our only outside expense was the telephone.

From the picture window of our living room, we could look down the hill, over the roof of the apartments across the quad and see Monterey Bay, with its own small Fisherman's Wharf, and it was indeed a lovely view. Every night the fog would roll in off the bay and envelope the Presidio in a soft mist, and every morning it would burn slowly away in the sunshine. We awoke each morning to the barking of the sea lions that basked on the boulders that surrounded the Coast Guard pier down on Lighthouse Avenue. I had grown used to this sound over the past two months before my family arrived. I had secured a special duty through the school which released me from all company and barracks details, odious jobs like CQ (charge of quarters) and latrine cleanup. All I had to do was arrive early at the classrooms down the hill from our barracks and unlock all the classroom doors. It was an easy job, and my getting to school a half hour early gave me a little extra study time each morning too.

Perhaps I should explain that there were two sets of classrooms for our Russian classes. For about the first half of our thirty-nine week schedule our classes were all held about a block down the hill from our barracks, in old wooden barracks-type buildings left over from World War II which had been converted into schoolrooms. Once we had successfully completed that part of the class – and a surprising percentage washed out or were re-cycled those first few months – we moved up the hill to the new, more modern classrooms, which were practically next door to the barracks buildings. Once I had passed that milestone, I relinquished my morning chore.

The climate on the Monterey peninsula is practically ideal, with temperatures ranging in the seventies year round. Summers were beautiful, with their cooling sea breezes; and winters rarely necessitated more than a light jacket or sweater. The fog I mentioned, while rather pretty and exotic to Midwesterners like us, we quickly found had some distinct disadvantages. I think we had only been in our new apartment about a month when one Saturday afternoon I decided to go out and wax our car, a still quite new '75 AMC Hornet wagon. I applied some Turtle Wax paste carefully and evenly onto a small section of the silver station wagon's roof and let it set for a moment and then began to wipe it back off and polish it. To my horror, I found that the top layer of paint was coming right off on my polishing rag. That fog rolling in and out each day, with its toxic salt air, had done its secret work. In Michigan we had been used to seeing cars with rusted fenders and rocker panels, corroded by the road salt used. Now I understood why I had been seeing so many cars with rusted roofs, hoods and trunk lids here in California. Every horizontal surface of an ungaraged vehicle fell prey to this lovely yet insidious salt air from the sea. We had no garage, of course, or even a carport. We had only a row of uncovered parking places along the road outside our apartments. There was nothing to be done. I put away my wax and rags, shaking my head. My beautiful almost-new car was doomed to the ravages of early aging, courtesy of the California coastal fog, creeping in each evening on little cat feet. The only thing I could do was to go out in the morning and wipe it down thoroughly whenever I remembered or had time, which wasn't very often.

The truth was, we didn't have to use our car all that much while we lived at DLI. I walked to class each day, and could even come home to lunch if I wanted. The Presidio chapel was just a couple blocks down the hill, as was a small Post Exchange (PX). And just across a blacktopped parking lot from our back door was a small base-operated convenience store where we would often run to buy bread and milk and a few other foodstuffs. Sometimes we would even send Jeff. He was seven by then and already beginning a life-long love affair with comic books. This little store had a well-supplied comics rack, so Jeff's incentive to run over and get milk or a loaf of bread was usually an extra quarter for a new comic. I wasn't much better. They also had a great rack of paperback books where I could usually find something if I looked long enough. That was where I found a paperback copy of *Shogun*, by James Clavell, the book which spawned the award-winning TV miniseries with Richard Chamberlain. (I'm not sure if I ever did finish *read*ing that book.) Sometimes I'd find more than one book. Days like that my impulse-purchase books came to more than the bread and milk I'd been sent to get. Treve soon concluded it was cheaper to just send Jeff.

It didn't take us too long to get out as a family and see the nearby sights, and fortunately we found things to do that were free or relatively inexpensive. The local beaches were ideal for family outings. There were two that were fairly close. The one we went to most often was the Seaside beach – or it may have been called Del Monte Beach, I can't remember for sure anymore. It was just off the highway in Seaside and it seemed unused and natural, meaning there weren't any boardwalks or snack or souvenir stands or any of those things today's kids associate with going to a beach. It was just a few miles of open sand alongside the highway on the way to Fort Ord. Treve would pack us a big picnic lunch and the boys would bring along some beach toys. We'd all get on our swim suits and bring a blanket and towels and a Frisbee to throw for Heidi, our dog. Some days we'd also take sweatshirts, as the wind along the beach could turn chilly. The boys and I would play along the waterline while Treve usually lay in the sun and worked on her tan. Jeff and Scott were never totally comfortable with the size of the breakers that would often come crashing in, and would venture out a little way into the receding waves, then come running back in near terror as the incoming breakers came charging in behind them. All three of us got knocked down by those waves on occasion. Heidi would run after the waves, barking furiously at them. After all, she was just as much a dumb Midwesterner as we were. Heidi probably enjoyed that beach more than any of us. There were usually few other people around, so we would simply turn her loose and she would tear crazily up and down the length of the beach, so delighted to be off-leash and unfettered. She would run and run and run, and then return to Treve and flop down on the blanket, tongue lolling, panting and grinning as only a truly happy mutt can.

Heidi was our first dog as a family. We had gotten her from the pound in Monroe in 1974, shortly after we moved into our first house in Riverside Manor. Getting Heidi was one of those all-American family rites of passage, I suppose. A wife, kids, and a first home – ya gotta have a dog too. And Heidi was perfect for our family. She was a mutt, product of a cocker spaniel and beagle mating. We called her a cockabea, reasoning it sounded better than beacock, more G-rated anyway. She was a lovely golden brown with the short coat of a beagle, and not very big, about twenty-nine pounds as an adult. Treve and I still remember the day we brought her home as a puppy, and how she was cruelly infested with fleas and ticks. We bathed her with flea soap and suds out in the sun on the driveway behind our house, using that same galvanized washtub Treve had used in our Fernwood apartment. We scrubbed her clean and tweezed and picked all the ticks off her while she stood docilely in the gradually graying suds and licked and licked at our faces, her little tail wagging. We were goners and loved her from the start, all of us, although she probably became more Treve's dog than anyone else's.

We had added a second dog, a purebred Lhasa Apso, about a year later, an impulse purchase from a pet store in Belleville. We dubbed her Svetlana Sukiyaki (after Khrushchev's daughter and the sixties pop song by Kyu Sakamoto), but she soon became just Suki to us. Although she quickly fit into our family, Treve and I made the difficult decision, when I went back into the army, that one traveling dog would probably be more than enough, so Suki was given away to a Belleville neighbor of the Zimmers, an elderly lady who lived alone and wanted a companion. Suki fit the bill.

The other beach we went to a few times was the one in Pacific Grove. The boys liked it better because it was smaller and situated in a sheltered cove, so the sea was much gentler there and they could actually get into the water and play in it. To get to this beach you went down some steps through a stone sea wall that surrounded the beach area. The area was also sheltered from the wind so was perfect for sunbathing. We went there a couple times with our across-the-hall neighbors, the Starrs. Jim was an Air Force sergeant, a Korean linguist who was part of the military staff at the school. Treve and his wife, Judy, got along very well, and they had a little girl who played with our boys sometimes.

You'll notice I said we went there a "few" times, or a "couple" times. Well, that's because we found out our second or third time there that the Pacific Grove beach was also a favorite place for the gay population of the area to get their sun and sand time in. And after we noticed some of these same sex couples, mostly guys, doing a little too much laying on of hands as they applied oils, lotions and creams, or lay entwined on towels nearby, we got a little uncomfortable about having the kids around to see this. "Not that there's anything *wrong* with that," as that famous Seinfeld episode went, but we didn't want to have to explain anything to the kids, and just felt … Well, we quit going there.

Carmel was probably the most beautiful beach we visited.

February 8, 2009

I'm back. But the beach at Carmel can wait a while. I'm going to tell some other stories right now. I've been napping. It's nearly two in the afternoon, the sun is shining so brightly outside it hurts your eyes, and I've been napping. But I don't think I was ever quite asleep. Rather I was teetering on the very edge of consciousness as I mapped my next move in my magnum opus, meaning this, this life I am writing – telling.

I heard a funny story from my cousin, Christine, not too long ago. Christine writes too. She is a poet. She is also a nurturer, a caregiver. She runs a daycare out of her house in Traverse City. One of her small charges for a couple years or so was the youngest son of Doug and Anne Stanton. Doug and Anne are writers too. Lemme see now, that's Chris, Doug, Anne and me – four writers already in this story, which I'm trying to keep reasonably short and to the point, but sometimes, if you want to get it right, so it all makes sense, and so your readers can see all the connections, you just can't keep it short.

Anne writes for the *Northern Express*, a small newspaper out of Traverse City, so, as a working reporter, she's kinda used to searching out a good story, then researching it and getting it written, because there are deadlines and such when you work for a newspaper, even if it's a weekly. And she writes good stuff too. I remember in particular an excellent piece she did a couple years ago; about a meth house in the Traverse City area. Methamphetamines, the home-cooked kinda stuff, in case you didn't know, have become the drug of choice for the very poor in rural areas of Michigan, and probably other parts of the country too.

Doug writes pieces for magazines, and I'm not sure whether he has the same kinda deadlines doing this as Anne does, but I don't think so. He also writes books. His first book was published several years ago. *In Harm's Way* was an international bestseller, and is, I am sure, still selling. It's an impeccably researched and reported historical book about the sinking of the *USS Indianapolis* in the closing days of WWII. For the past three or four years now, perhaps longer, Doug has been working on his second book, which will be called *Horse*

Soldiers. This book will also have historical significance as it is all about a secret expedition by U.S. forces into Afghanistan soon after the 9/11 attacks. I think that's what it's about. I haven't read it yet. It is scheduled to be published this spring, if the publication date doesn't get postponed yet again.

I first met Doug shortly after my own first book was published back in 2004. Well, actually I met his father first, and then later I met Doug. Here's where I tell you about how everything is connected, like I kept doing in my fourth book, the one about Bill Porteous. See, Doug was born in the Reed City Library, which seems very fitting, considering he's become such an important author. There's a simple explanation, and it's nothing like that book and movie about the girl whose baby was born in a Wal-Mart either. No, it's just that our library *used* to be the Reed City Hospital. Doug's parents are both Reed City people, now transplanted and retired to Traverse City. Doug's mother, Bonnie, went to high school with my brother Bill, the class of 1958. Doug's dad, Derald, was from the class of 1957.

Reed City is a pretty small town, so I could give you other more obscure kinds of town and family and neighbor connections here and just keep going on and on, but I'll try not to. The important thing was that I did hook up with the Stantons five years ago, and it was a very fortunate thing for me. First of all, they're great people and I enjoy their company. Secondly, Doug provided me with my first important endorsement from a known writer. This means he wrote a very cool blurb for *Reed City Boy*, which I suspect helped me sell quite a few books. Blurbs are like gold to authors, and I was very grateful to Doug for writing me one, although I kinda kidded him at first about how his mom made him do it, because his folks are closer in age to me than Doug is. He denied it, but I'm pretty sure Bonnie kinda made a suggestion at least. I also like to kid Doug about how long it takes him to finish a book, and point out that I've written four books while he's been working on this second one. He told me quite a while ago that this second book would be called *Horse Soldiers*. And I pointed out to him that both his books are named after John Wayne movies, and asked him what's the next one gonna be – *The Searchers* or *The Shootist*? Of course, the Duke made a lot of films so there are plenty of titles left to choose from. I don't think Doug finds this very funny, because I've used this corny crap with him a couple times now, and he just kinda politely ignores me now. But take my word for it. He'll have another national bestseller soon. I know, because I heard him read an excerpt from this book at a symposium up at Interlochen a few years ago. This auditorium was full of writers – and serious readers – and everyone there was leaning forward and listening with everything they had, because they didn't want to miss a word. It was that good. Doug can make history seem like the most finely crafted fiction. I don't know how he does it, but he does. Me, I just tell my stories.

So here's the story my cousin Chris told me just a month or two ago. We were talking on the phone and I asked her if she was still taking care of Doug and Anne's boy, Will. She said no, she wasn't, but she still saw Anne around town fairly often. And she told me about how Doug's book was finally nearly completed and he was working on the final revisions and only had like a week or two left to get it all sent back in to his publisher, which is Scribner's, one of the best and oldest publishing houses in the business. So Anne had taken time off from her job at the newspaper to help him get it all together. Anne, given her newspaper background, is used to deadlines and figured she'd help.

"I just saw Anne a couple days ago in town," Chris told me. "And it was so funny. I asked her how the book was coming, and Anne said, 'Oh, that *man!* I thought we'd have it done by now, but we don't. You know what he did yesterday? He seemed to be busy doing his revisions, so I went out to the store to get a few things. And do you know what he was doing when I came back?! He was taking a *NAP!* Do you *beLIEVE* that?! I mean, we have less than a *week* to get this in, and he was taking a *NAP!*'"

Chris was laughing as she told me this, and so did I. I don't know Anne that well, but I guess she might be wrapped a little tighter than Doug is, who, even when he's talking with you, doesn't seem to be a hundred percent there; he always appears to be maybe a few miles away, mulling something over in his mind.

But let me tell you about napping and writing. They are not necessarily mutually exclusive activities. When I said I was napping today – *see?* I'm *back!* – I was in that "miles away" place myself, never quite asleep, but not quite conscious either. I was thinking about what I was going to write next. And you've just read some of it. But what a tangled web our subconscious can weave, ya know? If I were as masterful a writer awake as I am when I'm half asleep, I would sell more books than Doug Stanton. Alas, when I finally get up, it's just me sitting here again at my PC, trying to make sense of it all once again, telling my life in bits and pieces, fits and starts, shits and farts, etc.

Last night as I fell asleep and again today while "napping," I thought about other, weightier things too. Fathers and sons.

I've been reading this novel the past few days – *another* reason I didn't get much writing done. It's by the British writer, Pat Barker, and it's called *Regeneration*. It's a look at the toll taken by war on the minds of men, and the story is set mostly in the mental ward of a military hospital in Scotland during the First World War. The book's major characters are based on real people – the poets Siegfried Sassoon and Wilfred Owen, and the noted psychiatrist, William Rivers. In the course of treating his patients traumatized by war, Dr. Rivers is forced to confront what it means to be a man and how important and problematic the whole father-son relationship can be.

Fathers remain opaque to their sons, he thought, largely because the sons find it so hard to believe that there's anything in the father worth seeing. Until he's dead, and it's too late.

I loved my father, and I have no doubt that he loved me. But that "opaqueness" that Pat Barker has her protagonist of nearly a hundred years ago consider is still, I think, a problem today. It certainly was – and still is – for me. In a later passage in *Regeneration*, Rivers further ruminates: "… the relationship between father and son is never simple, and never over. Death certainly doesn't end it."

My father has been dead for nearly twenty years now, but I don't think that a day goes by that I don't think of him at least once. I suppose I have, in the jargon of psycho-babble, "unresolved issues." I don't think they are serious – at least not any more. But for a time they were, and nearly destroyed my marriage.

When I read those lines in Barker's novel last night those awful times came quickly back and I did some ruminating of my own. I also did some rummaging about in my closet, in some boxes of old papers. And in one of them I found a letter I wrote in March of 1992. It's quite a long letter, and I remember writing it, scribbling furiously as the feelings and the heartache, and the pain and the sadness all came pouring out so fast I could barely get it all down. I remember crying – *bawling* – as I wrote it. The letter was addressed to my mother, but I never sent it. Because it was more to my dad than it was to Mom. Dad, who had been dead for over two years by then.

Never simple ... never over ... and death doesn't end it.

When I wrote that letter I had already moved out of our house in Maryland. I had two sons in college and a fourteen year-old daughter still at home. Treve and I had barely been speaking to each other for months. Our marriage of nearly twenty-five years seemed to be crumbling, falling apart. I was devastated. I didn't know what was wrong. And neither did she. We had gone to a marriage counselor a couple times, but it didn't seem to help. I still had this boulder on my chest. We stopped going. Not long after that I moved out.

I can still remember the day I moved. Treve was at work. It was raining. I sat on the edge of the bed in our room and looked out at the rain. And I wept. Our little dog, Chico, came into the room and jumped up beside me on the bed, and then he crept into my lap and licked my tears. He didn't whine. He didn't make a sound. He licked my face and sat quietly on my lap as I hugged him and cried. It sounds maudlin and melodramatic now, telling it, but it happened. Dogs know, I guess. I gathered most of my clothes out of drawers and closets and filled the back of my car. It was still morning. I had to go to work. My fully packed car sat in the NSA parking lot in the rain all day.

A friend from work who was going through a rather messy divorce let me occupy an empty bedroom in his house. I bought a single bed and tried to settle in. I was always so cold in that room; it was a cold that seemed to come from inside me and wouldn't go away. It was in that room that I wrote the letter.

I tried to fill my days during that time. I took a twice-weekly class in Japanese culture at the NSA annex. I began training to do volunteer work with the Hospice of the Chesapeake (which I completed and became a Friendly Visitor, offering respite to caregivers). I walked a lot, more than usual because I seemed mostly unable to read during those days. I couldn't concentrate. I wept easily, for no good reason. I still have a vivid memory of driving to work one morning when the Bonnie Raitt song, "I Can't Make You Love Me," came on the radio. I began to cry so hard I had to pull over and sit on the shoulder of the highway until I could get myself together.

Finally, I began seeing a psychologist.

I was very hesitant about going to see a counselor. Here's why I was afraid. I was working as an intelligence analyst at the National Security Agency. Most of my work was highly classified. Even though the NSA had set up this counseling office for "troubled employees," I still resisted making an appointment. My reluctance was part of an ingrained feeling that went back to earlier times in the military and the intelligence business. Because we have not always been the "touchy-feely" society that we are now; the kind of culture that thinks it has to bring a busload of grief counselors into school because a kid gets hit by a car or dies from meningitis or something. I always wonder about that. I think most of the kids probably could give a shit (unless the deceased really *was* a close friend), but it's always cool to have a big-ass assembly in the cafetorium while some child psychologist gives a lecture on *feelings*. And then if you want to get out of some more class time, you can sign up for a private appointment with one of the grief counselors. But I digress.

There was a time, you see, in my business, when if it got around that you were seeing a shrink or a counselor of any kind, you could lose your security clearance, *BAM*, like that. Good-bye, promotion; maybe even good-bye, career. I don't think things are that way anymore, in fact I'm pretty sure they're not, and probably weren't even back in 1992, but I wasn't sure, so I was a little scared about doing this. But I was even more scared about the way my whole life seemed to be going to hell, so I started seeing this guy, this newly-minted shrink, at the Agency office, out at the NSA office annex near BWI airport.

I call him new, because he was. This counseling service was new at the time, and it turns out this guy had been a linguist there at the Agency, just like me, who'd gotten tired of the intelligence trade and went back to school part-time and gotten a degree in clinical psychology just about the time that NSA decided to open this office. He was probably around my age, or maybe a couple years older. But regardless of how new this guy was to his job, luckily for me he was pretty good at it.

I think he pretty much figured out much of my problem at my first appointment. First of all he asked me why I was there. I told him my wife and I had split up, and I don't know what he might have said to that, because I began to cry right there in this new office in front of this guy I'd just met. He was cool about it, I remember that. He offered me a box of tissues and just sat there and waited until I'd pulled myself together enough to talk again. Then he told me that marital problems were always tough; and gave me a breather by taking down a kind of "family history," and of course one of the first questions he asked was whether my parents were living or deceased. Then he wanted to know when my father died. I told him. He took this and other information down. Then he put his notes aside.

"Tell me about your marriage," he said.

And I did. I told him about how we'd barely known each other when we married and maybe we'd been too young and how we didn't seem to have much of anything in common anymore – if we ever did – except our three kids, and two of them were in college and the other one was only fourteen and going through enough hell of her own, just from being fourteen, and things had just been so bad between Treve and me for the longest time, maybe even for a couple of *years*, and I just wasn't sure if I loved her anymore, or if she loved me, because we never seemed to talk anymore, and when we did it always turned into an argument.

It all came rushing out of me; I didn't know where it was coming from, but it seemed so good just to finally say all this stuff to another living person, instead of keeping it all bottled up inside they way I had been doing for what seemed like forever. Well, maybe it didn't feel "good," but it was a relief, no question. What I felt most was utter and abject misery to be where I was at that moment and to be confessing all this hurt and confusion. And I was afraid. Afraid of what was happening to me, to Treve, to *us*, if there still was an "us."

"So you've been pretty depressed," he said.

This is where, in most of my stories, I'd throw in a real funny line, a real zinger for a little comic relief. But I can't think of one here, not for this story.

Then this "doc" asked how things were going otherwise in my life, besides the marital problems. This kind of brought me up short, because I hadn't really thought too much about anything else for quite a while.

"How are things at work," he prompted.

And, after thinking about it a moment, I had to answer that things were not all that great in the work arena either. Because by 1992 I had spent nearly eighteen years of my life learning all I could learn about the Soviet Union and – for the last sixteen years – the Russian language. And by 1992 that same Soviet Union had slowly begun to disintegrate. The awful threat we had been guarding against for nearly fifty years was gradually revealing itself to be a toothless old bear that could barely feed itself. In other words, I was beginning to seriously wonder about my job security. Or, at the very least, would I have to start over again and retrain into some other job. And I should tell you right here that I flat loved my work at NSA. It had always seemed that I was doing something vitally important to keeping our country safe. And, as an added bonus, it was the most interesting job I'd ever had, and I can honestly say that I learned something new every day I went to work there for over twenty-one years. In short, I suddenly realized that I'd been worried about my job too.

I confessed I was still also worried that my very presence in his office would reflect badly on me and might threaten my security clearance and hence my job. The doc waved off this concern.

"We're not like that here anymore," he assured me. "The Agency wants its employees to be healthy in *every* way. Not just physically, but mentally and emotionally too. You absolutely did the right thing to come in. Don't worry about those things. You're safe. Let's concentrate on how we can help you start feeling better about yourself."

And that was how we began, how I began, slowly, trying to fix my life. I can't remember now how many sessions I had with the doc. Not very many. That first day we talked mostly about me, and about Treve too.

I'm not going to try to explain how Treve felt about this unhappy period of our marriage, because I can't know that. At the time it was happening, from my side, I saw her pulling away from me. I can analyze us a lot more easily now; hindsight is always so much more accurate. But you'll remember that Treve was only twenty when we married. She basically went straight from living with her parents to living with me. While it's true she was at Ferris for a couple years, that wasn't long. Certainly not long enough for her to get much of a sense of freedom, a sense of being her own person. That came later, over twenty years later, in fact. By 1992 our older son, Jeff, had already been in the army and was back home working and going to the community college. (He would transfer to Frostburg State and move out the following year). Our other son, Scott, was away at college, in Pennsylvania. Suzie was going through her own hell in junior high. After being a stay-at-home mom for twenty years, Treve had gone back to work, selling ads for the local *Pennysaver*. She'd been very apprehensive about joining a workforce so vastly changed since she'd spent just one year working as a beautician. But she quickly found out she was very good at sales, and was soon winning office awards. She blossomed and became more sure of herself than she had ever been. She was contributing and she felt good about it. She always faithfully banked at least half – sometimes more – of her take home pay from the *Pennysaver*. Our taxman told us she wasn't making enough to make it pay, because it put us into a higher tax bracket. But we didn't listen to him. He may have been right, but the money she saved put our kids all through college. She didn't want them starting their lives with huge college loans to pay back. And they didn't. And she is very proud of that.

As for the rest of her pay, Treve always let me know that that was "her" money, and I think I would have been okay with that. Except she was using it for a time as "party" money. Remember I sowed my oats between high school and college, while I was in the army that first time. Treve never had that. She went directly from being that "good Catholic girl" to being a "good Catholic wife." She'd never really got to kick up her heels and go out with the girls and have some fun. So that's what she was doing in 1992. And I didn't like it. Because some of her friends from the *Pennysaver* and the neighborhood were divorced and liked to party. Treve wouldn't admit it, but those women were out cruisin' and she was along for the ride. I'm not saying she was looking, because I don't think she was. It was that "negative potential" that bothered me. And so we fought. And we argued. And we maintained, for the most part, an armed truce – an extremely uneasy one.

I know now too that she went out to get away from me. I was not very pleasant to be around in those days, given to black moods and inexplicable depressions. She didn't know what was wrong with me, and neither did I. I was just angry a lot. She thought I was angry at her, and I was afraid she didn't love me anymore, and I had a hard time coming up with a good reason why she should. Things were falling apart. We were both miserable. It was unquestionably and unequivocally the worst time of my life.

I think it was during my second session with the Agency doc that he asked me to tell him about my father. Was I close to my dad, he asked me. And he wondered how I had handled it when Dad died.

The first question seemed innocent enough. I had to say no, we weren't particularly close. That I was always kind of a "mama's boy." My mother had four sons in just six years, and I was the fourth, the baby. Mom suffered a couple of miscarriages and a stillborn baby over the next several years, so I stayed the baby for over seven years. And I was Mom's favorite. Even I know that. And we are very much alike, Mom and I. We both share a love of books and music and quiet pursuits. I have never been terribly interested in sports or hunting or guns or other "manly" things. In 1951 my sister, Mary, was born, and, a couple years later, my brother, Chris. I wasn't the baby anymore, but remained, I'm afraid, a "mama's boy." Or at least I always felt that was how my dad saw me.

My paternal grandparents had a small farm next door when I was growing up, so there were always plenty of chores to be done. I was the son who hated to work in the fields or the garden. I preferred to stay in the house with mom and help clean house or do dishes – woman's work. I *did* work in the fields though. Dad required all of us boys to. Having grown up on a farm himself, a poor one, he wanted us all to know how a man made a living, by the sweat of his brow, so to speak. But I always did my best to escape back inside to my books as soon as I could.

So we're back to this question. How is manhood defined? And how important is the relationship between a father and a son. It's *damn* important, *that's* how important it is. I learned it the hard way.

Because I *yearned* for my father's approval as I got older. Being a man – being *perceived* as a man – becomes even more important after puberty, of course. I have often wondered if I joined the army right out of high school just to prove something to my dad. Although, since my dad never served in the military himself, it may have been a futile gesture. I certainly was a fish out of water in the crude world of basic training though. Perhaps that particular rite of passage went a long way toward turning me into more of a man. It was after that experience, I think, that I began to quit worrying, at least for a time, what Dad might or might not think about me or my manhood. In my early twenties I was ruled by sexual urges and in a rush to mate and reproduce. That was probably the period Barker speaks of in her novel when "sons find it so hard to believe that there's anything in the father worth seeing."

You know those lines from "Jackson," that Johnny & June tune: "We got married in a fever/Hotter than a pepper sprout ..."? Well in many ways that was Treve and I. We were following a script set by biology and previous generations from time immemorial.

When I reenlisted in the army in 1976, was I looking again for more approval from my father? I don't know. There were the other reasons I gave you earlier, but the mysterious ways of the subconscious sometimes surpasseth all understanding and all that. In spite of my two stints in the service, I still ended up working with words, not weapons. Teaching English finally gave way, indirectly, to a career in translating Russian. Words.

Back to the doc's second question. How did I handle my dad's death? Not well. I was the son who wept at the funeral home, at the funeral mass and at the cemetery. It was not a subdued, stiff upper lip kind of weeping either. It was flat-out bawling, with plenty of snot and tears. I was a bit of an embarrassment to my four brothers, I'm sure, who mostly regarded me uneasily and seemed to wonder what my problem was.

Then a couple days later I went back to work. I seemed to have recovered from the shock of Dad's death.

Then a couple years later everything fell apart. My job, my life, my marriage. Coincidence? I don't think so. Because I believe my doc went right to the root of my problem – my depressions, my black moods – when he asked about me and my dad and what kind of a relationship we had. Pat Barker nailed it in her book: *Never simple, never over. Death doesn't end it.*

All that unspoken grief, all those unresolved "issues," as screwed-up-ness is so genteelly called these days – all of it came back and bit me in the ass two years later. My counselor saw this right away. He recognized a clinical depression when he saw it, and he also recognized the cause. It took me a little longer.

First he offered to get me a prescription for an antidepressant. I declined. I was afraid of what it might do to me; that it might compromise the mental acuity I needed to do my job effectively. Because I think I was still terrified too that I could lose my job over what was happening to me. So he took another tack. He prescribed a rhetorical exercise for me – some "homework." He told me to write a letter to my father, and to tell him everything I was never able to say to him when he was alive; everything I wished I'd told him, but didn't; what I wished I'd said the last time I saw him alive just a few weeks before he died. I told him I would, but I didn't think I'd do it. It sounded stupid to me. What good could *that* do?

So I resisted writing that letter. For a few days. And then instead I began to write a letter to my mother, telling her finally that Treve and I had separated, that I'd moved out. And then, before I even realized I was doing it, I was writing that letter to my dad, the one I found again last night. Nearly sixteen years have passed since I wrote it, and Treve and I are okay again now, we have been for years. I've never shown this letter to anyone. And its angry scrawl still hurts, is still raw –

> *... I'm still grieving, Dad, almost two and a half years later ... I respected and loved you so much, but our brusque, hearty, Irish or French or German, or whatever kind of shanty Irish or mongrel mix we all come from just wouldn't allow us to show any tenderness or outward affection to each other, so you just had to kind of* **assume** *you were loved or valued by the person or people who meant the most to you in the whole world. And I am so* **angry***, and so* **disappointed** *in myself, and I have such deep regret that the last time I saw you in the RC hospital – when you were so sick and I knew you were dying and that I'd probably never see you alive again – that I couldn't just take you in my arms and hold you and tell you how much I loved you and how much you meant to me – and maybe then you would have told me the same thing. If I could have just done that, maybe I wouldn't cry now every time I think of you. But I didn't. Just that quick hug and peck on the cheek and a "you take care of yourself now" and out the door. And then I sat in my car in the parking lot and cried for ten minutes before I could get myself together enough to start that long drive back to MD. It would have been –* **should** *have been – so easy. But I couldn't do it. And I've been so fucking miserable ever since you died. I loved you so much, Daddy, and I just wanted to be able to hug and kiss you again the way I did when I was little, before I reached that unspoken age – seven? ten? twelve? – whatever it is, when it's no longer* fitting *or* proper *for fathers to kiss their sons ...*

There's more, but enough. There it was. Why my life seemed so screwed up. As a father and son, we had never really properly connected. We had both been held prisoner to that ridiculous John Wayne idea of manhood. Well, as old Roberto Duran so famously once said after being body-punched one too many times in his stomach full of steak in that title fight, *No mas!*

A simple thing, writing that letter, the one I hadn't wanted to write. It opened the damn. It helped me put things in perspective. I began talking with Treve again. And I found out she still loved me; and how hurt she had been by the way I'd been acting. Slowly, we began to listen to each other again. At my counselor's suggestion, we signed up together for Retrouvaille, a kind of non-denominational group counseling program for couples whose marriages were in trouble. Retrouvaille's unofficial motto is "God doesn't make junk" – a sentiment which implies that people are inherently good, and so is a marriage. After the initial couples weekend, we kept on going to follow-up sessions for several months, until we felt we could keep on respecting each other. I moved back home. For a long time we were more "careful" with each other. We learned to love each other again, and better. But most importantly, and perhaps for the first time, we became friends.

I am reminded here of some sage advice I once received from my good friend, Gene Ganske. Gene is nine years older than I am, a native of Mankato. Chuckling gently in that way only a true Minnesotan can, he told me, "Oh, marriage isn't really so hard, Tim, if you can just get past that initial twenty-five year period of adjustment."

In November of 1992 Treve and I quietly celebrated our silver wedding anniversary.

I don't write letters to my dad anymore, but I talk to him, nearly every day. Pat Barker is right. Death does not end the relationship between a father and a son. It goes on.

February 10, 2009

I felt a bit wrung out yesterday, so I took the day off and made a day-trip to Big Rapids. I picked up Treve's leather coat from the City Shoe Hospital on Maple, where it got a new zipper. Then I drove over to Ferris and parked on the edge of campus just east of the Automotive Tech Center. Every now and then I feel the urge to visit Ferris and wander through the buildings where I got the first two years of my college education. A lot of things have changed since Treve and I left there in 1967, of course. The Science Building and the Starr building were two separate structures separated by a parking lot back then. As a pre-teaching General Education student, I took almost all of my classes in those two buildings. And every evening, Monday through Friday, at five o'clock I would punch the time clock in the lobby of Starr auditorium and then walk over to the Science Building where I would begin my rounds of cleaning offices and sweeping out the classrooms and halls. I would mop up spills and messes and a couple times a week I would polish the tile floors with an electric buffer. It was not a very glamorous job, but it was one I could do almost in my sleep – and it paid the tuition.

Yesterday I stood at the eastern front entrance of the Science building underneath the old greenhouse and looked across the street at the lobby of Helen Ferris dormitory and remembered. In 1967 Treve lived on the third floor of that dorm, and sometimes while I was working she would walk across the street, just to see me and talk for a few minutes or to walk with me through the second floor offices while I emptied waste baskets. If Ed Howe, the main custodian of the building, happened to see us and he was in a good mood, he would tell me I could take off early as soon as I got my work done, that he would punch out for me. That was another advantage of the job. My hours were from five until nine, but I could usually get all my work done in the first two hours, after which I could sit at a counter in the janitors' room and study until nine. Ed was fine with this, as long as my work was done. He'd never gone to college himself, and encouraged me to "go for it."

Wandering through the Science Building yesterday was a study in the old and new for me. Pearson auditorium was still where it was supposed to be, but it seemed like almost everything else – rooms, stairways, lobbies – had all been rearranged. And all that stuff in between there and the Starr building was even worse. Ascending to the second floor in the Starr, I nearly got lost, and circled around looking for familiar indoor landmarks. There just weren't any. I stumbled across the office of Tracy Busch, a young history professor I'd recently met this past year, and told her how different everything was. She smiled sympathetically and said that's what she heard from a lot of alums that come through.

After finding my way back out again, I went across to Helen Ferris and went into the lobby, figuring I'd have to explain to whoever was manning the desk what I was doing there, and I was all primed to tell my story, about how my wife had lived here back in the sixties and I just wanted to see it again. There were students, both male and female, coming and going through the lobby as I stepped in, but none of them made eye contact with me, they just stepped around me like I was part of the lobby furniture. There was a tall thin girl wearing Sarah Palin glasses and a white hoodie sitting behind the counter, absorbed in something on her computer screen. She never looked up at me, even though I stood at the counter for a minute or two.

Finally, just to say something – to announce myself, perhaps, I asked her, "Is this a co-ed dorm now?"

Glancing up for only a split second and barely meeting my glance, she replied, "Yes," and went back to whatever she was doing.

The truth is, I already knew that Helen Ferris was co-ed now, because a couple years ago this summer Treve met up with two of her old suite-mates and another old Ferris chum who'd lived across the hall for a kind of mini-reunion. I called the housing office for them and got someone to come over and unlock the dorm, which was closed for the summer, and they were allowed to wander up and down the stairs and hallways and even see their old rooms on the third floor. Helen Ferris is occupied by honors students now, of both sexes.

What Treve and her friends – Marcia, Norma and Linda – seemed to marvel at most that day was how *small* the rooms seemed to them now, and wondered how they had all managed to live in such a confined space for two years or more. This little reunion had been my idea, probably because I'd been looking back at those times while I was writing my third book which chronicled those years. *Pinhead* had just been published and Ferris was still very much on my mind. Treve had resisted the idea at first, but finally came around and made the calls – to Marcia, down in Hartland; Norma in Holland and Linda in Howard City. Two others, Marilyn and Rinda, weren't able to come. But the four women who did show up that day – the "girls of the sixties" (makes me think of that K.T. Oslin song, "Eighties Ladies") – seemed to have an absolutely wonderful time, enjoying a leisurely lunch at Crankers, where they all seemed to be talking at once, catching up on forty years of life after college; and then walking through the dorm and the Rankin Center and Dome Room, where they'd all once danced at Friday night "mixers;" and finally visiting the college bookstore, where the out-of-towners bought sweatshirts and souvenirs. Through all of this I kind of hovered on the fringes, watching and listening, and remembering these women as the girls they had been back then – the images still crisp and sharp in that mysterious way that memory sometimes serendipitously keeps certain things while others are lost forever. The beautiful girls of Ferris State in the sixties. There are beautiful girls there now too of course, but they just are not the same. Maybe it's just me, but, well, then was better.

Since I was already invisible – that particular invisibility of being old in a place populated by the young – I sat down for a moment in one of the chairs in the dorm lobby and let the memories wash over me. Of Treve, with her shining helmet of short blonde hair, bouncing down the stairs and into that long-ago lobby to meet me, her brown eyes shining with happiness. Of those last minute clinches in the car, parked in front of the dorm just before curfew, when the lobby doors would be locked for the night. Of our being just one of many couples locked in passionate embraces, standing in the semi-darkness just outside of the halo of light that shone from the lobby, again just before curfew. Of golden warm spring afternoons when a row of baby-oiled young bodies lay prone in their two piece swimsuits on towels across the back patio of the dorm, soaking up those rays that no one knew could one day cause cancer.

Finally I got up and let myself quietly back out, still ignored by all. But that's okay. I remember what it was like to look at an old person, perhaps a bit put off by the gray hair, age spots and wrinkles, but certain that *I* would never look like that. Well, now I *do* look like that, and I'm okay with it. I like my life now just fine. In fact I love my life. And my wife. And I can't wait for her to get home again from her "Grammy" trip, so I can bring her coffee in bed and so we can spoon together again at night. Yes, I am in love with a grandmother, and I have missed her so much these past few weeks.

For the first half of her life, Treve was a sun-worshiper, always working on that "perfect tan" whenever the opportunity presented itself. She can't do it anymore. Sometime in her forties she developed an allergy to the sun. And now even brief exposure to bright sunlight causes a raised rash on her skin. Something about the change in body chemistry as we age perhaps. But even though we both now understand the harmfulness of the sun's rays, she mourns the loss of those golden brown days. She used to be fond of saying, "Brown fat looks better than white fat." She still says it, but wistfully. She's not fat though. Growing up with three older brothers who teased her unmercifully left her with a life-long inferiority complex about her own body. It's crazy, but there it is. To me she's perfect. Always has been. (To this she would respond suspiciously, "Just what is it you're *after*, Bazzett?")

We were both still enamored of beaches and sun back in 1976 and '77 when we lived in California, and Carmel offered the most beautiful of all the surrounding beaches. We were nearly speechless the first time we went to Carmel and saw that beach. The sand there is a blindingly pure white that we had never seen before. Remember that song from the fifties called "White Silver Sands?" That's how the sand was at Carmel Beach.

We probably didn't go there more than a half a dozen times in the approximately fourteen months we lived in California together. But it was always a special place to go. Even in the seventies the Carmel community was populated by what seemed like perfect people, mostly very wealthy. People like us would have been considered riff-raff to the natives, I suppose, but we didn't let it bother us. We still walked and gawked and took along our cheap picnic baskets and coolers and made camp for the afternoon on those sparkling white sands. Treve would work on her tan and I would people-watch. Well, woman-watch, would probably be more truthful. I know, I know. I just got done telling how much I love my wife; and I do, and I did then too. But that doesn't change the biological imperative that compels men to look at women, especially nearly naked women, and even more especially if those nearly naked women are walking up and down the beach all around him, nearly as far as the eye can see on a sunny California afternoon.

Because Carmel Beach was, no question, a girl-watcher's paradise. (Another old song – "I'm a Girl Watcher.") On a couple different occasions there were even women in monokinis to ogle. The first time I witnessed this, I'm sure my mouth probably just dropped right open. I've never been able to act very cool around bare breasts. You have to remember I grew up in Reed City, which is a long way from California. As a kid I didn't think there *were* any tits in Reed City. Too many churches.

Monokinis, for the uninitiated, are, to put it simply, a bikini minus the top, sometimes with long straps, which hide nothing. Fashion designers might want to put a finer point on it, but hell, I'm just a regular guy. To me monokinis just mean, hey, there they are, right out there for anyone to look at.

I can still remember a particular night on guard duty in Sinop, Turkey, back in 1964. I was sitting in the guard shack during my four hours off (after four hours on, patrolling the post's perimeter fence with my useless empty carbine), leafing listlessly through a fairly new issue of *Newsweek*. Suddenly my attention was riveted on this tiny black and white photo. You know those tiny photos inserted into magazine columns, the kind that aren't much bigger than a man's watch? Well this was a photo of a woman in a bikini with no top! Yup, yup, bare tits, right there in *Newsweek*, for cripesakes! Well, after about a half hour of minutely examining this ground-breaking photo, during which time I discovered there was actually a kind of strap on top, even though it covered nothing, I read the column around it. It was about this Austrian fashion designer, Rudi Gernreich, and his new invention, the "monokini."

Well, that magazine got passed around a lot at Sinop, as you might well imagine, and may have even caused a few cases of eyestrain. (*Nah*, probably not; there were plenty of *Playboys* in Sinop.) But I never actually saw a real live girl *wearing* one of those things until sometime in 1976 at Carmel Beach.

The woman wearing the monokini was beautiful of course, and she was flaunting it, as she strolled casually along the waterline with her much-older male companion, probably her very own "sugar-daddy," his arm around her waist. His arm, his bearing, his erect posture, told everyone: "This is *mine*. Eat your hearts out, guys."

This happened more than once at Carmel. I know I must have ogled shamelessly, because there were always some reproving glances and sharp words from Treve's side of the towel, even though she was kinda looking too. It was just too shocking for us not to look. I mean this kind of stuff was just so *unheard* of, so exotic to sheltered Midwesterners and good Catholic kids like us. So yeah, we stared.

We knew that Carmel was supposedly a hangout for Hollywood people, so we were always looking, star-searching, I suppose you'd call it. But if the famous folks were around, they stayed out of sight for the most part. We knew that Clint Eastwood kept a home there, and also owned a bar called The Hog's Breath Inn. We looked, but he was never in. And we knew that Doris Day lived there somewhere, surrounded by all her dogs, but never saw her either. I had only two celebrity near-encounters in Carmel. Once I thought I saw Kristin Nelson (Rick's wife) trying on boots in a shoe store I was passing by. I didn't go into the store of course, since all the shops in Carmel were way too expensive for us; but it could very well have been her, considering years later I read in a biography of Rick that she damn near spent him right into the poorhouse. He was practically broke when he died in that plane crash several years later.

And, on another visit one day, I was walking down the beach a bit further away from the crowds, and this enormous dog came galloping up to me, tongue lolling, and stopped to greet me effusively, jumping up on me and dancing and skittering around the way happy dogs do. It was one of those tall hairy breeds I often can't tell apart, a Scottish deerhound or an Irish or Russian wolfhound or something like that. And then this short, paunchy balding guy came running up behind him, apologizing for his dog's enthusiasm. I recognized the guy. It was Dub Taylor, a character actor I'd seen in several movies. He was most famous for playing the father of Michael Pollard's character, C.W. Moss, in the sixties film, *Bonnie and Clyde*. C.W. and his pop, if you remember the film, were the ones who supposedly ratted on poor Bonnie and Clyde, and caused that slo-mo ballet of a death scene where the two were shot repeatedly in that ambush by all those G-men. (I learned only recently that Taylor also played comic "sidekick" characters in B-westerns, to Wild Bill Elliott, the Durango Kid and Jimmy Wakely throughout much of the 1940s. He died in 1994.)

I told him how much I loved that movie and he seemed happy that I recognized him, and was even more pleased that I actually knew his name, since character actors rarely get much credit and hardly ever gain any name recognition. But that was it, my major brush with Hollywood. I got licked by the large dog of a pretty much no-name actor, and even shyly shook his hand, which, like mine, was all slimy with dog slobber.

Our boys loved Carmel Beach. They always took their pails and shovels and dug holes and built small cities in the sand and populated them with their toys, or "little rubber guys," as they called them. Since we really couldn't afford the trendy upscale restaurants in town, we usually picnicked on the beach, and sometimes walked a little way into town to buy ice cream cones or popsicles later. We always came home from Carmel semi-sunburned and exhausted and would fall into bed, sand and all for much-needed naps. And once the boys were asleep I could usually cajole Treve into joining me in a little of that oh-so lovely "Afternoon Delight," a song that played on the radio all that summer of 1976. And there was nothing quite so delightful as that particularly delicious combination of warm sun-browned skin offset by those small secret salt-tasting patches of pink and white, with the bedroom blinds drawn and the late afternoon sunshine filtering across the sheets. Mmm-*mmh!* Makes my mouth water, just remembering. California dreamin'. (Hurry home, Dear.)

Just inland a few miles from Carmel was the sleepy little village of Carmel Valley. We got off Highway 1 and drove down that road one day during one of our first trips of exploration along the coast. I only remember one thing from Carmel Valley – a place called the Thunderbird Bookshop & Café. As I remember it – and it's been a long time, so ... - the shop was housed in an old, sprawling one-story wooden building fronted with a gravel parking lot. In other words, it seemed very "country." We spent a completely enjoyable afternoon there. I cruised the well-stocked fiction shelves, in book-lovers heaven. Treve found a book that looked good and sat there and read the whole damn thing that afternoon. There was a large section of children's books with some big cushions on the floor and the boys settled in there, hardly making a peep for the four hours or so we spent there reading and browsing. We didn't even have to stop for lunch, because the tables where you ate were also surrounded by shelves of books, and the staff only nodded their "go-ahead" looks when I glanced their way while eating and pulling a book off the shelf next to me. The food was advertised as "home-cooking" and it was – huge sandwiches made with thick homemade-style bread, and steaming, fragrant, hearty soups of all kinds. We grazed and browsed the afternoon away that day and finally left only reluctantly, carrying away a hefty take-home bag of books, and probably a doggie bag or two of sandwich leftovers too.

Not too long after that magical afternoon, the Thunderbird moved up the road to Carmel, taking up residence in a modern new building where there was more room for books, customers and eating. I suppose they were upgrading, or upsizing or something. And while there was a fireplace and plants and such touches in the new building, it never seemed quite as magical to us as the old place down in the valley had. We went to the new store a few times, and while we always came away with new books, it was a much more generic bookstore kind of experience. There was also a very large and quite new bookstore right on the main drag in Pacific Grove that I used to frequent, but I can't remember the name of it. In fact, just now when I tried to find the Thunderbird on-line, I found information that indicates it may have closed up and quietly gone under a few years ago. I hope that's not true, but if it is, it's not so surprising, given today's economy and sorry state of affairs for the books and music business in general these days.

February 11, 2009

Just in case you haven't noticed, books and music – and sometimes movies too – have always been an important part of my life, and I certainly wasn't going to let the fact that I'd quit teaching, gone back in the army and moved to California change any of that. We were all still reading, still listening, still watching.

One of my favorite places in Monterey during the time we lived there was Cannery Row. You probably think it's because that was the street made famous by John Steinbeck in his books and stories, right? Because, after all, I was an English major and a teacher, right? We-ell, no, not exactly. I mean I *did* like Steinbeck and had read a few of his books, and I *did* take a quick gander at the old canneries and the stores and restaurants that the place was famous for, but the place I liked the best and the boys and I always made a beeline for whenever we went down to the Row was Odyssey Records. It was a huge music store, with rows and rows of record bins, and it carried not only the newest stuff but also carried a lot of classic rock and pop and jazz and classical and … Well, Odyssey just had it *all*. If you were a music lover, it was simply an exciting place to be. There was always music playing in the place over a state of the art stereo system and you were greeted by displays near the door of what was new. And one of the really cool things about Odyssey was that all the very latest records were always on sale for at least the first few days of release. So, as a former student of *Billboard* magazine and its charts, I usually knew just what I was looking for, and I grabbed 'em freshly waxed. These were records, of course. Remember *records*? Oh, never mind …

This was California – Beach Boys country! I scarfed up their newest album, which featured that quintessential live party song, "Ba-ba-ba, Ba-barbra Ann." And this was the TV era of *Kojak* and Mistah Kotter. The Four Seasons big comeback album that year, with its title track "Who Loves You (Pretty Baby)?" ripped right outa Unca Telly's mouth, had just delivered a monster hit with "December 1963 (Oh What a Night)."

The very first album I bought once we got settled into our new digs on Bellegarde Way was the Starland Vocal Band with that infectious and horny tune "Afternoon Delight," mentioned earlier. Another California album the boys and I both remember well was young Dean Friedman's debut disc, with its Top 40 hit, "Ariel." Probably not many people remember that tune, but it was so way cool, with its undisciplined run-on dopey lyrics about this nice Jewish kid who fell in love with a girl named Ariel, a hippy, pot-smoking vegetarian. For example:

> I picked her up in my new VW van
> She wore a peasant blouse with nothing underneath
> I said, "Hi." She said, "Yeah, I guess I am ...

Or its operatic aria-like and suggestive final chorus which wraps up a last verse about eating spaghetti and watching TV together until the channel goes off the air with the national anthem – "We made love to bombs bursting in – Aaaaa-ariel." Great stuff. Where are you now, Dean Friedman? Another one-hit wonder album we got was by a guy named Henry Gross, whose hit single "Shannon" was playing one day when we came into the shop. Who remembers Henry Gross, or the song?

My son, Jeff, got his very first KISS album at Odyssey Records, the *Rock and Roll Over* LP, which featured the then-current Top 40 hit, "Hard Luck Woman." I will confess that I liked that song too, so was something of an accomplice in introducing my then barely eight year-old son to this flamboyant group of the outrageous makeup, costumes and platform boots. It wasn't until years later I heard all that stupid crap about KISS being an acronym for "Kids In the Service of Satan." Bullshit. As Jeff became fond of explaining to me in later years, Paul Stanley and Gene Simmons were (like Dean Friedman) just a couple of nice Jewish boys who also happened to be great showmen and extremely astute businessmen. They're still performing and selling records more than thirty years later, so Jeff is probably right.

And there was the new LP by John Sebastian (formerly of The Lovin' Spoonful) which featured the theme song from comedian Gabe Kaplan's runaway hit sitcom, *Welcome Back, Kotter.*

Many of these songs had already been playing in heavy rotation on Monterey's KMBY (the local AM pop station) for several weeks before Treve and the kids got to California, so I was primed. But the Kotter song held special significance for me and several of my new "retread" friends there at DLI. Because the guys I gravitated towards, quite naturally, I suppose, were the older guys, and many of them were on their second enlistments, "prior service" types like me. But even among them, I was invariably the oldest. Because, let's face it, most guys who do end up back in the service after some time out don't usually wait over ten years to make up their minds. In any case "Welcome Back" usually brought a wry grimace to our faces whenever we heard it that year.

Chuck Squires was one of the first of these guys I met, and Chuck and I remained good friends for the next two years, or throughout our AIT. Chuck was nine years younger than I, but the age difference didn't seem to matter. He had a long lantern-jawed face and an easy laugh. We liked each other from the first day we met, which was, I think, even before our Russian classes officially started, while I was living in the barracks and we were all just hanging around waiting. (There's always plenty of that "hang time" no matter where you go in the army, even if all your paperwork is in order.) Chuck was married, but he and Jake had no kids yet. Yes, his wife's name was Jake. I'm pretty sure it was just a nickname and that she had a proper "girl's" name. In fact I probably knew what it was once, but I sure can't remember anymore. She was always just Jake to everybody when we knew her and Chuck. They had met when they were both enlisted in the army and overseas. I don't think Chuck was out of the army even a year before he came back in, so he didn't have to do basic again. They had found a small, no doubt horrifically expensive, apartment in Monterey a few blocks down the hill from the Presidio. (Monterey and Pacific Grove, by the way, were the flanking towns on the sides of the hill where the Presidio, with DLI, was located. So whenever I talk about things being just "down the hill" or "up the hill" I'm being quite literal; practically everything was up or down in this area. The streets leading to and from DLI were all fairly steep, and sloped precipitously down to the bay.) Either they were living on their savings, or else Jake had found a job – or both – because housing and rental prices on the Monterey peninsula were simply out of sight.

Chuck and Jake were quick to welcome my family once Treve and the boys arrived. My boys can still remember visiting the Squires' small apartment for a dinner of homemade tacos – a relatively new taste treat for the Bazzetts. Prior to that I'd been the only one in our family to eat tacos, and then only the Patio brand frozen kind, along with some lettuce and mayo and a beer. But Jake was the one who showed Treve how to make the filling and fix the shells and build a real taco. Tacos still remain a favorite supper staple with us more than thirty years later. The Squireses ... (Hmm ... "Squireses"? Looks strange, don't it? But Jones becomes the Joneses, so ... I think I'll just use the singular, even when I mean both of them, okay?) The Squires quickly became fairly regular guests at our home and table that year, and we often did things together.

The Squires were practicing Mormons, or Latter Day Saints, at the time, and I remember one interesting weekend when they invited us all to an open house at their Stake, which is, as I understand it, the equivalent of a parish or congregation. What we found very interesting was the variety of canned and dried foods that were on display in jars, cans and plastic bins that night. Apparently one of the tenets of LDS teaching includes a requirement to have a three- or six-month supply of food stored in the home. We saw a wide variety of dried fruits and other foods and were invited to taste them. We found we all quite enjoyed the flavor of dried bananas, a snack I still pick up now and then when I see it in the store. The Stake hall that night was filled with kids of all sizes and ages and most of the women were dressed in long modestly styled dresses that looked like something from the previous century. Their hair was invariably long and worn pinned up or down and brushed out. The men and boys were all dressed in good, "Sunday-go-to-meeting" kind of clothes, with lots of white shirts, ties and polished shoes in evidence. The Mormons were obviously putting their best feet forward for the occasion. We learned about the traditional "family home evening," celebrated by Mormon families at least once a week, when the TV would be turned off and they would play games together or other "wholesome" activities. It was, in fact, a very enjoyable, entertaining, and informative evening. And when we left I got a copy of *The Book of Mormon* to take home. It wasn't forced on me; I was happy to take one. In fact I read many passages from it later. I had read books about the Mormons, and about Joseph Smith and Brigham Young before, but I had never read this particular "lost" book of the Bible, and found it most interesting.

Chuck was from Mesa, Arizona, and had been raised Mormon, but Jake was a convert. They were not to be my only Mormon friends though. There were several others in my DLI class and a few of them also became close friends. Tim and Heidi Steele were neighbors in the apartments we lived in, down the hill (there it is again) to the left from us. I think they had two little boys at the time, though Tim was several years younger than I was. A native of Phoenix, Tim had already done a partial tour in the Air Force and was back in uniform again, this time in army green. Heidi was a waifish Mia Farrow kind of blonde beauty, with perpetual dark circles under her eyes – those two babies, no doubt. The kids were named after the evangelists, as I remember – at least I'm pretty sure there was a Matthew, and maybe a Mark. I only found out recently that Tim and Heidi had actually met and married at DLI a couple years before we met them. I'll be darned. Shades of those quickie DLI courtships and marriages that I mentioned earlier and Debra Dickerson described in her book, *An American Story* – except *this* one turned out *well.*

Here's how Tim Steele described it himself in an e-mail I received just today in response to a general request I'd put out to the guys for memories or stories of our DLI years –

Heidi and I are still together; this year will be thirty-five years. We actually met and got married at DLI. A marriage that shouldn't have lasted a year. She was army and I was USAF. She studied Russian and I studied Vietnamese. No way we were ever going to be assigned to the same area. As it was, the USAF released me, because the Vietnam war was over and there was no need for so many linguists. Heidi continued on for a while, but when she found out she was pregnant, she didn't want to stay in the army any longer. So she got out and I joined the army, and that's when we all met.

Another Mormon classmate was Steve Egbert, who also lived off-post, with his wife, Kathy. No children there either.

Steve and Chuck were always my stiffest competition in the battle for top grades and class ranking during our months at DLI. The prize for the top graduate of the class was considerable. You received an immediate promotion to the next pay grade. As prior service types, we were all E-4's, but as married men we all wanted that extra pay grade badly. Egbert ended up winning it and I think I was second and Chuck third, or maybe vice-versa. In any case, Chuck and I both ended up making Sergeant (E-5) before we left Monterey anyway. But we did it the hard way, by going before a promotion board. With his recent service record, Chuck got promoted first. I had to work a little harder. First, I applied for reinstatement of my old military occupational specialty of manual Morse intercept operator, (MOS 05H), which was granted with surprising alacrity considering how long I'd been gone. Then, in order to amass the proper number of points needed for promotion, I took a whole raft of dirt simple army correspondence courses I ordered through the Fort Ord education center. When I'd gotten enough points together I got my name onto a promotion board list. Suffice it to say I jumped through a bunch of fairly low hoops, but I got the promotion before I left DLI.

Treve has her own vividly purple memory of the day I got promoted to sergeant. She accompanied me that day to the ceremony, which was held on an upper floor of the Rialia Building. There was an official photographer there to take pictures of wives or other family members pinning the new stripes onto the sleeves of the promotees. Treve, being still relatively new to the arcane ways of the military and the differences between the services of stripes and other insignia of rank, made the mistake of placing my new sergeant stripe upside down on my uniform sleeve as the photographer snapped the picture. We still have that photo. Of course the group of people gathered for the ceremony all got a big laugh out of her unintentional gaffe. No one who laughed really intended to be unkind, but Treve was terribly embarrassed by her mistake and couldn't get away fast enough once the ceremony was over. She was wearing a beautiful white pant suit with matching new white sandals that day. The sandals were new enough that the soles were still quite slick, and as we started down the stairwell on our way out of the building, she slipped on the second step and fell all the way down the stairs, which were made of poured concrete with metal treads. Treve literally bounced, on her butt and one side down more than a dozen steps. At the time we were alone in the stairwell, but all she could think about when she hit the bottom was that she had screwed up yet again, so she quickly jumped to her feet, in spite of what must have been excruciating pain.

"*Geeze*, Hon," I exclaimed in concern. "Are you *okay?*"

Wincing in pain, but glancing fearfully back up at the top landing and the door there, she replied, "I'm *fine. C'mon.* Let's get out of here."

And so we did, with her limping the few blocks back home to our apartment. I was afraid she might have broken something in that terrible tumble – a shin, a foot, some ribs – *some*thing. But she insisted she hadn't, and she was right. Later that afternoon, however, a giant purple bruise with a raised lump in its center emerged across the top side of her left thigh, which did prove to be very painful. She wouldn't hear of going to a doctor though. It took weeks for that bruise to go away and it went through a successive rainbow of colors as it gradually dissipated. In fact, the bruise was so spectacular in its initial stages that I took a photo of it – a picture of her posterior for posterity. We've got that photo here somewhere too. In any case, that awful body-bouncing fall is how Treve mainly remembers my promotion to sergeant. That and the humiliation of the upside-down stripes, which mistake she explains by noting that many of our neighbors there at DLI had stripes that went on and were worn that way. Yes, Dear, but they were in the Air Force.

But no matter.

Egbert, in addition to being consistently at the top of our Russian class and a kind of linguistic egghead (he also knew a little Chinese Mandarin), was very handy mechanically too – one of those guys you'd want to have around the house. I remember this because I spent one afternoon over at his apartment standing around in the parking lot feeling useless while he replaced a faulty thermostat in our car and then installed a new chrome-plated temperature gauge I'd picked up at Western Auto, mounting it handily under the dash. It took him a couple hours at least, and he got all greasy in the process, but he wouldn't take any money for his efforts, even though I knew living off-post had to be killing them, even with Kathy's job.

"Let's just call it a favor between friends," he told me as he politely refused my offer of payment. Steve was that kind of guy. I know he was a few years my junior, but he always had a kind of dignified reserved about him, a professorial air almost. Hell, *I* was the one who'd been a professor, or an assistant prof at least, but I always had a bit of the goober about me; still do, I'm afraid. Must come from growing up in Reed City. I'm not sure where Steve came from. Nebraska or Kansas maybe.

So that was my trio of close Mormon friends: Squires, Egbert and Steele. As I said, however, there were quite a lot of Mormons in uniform at DLI, and there's probably a good reason for this. Part of the Mormon faith is a requirement for all the young men to go out on a mission, preaching the gospel and the Mormon faith at some time after they've completed school. In fact, I remember that my first exposure to Mormon missionaries came in Germany in 1964.

I was coming down the Steppenstrasse in Kassel one beautiful fall day when I saw a small crowd of people, Germans, gathered around two young men. Both were wearing dark shoes and trousers, with white shirts and ties. One of them was standing on one of the lower steps putting his head just above the heads of the crowd. This young man was holding a Bible and speaking in tongues – well, the German tongue, actually, and he sounded very fluent. He seemed to be mildly exhorting the masses about something, but I couldn't really tell what he was saying, since at the time I didn't speak any German beyond a few filthy phrases I'd picked up from my more experienced army buddies. Curious, I stood at the back of the small knot of people listening, trying to figure out what was going on, but the "sermon" was over. The young man got down from the step and said a few words to one of the onlookers and then the crowd began to disperse. I started to leave too, but my GI haircut and cheap PX civvies must have given me away, because the other young man came up to me through the crowd and stuck out his hand and introduced himself – in perfectly American English. Because he and his pal were Mormons, from Utah (or "Happy Valley," as Steve and Chuck sometimes wryly referred to the state where the Mormon Church is headquartered). And that's when I first found out about the missionary duty for all able-bodied young Mormon men.

Foreign languages are important in Mormon education then, at least for the boys. My theory is that some of these young men found they enjoyed working with words and learning new languages, which is how so many Mormons ended up in the military at DLI.

February 13, 2009

Shivers! It's Friday the thirteenth. But I'm back at the computer again. Yesterday was a housekeeping and maintenance day. A few loads of laundry, a little cleaning, and a trip to the store for some staples, since my sweetie will be back on Sunday. Also drove over to visit with my housebound friend, Bill Porteous, whose story I told in my last book, *Love, War & Polio*. We talked about books and also discussed the current grim economic situation, and wondered if President Obama's proposed economic stimulus package would have the desired effect. Bill is doubtful that it will, and not just because he's a Republican. A boy during the Depression, Bill knows about hard times. And as someone who was a banker for over forty years, he is simply appalled at what all the so-called financial experts have done in recent times in their greed for ever higher profits. Me too, Bill.

So let's go back to Monterey in the seventies – happier times, at least for us. We have a lot of very fond memories from those days, but perhaps one of the best for all of us was the Christmas we spent on the Presidio. Not only was it our first (and only) California Christmas, but it was made even better by the fact that Treve's mom and dad flew out from Michigan to spend it with us. It was the first time that Wanda, Treve's mom, had ever flown. She was scared to death about getting on an airplane, but she bit the bullet and did it. She had to have a few drinks at the airport and then a couple more on the plane to overcome her nervousness, so by the time we met them at the Monterey airport, she was feeling just fine. She had decided she was not going to let her silly fear of flying keep her from her only daughter and her grandsons at Christmas time. Well, *I* was there too of course, but it was Treve and the boys that did the trick of getting her on the plane, no question.

Wanda and Chet stayed with us for about ten days, I think, arriving a couple days before Christmas and leaving shortly after New Year's. But we packed a lot of stuff into that time. One of the things they wanted was to see their friends, the Sobeckis, who lived not far north of Monterey, in either Sunnyvale or Mountainview – one of those Silicon Valley settlements. Felix and Treva Sobecki were Treve's godparents.

Wanda had in fact named her only daughter after her best friend, an act Treve rebelled against by the time she hit puberty and unofficially changed her name to a "more American" one, Terri. Unfortunately, her name change just never took within her own family. Our friends throughout the years have often been confused when they hear me call her Treve, since they know her as Terri. Her secret usually comes out in the end though. Frankly, I like Treve just fine – it's unique, and it suits her. The only time I'd ever heard the name Treve before was in a book I'd read as a boy. The book was called, simply, *Treve*. It was one of those Albert Payson Terhune books about his Sunnybank collies, dogs with names like Lad, Lady, Wolf, Bruce, Buff , and – yes, Treve. I went through a dog book phase when I was ten or eleven and read all the Terhune books I could find.

Treve hates it when I tell people this story. She thinks it implies she was named after a *dog*. Nope, she was named for her godmother, Treva Sobecki, whom she grew up calling "Aunt" Treva, although they were not related.

So the Sobeckis traveled down to Monterey and spent a day reminiscing and playing cards with Chet and Wanda. Cards have always been important in the Zimmer household, particularly gin rummy. Treve and her mom played endless hands of gin during that visit, and Chet played just as many hands of cards with Jeff and Scott, usually War or Go Fish. But the game we all played the most that week was a new one we'd just gotten for Christmas. It was a word game from Parker Brothers, called Boggle. It consisted of a square tray with sixteen six-sided die with letters on each side of the dice. You fitted a transparent square dome over the tray of letters to shake them up at the beginning of each game, which was timed using a small plastic hourglass egg-timer. Aw, hell. I'm not gonna try to explain it. *Some* of you must remember Boggle! The object of the game was to make as many words (of three letters or more) as possible from that sixteen-letter grid during those three minutes. The words could run vertically, horizontally, or diagonally. At least I think that's the way it worked. It's been a long time since we played. In fact, I couldn't even remember the name of the damn game when I started to write this. I had to go down in the basement and dig around in our game cupboard until I found it. *Ah! Here it is! BOGGLE! That was it!* You *old* people reading this know the kind of blank-spot mind-fart I'm talking about, when you can't come up with a particular word you want. But you're also the same old people who should be able to remember this game too – one of the great pre-computer games requiring pencil and paper and a brain.

Treve's dad, Chet, was a compulsive crossword enthusiast for many years after he retired from Ford, so he went absolutely bonkers over Boggle. Once we started playing – and we played nearly every night after supper for a week or more – he just didn't want to stop.

"Just one more," he would entreat us as we began rubbing our eyes and yawning. I think one of the reasons he enjoyed it so much was that most of the time he was beating the pants off us – and he was *lovin'* it. *Take that, English teacher* – from a guy who never went past the sixth grade in school. We would often play until one or two in the morning.

Which was a bit problematic for me, because I was working some of those days. Well, working would be too strong a word for what I was doing, actually. Since Treve's folks were there for nearly two weeks, and I didn't want to burn up too much leave, I had opted to report to the student company supply room each day to pull work details around the company area. I had graduated from the Basic Russian course just before Christmas break, and I had been chosen to begin an intermediate level course in January, so we were going to be staying in Monterey for another several months, something we were all quite happy about. The "work" details that week were pretty light duty. I'd report in around nine AM each morning, along with a couple dozen other guys, and we'd be sent out to "police" the company area, which means picking up trash, cigarette butts or whatever. The truth was, the company area was usually pretty clean; there was very little to pick up. So we'd go out and wander around up and down the hill and through the small ravines choked with the ubiquitous ice plant that grew everywhere on the grounds of the Presidio and throughout the Monterey area. Ice plants were weird. They are a succulent species of green plant and, if you walk across them, as we often did in our shoes or combat boots, they kinda push back, they're so springy. It feels like you're walking on top of human bodies or something. A little creepy at first, but we got used to it.

Anyway, we "casuals" would walk around looking down at the ground, occasionally picking something up, or pretending to. Gradually though, we would separate and wander off on our own particular agendas until we had to report back to supply, usually around eleven, at which time we were set free for a two-hour lunch break. Or sometimes the supply sergeant would just tell us we were done and send us on our way. After all, it was Christmas time. We didn't really do shit that week, but we were saving our precious leave time. So I was usually back home with Treve and the boys and her folks by early afternoon, or, like I said, sometimes I was done by eleven, after just a couple hours of basically goofing off in uniform.

During the Sobeckis' day at DLI, Chet wanted to take everyone out to dinner – someplace ritzy, as he put it. Treve suggested the Sardine Factory, which was certainly top-of-the-line as local restaurants went, so much so that I was just horrified. I knew how expensive it was and didn't want Chet spending that much. But, since he insisted that sounded like the place to go, I volunteered to stay home with the boys. The other adults tried to change my mind, but I am not a ritzy place kinda guy, and held my ground. I said I'd take the boys to McDonalds, which was *their* favorite place to dine. Treve still loves to tell friends about her dining experience at the Sardine Factory with her folks and godparents that day.

"It was so *rich*," she says. "There was all this thick carpet and candles and wine and white linen table cloths. And I still remember how the waiter actually placed our linen napkins right on our laps. I was just shocked!"

That's the detail that usually gets into the telling, how this waiter was whipping those napkins around and reaching down in their laps. Hmm … Cheap thrills for a waiter? I'm sure Chet got a thrill when they brought the bill. This was over thirty years ago, but I think the bill might have topped two hundred bucks. Probably that "good" wine had something to do with it. I'm glad I wasn't there. I'll bet the boys and I enjoyed our Big Macs every bit as much as they enjoyed their steak and seafood – and the waiter with the hands. But for Treve it's one of those lasting memories, so I guess it was worth it.

Not that we didn't eat out on occasion in Monterey, but we didn't frequent upscale places like the Sardine Factory or the Spaghetti Warehouse. When we wanted a sit-down meal we went to Grandma's Kitchen, where they served big helpings of good food of all kinds and breakfast all day. Or we'd go to Sambo's, once a large chain which has almost completely disappeared now, a victim of political correctness. I think there is only one left now, the original Sambo's in Santa Barbara. I grew up hearing the story of Little Black Sambo, so I guess I never gave the chain's name much thought, or the decorative murals on the walls of Sambo and the tigers. When I was a kid, we had a children's record with the story of Little Black Sambo and I can still remember singing along with the song –

> *I'm little black Sambo, little black Sambo*
> *Dressed in the prettiest clothes*
> *My jacket is red, my trousers are blue*
> *A green umbrella and purple shoes …*

The Story of Little Black Sambo, written by Helen Bannerman well over a hundred years ago, is still around, and you can still buy it, even under that title. But it has also been re-printed under the name *The Story of Little Babaji*, or in a Little Golden Books edition called simply *The Boy and the Tigers*. Either way, kids today probably won't ever hear that cool little song I learned. And kids *love* the song. I know, because I sang it once to Treve's niece's little daughter when I was reading her the story.

Little Caroline looked at me with big eyes while I was singing, and, when I finished, she immediately said, "Sing it *again!*"

See?

But those Sambo's restaurants, which were pretty much just Denny's under another name, are all gone now.

Come to think of it, there was one trendy place where Treve and I ate several times. It was on a second-floor level right near the middle of Cannery Row. I can't remember the name of it, but it specialized in soup and sandwiches, and that place was where we first encountered alfalfa sprouts as a sandwich topping or garnish. Having grown up in farming country, I'd always thought of alfalfa as strictly cow feed. It *is* a kind of grass, after all. But there it was, on top of our ham and cheese on rye, so we figured, well, what the hell – when in Rome and all that. And it wasn't bad, kind of a bland roughage. Californians probably figured it was good for your colon health or something. Makes me think of that Steve Martin film about L.A., where Sarah Jessica Parker takes him to this parlor where they paid to get something called a "high colonic." I'm still not sure exactly what that is, but judging by the little dance Martin was doing afterwards, it must have something to do with getting your plumbing irrigated. Alfalfa sprouts, artichokes – nearby Castroville had a sign at its city limits boasting it was the "artichoke capital of the world" – lotsa new stuff for Midwesterners to take in. As a kid I used to hear folks around here refer disparagingly to California as "the land of fruits and nuts" (like Sambo's, another one of those very politically incorrect things nowadays). But uh-uh. We've been there. *Veg*etables – and alfalfa and other grazing grasses.

But no matter.

I was talking about that magical long ago California Christmas we spent with the Zimmers in 1976. And one of our fondest memories of that time is going Christmas caroling around the apartment complex quad, with Chet on harmonica and George Brown on guitar. Wanda, the boys and Treve and I were singing, of course. And ya gotta remember that Christmas in Monterey was – is – nothing like Christmas in Belleville or Reed City, where the snow is sometimes already a foot deep by then. It was shirtsleeve seventies when we all went out caroling, picking up a few friendly neighbor kids along the way. What we quickly found out, much to our embarrassment, was that there were very few carols we all knew more than just a few lines to. So we'd start out strong with the first few lines, then kinda start humming and faking it until the song just sorta petered out. Finally we found out that we all knew most of "Rudolph the Red-Nosed Reindeer," so we ended up really *working* that one every time we stopped to serenade someone. We weren't exactly model carolers, but we sure had fun that night.

George Brown was a guy I'd met during my stay at the Booth Hotel down in Fort Leonard Wood. He'd come along a few weeks behind me in Minuteman training, and may have gotten slightly recycled, because George was just a bit on the heavy side. He was tall too, so he could have carried a few extra pounds without any trouble, but, by army standards, George was always just barely borderline fat. Like me, George had been a teacher for a while, and for reasons of his own, ended up back in the army again and came along to DLI to learn Russian. He was never in my class there, always a month or two behind, but eventually he ended up in Augsburg (Germany) too, where we would see him again.

The boys always liked George. He was single and lived in the barracks at DLI, but would often come over to our place for dinner and bring along his guitar and play and sing songs with us. I think he may have even tried to give Jeff a few lessons on a cheap second-hand guitar we bought from someone who was moving out shortly after we moved in on Bellegarde Way. George had a generally jovial air about him, almost the stereotypical "jolly" fat man, although we would never have put it that way. He was the ideal houseguest, always offering to help with the dishes or any other odd jobs we might have to do. He babysat for us with the boys on more than one occasion, and went with us to the Monterey County Fair that year too, going on the rides with the kids and buying them cotton candy and other treats. Sometimes we would all go together down to Dennis the Menace Park, a popular local playground with huge plywood cutouts of that comic book character and where the main attraction was a massive genuine steam locomotive sitting stranded forever on a short piece of track, where kids could climb around on its cowcatcher or in and out of the cab and pretend to be engineers.

In fact George may have stayed with the boys and dog when we made a trip to San Francisco during a long Columbus Day weekend. We stayed at the Americana Hotel, just a few blocks from Union Square. The hotel seemed fairly nice, but I can remember when we went out for a burger one night we got panhandled two or three times in just a couple blocks and saw winos sitting in doorways along the street, nodding off and still clutching their brown-bagged bottles of Thunderbird. It seemed very seedy, if not a bit threatening. In a postcard home to my folks, I commented: "It's kind of a strange city – part of it like downtown Detroit and part of it pure California." During our two days there we probably walked forty or fifty blocks both days. The streets were so steeply vertical that I didn't really feel comfortable driving them; and the storied streetcars – "where those little cable cars, climb halfway to the stars" – were always so jam-packed with people we could never get on. Although I don't think I said jam-packed at the time.

I remember hollering in frustration to no one in particular as yet another crowded trolley passed us by on its climb up the next hill, "Why are they all so fucking *full?!*"

"*Tim!*" Treve admonished me, looking warily around. "Be careful what you say. Someone might *hear* you."

Not that I cared. My butt hurt. Try walking dozens and dozens of blocks straight up or straight down, hill after hill. Because that's where it gets you after a while, right in the ol' gluteus maximus. I didn't leave my heart in San Francisco; it was more like a good portion of my ass, where as Treve is always quick to point out, I can't really afford to lose anything.

"He doesn't *have* any ass," is how she delicately puts it.

But we saw the sights, by God. We were there to tourist, and by golly we touristed our tired asses off that weekend. We went to the Wax Museum, ripped through Ripley's Believe It or Not, and walked all over Fisherman's Wharf, where we climbed aboard the *Balclutha*, an authentic sailing vessel from the 1880s, just like the ones that once regularly rounded Cape Horn carrying all manner of goods to California and points north.

By Saturday evening we'd had enough of walking, and drove to the House of Prime Rib for a fine dining experience that Treve still talks about. It ranks right up there with her Sardine Factory adventure, only without the waiter's hands in her lap. On Treve's list of important things in life, prime rib is waaay up there, much more important than sex, I am sad to say. But speaking of sex, you'd be surprised just what a girl will do for you once you've indulged her and wined and dined her properly. I kept that in mind as I ate my delicious creamed spinach (a new taste treat for both of us). I could get real graphic here, but I won't. Somebody's mother might be reading it. Suffice it to say that we *both* thoroughly enjoyed our last night in San Francisco.

We traveled back to Monterey on the coastal highway and I remember we stopped that Sunday in the little village of Half Moon Bay, and got out and walked up the main street and around on the residential side streets too, looking at the small run-down homes, probably wondering what kinds of lives went on in those houses here on the very western edge of America. And just stretching our legs, relieved to be out of the city. There was an enormous pumpkin patch on the edge of town where they were selling pumpkins for Halloween – pick out your own and take it with you. It's probably part of being brought up in a small town, but I think I almost have fonder memories of that half hour or so spent in Half Moon Bay than I do of the whole weekend in San Francisco (except for that simply lovely Saturday night I just mentioned).

We also made a couple day trips to the Bay area with the boys during our time at DLI. One was to Marine World/ Africa USA where we saw a lot of animals and also watched the killer whales perform. Another time we visited the Great America amusement and theme park, where probably the ride we remember best was called Loggers Run, where we rode a hollowed-out log boat placidly about in an elevated flume overlooking much of the park. We had picked this ride because it looked safe and not so intimidating to the kids. But then, at the end of the ride, we went whooshing suddenly down a sixty-foot drop to splash into a pool at the bottom. Treve was sitting in front with Scotty in front of her. Talk about a few seconds of utter terror as we approached the drop-off. But it was over before we knew it, and all we really got was wet.

Our biggest tourist adventure in California was probably our trip to Disneyland in the spring of 1977. It was Easter week and I took a few days of leave, thinking it was the perfect time to make that trip. The boys wouldn't miss any school, and, well, it was *Dis*neyland. We couldn't live for a year or more in California and *not* take our kids to Disneyland, right? Right! The trouble was, practically every other family in California, natives and outlanders like us alike, must have thought the same thing, because the park was so jam-packed with visitors that week that the lines were interminable, often taking much longer than the rides or attractions themselves.

But I'm getting ahead of myself, because the trip there has its own story. We left early on a Saturday morning and were not quite halfway to Anaheim, just north of San Luis Obispo, when we blew a tire on our Hornet wagon. And I mean it *blew* – BAM!

Treve screamed, "Omigod, what was *that?!*"

And Jeff and Scott, in the back, were suddenly up on the edge of the seat, watching wide-eyed over my shoulder, both of them at once asking us what that *noise* was.

"A tire!" I answered everyone, none too calm myself as I wrestled with the steering wheel just trying to stay on the highway. I managed to guide the car onto the shoulder and parked precariously above a deep storm ditch and sat there for a moment, my heart beating wildly.

"Well, shitfire," I muttered to myself, slumping in my seat. Because there's just nothing like a flat tire to make your day, especially when you're on vacation and your car is packed halfway to the roof. And it wasn't just flat, I discovered when I finally got out and walked around the back of the car to inspect the damage – the right rear tire had been quickly reduced to rubber shreds.

"Shit." I said glumly, staring at the mess.

So we got the boys out of the car and had them sit halfway down the embankment of the ditch, safely away from the traffic that continued to whiz obliviously by in the bright California sunshine. Then Treve and I carefully unloaded most of the luggage out of the back of the wagon to get at the spare tire well, which was under the floor.

I had never really even looked at the spare tire or jack assembly before, although we'd had the car over a year by then. It was one of those folding, accordion type jacks and I had no idea how it worked or where to attach it, and stood there holding the jack assembly and tire iron in my hands looking at them.

"Don't you know how to use it?" Treve asked me tentatively.

"Nope," I replied. "But I guess I better figure it out, huh?"

Just then Jeff, almost eight, climbed up the bank to stand beside us, listening in. Pointing to the upturned trunk lid, he asked, "Aren't those the directions, Daddy?" I looked up, and sure enough, right there in front of me, stenciled on the back side of the tire well's lid, were complete printed instructions on how to operate the jack, where to attach it and how to inflate the space-saver donut tire. And, since Jeff was the only one bright enough to notice this handy feature, I let him stay and help me change the tire while Treve and Scott rested down the embankment. Then we re-loaded all our stuff back into the car and limped slowly down the road and into San Luis Obispo, where we spent probably close to two hours waiting for a tire store to have the correct size tire delivered and then put on our rim and back onto the car. We didn't want to spend the next week without a spare, after all. All of this unexpected crap kinda dampened our spirits about our big Easter vacation, but finally we were back on the road again, en route to the magic kingdom. I was in kind of a foul mood by this time, thinking to myself, *this fucking place better be worth all this trouble.* But Treve got the boys singing something and pretty soon they'd jollied me back into a happier frame of mind.

We got our first look at and whiff of Los Angeles' famous smog when we were still miles north of the city, and even had to roll up our windows against this brownish scrum as we descended into the valley. And we did not have air conditioning. But Anaheim, when we finally arrived, seemed somehow cleaner, and the boys were very excited to find out that our motel had water beds, a brand new experience for all of us, and one which might have been nearly as exciting to them as most of the park's rides, many of which simply frightened them. The high rides and various roller coasters were out of the question. Even the saucer and teacup ride, a fairly tame one, scared them. When we started up the steep winding stairs to the lofty tree house of the Swiss Family Robinson, Jeff froze about halfway up.

"It's too *high*, Mommy," he quavered. But we managed to keep him going, telling him to stop looking down then. There were other people behind us and no room to go back down. Captain Hook's pirate ship was better. Both kids had fun clambering about on it. And we all enjoyed the musical shows in the small theaters, performed by enthusiastic talented young people, all trying to break into show business, I suppose. The river boat ride through the jungles of Adventureland, with the animatronic hippos and elephants was also a bit intimidating to them. But they loved the small boats we took through the tunnels of It's a Small World, and the displays of children from other countries and the lively music that accompanied the ride. We found that attraction just as we exited the park and nearly missed it altogether. The kids were singing that song for days afterward.

Our second day we went to Universal Studios and did that tour. We visited TV and movie sets, watched a Wild West shootout and fake fist fight, met Jack Albertson (then co-starring in the TV sitcom, *Chico and the Man*), and *Baretta's* pet cockatoo, Fred (or maybe a stunt double). We traversed the spinning tunnel of Bigfoot from the *Six-Million Dollar Man* show, visited the TV home of Beaver Cleaver and his family, and crossed a precariously tipping railroad trestle on a small tourist train.

We were still riding that little tourist train along the edge of a small lake when something happened that was no doubt burned forever into poor Scotty's five year-old brain. Scott was at the right-hand end of a bench seat that held four abreast. He was sitting next to Treve, and there was a middle-aged Japanese couple sitting on the other end. Jeff and I were sitting behind them. Suddenly, without any warning, the track we were riding on tipped to the right and a larger-than-life *extremely* realistic-looking great white shark – yes, the one from *Jaws* – came roaring and lunging like hell itself, splashing up out of the lake water straight at the tram. Before anyone else could even react, poor Scotty, nearly in the shark's jaws and absolutely terrified, had clawed himself across his mother and catapulted himself across the tram and into the lap of a very startled Japanese gentleman. Scotty didn't scream, and I don't think he even cried – then or later – but man, what terrific *reflexes* the kid displayed. That poor kid.

We still tell that story today, and Scott usually smiles. The truth is I don't know if Scott even remembers that incident. It may have been the kind of traumatic thing you just block out of your conscious memory. Maybe it's a "memory" that he only has because he's heard us tell the story so many times. If we'd known that was going to happen, we certainly wouldn't have put the littlest kid in the scariest seat on the train. Oh well. Sorry, Scotty.

That was our Easter vacation, 1977. Probably the most vivid memories for the kids – and maybe for Treve and me too – are the flat tire and the water beds. And to this day probably the only thing that comes to mind for all four of us when we hear San Luis Obispo mentioned is that blowout.

Many years later, after our kids were grown, they would often teasingly call us bad parents because we never took "real" vacations during all the years we lived in Maryland, only those once or twice yearly trips to Michigan to see the grandparents. Well, what you have just read is my proof that we did – at least *once* – take the kids on a proper vacation. Of course it was over a year before Suzie was born. But the boys did see Disneyland, and it was years before Disney World even existed. And it was that latter attraction that all their Maryland childhood friends visited while we were driving west to see grandpas and grandmas, something we had decided was more important than visiting an elaborate tourist trap in Florida (and a helluva lot *cheaper* too). In retrospect, both Treve and I think that our boys, at seven and five, were still too young to fully enjoy a place like Disneyland. But we still have those warm and fuzzy family memories: of a flat tire on 101 near San Luis Obispo, the gurgling water beds that lulled us all to sleep – and a giant white shark that almost ate our second-born son. It's a small world after all.

February 16, 2009

She's back, and I am so happy. Our house feels like a home again. My experiment – can I write a book in a month? – has failed. And I don't care. I've made a pretty good start, and what I found out instead is how much I miss my wife when she's gone, even though we might bicker and carp at each other way too often when she's here. I picked Treve up at the airport in Grand Rapids yesterday, after driving in and out of snow squalls to get there. We spent most of the evening grinning at each other, we were both so happy she was home again. After a month of living in constant proximity with the kids and grandkids, she was pleased to just sit in her chair last night for at least two hours and relish the quiet. She didn't even turn on the television. And I sat in my chair across the room and looked at her and smiled.

Today life is nearly back to normal. She wondered why I hadn't dust-mopped the dog hair out of the corners of the bedroom and why the tub hadn't been scrubbed and later yelled at me *not* to do the dishes after brunch, because the dishwasher hadn't been used in over a month and she needed to fill it and run it soon. Ain't love grand?

February 19, 2009

Yes, it really is hard to get back in the saddle with this writing thing when your honey's back home again. I've been sitting in the living room just looking at her and smiling for a couple of days now. Well, we did some other stuff too, but I'm not gonna talk about that.

Speaking of which, she has plans to go see *The Vagina Monologues* at Ferris tonight. She's going with Mary Murnik, our back fence neighbor, who teaches biology at Ferris. I had suggested that *we* go to see it, but Treve nixed that, telling me she just wouldn't feel comfortable at a show like that with me there, so … Oh, well. Who wants to go see a dumb ventriloquist act anyway?

It's snowing and blowing like hell outside this morning, "beginning to look a lot like Christmas," as the song goes. I know it's February, but I'm trying to segue into something here. Various friends and members of my family have pointed out that I didn't tell any Christmas stories in my first book, so I'm gonna try to rectify that oversight here.

I've been thinking back and trying to remember some Christmases past – things that stand out in that mess we call memory, ya know?

It must have been around 1952 or thereabouts, as near as I can figure, that I absolutely lusted after a rather realistic-looking lever action toy rifle made of black metal with a wood stock and front hand grip. I would have been eight. No it wasn't that classic Red Ryder model Daisy air rifle that little Ralphie fantasized over in *A Christmas Story*. That came a few years later. It was a cork gun, i.e. it shot corks. Remember those? The thing is, there were two models. One was a kid-size model and the other one was closer to real size, maybe a foot or so longer. I was a kid, of course, but I was very tall for eight years old, and I had surreptitiously hefted both models, taking them carefully down from the top shelf of the special seasonal toy section in the basement of Gambles hardware store and holding them up to my shoulder, cardboard packaging and all. It wasn't a perfect arrangement, what with the box, but even I could tell that the junior size model was too small for my longer arms. And the bigger one made a much more satisfying *thunk* when you fired it than that piddling little one, which had, in comparison, a puny, tinny sound. The bigger rifle was probably an additional four or five dollars, and I knew Mom and Dad always looked for the bargain whatever they were shopping for, given that there were five kids and they had to stretch their dollars. But what kid wants to play with a toy gun that's so small it actually *looks* like a toy? So when I started my hints and lobbying, probably shortly after Thanksgiving, about what I *really* wanted for Christmas that year, I always managed to "subtly" emphasize that "there are two models of this rifle in the toy section of Gambles and the little one's too short for me, but the big one is just right, I mean, it's *perfect*, and I really really *really* want that one." Geeze, I even sounded like Ralphie. But my "need" predated poor Ralphie's by at least thirty years.

Of course in today's world, toy firearms and weapons have become so politically incorrect that they are seldom given as gifts, and may even be difficult to find in toy stores, but I grew up in the days of cowboys and Indians (*more* political incorrectness), and white hat heroes like Gene Autry, Roy Rogers and Hopalong Cassidy. Guns were absolutely essential for all little boys back then. I already had a set of twin six-shooter cap guns, but in order to complete my Wild West ensemble, I just had to have that rifle, to slide into my make-believe saddle boot on my make-believe mount. You needed a rifle to pick off those bad guys from a distance as you crouched behind a rock or hid behind the trunk of an apple tree. It was essential for ambushes and bushwhacking.

I'm pretty sure that I visited that lethal-looking corner of the basement in Gambles at least two or three times a week during those weeks leading up to Christmas, fondly stroking the varnished stock, and sometimes, after looking carefully around, taking the rifle down in its open-fronted package and cocking and firing it, just to hear that soul-satisfying thunk. I know I thought more about that rifle than I did about the baby Jesus that year, but I don't remember feeling any guilt over my misplaced greed.

I probably ought to squeeze in here something about how much I loved the solemn ceremony of the hymns and colorful vestments and incense and candles of the midnight mass at St. Philip's church, because I did. It was really a big deal, and it may even have been the first year I was old enough to be an altar boy and actually participate in all that stuff from up in the sanctuary. But when you're just eight years old, singing and vestments and Latin and candles can't compete with a cork gun with a real lever action and a front sight and a genuine wooden stock that fits just perfectly up against your shoulder and, and … Well, you old guys out there know what I'm talking about. You remember.

I got the kid-size model. I was so crushed. I wanted to cry when I unwrapped it. But I think I smiled bravely, or at least I tried to. When Mom asked if that was what I wanted, I nodded my head, an enormous lump in my throat, sitting there holding that *baby*-sized weapon while my brothers happily opened their own presents, exclaiming and laughing. Ain't it funny how a sixty-five year-old man can still so vividly remember a dumb thing like that – something from *fifty-seven years* ago?

But it ended happily, although I felt just a tiny bit guilty about what I did. And what I did was I took some money I got in Christmas cards from my grandparents and I exchanged the small rifle for the larger one a few days later. I never took the original gift out of its box. And I smuggled it out of the house the next day and almost ran down the road from Holdenville and across the bridge into town, looking guiltily around as I entered the hardware store and made the exchange, feeling like Judas with his thirty pieces of silver. I took the bigger rifle home with me, and I took it out and played with it a little, but somehow it wasn't quite as wonderful as I'd expected it to be. I don't know what it was, maybe just knowing that Mom and Dad had done the best they could, but it hadn't been enough for me. I was an ungrateful son. Somehow I knew this, I think, and it spoiled some of the magic of that toy gun.

On second thought, maybe it didn't end so happily after all.

I remember another Christmas a few years later, at our house on Church Street – the "old Morefield place." Carolyn Beilfuss lives there now, and has for many years. She was

Carolyn Crane when we were in high school together.

But no matter.

The reason I remember this particular Christmas is because I was being a smart-ass that year, and opted to make some practical joke kinda gifts. My brother Bob, who is just sixteen months older than me – I think, I've always been bad at math – used to enjoy picking on me. He was really good at pushing my buttons and then acting innocent when I'd react. He enjoyed getting me into trouble with Mom and Dad and stuff like that. I mean we were roommates for the first eighteen years of my life, but it was never a good match. If we'd been college roommates, I'd have moved somewhere else after one semester, ya know? But you can't do that at home, with a brother. You're just stuck, and you live in this uneasy kind of armed truce.

So that particular year I decided I'd "get" Bob for Christmas. I don't know if younger people ever hear this anymore, but back then, in the fifties, one of the threats parents used to make in that time leading up to Christmas was, "If you're not good, you're gonna get a lump of *coal* in your stocking."

Not that there's anything wrong with coal, of course. A lot of people still heated their homes with coal furnaces. We did, there in the old Morefield place. And Dad sold coal to a lot of those homes, hauling it from his coal yard at the Kent Elevator. I even helped deliver a lot of that coal in the next few years.

So anyway there was plenty of coal around our house, in the coal bin next to the furnace in the basement. So yeah, I decided to gift Bob with a lump of coal. But instead of just putting a briquette of coal in Bob's stocking, I super-sized my practical joke. I found a huge chunk of coal in the bin downstairs – probably at least a ten-pounder. I wrapped it up in newspaper, and then put it inside a big cardboard box wrapped in pretty red and green Christmas paper. I even put a bow on it. And a card that said, "To Bob, from Santa." You should have seen the eager look on Bob's face when he pulled that present out from under the tree. Because we all knew that "from Santa" meant something from Mom and Dad. And this was something impressively *heavy*, so Bob must have figured it was something really *good*, ya know?

Well, man you shoulda seen his face when he opened up that coal. It was pure shock.

"What is it?" Mom asked, perplexed.

"Coal," Bob said, still stunned.

Mom looked around at the rest of us. I was the only one grinning – probably laughing out loud by then.

"*Tim*, did *you* do that?" she asked me accusingly.

"No," I said, shaking my head and laughing. "Look at the card. It's from *Santa*. Bob musta been really *bad* this year."

Bob was giving me a really dirty look by this time, a look blacker than the coal sitting in his lap. "That's not funny," he said.

"That's a *terrible* thing to do on *Christ*mas," Mom said, shaking her head and somewhat dampening my good cheer, but not completely. I tried to look a little ashamed, but didn't quite succeed.

Suddenly, however, I didn't have a good feeling about the *other* joke gift I'd placed under the tree. It was for Dad.

Dad used to have this expression he'd use whenever he saw one of us kids looking unhappy or put upon, usually when he was assigning us some particularly onerous task, or interrupting us in something we enjoyed. He'd say, "Whatsa matter with you? You look like you got a cob caught crossways."

Well, sometime during the course of our youth, we'd heard the origins of this expression, which probably came from the days of the Great Depression, or maybe even earlier. Poor folks apparently used to keep a bucket of corncobs in the outhouse to use once the pages of the Sears or "Monkey Wards" catalogues were gone. While I do remember the catalogue pages – particularly those shiny ones, often painful no matter how much you crumpled them first to soften them – I never had the pleasure of trying a corncob. But that phrase of Dad's had always fascinated me, so I had this bright idea that Christmas to play a joke on Dad. I'd gone out to the corncrib behind the house and gotten a cob of corn and shucked it down to a bare cob. Then I got out some brown shoe polish and smeared it liberally over the naked cob. I found a plastic box with a royal blue plush-looking interior that had held a new watch once and placed the cob smack on that blue material. Then I closed the box and wrapped it in colorful Christmas wrap with a "To Dad from Santa" tag.

Dad didn't get it, even though when he opened the package he looked, in fact, like he had a cob crossways. I wasn't grinning this time, but everyone immediately looked at me when Dad opened his mystery gift.

"What th- …?" said Dad, then also looked to me.

"You know, a cob crosswise," I muttered lamely, trying to smile and failing miserably.

"*Tim!* It's *Christ*mas! What were you *think*ing?" Mom scolded, as Dad glowered and Bob grinned hugely.

My practical joke Christmas. Didja ever wonder why some things *seem* funny when you're planning them, but …? Never mind.

Once again, kind of a shameful Christmas memory. Maybe I'd better try for a happier one.

Let's jump ahead to Christmas 1978, in Augsburg, Germany. Not that there weren't plenty of happy memories in between, but this particular one stands out.

It was our first Christmas overseas. We had a new baby. Suzie was just four months old.

March 4, 2009

Geeze. See what happens when the old lady gets home? All your carefully laid plans to write another book go right out the window. Seriously though, it's not her fault. I've just been reading and loafing ever since she got home, and coming up with all kinds of dumb excuses to myself for *not* working on this book. And that "old lady" crack is made with love. She is my special lady, even if she is getting older – something she'd rather not talk about. We all are though. Getting older, I mean. We have lately begun calling each other Earl and Opal, after the old couple in the *Pickles* comic strip.

But no matter. Back at it, Bazzett.

Christmas in Augsburg, 1978. There are a lot of reasons that Christmas stands out in memory, and probably in Treve's too, since that was the very first time she was separated from her parents during the Christmas holidays. They'd even flown to California in 1976 to be with us over the holidays, as I've already mentioned. In 1977 I made it back to Belleville for Christmas from Fort Meade, where I was about halfway through my second TDY before going overseas. Treve and the boys were living with her folks then; in fact, they lived with the elder Zimmers from August 1977 until March of 1978, when we left for Germany.

By Christmas time of '78 then, it was finally beginning to sink in with Treve that we really were thousands of miles from home and our extended family. Of course one of the iron-bound traditions of the Zimmer family was the making and consumption of that very Polish delicacy, pierogies. The problem was Treve had never made them herself. She had only been in on the consumption end of things. And she decided about a week before Christmas that by God if she wasn't going to have her mom and dad around for Christmas then she had to at least have the pierogies. But she had no recipe. So she told me she would have to call her mom to get directions. Not having grown up Polish, and not being terribly fond of pierogies yet (and I say "yet" because I did learn to enjoy them more as the years went on), I was simply appalled at the idea she would consider making a transatlantic phone call just for a recipe.

"Geeze, Treve," I remember saying. "A phone call like that will cost us an arm and leg! Can't you just write and ask your mom to mail you the recipe?"

"*No*, it's too *late!*" she replied emphatically. "It would never get here in time, and you *know* it. You just don't like pierogies. Well, I don't care *how* much it costs! I'm calling Mom and that's all there is to it. We're gonna have pierogies for Christmas Eve dinner just like I've always had for as long as I can remember. And you're not stopping me!"

What could I say? She was right. Letters did take at least a week to reach us from the States. And I really didn't care if we had pierogies or not. Treve was adamant though. The next day – or maybe it was night, what with the time difference – she called home.

I can still remember pacing up and down the living room while she talked with her mom that December, checking my watch every few minutes and counting the dollars this was gonna cost me. Of course she and her mom hadn't spoken to each other since March, and we'd had a new baby and all since then, so they had to catch up on all that and other news.

Visions of dollar signs danced in my head while I paced and fumed and kept whispering loudly, "Get to the *point*! Get the *recipe*, dammit! That's why you're *calling*. Re*mem*ber?!"

But Treve and Wanda were in high gear by then. Treve had that first cigarette going, and I know Wanda did too. In the seventies you couldn't make a call or answer the phone without lighting up.

"Oh, *shush!*" she said, waving me off. "We haven't talked in months. Leave us *alone!*"

I was beside myself, but there was little I could do. Finally, after what seemed like hours but was probably only ten or fifteen minutes, Treve asked her mom to read her the pierogies recipe. She was quiet a moment, then looked over at me and said, "She says she doesn't have a recipe. She's never written it down. She learned how to make 'em from her mom."

"Well, forget it then. Hang up, ferChrisesakes!" I said, biting off my words in frustration.

"NO!" Treve replied. "Why don't you just go away?"

And then, over the course of the next twenty or thirty minutes – yes, *TWENTY OR THIRTY MINUTES AT TRANSATLANTIC TELEPHONE RATES!* – she patiently picked her mother's brain, taking notes and walking her slowly through the whole process of pierogi-making, or perhaps vice-versa. They talked about ingredients and beating the dough and mixing and preparing the filling and then assembling the final product and boiling them and cooling them and then frying them. I mean, it was absolutely *excruciating* for me to listen while I paced and moaned and tore at my hair. But she finally extracted what seemed to be a reasonable facsimile of a recipe for pierogies. Then she wanted to put Suzie on the phone to talk with Grandma – Suzie who was only FOUR MONTHS OLD!

"*NO!*" I shouted, nearly hysterical. "Absolutely *NOT!* You're *DONE!* Hang *UP!*"

And, pouting just a little, she did. And the next day she worked most of the day making pierogies for the first time in her life. I was going to say, "all by herself," but that wouldn't be quite true. And no, *I* didn't help. But I had a friend from work who was over visiting that day, and *he* helped.

Francis Tyler was the civilian rep from NSA who was working at Field Station Augsburg during much of my tour there. Francis was hard to miss in a crowd. He had bushy hair and sideburns of a bright orange color, kinda like Bozo the Clown had. He was several years younger than I, but we seemed to have quite a lot in common. We'd both been seminarians once and so shared that "good Catholic boy" background. But more than that, we had a lot of the same tastes in books and music too. I'd met Francis at work and got to know him pretty well when, as part of his official duties, he helped to teach a Russian refresher class to a group of the military linguists at the site. It was pretty basic kind of stuff, but I enjoyed it and Francis and I became friends. We both really enjoyed our work at the station and he taught me a lot about my newfound trade. He was single and lived alone. He ate lunch in the field station cafeteria every day, while I usually brown-bagged it. But every now and then he'd entice me down to join him in the cafeteria, usually by telling me something stupid, like there were radishes in the salad that day. I took pity on his bachelor lifestyle, so I started inviting him over to our apartment for a meal now and then, and Treve and the boys quickly came to enjoy his company too. Jeff and Scott still remember "the Francis laugh." Francis often laughed very silently – no noise at all, just a grin and a slight bobbing of his head and shoulders, a lot like Fozzy Bear from *The Muppet Show* used to laugh. This silent laughter was probably a holdover from goofing off during night time "grand silence" in the seminary. Anyway, Francis was at our place the day Treve was steaming up the whole place boiling and stock-piling pierogies. So he volunteered to help her stuff the filling into the dough and then pinch the whole thing together, a time-consuming and tedious process, especially when you're making a hundred or more. I was probably watching the baby or playing with the boys. Or maybe I was still sulking over that excessively long phone call; I can't remember.

Anyway, the reason I remember Francis's role in pierogi-making is that when they reached the end of the filling, they found there was still quite a lot of rolled out dough still left. Treve didn't have any more ingredients – potatoes, cheese and onions – to make more filling, but she didn't want to waste the leftover dough. We'd had tacos that day for lunch, and it was Francis's suggestion that we use the leftover taco filling in the leftover dough. Treve was at first appalled at such an idea, but then she thought about all the trouble it had been to mix and beat and form that dough, so finally decided *why not?*

I know she and I both still remember it, but I wonder if our boys remember the only Christmas we had Mexican pierogies to eat. Francis Tyler didn't just help us make pierogies that Christmas. He made us a lasting special memory. We never had taco-pierogies again, but I have to tell ya, they weren't half bad, actually.

But all this is really only a small part of what made that first Augsburg Christmas special. What made it really great was that we opened up our home – and our hearts – to several other people on Christmas day. I was a shift chief in the transcription shop, which means I was in charge of the efforts of several other Russian linguists who worked rotating shift with me. I'd made Staff Sergeant just a couple of weeks after I arrived in Augsburg – which ruffled a few feathers, I suppose, because here I was a "new guy" on station, but I outranked most of the people who were training me. It was initially a little uncomfortable, but they got over it. The thing was, I pushed as hard as I could to get that promotion while I was still in training at Fort Meade the last month before I left. I asked for a promotion board to be convened and at first my request was denied. The administrators at the training company said I had to be working in a specific MOS in order to be boarded. Well, I spent a few hours in the company orderly room reading through the army regulations on promotion boards and found that an exception could be made. I pointed this clause in the regs out to the company clerk, who wasn't too happy about being corrected. The end result, however, was that I did get a promotion board. I aced it and got the highest recommendations. The promotion to E-6 caught up with me very soon after I started work at the field station. I was a very happy soldier.

But no matter. Well, it *did* matter, but we're talking about ghosts of Christmas Past here, not promotions.

I was supposed to work on Christmas day, but my platoon commander gave me the day off. I had invited several of the linguists on my trick – younger troops who lived in the barracks – to come to our place for food and drinks that day. I had first cleared this with Treve, of course. So it was a pretty big production for her to get everything ready that day – and this was *after* we'd already had our own Christmas morning with the kids' presents and everything. (We'd gone to midnight mass at the field station chapel the night before.)

So anyway, Treve was busy pretty much all day that Christmas, with a turkey and a ham and stuffing and all that stuff that goes with a major holiday feast. A couple of friends of ours, John and Ruth Williams, whom we'd known since DLI, came over to help too. Ruth made her special homemade potato rolls. We knew they were scrumptious because she and John usually baked them on Sunday mornings and they knew we walked by their third floor apartment in another building on our way to and from mass, so whenever Ruth had fresh rolls she'd put a big sign in their window for us to see on the way home. It would say, "Tim and Terri, Come up for breakfast," or something to that effect. And we did. And those warm rolls were just soooo good. John and Ruth didn't have any kids yet then and they loved ours. And the boys liked them too.

So Ruth made her potato rolls and brought them, and John had made this mulled wine and cider stuff that he brought along to heat up, to provide some special Christmas cheer of the "spirits" kind. Our neighbors from across the hall, the Olivases, were gone for the week and had given us a key to their apartment so we could use their stove and oven, which we did, what with all the stuff Treve was making. I mean she baked two or three pies and a few batches of cookies too.

Around four-thirty or so then, some of my people from work started arriving. There was Kate Philbin, a redheaded girl from Huntington Beach, California. And her friend, Chris Jorgenson, came with her boyfriend, Joe Newton, who brought along his guitar. The food was all ready, and everyone loaded up a plate and ooh-ed and aah-ed over all the stuff. Everybody sampled the warm mulled drinks and there was also beer and soda and a few bottles to mix drinks. We all sat around the living and dining rooms and swapped stories about Christmases past. There was lots of laughing, smoking – I *toldja*. Just about *every*body smoked then and it seemed normal.

One of the non-smokers arrived a couple hours later. Dan Beck was probably around twenty-two or so and was another person who had become something of a "regular" at our apartment since we'd been working together. He lived in the barracks and he was a runner, something not all that common in the seventies army. At least two or three times a week he'd put on some sweats and run from his barracks all the way into town. It would seem he was into fitness, but I think not. Because on the way back from his run into town, he would usually stop at a bakery and buy a big bag of pastries and then run over to our place to share them with us. The boys always loved to see Dan show up. It meant donuts. The funny thing about German pastry was that it never tasted quite as good as it looked. The German bakers tended to skimp on the sugar, perhaps a holdover from wartime rationing. But we soon learned to add a little powdered sugar whenever necessary. Dan liked to eat the pastries and donuts too, so, like I said, I don't think he was really running for the fitness. He just liked to run for the pure animal joy of it. And Treve was always glad to see Dan too, because he was also a very handsome young man, with a head of dark curly hair that she just loved to stick her hands in. She was a hair dresser, remember?

So Dan came in around 6:30 or so and he brought along his family. His mom and his twenty year-old blonde sister, Heidi, were in town to celebrate Christmas with Dan, all the way from Seattle, I think it was. Dan had called earlier and asked if he could bring his family and we'd said sure. Three more people came in, then, and loaded up plates and made drinks and found places to sit, perching on chairs or arranging themselves on the floor. We had bought a new pad and an orange carpet (remember how popular *orange* was in the seventies?) at the PX when we'd moved in, so we had a pretty comfortable floor. I'd sat and lain on it enough to know. People got seconds on food and there was more talk, more stories. Joe strummed a few tunes on his guitar and we sang a little. Later I put on some of the new records I'd gotten for Christmas. I can remember a Dr. Hook album with a pretty song called "Sharing the Night Together." And there was Charlie Pride singing about burgers and fries and cherry pies and how "it was simple and good back then." Suzie stayed up late and got passed around from hand to hand and smiled and cooed and charmed everyone. Our boys had gotten this new cowboy game – a pistol that shot a beam of light at a "bad guy" with mask that you'd set up across the room. If you hit the right spot on this guy with your light beam, he'd fall over. So they were playing this with all of our company. I was the only one that couldn't seem to get the hang of it, but I didn't care. It was just so great having everyone there.

There was something almost magical about that evening. I wish I could better describe it – a sense of good fellowship, peace perhaps. "Peace on earth, good will to men." Maybe that's what we were feeling. But looking back, I see the contradictions. If it hadn't been for the Cold War, probably none of us would have been there. We were the peacekeepers.

The party finally started to break up around ten or ten-thirty, I think. People seemed reluctant to leave. The Becks were the last to go, and I remember Dan's mother taking our hands and telling us how much they had enjoyed the evening, especially after feeling a bit disoriented at being in a German hotel earlier on Christmas day.

"But being here with all of you tonight was almost like being at home again," Dan's mom told us. "This may be one of the best Christmases we've ever had. Thank you *so much* for inviting us."

It was perhaps one of our best Christmases ever too. Just being with all those people – friends – made it so. I for one will never forget it – sharing the night together.

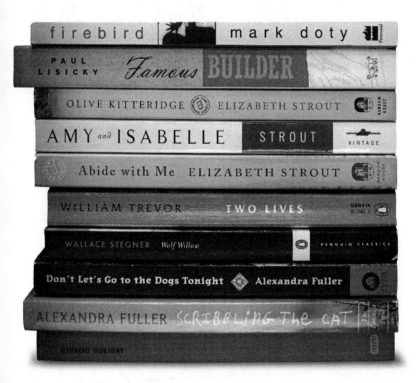

March 5, 2009

Today is tax day for us. We have an appointment after lunch with our accountant, Patrick Kailing. I hate taxes, but figure it's the price of admission for living here in the U.S., which may have its problems, but I wouldn't want to live anywhere else. And they say the only certain things in this life are death and taxes. I'll take taxes.

Let's talk a little more about our life in Augsburg. We got there in early March of 1978. Treve and the boys had been living with her folks since August of '77. She'd gotten Jeff and Scott into Savage Elementary School just a mile or so down the road from her parents' place on Martinsville Road, and they'd made some friends and seemed to be thriving there, possibly deriving a bit of cachet from having lived in California for over a year.

I'm sure it wasn't an automatic easy adjustment for Chet and Wanda, having their daughter and her two children move back in with them for several months, but I can't remember them ever complaining about it. There was only one unpleasant occurrence during that period. I remember Treve calling me at Fort Meade to tell me that she and the boys had "moved out" and were staying with a friend of hers. She and her dad had had an argument over something one night that escalated into some nasty shouting, so she just packed up the kids in their pajamas and threw a few things in a bag and left the house. I was really upset about it and asked her if she wanted me to fly home and bring them back to Maryland with me, but she assured me she'd work it out. And she did, undoubtedly through the intercession of her mom. I think they were all back at the Zimmers after a few days. But in the meantime I passed some anxious hours worrying about "the situation at home." I can vividly remember riding the shuttle bus from our barracks to class at the NSA complex one morning soon after Treve's call and watching a blood-red sun come up, and the words from this old song by a one-hit group called Cyrkle suddenly popped into my head.

And I think it's gonna be all right
Yeah, the worst is over now

The morning sun is shining
Like a red rubber ball ...

I know I'd been praying hard about it all, and somehow those dumb song lyrics and that rising sun seemed like a sign, and gave me comfort. In any case, as I soon learned, it seemed the worst *was* over and things got better in Belleville.

The truth was Chet loved having the two boys living there. Treve still remembers how he used to look forward to their return from school each day, and would even go out and stand at the foot of the driveway to meet the school bus. Grandma would have a snack ready for them and Grandpa could hardly wait to see what kind of homework they might have so he could help them with it. He especially liked helping them with their math. He might not have known how the "new math" worked, but he knew how to solve a problem, which may have caused a few problems with the kids' teachers, but Chet's heart was certainly in the right place.

This interest in the boys and their homework was a source of some surprise to Treve, because when she'd been a kid in school her dad was never around much. He was always at the Ford plant, working – and not just normal hours, but all the overtime and double time he could get too. But she shouldn't have been surprised. Chet's kids had all grown up and moved away practically before he realized it, he had been so busy. Now that he was retired he had time to spend with these grandsons who'd been suddenly dropped in his lap, so to speak. And he loved it.

This made our leave-taking in March all the more wrenching for all concerned. I will never forget saying good-bye to Chet and Wanda that day in March. Wanda was openly crying and so was Treve. Chet was struggling, his face so stern that he looked angry. But by the time we got everyone in the car and began to back out of the driveway, there were silent tears running down his craggy furrowed cheeks too as he and Wanda waved good-bye to us from the side porch. My own eyes were filled with tears too and I think Treve and I were actually unable to speak until we'd gotten past Toledo and onto the Ohio Turnpike. We both figured it would probably be at least three years before we saw them again. As it turned out, Treve flew home from Germany with Suzie about a year later for a two-week visit so her folks could meet their new granddaughter, who was about six months old by then.

Jeff and Scott probably still have some fragmented and pleasant memories of our first couple weeks in Augsburg during which we were billeted in the American Hotel, which was actually a traditional German hotel which was owned or leased by the U.S. to serve as transient quarters for military families. I also remember spending a couple of nights at another American hotel in Frankfurt, where the Replacement Depot or "Repo Depo" was located. Once I'd gotten my orders cut and approved and stamped there, we took a train to Augsburg.

At the hotel in Augsburg we were given a double room, which was quite a large area with two double beds and a couple big bureaus for our clothes. The hotel had a restaurant where the army paid for all our meals, and the food was just excellent. Treve and I looked forward to supper every night, and I think we may have tried nearly everything on the menu during our stay there. Our favorite entrée, which we sampled several times, was the cordon bleu, which I don't think either of us had ever tasted before then. We also liked the homemade German noodles, called *Spaetzle*, which was usually served as a heaping side dish with another house specialty, *Wiener Schnitzel*. During our three years in Augsburg we would often order this delicious combo at another local restaurant called Lamb's, located not far from our apartment.

I remember that the staff at the hotel were all super solicitous with all of their guests, bringing us fresh linens twice a week and even offering to make up the beds, but Treve always preferred to do that herself. She remembers how pampered and indolent she felt during those days, lounging on the bed reading magazines during the day and taking just a short stroll down the hall to the restaurant (our room was on the main floor) for a leisurely lunch while the boys were at school. The kitchen staff prepared brown bag lunches for all the school age kids to take with them each day, and even gave them a choice of sandwiches and desserts to pack.

There was a barber in the hotel, and haircuts were very reasonably priced – probably subsidized by the military. I got my hair cut there once, and both Jeff and Scott got their very first barber shop haircuts there from Hans the barber. Jeff was almost nine and Scott was six, and up until that time only Treve had cut their hair. They both thought it was very cool to sit in a real barber chair in a real shop, instead of in our kitchen.

The kids got those haircuts just before Palm Sunday. We found out there was a Catholic church just a few blocks away from the hotel, so Sunday morning we all put on clean clothes and walked down to the church, an impressively old and huge stone edifice. We got there just before Mass began and found seats in one of the side sections of the knave. It was an educational and memorable experience for us small town folks. First of all, when we entered the church we were each handed a stalk of pussy willow, not palms. Then when we took our places in the pews and started looking around we noticed that everyone – everyone except us – was dressed to the nines. Suits and ties were standard for the men, and the women were all in tailored dresses or suits, with hats and even quite a few furs. And looking around the church in the moments before the processional we were also a bit nervous to note that our two boys seemed to be the only children in church. But then the processional began and we did see some children in choir-robe-type outfits carrying pussy willows come in as part of the whole shebang – but not very many. And the *music*. It just blew us away. It was not the organ we expected to hear, there in the land of Bach, but instead a resoundingly majestic brass section held forth: trumpets, trombones, tubas and a few things I didn't recognize. It was really amazing. The service was conducted in German, but the rituals were the same. We made our Sunday duty and got a lesson in how the Germans did things in Church. We did feel a bit out of place in our American dressed-down state and being the only ones there with kids, but the people were very pleasant, and we received quite a few smiles and *Gruss Gotts* as we exited the church after mass to head back to the hotel for brunch.

It was our first and only Pussy Willow Sunday.

We did not have a private bathroom in the hotel. There were communal toilets and showers, one for men and one for women. So I would take the boys for their showers every couple days, which was also kind of a new experience for them. But what they were most fascinated by were the German-style toilets and the way they were designed. They noticed right away that their poop didn't plop directly into the water in the commode. It fell instead onto a kind of shelf at the front of the ceramic stool, and then was washed off and down the drain into the water when you pulled the overhead chain. For some reason both the boys found this both fascinating and funny, and seemed to want to go crap more often than they might have usually, purely for the entertainment value, I'm sure. Ain't it funny the stuff you remember when you have kids?

A school bus came to the front door of the hotel each weekday morning to pick up the kids and take them to the American school over near the Cramerton apartments, where we would end up being assigned permanent quarters after two weeks in the hotel.

I was busy during those two weeks with all kinds of annoying paperwork that came with every PCS (permanent change of station) in the military. Our car had been put on a boat in New Jersey, but would not arrive in Bremerhaven for another two to three weeks, so I was mostly on foot or riding shuttle buses back and forth between various offices on four different small installations, or *Kasernes*, scattered about town. I was assigned to the 1st Operations Battalion, which was on Sheridan Kaserne, but I had to schlep paperwork back and forth between there and Flak Kaserne and another one, the name escapes me now. And the operations building was outside of town on Gablingen Kaserne. I found out within a few days after arriving in Augsburg that in order to be eligible for government family housing (Cramerton) I needed to extend my enlistment another year. This might have made me angry, but there had been hints about this before we'd left the states, so I sucked it up and made yet another trip to some admin office and signed the necessary paperwork for the extension. It seemed to rain nearly every day and somewhere in the midst of all this I came down with a bad case of the flu, which affected me at both ends. I bought a box of Pepto-Bismol chewable tablets to carry in my pocket, and made sure every time I had business in a building that was new to me that the first room I located was the latrine (which is military for the crapper, in case you didn't know). It was kind of a miserable time for me, but at least we had a place to sleep and everyone was eating well. And the boys had taken pooping to a new level of fun with those funny German toilets with a shelf and a chain.

The apartment we finally got after a couple weeks was fine. It was so great to finally have our own bathroom again with a shower *and* a tub, and a normal American-style toilet too. We had three roomy bedrooms a large living room and dining room and a small-ish galley style kitchen. There were certain disadvantages and idiosyncrasies of the place to get used to but we were happy to be settling in again and making a home. We were on the third floor of a four story building, but the space over us was empty – used for storage and parties (which didn't happen very often, thank God). So it was a lot of steps to carry groceries, but we were still pretty young and didn't notice it that much. Well, maybe Treve did for those first several months, since she was about three and a half months pregnant when we arrived, and the laundry room (which had several washers and dryers used by six families) was down in the basement, as was our personal goods storage closet. Our household goods arrived quickly after we'd moved in. The only furniture we had shipped was our king-size bed, a TV and stereo. Everything else was just boxes of clothes, books, records, toys and miscellaneous stuff. The army provided us with any furniture that we wanted. So we had a couch and a couple of chairs, a whole dining room set and bunk beds for the boys brought in. After Suzie was born, we bought a new gold plush rocker-recliner at the PX. That chair got used nearly to death. Treve sat in it to nurse Suzie and rock her. And the boys liked to settle into it and rock it like a bucking bronco while they listened to music. It was the most comfy seat in the house.

The only thing we were missing to make the new place home was Heidi, our dog. Once we were moved in though, we wrote Treve's folks and made arrangements for them to ship her by air freight and we picked her up in Munich. We all drove down to the airport there to pick her up. Our vet back home had suggested a sedative for her for the trip, which was a pretty long one for a little twenty-nine pound dog in a crate. So when her crate was finally brought out to us and we got her out, she was pitiful to behold, very wobbly on her feet, although she tried her best to wag and greet us. But by that night, after we got her home, she was fine again, and she made the apartment seem even more like home. Dogs can do that, ya know. Maybe it's those little dust-bunnies of dog hair that you find wisping about in all the corners and behind doors. In any case, our family was finally all together again.

Speaking of Heidi made me remember another unusual event our first year in Augsburg. Like all of our dogs have done, Heidi slept pretty much anywhere she chose to at night – sometimes in the boys' room, sometimes in the living room, but since she was more Treve's dog than anyone else's, she usually chose to sleep in our room, either on the foot of the bed, or sometimes next to the bed or even under it.

One morning about two weeks after Suzie was born, we were awake early, around 5:30. We had Suzie in a bassinet in our room, and Treve had just taken her out and was sitting up in bed nursing her. I was about half-asleep beside her when the bed began to vibrate just slightly. Still groggy with sleep, I raised my head to look over at Treve and the baby.

"Is Heidi under the bed?" I asked Treve, thinking maybe the dog was down there scratching herself, causing the bed to shake.

"I don't know," she replied, looking a little uneasy herself.

Just then Heidi came in the bedroom door from the hall, whining and glancing around behind her, then came over and jumped up on the foot of the bed, which was still moving.

I sat up and looked around the room. "What the hell ...?" I said.

Suddenly there was a steady tinkling sound coming from the vanity across the room and we looked over and saw that the vanity was vibrating too, and all Treve's little makeup bottles and perfumes were jiggling and bumping and tinkling.

"*Jee*-zus!" I exclaimed, jumping out of bed. "I think it's an *earth*quake!"

Treve's eyes were huge as she continued to nurse the baby. "*No*," she said. "It *can't* be."

Then it stopped. The shaking and vibration were gone. I went into the boys' room. They were still sleeping soundly. I stalked through the house, looking out all the windows at the early morning sky. But I saw nothing to explain this eerie movement of the building, of the *earth*, maybe. I came back into the bedroom where Treve continued to nurse the baby. "What should we do?" she asked.

"Nothing, I guess. It seems to be over."

But I couldn't sleep after that, so I got dressed and took Heidi with me down the stairs and outside. It was already quite light out and another guy from the building across the parking lot was coming out too. I didn't know him, but we both looked across uncertainly at each other, probably both wondering the same thing. I asked him, "Hey, did you just *feel* something a few minutes ago?"

"Yeah, I sure did," he replied. "You felt it too, huh? My wife said I was crazy."

"I think it was an earthquake," I said.

"Me too," he agreed. "Not a very big one, I guess, but it was a little spooky, wasn't it?"

"Yeah."

Then he got in his car and drove away. I followed Heidi out into the field and watched while she took care of her morning business. Then we went back inside together.

The next day I read in the paper that there had indeed been an earthquake. There were photographs of buildings split in half with furniture hanging crazily out into thin air from the damaged structures and crowds of people standing in the street. The pictures were taken in Stuttgart, I think.

It did indeed seem crazy to us. We had recently lived for more than a year in fault-ridden quake-prone California and never felt even the tiniest tremor. And now after less than a year in Germany, we had experienced our first earthquake.

Tonight I got on-line and Googled "earthquake Germany 1978" just for grins, and by golly I found out just exactly what we'd felt that morning over thirty years ago. On the morning of September 3, 1978, an earthquake of a 5.2 magnitude shook southwest Germany. Its epicenter was just south of Stuttgart in the small town of Albstadt, which is, I believe, approximately a hundred miles west of Augsburg. The damage was estimated at fifty million U.S. dollars.

Nope, it wasn't Heidi scratching herself under the bed. As Carol King so famously sang, we had just "felt the earth move under [our] feet."

March 11, 2009

Yup, I've been loafing again. No excuse. Except, of course, the usual one. All those good books to read. And I've read a few since I last logged onto this journal. But no matter.

Let's jump backwards again, to DLI again – happy times, for the most part. I successfully completed the basic Russian course shortly before Christmas of 1976. I finished either second or third in my class, I can't remember for sure anymore. Steve Egbert and Chuck Squires were right up there with me; Steve was the honor graduate who got the promotion to E-5, as I've already told you. But there was another reason that we were so anxious to do well in that initial course. We were all competing, we thought, for slots in the special intermediate Russian class that would begin in January. I say "we thought," because we found out sometime in the last part of our basic course that only a small number of us were actually interested in getting into this add-on accelerated course. Because, unless you were prior service, an extension on your enlistment was required to qualify for this extra seven or eight months of training. And few of our young first-timer classmates were much interested in extending their enlistments. So the new class that began in January of 1977 was a small one, just six men, and four of us – Egbert, Squires, Steve Davidson and I – were all prior service. The other two, Joe Jenkins and Bob Protosevich, were on their first enlistment, but both were smart enough to recognize the value of the additional training they would receive. The six of us would remain together as a group for the next fourteen months. We would leave Monterey in August, but then we spent three months at Goodfellow Air Force Base in San Angelo, Texas, and another four months at Fort Meade, Maryland, for additional technical training. If you've been paying attention here, then you've probably figured out that I was in a training status for over two years before I finally went overseas and began to practice my new trade.

The add-on intermediate Russian course was called the LeFoxe program, and I can't remember anymore why. I think it had something to do with the equipment we operated once we got overseas. And when we finally did get our orders we were split up. Three of us went to Augsburg and the other three went to Field Station Berlin.

Shortly after our class began, another student was added. Fawn Trowbridge was a civilian, a Russian major who was, if I remember correctly – and I may not – a grad student from UC at Santa Cruz, just up the road a piece from Monterey. I remember feeling a bit uneasy initially about sharing a classroom with a graduate student who'd already had four years of Russian, wondering if I'd be able to "compete" with someone who'd done all that study. I suspect maybe the other guys might have had similar thoughts. But we needn't have worried. First of all, Fawn was a very friendly and personable young lady, and we all quickly developed an easy rapport with her both in and out of the classroom. But what surprised us the most was learning that our just-completed nine months of intensive study had put us not only on a par with a grad student in Russian, but actually gave us an advantage. Our understanding of the language was probably superior to Fawn's, at least when we first began. We suddenly began to fully appreciate the quality of the instruction we had been receiving at DLI, and to this day I believe that there is probably no other school in the U.S. that will provide you with a better understanding of a foreign language in such a short time. Fawn was a very bright girl though, and if she had been behind us, it didn't take her long to catch up. The LeFoxe class of 1977 was an extremely competitive environment. We were "immersed" in the language and the culture, and I know that all seven of us pretty much worked our asses off learning as much Russian as we possibly could for the next several months. I think our classes were from eight to noon, with a one-hour lunch break, and then more classes from one until four. Five days a week, studying nothing but Russian for six to seven hours a day, with lists of vocabulary to take home and learn, tapes to listen to, recitations to memorize, compositions to write, translations to do. Our teacher for those seven months was a lovely single lady of indeterminate age, perhaps fifty-ish, named Lyubov' Yakovleva. Her Christian name is Russian for Love, and it suited her. She was always extremely patient with us, and I think we all grew to love "Lyuba" before we were finished. Her English was a very precise British English – learned,

I believe, at Cambridge. Not only did she correct our much mangled Russian, she also, on occasion, corrected our English. I can still remember a very odd English idiom she used: "Well, dog my cats!" We told her there was no such phrase, but she insisted that it was a common one. Many years later I learned that she was probably right and we were wrong. I heard that very phrase used by the British actor, Arthur Treacher, in a Shirley Temple film from the thirties. Ms. Yakovleva was an excellent teacher, and we were lucky to have her. But learning Russian was a full time job, no question, and we buckled down and worked.

But somehow we found time to play too. Some of us would get together on occasion for pot luck suppers. I remember one Friday or Saturday night when we had a pot luck supper and played "Name that Tune" at our apartment. Chuck and Jake were there, as were Steve and Kathy Egbert, Steve and Cathy Davidson, and Joe and Lou Jenkins. We had various dips and chips and Egberts brought a mess of abalone and showed us how to fry it in oil and everyone thought it delicious. I know I did. I had spent a couple of weekends putting together a homemade "tune" tape from my record collection and we spent the next couple of hours in this more pleasant form of competition, remembering old songs which triggered myriad memories which were shared, and we all got to know each other a little better.

Music has always been important to me, of course, and I can also remember my first visit to Tower Records in San Francisco. Tower was once one of the premiere chains of music stores, operating not just in the U.S. but in several foreign countries as well. But I do remember well once making a day trip to Frisco with our LeFoxe class, where we visited a Russian Orthodox church with its onion-shaped domes on the outside and colorful statues and icons inside. I can't remember what else we might have done as a class that day, because it was all overshadowed by the trip I made at the end of the day with Chuck to the Tower Records store at the corner of Bay and Columbus.

Chuck and I had driven up together purposely so we could shop a little after the class activity was over. One of the things both Treve and I admired about Chuck was that he seemed absolutely fearless about driving in places he was unfamiliar with. He and Jake had recently traded in their pickup for a shiny new banana-yellow VW Rabbit with a five-speed and diesel engine. You may remember that there were flare-ups of gas shortages and gas price increases throughout much of the seventies, so diesel engine passenger cars became quite fashionable, and, since diesel fuel was actually cheaper than gasoline then, they were also economical.

But even Chuck was a bit challenged maneuvering up and down the steep hills of San Francisco that day, particularly when we encountered stop signs or traffic lights at the top of a hill. I can still remember him revving the engine and rocking back and forth, using the clutch, hoping like hell he wouldn't stall and roll backward into the cars behind him. But he didn't. And we made it to Tower that afternoon.

That store seemed like the promised land for music lovers and record collectors, with its rows and rows of record bins in long aisles which seemed to stretch almost to infinity. Several times larger than Monterey's Odyssey Records, I think the store may have been a supermarket in an earlier life; it was that huge – and *filled* with records. I was absolutely overwhelmed, and I hadn't brought a list of what I'd like, so I was moving manically from aisle to aisle and flipping frantically through the endless choices. I know I found a couple new records by Cliff Richard, an artist I'd discovered during my first army tour back in the sixties. Cliff, now "Sir" Cliff Richard, was touted as "the English Elvis" from his beginnings back in the late fifties. He has been a force on the British music scene for over fifty years now, but never really quite caught on here in the U.S., except for a few widely scattered Top 40 hits. One of them, "Devil Woman," was on his *I'm Nearly Famous* album, which I'd bought at Odyssey on Cannery Row. And years later he had a duet or two with Olivia Newton-John that also made the charts. And I may have picked up a Jesse Winchester album called *Nothin' But a Breeze* that day too. Winchester was a talented musician who was perhaps most famous in those days for eluding the draft by moving to Canada. My hour or so at Tower that day was both exhilarating and frustrating. There was simply not time enough to look at everything; and

I certainly didn't have enough money to buy all I'd have liked to. Hard choices. Years later, when we lived in Maryland, the Tower Records in Annapolis became one of my favorite places to visit. All of those stores are gone now, bankrupt and shuttered back in 2006. Records – the real stuff, *vinyl* – have, of course, been pretty much gone much longer than that. Also gone are the short-lived eight-track tapes that were popular in the mid-seventies. In their case, good riddance. But I still miss the ebony elegance of vinyl and the larger cover art and more easily read liner notes that accompanied records. At one time I owned a collection of nearly two thousand albums. No more. I got rid of most of them when I retired. After hauling many of them halfway around the world and back, I finally decided enough. I had begun my CD collection by then. More than half of my record collection ended up stacked in boxes on a loading dock outside a Salvation Army store in Glen Burnie, Maryland. It felt kinda like "the day the music died" all over again, but I'd made up my mind I was not going to haul them all from Maryland to Michigan. Nope. Enough. *No mas.*

That trip to Tower with Chuck lives on in my memory though. And Chuck figures in another important musical memory too. In the spring of 1977 I learned that Rick Nelson was doing a concert at the Catalyst, a night club in Santa Cruz. I told Chuck about it and he never even missed a beat. "Wow! Ricky Nelson? Let's go. I'll drive." That was Chuck. I forgave him for not knowing that it was "Rick" in 1977, that he hadn't been "Ricky" for more than twenty years. After all, Rick hadn't had a Top 40 hit for several years by that time. Not since his comeback song, "Garden Party," which he'd written after a disastrous appearance at Madison Square Garden when he'd been booed for his long hair and new music. The crowd in New York was there for an oldies show that night; they'd wanted Ricky, not Rick.

So Treve and I crammed ourselves into the back seat of that yellow Rabbit with Chuck and Jake up front and headed for Santa Cruz that Saturday night. I brought along about a dozen of my Rick Nelson albums, hoping I could get them signed.

It was a long night. Rick and his Stone Canyon Band were scheduled for two shows, an eight o'clock and a later one. We got there for the early show, but no Rick. The club was only half full, so I think the band wanted to wait for a full house. There was a house band playing while we waited for the main attraction. I didn't remember them, but I recently exchanged a couple e-mails with Chuck and he did.

"And the first band was The Skunk Band, from San Francisco," he wrote, and I could almost hear him laughing as he wrote it.

Whoever they were, they were forgettable. Finally they packed up and cleared the stage though, and the musicians from Rick's band came on stage and began setting up their equipment. I recognized the steel guitar player, Tom Brumley, from pictures I had on my albums. (Yes, there was a steel guitar in Rick Nelson's band, which was the epitome of the California country-rock sound, very much like the Eagles.) So I went up to the stage and talked with Tom and showed him the albums I'd brought. Brumley, who was an older guy with a kind of blonde comb-over to hide his badly receding hairline, looked at the albums, some of them bought in Germany in the sixties, and told me to come backstage when the concert was over, and he'd introduce me to Rick.

Holy crap! I was gonna meet Rick Nelson!

I was thirty-three years old in 1977, but I had been a Rick Nelson fan since he'd been Ricky. Since his first hit single, a cover of Fats Domino's hit, "I'm Walkin'," in 1957. And now, after twenty years of listening to his music, I was going to shake his hand, talk with him.

I did not watch the TV show that made the Nelson family famous when I was a kid. *The Adventures of Ozzie & Harriett* was not featured on any of the two and a half channels we received on our early black and white TV sets in the fifties. I knew about the show, but I never saw it until many years later when it showed up in syndication. But I remember finding Rick's first record among the new 45s at DeWitt's Radio and TV, which was the only store in Reed City that had a decent assortment of popular music. "I'm Walkin'" was on Verve, a label famous for its jazz. I'm not quite sure how that happened. But I didn't care. I loved it from the first time I heard its big BOMP-BOMP BOMP-A-DOMP-A-DOMP intro notes. I already knew the words, of course, from the Domino version. But this was different. Because Rick wasn't black, and he wasn't some older guy. He was just a kid, like I was, and I think that was a major part of his appeal to kids all over the U.S. His parents' radio and TV shows, where he'd been part of the cast since 1949, provided him with an immediate audience and, for the next five or six years, everything Ricky Nelson touched turned to gold. His picture was constantly on the covers of nearly every teen magazine published in the late fifties and early sixties. While Elvis was in the army, Nelson dominated the charts and was the most popular singer in America. After an unprecedented string of hits with Imperial from 1957 through 1962, Rick signed a twenty-year million-dollar contract with Decca records, after which his career began to fade, particularly in the face of the Beatles and the "British invasion" which began in 1964. He kept on making records, but people weren't buying them. Except for me. I have most of them. Even the ones no one remembers.

When Rick and the Stone Canyon Band finally came on, it was close to ten o'clock. We'd been there for nearly three hours already. But the club was packed by then. The whole place suddenly went completely dark while the band made their way onstage. Then the announcement blared through the dark: *Ladies and gentlemen, Rick Nelson and the Stone Canyon Band!* Then the lights came up and the band thundered into their opening number, one of Rick's classic rockers, "Believe What You Say."

The truth is I don't remember a whole lot about the concert itself. It was loud like thunder though, and it seemed everyone was on their feet for the whole hour-plus that the band performed. I know they did a lot of Rick's old hits and also some soft country-rock numbers from his later period, songs like "Easy to Be Free" and Dylan's "She Belongs to Me" and "Sky Pilot" – tunes from the *In Concert* and *Rudy the Fifth* albums. I know the show went by all too quickly, but I knew that I was going to meet the man when it was over.

And I did. Brumley came out and got us and took us backstage and introduced us all to Rick. Treve and I both had our pictures taken with him and he took his time looking over the albums I had brought for him to sign, lingering over a few on the Brunswick label I had bought in Kassel in 1964.

"I don't think I've ever seen these covers before," he told me. "Cool, though."

Maybe it seems like I'm making too much out of this short meeting, but I'd been listening and singing along to Rick Nelson's records for twenty years by then, from when I was thirteen, so it was a big deal for me. You're probably supposed to outgrow stuff like that, but there was something about Rick Nelson and his music that kept me a loyal fan, even after his star faded. He was that good, white-bread kid, a lot like me. I know there were stories about his being a coke-head and a druggie in the later years of his life. I don't know if they were true or not. I guess I don't care. I still listen to his music on occasion, and I still remember the night I shook his hand and we talked for a few minutes about music and records. I know that most people think of the plane crash that killed Buddy Holly, Richie Valens and the Big Bopper as "the day the music died," but for me it happened all over again with the plane crash in Texas that took Rick Nelson on New Year's Eve 1985.

Ain't if funny the things that stand out in your memory? Chuck and Jake Squires, Treve and I – and Rick Nelson – Santa Cruz, 1977.

March 12, 2009

I'm back, and I didn't wait until after supper today. It's actually still morning. Brought my wife her coffee already this morning – twice, in fact. Sat in my chair by the front window with my own and wrote a few notes in my daily journal, which I've been keeping for about five years now, and watched the sun come up. Our two dogs, Daisy and Barney, are always hovering nearby during this time, because after they've been let out and back in they know it's "cookie time." They get a small ration of dry kibble in the morning to keep them until their main meal of the day, around five o'clock. Daisy always scarfs this breakfast down as fast as she can upon coming back in. She has no clue about higher things like deferred satisfaction. Barney, our smaller dog, apparently does. He usually tries to beg a biscuit or two from me before he goes back out in the kitchen to eat his kibble. And he's so damn cute he usually succeeds. He's so fat he waddles, which makes me feel guilty. Barney has always been big for his breed. He's a Tibetan Spaniel. But with all these extra snacks, his butt – and all the rest of him too – is just plain too big.

Treve was watching the news this morning and learned that *Sesame Street* has been hit by this recession in the form of a twenty percent reduction in staff. I sure hope they didn't dump Bert and Ernie, or Big Bird. I wonder if Oscar got the sack. He was always a bit prickly, ya know. Too grouchy for his own good.

Yesterday I took our car over to Crossroads Chevrolet to have it checked out. For the past couple of months the air bag warning light has been coming on intermittently, along with an ominous menu message, SERVICE AIR BAG. We haven't run into anything, so I don't know what's wrong. I sat around the waiting room for an hour or so, and then the service manager, Travis, told me they couldn't figure out the problem and would have to call a tech rep in Detroit after lunch to try to get some advice. So another young fellow, Adam, gave me a ride home. One of the nice things about living in a small town like this is that "six degrees of separation" thing. I learned Adam's last name is Erbes. His grandfather is Garth Erbes, who is the older brother of Lamont. Lamont and his wife, Nancy (Hays) were both in my class in high school. I don't think that's even six degrees, actually. More like three. Adam is a good-looking young guy who bears a striking resemblance to the actor, Noah Wyle, who has played Dr. Carter on the TV show *ER* for the past fifteen years or so. Of course he looks like Wyle did when the show started, not like he does now. I told my wife this. She's a big fan of the show, and Wyle in particular. She was disappointed that she missed Adam when he brought our car back to us later that afternoon, when they determined they needed to order a part.

Travis Wekenman, the service manager, was another of those "six degrees" cases. His grandmother is Esther Wekenman, whom I see in church just about every weekend. His dad is Neal, brother to Brian, who died probably twenty years ago or more, way too young.

Meeting Travis got me to thinking about Brian, who worked alongside me nearly forty years ago at a summer job on a pipeline. It was the summer of 1970 and I had just completed my master's degree at CMU. I had landed a teaching position in Monroe starting in September, but I needed to make some money in the meantime. I also had to move my family – Treve and our year-old baby, Jeff – out of married student housing at Central. I borrowed an old pickup from my cousin, Dan Whalen, who was a Michigan State trooper posted in Mount Pleasant at the time, and piled most of our stuff in it and hauled it downstate to store at my in-laws' home in Belleville for the summer. Then we moved in with my folks in Reed City – a temporary arrangement, of course. I had gotten my old summer job back with the Great Lakes Gas Transmission Company (GLGTC) at their Lake George pumping station located out in the middle of the woods north of Farwell. Brian Wekenman had a job there that summer too. He had either just graduated from college or was a senior that year, I can't remember. He'd been on an athletic scholarship out in the Dakotas somewhere. He probably got the job through his uncle, Jack Rolston, who was a full-time regular employee there.

I had worked on the pipeline the first time during the summer of 1968, between my junior and senior year at Central. (The summer of 1969 I was already in grad school.) I can't remember how I happened to get the job, but I was grateful to find it, as it was my first "married" summer and I felt a heavy responsibility to be an adult – to be "responsible" and provide for my bride. The company tried to hire a couple of students each summer, I think. I was one and the other one in 1968 was Alford Collins, another CMU student. I located Al this past year. And recently I phoned him. He's retired now after a long career as a design engineer with Ford. I was afraid he wouldn't remember me, since we only worked together for those three months and then never saw each other after that, since he was a math and science major and I was in English, so we were never in any of the same buildings at Central. I needn't have worried. As soon as I identified myself and mentioned we'd worked together forty years ago at GLGTC, he responded, "Yup. I painted the white, you painted the red."

He was talking about the cedar posts we spent much of that summer painting, to be used as markers along the pipeline from the Straits of Mackinac all the way down to St. Clair, just north of Detroit. It didn't take Al and me very long to find something in common. We were both veterans. He'd done four years in the Air Force. Veterans can always find a common bond. The branch of service doesn't matter. We all have our own "war stories" and other lies to tell each other.

But we went beyond the usual war stories that summer. I was still pretty newly married and Al, who was a few years older than I, was about to be married. In fact, he was living that summer with his soon-to-be in-laws on their farm north of Midland. His fiancée's family had emigrated from Germany in 1954, after fleeing the advancing Russian army in East Prussia during the war. We talked a lot about our families that summer. I told him all about growing up in Reed City, and about Treve and how we met at Ferris; and he talked about his girl, Traudy (Waltraud; at the time I was so dumb I thought he was calling her "Troutie," which I thought an odd nickname) Spittka, and how he grew up "here and there," the son of Baptist ministers. I can't remember anymore what he might have told me back in '68 and what he told me this past summer when we talked on the phone and exchanged a few e-mails. Al's boyhood was not a very easy one. Here's what he had to say about it last year.

My parents were both Moody Bible Institute graduates,
who graduated back in the early '30s. They were both
conservative evangelical fundamental Baptists and reared
my sister and me to be the same. My father's forlorn cry
before he took the belt down from the nail on the kitchen
wall and "laid the belt to me" was, "What are you trying to
do, drive me out of the ministry?" This helped to establish
my priorities and show me where the "family" stood in
relation to the "ministry." But then he told me how his
father beat him with a buggy whip for cutting across the
corner of his neighbor's farm when walking home from
school one day. So rearing children changed a lot from the
1920s to the 1940s. What was acceptable as normal was
later sometimes called cruel behavior …

Al told me too how he had moved around a lot as a kid,
following his father's many ministerial jobs. He lived in little
towns in Indiana and Michigan during the fifties and went to
three different high schools in four years, finally graduating
when he lived in Ocqueoc, Michigan, which he called "the
small town of small towns."

It consisted of a T in the county road. At the T there were
four houses, a bier [sic] garden and combination post office,
gas station and general store. We lived a half mile out of
town between the state forest fire tower and Ocqueoc Gospel
Assembly church, where my dad was the pastor. Here I
was graduated from high school [1959], then graduated
from Moody Bible Institute [1962], and graduated from the
USAF [1962-1966] …

Traudy, Al's wife now – maybe I should add "still," in light
of the fleeting nature of many of today's marriages – spoke no
English when she arrived in the U.S. with her parents and four
siblings. But she quickly learned it, "the hard way, by living
it in school." She did well in high school and then moved to
Canada, where she worked for seven years and saved her
money for college. She moved back to Michigan to attend
CMU, where she met Al, just back from Vietnam and freshly
discharged from the Air Force.

Traudy laughed at the way I swung my arms when I walked
(12 inches to the rear to 15 inches to the front) and how

I pivoted on my "outside" foot to make a "square corner" when coming up to her house. I remember thinking that "parade rest" did not seem to be appropriate when I was talking to her, but I didn't know what else to do with my arms. We went to the First Baptist Church of Mount Pleasant together, sang in the choir together, and had many a pizza from Giovanni's together. She worked in the CMU Biology Department as a secretary and I worked in the adjacent Physics Department as a laboratory assistant. We were married in September 1968 and found a nice set of rooms at 219 North Fancher to live in. I graduated in 1969 and began my career at Ford Motor Company as a design engineer ...

If you're wondering why I'm including all this stuff about Al Collins, a guy I only knew for a few months forty years ago, it's because I just loved the way he told it. I sense a natural story-teller in Al. Have you ever stopped to consider how many wonderful and interesting stories there are out there that never get told, or at least never get written down? Al's story is simply a good one, so I thought I'd share this little bit of it.

And I *will* get back to Brian Wekenman and the summer we worked together. I promise.

Red and white. Those were the colors we painted cedar posts for most of the summer of 1968. I would paint the whole post white, then Al would paint the top foot or so of it a bright red. And sometimes we'd trade jobs. And yes, it was excruciatingly boring at times, but we found ways to amuse ourselves. Mostly we talked. And I think I may have brought along my little Sony transistor radio so we could listen to some music too. Al was a very funny guy, who possessed an outrageously irreverent and quirky sense of humor, especially when you consider he'd grown up with Baptist ministers for parents and had attended Bible college himself. I think by the time I met him, he may have been distancing himself at least a little from all that strictness. And although I can't remember any more what we laughed *about*, I do know that we laughed a *lot* that summer.

There was one day in particular that I remember. I think perhaps I had seen something on TV that involved some acrobats or something, because I was telling Al about it, how these people did this balancing thing on a round pipe or cylinder. It gave us the idea that we should try it ourselves. We had the necessary materials right at hand there in the shop where we were working – scrap plywood and all those cedar posts. We found a piece of plywood that was probably about two by three feet and we set it on top of a post that was lying on the floor. The object of this trick was to stand on the board and balance it on the post, which required a constant rocking motion to keep your balance and to keep the post from rolling out from under the board. It looked easy when I saw it on TV, and Al agreed, sure we could probably do that.

"Here," Al said. "You go first. I'll hold the board in place while you step up onto it."

Yeah, right. "You go first." But I wasn't thinking that at the time. I was simply intrigued by the mechanics required to stay balanced on the log, so I stepped up onto the board. Al let go, the log let go, and down I went, *ker-splat* right onto the concrete floor of the shop. Holy *CRAP*, did that hurt! I tried to throw out my arms to break my fall, but only succeeded in spraining a wrist and still went right down on one side. It was one of those *OW! OW! OW!* kinda moments. At first I couldn't even catch my breath it hurt so much, besides which the wind was knocked completely out of me. I lay there on floor gasping for breath and muttering *ah, ah, ah* weakly. I didn't have enough wind for the *OW's*. Al was torn between concern for me and laughing at how quickly I'd gone down.

"Tim, are you okay?" he asked, giggling just a little.

"*ah, ah, ah* – you *bas*tard!" I managed to get out between gasps.

"Jeez, I'm *sor*ry," he said, then sputtered a little more.

After a few moments, I was finally able to sit up, but it hurt like the devil. "Okay," I said, gritting my teeth against the pain. "Your turn."

"Ooh no," Al said. "You think I wanna bust *my* ass like that? No way, man!" Then he allowed himself a good laugh. "*Man*, did you go down *fast!* I thought you'd manage a couple seconds at least. But wow! *BAM!* That was *somethin'*, man!"

More hearty nervous laughter.

Although I soon agreed with Al about what a sight I must have presented, as well as how *stoopid* I'd been to attempt this trick, it was quite a while before I was able to laugh – or even *breathe* – normally again. I never went to the doctor, but I'm pretty sure I may have cracked a rib or two in that split second of horseplay. We never let on to our bosses about it, of course. We didn't want to get in trouble, after all. We needed those jobs.

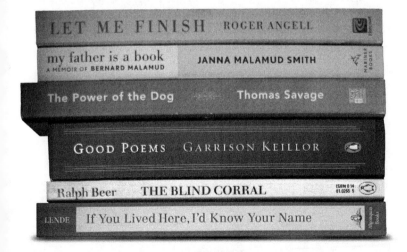

March 16, 2009

Another interruption – in the form of warm spring weather, which took us outside. Do you ever wonder what "famous authors" do when they're not writing (or napping)? Well yesterday this one spent nearly two hours cleaning up a winter's accumulation of dog doo from our back yard. It's been a very long winter, with deep snow in the yard since last November, so there was a *lot* of crap out there, lemme tell ya. So Treve and I worked, scooping and bagging and raking and burying. Picking up poop can be a maddeningly frustrating chore. We have a couple of garden trowels we use to shovel up the individual piles and then dump it into a plastic bag. The problem is there are usually at least three or four turds – sometimes more - to each pile, and it seems like for every turd that stays on the trowel two or three roll back off, so you often end up scooping the same turd two or three times. It's kinda like roundin' up cattle. There's always a maverick or two slipping away from your loop and headin' off into the brush or down into a draw. "Git along, little dogies ..." All that bending and stooping is pretty hard on your back. We really should get us one of those long-handled poop-scoopers. Anyway, I dug three medium-sized holes out at the back of the yard and buried probably twenty-five or thirty pounds of shit. Treve preferred the traditional method of bagging it and saving it for the garbage. But she probably had nearly as much as I did by the time we were done. Our dogs napped in the sun while we were doing this, or periodically got up and came out to inspect our progress. Daisy even offered up a couple fresh piles while we were at it. I think she's always afraid when she sees us doing this particular chore that she'd better hurry and mark a place or she might come rushing out one night after supper and be unable to find the bathroom. Anyway, we worked, they slept. Makes ya kinda wonder who's really in charge, don't it?

I meant to write here yesterday, but by the time I came in, all sweaty from my efforts and the sixty degree temperature, and took a shower, I had to take a nap. Then it was time to feed the dogs, and ... Oh well, you probably get the picture.

But no matter.

Al Collins and I managed to keep our jobs at the pipeline, in spite of the shenanigans we often engaged in to break the boredom. But every now and then we would go "on the road" for an overnight or two. I remember one particular job we did down near St. Louis, Michigan. Someone had reported smelling gas near a main valve there, so we took a trip down there. We traveled in the company pickup, which had a four-door crew cab. Four of us went: our foreman, Rocky Anderson; Jack Rolston; and Al and I. Al and I though it kind of interesting, once we got there and started to work, how much the pipeline crew was like an army or air force detail: one or two guys to do the actual work and two or more to supervise. We spent a day and a half digging out the pipe below the valve that had been reported. We used special copper-tipped shovels and picks. You don't want any sparks flying if there is any possibility of a gas leak, unless you want to find out where "kingdom come" is actually located. At first both Al and I did the initial digging around the valve, while Jack and Rocky stood off at a respectably safe distance and smoked and bullshitted. But once we got the hole started and were a few feet down, there was only room for one person at a time down there. So Al and I took turns at the top of the hole, manning a bucket with a rope on it, to pull the dirt back up out of the hole and dump it off to the side. At about six feet down, water started seeping into the hole. But we were prepared for this and set up a sump pump and hose to suck the water out. Even so, whoever was down there doing the digging was usually standing in several inches of muddy water. It was clay, and hard going. And the sun was hot. Every now and then, Rocky would lower a "sniffer" instrument down to check for gas fumes.

It was hard, boring work. Al and I, who were, of course, the "designated diggers," got sweaty, irritable and bored. We were both wearing rubber boots that came nearly to our knees, which served to keep our feet mostly dry. The tops of the boots were quite wide, so Al devised a little game to relieve his boredom. He gathered a little pile of pebbles and dropped them down into the hole one at a time, trying to get one down the top of one of my boots, kinda like that game we used to play at birthday parties as kids, the one where you stand and try to drop a clothespin into a milk bottle. He got pretty good at it, which was pretty damned annoying. If you've ever tried to walk with a stone in your shoe, then you know what I mean. Of course, when it was his turn in the hole, I'd get him back. There was a lot of muttered cursing down below and chuckling up above; but in this way we managed to amuse ourselves and got through the heat of the day.

We never did find any evidence of a gas leak, though we dug down eight or nine feet, sniffing all up and down that pipe every several minutes. Rocky figured it wasn't safe to go any further down. He didn't want to take a chance on the sides of that hole collapsing in on one of us and killing us. "Just imagine all the paperwork I'd have to do if that happened," he said, chuckling. So the next day we filled it all back in, packed our sump pump, sniffer, and special picks and shovels back into the bed of the truck and headed home to Lake George.

The best thing about those overnight ventures for Great Lakes was that we would be given per diem cash before we left. We didn't have to account for the money, so we usually ended up a few bucks to the good if we were frugal while on the road. Rocky and Jack usually liked to go out for a good steak dinner at a nice restaurant at the end of a day, but Al and I were fine with a quick burger and fries, a meal which left us with a small profit. On one trip we'd been checking and replacing those red and white marker posts along the line and ended up at the southern end of the pipeline in Michigan, near St. Clair. That night Al and I went out after supper and killed some time at a nearby K-Mart, where I bought an album by John Phillips, a member of the then-popular group, the Mamas and the Papas. *John, the Wolf King of L.A.* was Phillips' only solo album, but it was a wonderfully melodic collection of songs, which featured his hit single, "Mississippi," with its catchily bouncy refrain, "Down on the bayou, why, you never know just what you're doin'."

I know. You're probably thinking, So what? But music, and my life circumstances when I first heard or purchased it, I always seem to remember.

But no matter.

One incident I still remember happened on Route 27 (now 127) when we were heading north late one afternoon just south of Mount Pleasant. Jack was driving the truck with Rocky riding shotgun, and Al and I were in the back. Up ahead of us we noticed another pickup towing a horse trailer with a horse in it. Jack was hanging back, well behind the horse trailer; there was a State Police cruiser about a half a mile up the road, so he was cooling it. A young kid and a blonde in a shiny red Mustang came barreling past us in the passing lane, but then the driver saw the police car, so he whipped back over into the right hand lane, right behind the horse trailer. Just then the horse in the trailer lifted its tail and, before that young driver could react, a chain of horse turds – fist-sized balls of shit – came flying out over the tailgate and splattered onto the Mustang's hood and up over its windshield and roof.

We all had ringside seats to this explosion of horse shit. Jack exclaimed, appropriately, "Holy *shit!* Lookit *that!*" and started to laugh, as he eased over into the left hand lane to go around the red Mustang, which suddenly slowed down. We could see the driver, his face red and his mouth working furiously as we sped by, all of us laughing and waving. The truck and horse trailer continued on its way, the driver oblivious, the horse probably feeling much better.

Al and I both craned around in the back seat, watching the shit-splattered Mustang pull over onto the shoulder. Jack was laughing so hard he had tears running down his cheeks. "There's a lesson for you, guys," he wheezed. "Always give a horse trailer plenty of room."

Thanks, Jack. It's a lesson I've always remembered.

The summer of 1970, for lack of anything better to do, and because I felt, with a wife and now a son too to support, I really needed to keep making some money, so I got hired back on at the pipeline at Lake George. The same regular guys were there, including Rocky and Jack, so it was a fairly painless transition for me, almost a kind of vacation, since I knew that, come September, I would be entering the work force full time, as an English instructor at Monroe County Community College.

One of the really odd things about that summer of 1970 is that Treve and I have almost no memory at all of living with my folks in Reed City. I know that we lived there for at least nine or ten weeks, and yet when I probe my memory

– or Treve hers – we come up almost completely blank. I recently read that it is normal for people my age – sixty and older – to begin to lose some of their short term memory while their long term memory – of things that happened a long time ago – gets better. Well, generally I have found this to be true. But those two-plus months of living on Church Street the summer of '70? It's just *gone* – into a black hole of memory somewhere. This gap bothers me perhaps more than it should have, because I think that if I could lose a whole two months from my life that easily, why not two years? Indeed, why not twenty? In fact, I only recently read a disturbing, and rather sad, article on-line about Bjorn Ulvaeus, former front-man for the musical group ABBA. The poor guy isn't even sixty yet, but he recently revealed that he is suffering from an unexplained memory loss. He has no memory at all of the year the band won the Eurovision song contest which catapulted them into the world spotlight in the mid-seventies, and he has lost other large chunks of his life too. He has been studying old videos and photos, trying to recapture those mysteriously lost years.

It's a terrifying thing to consider, I think, losing one's memories that way. It's like losing parts of your *self*. Perhaps that's why I am trying so hard (well, *pretty* hard, when I'm not napping or reading) to get as much of it down on paper as I can. I mean I did somehow lose that chunk of time we spent with my family in June and July of 1970. I know I said Treve can't remember it either, but that's par for her. She always says that she was too busy just being a wife and mother to pay much attention to what was going on around her all those years past. And I guess that's a pretty valid excuse, when you come right down to it.

But no matter (I *hope*).

I do remember a few isolated things from my job that summer, the year Brian Wekenman was the other summer hire. I know one of the advantages of living in Reed City was carpooling. Since Brian's Uncle Jack Rolston was driving to Lake George to work every day anyway, we rode with him a lot. In fact, I think Jack drove most of the time. He and his wife, Lois, lived in a small mobile home park just west of the

Kel-Reed plant on East Church, so he would usually come by and pick me up, and Brian too.

My folks had nothing but good things to say about Jack Rolston, mostly because they remembered how kind he and Lois had been to my brother Rich when he was in basic training at Fort Leonard Wood in 1961. Jack had been in the army then too, on permanent assignment with the Army Corps of Engineers, which was headquartered at Leonard Wood. Because he was permanent party, he was able to come get Rich from his basic company and take him home for a good home-cooked meal now and then. Mom and Dad never forgot that. And their assessment of Jack was accurate. He was a good and honorable man.

He was also easy to tease, and to get a rise out of. And his nephew Brian knew that. Because Brian, as I remember him, was a very fun-loving sort of guy who enjoyed playing a practical joke as much as anyone. One of the few memories Mom has of that summer we stayed with them is of me calling her and Dad from the Glass Bar out at Hawkins one night after work. Brian had either been the driver that day or else had talked Jack into taking us all directly to the bar – do not pass GO – that Friday night. I was 26 that summer, so I think Brian was probably at least 21. So it's not that there was anything illegal or anything going on. I just was not a bar-goer, and never have been. At least not since my first army enlistment, when I used to practically *live* at one particular bar in Germany whenever I was on break. So I'd pretty much gotten that out of my system. But Brian insisted. *Party-time!* So I was stuck. My one-beer limit didn't last long. Dad came and got me while Brian partied on.

Brian loved to have fun, and sometimes it was at the expense of his Uncle Jack, who was, when I knew him, a pretty straight-arrow sort of guy. I wish I could remember who some of the other regular crew members were there at the pumping station north of Farwell, but I can't. I just know they were all a pretty easy-going bunch of guys who were always looking for some diversion, anything to relieve some of the boredom of the work they did from day to day. One of the jobs that Brian and I were given to do that summer was a little daunting. We had to change all the spark plugs on the giant Cooper-Bessemer engines used to power the pipeline. Each one of those engines was about the size of a one-car garage that you had to climb up an iron stairway to get at, so yeah, my first reaction was probably something like "are you *sure* you want *me* to do this?" *Me*, who'd never even changed the spark plug on a power lawn mower? But Brian never even batted an eye. He just gathered up the new plugs, got us some socket wrenches and, by God, we changed those spark plugs. I amazed myself, particularly when the engines actually started back *up* again without a hitch when we were all done.

Brian had a kind of blonde, bronzed young Apollo look about him that undoubtedly made him very popular with girls, and this had given him an air of confidence and competence, even then, at the age of only twenty-one or so, that it would take me years to acquire. And that cocksureness of his was complemented by just a bit of deviltry that he found hard to suppress. And sometimes he didn't.

Jack Rolston was a shy man, easy to tease, and Brian was pretty unmerciful with his uncle. Jack blushed easily when he was flustered, so Brian was always looking for new ways to embarrass him. It wasn't meanness on Brian's part; it was just an overdeveloped sense of fun – or tomfoolery, to use a more archaic term. Because there was never any question in my mind that there was a genuine affection between the two men. Family was very important to both of them.

But here's what Brian cooked up. One afternoon all the men were sitting around in the crew's break room. Brian was thumbing through a dog-eared old men's magazine from a stack on a table in the corner. Nothing nasty, just one of those masculine periodicals from that era, like *True* or *Argosy* or one of those. Some of these magazines had been around forever, so we'd long since glanced through the feature articles. So Brian was studying some of those boxed special advertisements in the back pages of this magazine, and he called me over.

"Hey, Tim, look at this ad for something called 'instant pussy,'" He whispered. "Whaddaya suppose that is?"

My interest piqued, I looked at the tiny ad he showed me. There were no details. Just those words in block print, and a mailing address. For just $3.99 plus shipping and handling we could find out what it was, but I wasn't that interested. "I dunno, Brian," I said. "And I sure ain't gonna fork over five bucks or more just to find out either."

Brian looked thoughtful for a moment, then his face lit up. You could almost see that cartoon light bulb in a bubble over his head. "Hey, you know what we should do?"

Almost afraid to ask, I replied, "No. What should we do?"

The other regular maintenance crew guys were all sitting over their coffee at the other table. Brian looked carefully over at them, then leaned in a little closer. "We should send for this and have it mailed to Jack."

"Naw," I said. "Lois'd kill him."

"No, no," Brian whispered. "We'll have it sent to him *here*, at the office."

"I don't know, Brian. We don't wanna get him in trouble."

"Oh *c'mon*," he said. "Can'tchu just see the look on his face when he opens it? It'll be *great!*"

I must have still looked skeptical, but Brian obviously didn't want to do this on his own, so he said, "Okay, just gimme two bucks. I'll pay the rest. C'mon it'll be *so funny.*"

So I agreed and slipped him a couple of ones, which he tucked in his jeans pocket, chortling already in anticipation. "I'll send it in tonight. This is gonna be fun."

About two weeks later we were all at lunch in the break room when Rocky came in from the office, carrying a plain brown envelope. "Mail for you, Jack," he said, handing the small packet to him. "Since when you gettin' mail here at work?"

"Hell if I know," Jack replied. "I didn't order nothin'." He looked curiously at the package with his name on it, then opened it up. Everyone at the table was watching …

Remember those Saturday matinee serials – the "cliffhangers?" Well, I do, and I'll continue this soon. But probably not tomorrow, because tomorrow is Wednesday and St. Patrick's Day, which has always been special to Treve and me. We met on St. Paddy's Day in 1967. Two months later we got engaged. And six months after that we were married. I was a much faster worker back then. (It's all in my third book, *Pinhead*.) So tomorrow we're going out to lunch. We'll go early; we both agree we'd like to be back home by nap time.

Stay tuned.

March 20, 2009

Well it's Friday; sometimes one day off can stretch into two or three. Remember what I said about writing being all about discipline. I still don't have it. And on Wednesday I got this book in the mail from Wyoming. I'd arranged to swap some books with this author there, Ted Judson. I had read about this book of his on Amazon. It's a novel called *Tom Wedderburn's Life*. He paid to have it published about five years ago. When we talked on the phone, Ted readily admitted that the book, his first, did very poorly sales-wise, although he still thinks it's his best work. (He has since published two books of science fiction that have done much better.) Well, I haven't read Ted's sci-fi books (yet), but I have to say that *Tom Wedderburn's Life* is perhaps one of the best books I have read in years. I'm nearly finished with it, and I had to practically physically tear myself away from it in order to get back to my own writing. I will reward myself by finishing Ted's book later today or tonight. It is without question one of the best swaps I've ever made.

Treve and I did make our nostalgic jaunt down to Ferris on St. Paddy's Day. It was an absolutely gorgeous pre-spring day with temperatures hovering in the low seventies. She took along a shopping list of sale items she'd found in a Walgreens flyer, and that's where she wanted to go first. I teased her a bit about how "romantic" she was, wanting to go to Walgreens to mark our special day. She countered by saying that we had never been to Walgreens in Big Rapids. True enough. She added, "I'm not sure if we've *ever* been to a Walgreens."

I had to remind her that our regular drugstore in Mount Pleasant, back when we were first married, was in fact a Walgreens, at the corner of Mission and Bellows. A friend from Ferris, John Tillotson, had been one of the pharmacists there.

"Okay, *okay*," she conceded. "Who remembers *that* far back?"

Well, *I* do. It's always good to have at least one romantic in a marriage – someone who remembers important things, like crummy old first apartments and where we bought our cold medicines.

So we shopped at Walgreens Wednesday, and then lunched on delicious Reuben sandwiches at Schuberg's bar downtown, which was crowded with St. Patrick's day revelers. After that we drove over to St. Paul's chapel and went into the lounge area and small library-meeting room, the place where we'd met forty-two years ago. There was no one else there, so we did a little old-folks making out and remembered. Then we drove over and parked by the Rankin Student Center. We walked into the empty Dome Room where Treve looked around and then did a couple of quick dance steps and told me, "It was right about here that I once fell flat on my butt showing off while dancing at one of those Friday night mixers. I was so embarrassed."

We walked down the hall and into the PUG snack bar, where we'd both spent many hours drinking cokes, listening to the juke box and checking out the opposite sex so many years ago. It's not the PUG anymore. Now it's a Quizno's franchise, and the jukebox is gone too, replaced by a couple of huge flat panel TV's in opposite corners of the cafeteria. It wasn't the same at all.

Then we walked over to Helen Ferris dorm, hoping to just stand in the lobby and remember all the times I'd picked her up and delivered her back there during the spring and summer of 1967. We couldn't even get inside the building. Since my last visit there a month or two ago an electronic card-swipe security system has been installed and activated. It's a different world now.

But our day on our very own memory lane was a successful one. No regrets. Ferris has changed and so have we, but no regrets.

But I know you're all (all six or seven of my faithful readers, that is) still waiting with bated breath to find out what the hell is "instant pussy," right? *No?* Well, I'm gonna finish the story anyway.

What Jack found in the package was a small, innocuous-looking capsule filled with what looked like a dark grey powder. It was sealed in cellophane and stapled to a small typed sheet of paper which read:

"Thank you for your purchase of INSTANT PUSSY. We hope it will bring you many hours of pleasure. To activate your INSTANT PUSSY, please place the enclosed capsule in a container of hot water."

All the crew members were by this time gathered around Jack and reading this important message over his shoulder. A chorus of catcalls and *Wooo's* erupted from the men as they read these brief "instructions."

"Whoa, Jack! Instant *pussy*? Whatsamatta, man? Ain'tcha been gettin' any at home lately?"

Peals of raucous laughter accompanied these comments and the men took turns thumping Jack on the back and issuing more similar cracks, like "You sly dog, Jack!" and "What the hell *is* it, anyway?"

Jack, in the meantime, had turned beet-red with embarrassment and was sputtering out genuine if ineffectual protests of innocence. "*I* never ordered *this*," he choked out, turning the brown wrapper over in his hand to look again at the address. "What th-, *who* the hell ...?"

Brian, hovering at the back of the crew, was silently convulsing with barely contained mirth, his shoulders shaking with silent laughter as he looked over at me, winking and grinning. Then suddenly he put on a somewhat more serious face and, shaking his head, exclaimed, "*Jack!* What the hell are you *doing*, ordering something like that?!"

Jack just stared at Brian, his mouth open and working soundlessly. One of the guys grabbed an empty coffee mug from the table and ran over to the sink and filled it with hot water and hurried back over and set it carefully down on the table. "C'mon, Jack, let's *activate* that sucker. Maybe we can *all* use it!"

"No way," said Jack, and protested once again, "I did *not* order this thing. I don't know who *did*, but it was *not* me!"

But he was preaching to an empty church by then. The guy who'd supplied the cup of water had already grabbed the plastic pouch, torn it open and dropped the gel cap into the hot water.

All eyes in the room were on the capsule as it gradually dissolved and sloughed away from its contents, which instead of spreading out and dissipating into the water remained for a second in a compact mass, and then, very slowly, unfolded itself several times and finally straightened out into the unmistakable shape of – a cat. A gray *PUSSY* cat.

A mixture of groans and guffaws filled the room. Jack's face began to resume its natural ruddy hue. A chorus of *Shee-its* and other less genteel epithets flowed about the table as the men gave Jack some final thumps on the back and "better luck next time, ol' man" kinds of comments. Break time was over and we all headed back out to go to work. Except Jack, who was still standing there turning the package over in his hands, peering again at the address sticker, trying to figure out, I suppose, "why me?"

I don't know if Brian ever owned up to this dirty trick. I know I never did. Jack continued to get ragged on about his "mystery" package for the rest of the summer. He took it in stride and with good humor, although he continued to regard everyone in the crew with a certain suspicion every time it came up. What the hell though. It was just guy stuff, and, as women are so fond of saying, "boys will be boys."

March 23, 2009

Took a long weekend to catch up on some reading. I got some terrific books in the mail last week, the result of a couple of swaps I'd engineered by e-mail with some other authors. Ted Judson's fictional memoir, *Tom Wedderburn's Life*, was a can't-put-it-down, absolutely mesmerizing read. I'd found the book by accident, just noodling around on Amazon. Judson, who is by no means a famous writer, is a teacher in Riverton, Wyoming, and his book is about a Wyoming man a generation older than Ted. It chronicles Wedderburn's life from childhood into old age, including his Marine Corps service in the Pacific during World War II. The only unfortunate thing about the book is that it was put out by one of those vanity press companies that provided no proofing or editing services and printed a book that is simply riddled with typos. But the story itself is strong enough that you can overlook this problem. I loved the book. Also received four books from a swap with Neal Bowers, who recently retired from Iowa State, where he spent thirty years or more as a professor. Reading a book of his poems, *Out of the South*, quickly made a disciple out of me. Then I read his "mystery-slash-memoir," *Words for the Taking*, about an unscrupulous plagiarist, who stole several of Bowers' poems. It doesn't sound very interesting on the surface, but it turns into a riveting read, as Bowers finds out more and more about this "word thief," who turns out to be a psychopath and pedophile, among other things. I've still got a novel and a book about cats from Bowers' package left to read. So many books …

It's odd. I've been feeling guilty for the past few days about not writing, and now here I sit, ready to write, and draw a complete blank. How very frustrating. I know there are more stories inside the old bean, but they seem to be hiding right now. Here's the thing though. When I'm lying in bed at night – or at "naptime" – right on the edge of sleep, my mind is literally alive with ideas. Or when I'm getting in or out of the shower, say. All these witty things to say keep flashing through my mind, and I think, I've gotta get this down on paper. This morning, for example, when I was stepping into the shower, I was thinking about hemorrhoids, and how it might be interesting to write about them. Then I thought, gross, Bazzett. People don't want to read about hemorrhoids. At least, that's what Treve would most certainly say. Nevertheless, they are often on my mind these days as I sit here on my donut cushion on top of a pillow piled precariously on the seat of my desk chair. I have learned in the past few years of writing, for example, that it's not a good idea to sit too long in front of this damned computer. If I do, I pay for it in the end. Get it? ... Never mind.

Meanwhile, back in Monterey. My brother Rich came to visit us at DLI once. I talked a bit about Rich in *Soldier Boy*, since our army tours in Germany overlapped a bit back in 1965 and we managed to see each other a couple times then. But then I went back home and off to college, and Rich took a European out, which means he was discharged from the army in Germany. As an electronics specialist, his skills were much in demand by American companies who had interests in Europe and Asia, so Rich quickly found employment with one of them and never really went back home again, other than for an occasional visit. He traveled all over the continent between jobs in Germany, Greece, Spain, Italy, you name it; he probably went there. He even did a couple extended tours as a civilian employee in Vietnam during its peak years. He never talked to me too much about that. I often wondered if he might have been a "spook" for the CIA, an agency that maintained a large presence in Southeast Asia in those years. I guess I can safely speculate on that now, since Rich died of cancer in 2001. He had just retired after more than thirty-five years of globe-trotting for various companies. Another one of those it's-not-fair kinda things. In any case, whatever secrets he might have kept died with him.

When Rich came to visit us in Monterey he had just returned from several months on a job in Kuwait, where he told us he had been installing new high tech air-traffic control systems at airports there and also conducting training classes for the natives who would operate those systems. He told us that the pay was fantastic, and he'd signed on for a year of work there. But his bosses and the host nation expected him to work about eighteen or twenty hours a day. He'd hung in there for as long as he could, but the grueling schedule finally took its toll and he just said, *enough*, packed up his stuff and headed back to the states. So he was en route home, which was, I think, in Georgia at the time, and he stopped in California to see us. He was visibly exhausted when he got to our place, with dark circles under his eyes and a kind of wrung-out puffy look about him. Treve fed him up good and we let him sleep as much as he wanted. I think Rich stayed with us for about five or six days, maybe a week, so after a couple days of rest and good food he was feeling more himself again.

My big brother was never a very social animal. A loner, I suppose you'd call him. He never married. His excuse was that all his traveling never gave him much opportunity to meet women. And, by the same token, his peripatetic lifestyle didn't make him a very good candidate for marriage. (Don'tcha just love that word, *peripatetic*? I like to use it every now and then.) He'd never be home. But the truth is Rich was just painfully shy with women. Part of it perhaps went back to his school years in Reed City, where he'd skipped a couple early grades at St. Philip's Catholic school. So by the time he graduated from high school here, at just sixteen, he was always the youngest – and probably the most socially awkward – in his crowd. He was always one of the tallest kids, but because he was growing so fast he was not very well coordinated and never went out for any sports. Oh, he had friends in high school, both boys and girls, but I don't think Rich ever had a real date in his high school years. I'm not sure about his two years at Michigan State, but I don't remember him ever bringing any girls home during that period. And then he worked at the Kent Elevator with Dad for the next few years. And nope, I don't remember any girls from that time either. There were a few girls who ran in a crowd with him – Barbara Sutliff and Ginnie Keelean, for example – around town and out at Indian Lake in the summertime for swimming and water skiing. But dates? I don't think so.

After Rich died, we found some photo albums in his house from the years he spent overseas. And in one there are several snapshots of him with a very pretty girl outside his villa in Bangkok, Thailand, a place he loved and where he had jobs off and on over the years. But there were no notes, no names or captions to go with the photos, so the story behind those pictures, if there is one, will simply never be told. Rich was always a very private person. But I'd always looked up to him.

I remember sneakily borrowing his shiny black penny loafers to wear a couple times when I was in high school, even though they were a size or two too big for me. They say you can never really know someone unless you've walked in his shoes. I guess even then I was trying to fill Rich's shoes, to bridge that five-year age difference and be just a little closer to my big brother, to know him better. Or maybe I just liked his shoes.

Anyway, we were happy to have Rich around for a few days that spring in Monterey. We let him take our car to go exploring around the peninsula. Treve and I both still remember the time he took along both our boys and Heidi, the dog, to go with him for the day. We were probably happy to have some time to ourselves for a day (nudge, nudge, wink, wink; if ya know what I mean). But by supper time, when they'd been gone for five or six hours, we began to worry a bit. Treve was more worried than I was, and kept going to the kitchen window to look outside to see if the car was coming up the street. But they finally got back okay, too late for supper, but Rich had fed them all a couple times and the boys and Heidi had run and run on a beach somewhere and were all pretty exhausted. I think we may have grilled him a bit – *why didn't you* call *us*, and *where* were *you* kinda stuff – but, never having been a parent, Rich was pretty oblivious to our worrying. The boys testified enthusiastically to having had a really *fun* time with Uncle Rich – hamburgers and French fries and milkshakes and stuff, and they got to collect shells and play in the sand on the beach. Which was pretty obvious – they both needed hosing off. And Heidi's tongue was hanging out about a foot for a while after she got home, before she plopped down in the living room and slept like a rack of roadkill.

Treve must have forgiven Rich by the next day, because she got it into her head that we should "fix Rich up" with a friend of ours. Her name was Margie – with a "hard g" – and I think we may have met her at a parents' open house night at the kids' school, where Jeff was in second grade and Scott was in kindergarten. Margie was a divorced single mom and had two kids the same age as ours – Gary was in Jeff's grade and Michelle was in Scott's. Treve and Margie apparently hit it off right away, because Treve had agreed to look after her two kids after school each night for a couple hours until Margie got off work from her job at a local dentist's office and could come to our house to pick them up. Treve made a few bucks and Margie knew her kids were safe and being looked after. It was a pretty good arrangement for everyone concerned, maybe especially for Scott, who seemed to be a little sweet on pug-nosed freckle-faced Michelle, in a very shy five year-old sort of way, of course. And Jeff and Gary enjoyed playing together after school too. And Margie, who was about Treve's age, wasn't bad to look at herself, truth be told, in a trim, girl-next-door, blonde freckly kinda way. She sometimes stayed for dinner when she came to pick up her kids, and we even went to her apartment for dinner once or twice.

So we invited Margie over for dinner one night while Rich was there. We fed the four kids early, so the "adults" could have a nice quiet meal. Treve fixed a real nice dinner and we may have even had candles on the table, and I probably put some soft music on the stereo. Margie was very charming and sweet, and seemed to like Rich okay. But it just didn't work. Rich, who had been talking to us nearly non-stop for two or three days by then, telling us all about his travels and his job, just kinda froze up with Margie there. She would ask him questions and try to draw him out, but he just seemed to get all tongue-tied and would turn red and stammer out a terse answer and then clam up again. He was just so uncomfortable, having this, this *woman* there – and a most attractive one at that. I think we all took a walk after dinner, but it didn't get any better. Rich just seemed incapable of feeling comfortable with Margie there. Conversation was strained and the evening just finally kinda petered out and Margie took her kids and went home. Of course maybe part of Rich's discomfort was knowing there were a couple kids as part of this potential equation, but I don't really know. Mostly I think it was just Rich's lifelong shyness with women that got in the way. He was what he was and he wasn't going to change – *couldn't* – just for a pretty face. Once Margie left, he seemed to breathe a huge sigh of relief, and resumed talking with us again. I don't know if Margie was disappointed, but I remember Treve was, a little anyway. Her attempt at matchmaking had failed dismally. I remember telling her later that night, after we went to bed, "Hey, it's not *your* fault. You tried. You did everything just right. It's just Rich. He's just not marriage material."

Treve and I were just talking about those times today. Rather uncharacteristically, she remembers Margie and her kids well. I wondered if we had any pictures of them. She wasn't sure, but reminded me that she had a newspaper clipping with a photo of her and Gary. How they got into the Monterey papers is a story I had completely forgotten, but sure enough, we still have the newspaper.

March 30, 2009

Another week gone by without writing. Reading though, that's another matter. I got my copy of Darryl Ponicsan's new book in the mail last week and read it. Actually it was an Anne Argula book, Darryl's pen name. He writes these PI novels now under this female nom de plume, and his heroine is a private investigator named Quinn, menopausal and funnier than hell. Anyway, I read the whole thing – this new one, *Krapp's Last Cassette* – in a couple of days and wrote up a blurb for it on Amazon, an activity that takes up more of my time these days than it should, I suppose.

And Friday I went book-bumming up to Cadillac with my back-fence neighbor, Jim Murnik. We spent about an hour looking through the used books at The Book Nook on Pine, and one of the books I brought home is this really great memoir of growing up in South Dakota called *Portable Prairie*. I've already read nearly half of it, so I might comment on it later. But first I guess I should finish the story I started, huh? The one about Treve and Monterey and the newspaper clipping.

Somehow Treve got roped into participating in a disaster drill that was held at the Monterey airport. I mean she volunteered, but she doesn't really remember now how she got involved. It was a pretty big deal at the time though, with the Air National Guard, the Navy, and local fire departments cooperating with the airport authority, the Red Cross and local hospitals, both civilian and military. I mean, it really looked a lot like the real thing, with fire engines and ambulances and airplanes and helicopters. It was realistic enough, Treve remembers, to frighten our son, Jeff, who didn't want anything to do with playing one of the "injured survivors" of the simulated airplane crash which precipitated the exercise. So Treve pressed Margie's boy, Gary, into service instead, and he shows up in the newspaper photos as her "son." Just to give you and idea of the "realism" of the exercise, here's how the Monterey Peninsula Herald reported it in the July 1, 1977, Friday edition:

> … *the Thursday night practice run to cope with local disaster was grim.*
>
> *This was the scenario:*

At precisely 7 p.m. an Air National Guard C-130 Transport plane landed on Monterey Peninsula Airport runway 10, broke a wheel, sheered left across runway 24, lost both main landing gear and the nose wheel and slid to a stop.

One engine was ablaze and fuel was pouring out onto the ground.

With this theoretical disaster outlined, the vividly real emergency exercise rolled into operation to rescue the 100 or so men, women and children aboard the plane ... [fire] trucks and crews sped clanging and screeching. Firemen in silver asbestos suits leaped out to hose out the simulated fire, backed by beeping and clanging red engines from the U.S. Navy and California Forestry Division.

The open cargo hold revealed a tangle of bodies and cries, mostly Monterey Peninsula College students who volunteered for the disaster exercise and had spent hours preparing wounds to match symptoms scripted on cue cards.

In moments, the concrete taxiway was strewn with injured, with rushing firemen carrying off groaning victims on wood stretchers and calming the frenzied, the hysterical, the shrieking, hugging them down soothingly to the ground.

Bloody wrists and legs, broken bones, repulsive charred skin and regurgitated food covered writhing bodies – special effects and makeup – matching the real thing. Calves' brains covered heads simulating open wounds, sausage casings stuffed with baby food starkly were exposed as intestines, old blood from blood banks splashed ... two bodies lay decapitated (mannequins) in the humanity-choked hold ...

Treve still remembers how real the makeup and simulated injuries looked that day, so it was no wonder, I suppose, that Jeff simply backed away from it all. Gary, on the other hand, seemed unfazed, later telling everyone how "cool" it all had been, and that he'd been in the newspapers and on television too.

Less than a month after that disaster drill on the airport tarmac, we were packing up again to leave Monterey. My LeFoxe Russian class successfully completed, it was time for us to say good-bye to our idyllic California interval. We lived in Monterey as a family from June 1976 until August 1977, fourteen months of mostly happy, memory-making times.

I say "mostly," because there was one very *un*happy time. In the early spring of 1977, Treve learned she was pregnant, but then at about ten weeks she suddenly miscarried. Thirty-two years later, she still has vivid memories of the day it happened and how she knew immediately she had lost her baby, when she began to bleed heavily. She sent me to a neighbor's to try to find more sanitary pads when her small supply was quickly used up. I got her to the hospital at Fort Ord as quickly as possible, but it was too late. The doctor's well-meaning and kind assurances that this was just "nature's way" of telling us something wasn't meant to be were small comfort. That afternoon, in a curtained alcove of the ER at Silas B. Hays Army Hospital, we clung to each other and cried for the loss of that tiny life that had been, however briefly, a part of us.

The bulk of our Monterey memories, though, are sun-soaked happy ones. Our younger son, Scott, was only five that year, but he still remembers his first year of school. He started kindergarten at Larkin Elementary School at the edge of the Presidio and he still remembers, as do Treve and I, attending a pool party at his teacher's home in Monterey – an event that seemed a very California kind of thing. And Scott and Jeff both also remember a huge unit picnic held on the Presidio, an event officially designated Organization Day. All the DLI students were in civvies, i.e. jeans and shorts and tee-shirts. There were beer tents and burgers, hot dogs, pop, ball games and tug-o-wars between company teams. I can still remember watching a couple of tug-teams compete, pulling mightily on a thick knotted rope that stretched across a large pit that had been dug and filled with water – a mud hole, actually – and seeing the losing tuggers get dunked in that gooey brown soup. What the boys remember most about that day was the outdoor concert held on the parade ground on a stage that had been erected there for the day. I can't remember anymore where the band was from. They called themselves Savannah and sported the then-fashionable long hair, tie-dyed tee-shirts and torn jeans. And they were very loud. Jeff and Scott, who had only recently discovered KISS, were absolutely mesmerized. The high point of their day was, unquestionably, getting to meet all the boys in the band when they took a break. They were selling an album they'd made, so I bought one for the boys, and all the band members autographed it. I talked with Scott about this album a few months ago. He still remembered it, and said he could picture in his mind just exactly how the cover looked –

> *Savannah. It was written in a script font, in a big star on*
> *the cover of the album. White type on a red background ... I*
> *don't have it, but Jeff might. I don't remember a single song,*
> *but I DO remember being there and getting the album ...*

Five years old, his first person-to-person brush with "fame." Of *course* he remembers. Many years later Scott got to meet the real deal, Gene and Paul and the other members of KISS. But he was much older then – in his twenties already – so I wonder if that meeting was quite as exciting as that hot summer afternoon in 1976 when they met Savannah, a long-forgotten California garage band I can find no mention of on the internet.

My own memories of California are a mixed bag of all the grueling hours spent cramming and drilling to learn a very different and difficult language, interspersed with more pleasant times spent with my family and our friends. And the latter memories are, of course, the ones I remember best. The days spent at the beach and watching my two little boys digging busily, constructing castles and moats, while Treve lazed in the sun and I threw sticks of driftwood for Heidi to chase and bring back to me. There were the community cookouts that happened spontaneously on the lawn inside the quadrangle of brick apartment buildings on Bellegarde Way – the lazy, elongated Saturday and Sunday afternoons when the adults would grill burgers and hot dogs, and dishes of macaroni and potato salads would be brought out to be shared in pot luck feasts. The kids climbed trees and rode their bikes and skateboards down the sidewalks and dogs frolicked among them. Pinochle and poker games would be dealt on blankets where husbands and wives would hunker together and bicker good-naturedly: "Who dealt this mess?" or "You in or out?" I look at old photos and I recognize the Starrs and the Lutes, the Sweeneys and Schillingers, and others. There was a kind of camaraderie in those shared afternoons that could never be matched in civilian life. We were all military – army, navy, air force – and we all knew these days would pass, and we would all go our separate ways one day, so we made the most of those times. They were our own "chocolate days, popsicle weeks" – halcyon times that would never come again. Looking back now at all those young couples – those families – that we were nearly makes me weep. I am, however, so thankful that we had those days, and those friends. Thinking back, I become lost once again in my own "California Dreamin'."

By early August of 1977 our California life was done. The movers came, we packed our things, carefully separated and labeled either for long-term storage or short-term storage to be shipped overseas when the time came. Because by the time we left Monterey, we already knew that we would be headed to Field Station Augsburg in Germany, but not right away. First I had two more places to go, for still more training. But I would go to these places alone, because they were considered "temporary duty" stations, or TDY's. My first stop would be Goodfellow Air Force Base, often fondly referred to by GI's as "Goodbuddy," in San Angelo, Texas, for eight weeks of training. Following that was another twelve weeks of training at Fort Meade, Maryland.

I was given a couple of weeks leave before I left for Texas though, so after I'd put Treve, the boys and the dog on a plane home, I set off on a cross-country drive to take our car back to Belleville. Bob Protosevich, one of my LeFoxe classmates, accompanied me on this marathon non-stop trip to share the driving chores. It was – and still is – the longest drive I have ever made, close to 2500 miles.

Our plan was to take turns sleeping in the back of the station wagon, but whatever sleep we did get over the next couple days or so was not very restful sleep. Bob was going home to Chicago, so we drove north from Monterey to Sacramento where we picked up Interstate 80 and followed it all the way to Chicago. My memory of that trip consists mainly of watching the white line and pavement unfurl endlessly and mostly monotonously before me. The climb up through Donner Pass was a bit unnerving as I felt the car slow, working gamely against gravity as I kept the gas pedal to the floor. I remember the lights of Reno, then Elko, and passing through Salt Lake City at night. Then Rawlins and Laramie and across the Wyoming plateau where pronghorn antelope raced beside the road and coyote carcasses dotted the shoulders. We cut across a corner of South Dakota and then began passage of the endless plains and cornfields of Nebraska and Iowa, which we thought would never end. And finally Illinois, and Chicago, where I left Bob behind. The final leg, from Chicago to Belleville nearly finished me. I had not realized how exhausted I was until I found myself drowsing over the wheel somewhere outside of Gary. It frightened me enough to pull off at the next rest stop, where I doused my face with cold water in a restroom and bought a small box of No-Doz pills which I popped with swigs of Coke as I drove across the bottom of Michigan on I-94. All that caffeine did the trick; woke me up and somehow got me safely back to Belleville – and *kept* me up for several more hours in spite of my long and nearly sleepless marathon journey. I remember arriving at the Zimmers around three or four in the afternoon and finding no one home and the house locked. They were shopping or something. I was so very wide-awake by this time – Coke and No-Doz are a *killer* combo, lemme tell ya – that I pulled the car around the house, got out the hose, and washed the car and was cleaning it all out inside when Treve and her mom and the boys got home an hour or so later. Treve still remembers how manic and demented I seemed, babbling nearly incoherently about my trip. I didn't get to sleep until after midnight and didn't really completely wind down until sometime the next afternoon when I finally crashed and slept for about twelve hours straight. Bob and Tim's excellent adventure was over.

April 2, 2009

I finished reading M.J. Andersen's lovely memoir, *Portable Prairie*, a couple days ago and was struck by one of her lines. She had taken a trip back to the land of her ancestors and was driving with a friend across the northern part of Denmark, into Jutland.

She writes –

I felt uncannily oriented … I even felt a familiar upwelling of boredom, the kind associated with long childhood trips past infinite fields, where there was so little for the eye to seize on.

I suddenly remembered, reading this, a trip our family had taken into the Upper Peninsula over fifty years ago – a camping trip. I probably remember it mostly because it was the only such vacation we ever took together. Dad had somehow appropriated a large mildew-smelling old brown canvas tent. He brought it home and we all helped put it up out in our front yard. We were living in "the old Morefield place" on West Church at the time. My brother Bob and I helped Dad lay out the heavy old tent, then raise the center pole and stake down the corners and guy ropes. The idea was to leave the tent up for a while so it could "air out." It was summer vacation and Bob and I were probably about thirteen and twelve or so at the time, an age when sleeping outdoors could still be an adventure. So we took pillows and blankets out and slept in the tent for a few nights while it aired out. I remember one night when we both sat up straight in our blankets, all our senses alert, when we heard a snuffling sound and soft padding steps outside the tent. A moment later, a small black muzzle poked through the tent flap, followed by the whole animal. It was just Bootsy, a small black terrier-mix, who belonged, at least technically, to Petersons, the neighbors at the foot of my grandparents' driveway. But Bootsy was one of those "free range" dogs that was so common to small towns and neighborhoods back in the fifties. In her heart she belonged to no one at all, but was a friend to every kid on the block. That night she came wagging into our tent and, after happily washing both our faces, she did that doggily universal three-times turnaround and plopped herself down between us, sighed contentedly and went to sleep. The moldy old tent, and the kids inside it, had passed muster.

Not long after that, we packed the tent and our other luggage on top of our Chevy station wagon and set off on our great family camping adventure – Mom and Dad, Bob and I, and our younger siblings, Mary and Chris. Rich and Bill, our two older brothers, who were both in high school – Rich might have even been in college by then – stayed behind to work at the elevator.

Dad had mapped out a vague route for our vacation. We would drive north, take the ferry across the Straits to St. Ignace, and then on up through the Porcupine Mountains. I'm not sure exactly how *much* planning he and Mom put into the trip, but Dad was like a lot of fathers back then when it came to a vacation. The main thing was to cover as many miles as you could each day, so you could cite those figures later on to your male friends when you talked about the trip. The more hundreds of miles you logged each day the better. Or at least that's the way it seemed to us kids. Mom was probably a little more realistic about traveling with children. We didn't have mobile DVD players to fasten to the back of the front car seat then, as kids seem to need now for a trip, but we did have comic books, and Mom allowed us to lay in a good supply of them from our stash, and may have even thrown in a few new ones too. She did warn us, however, that we'd better not spend *all* of our time in the car reading comics. This was, after all, a "vacation," and we were expected to take advantage of this fact and pay attention to what was going on *outside* the car as we traveled.

This advice was not hard to follow for the first few hours of our trip, as we passed through the "big city" of Cadillac, then continued north up 131 through the smaller towns of Manton, Kalkaska and Mancelona. These latter towns were not much to look at back then though, and our attention to the outdoor wonders of northern Michigan soon began to wane. Somewhere up north of Petoskey, Dad stopped for gas at a country crossroads station that boasted a black bear inside a pen. We kids all piled out of the car to get a closer look at this denizen of the wild. Bob and I had both, by this time, read

Ernest Thompson Seton's classic stories, *Wild Animals I Have Known*, as well as the same author's *The Biography of a Grizzly*. After reading these naturalistic tales, as well as James Oliver Curwood's stories of wolf dogs and other savage wild animals that ripped and tore and disemboweled, we were more than a bit disappointed by this tired old fly-blown bear whose only talent, it seemed, was the ability to slurp a soft drink from a bottle. We dutifully bought the bear a bottle of pop and watched him consume it, which only took a few seconds. I think we felt vaguely cheated. I remember looking furtively around for a stick that I could use to stick through the fence to poke the moth-eaten old guy, hoping for at least a small roar rather than the disappointing snuffling and oinking sounds he was making, but Mom was there, and I knew she'd never allow it, and it was time to get back in the car and head for Mackinac. Dad wanted to get across the Straits and up into the UP before it got too late.

Back then you had to wait in line for one of the ferry boats to drive your car onto and make the passage across the Straits to St. Ignace. We had a long boring wait for the ferry that day. Mom let us get out of the car and we killed time watching the flocks of seagulls that littered the lot and amused ourselves by rushing at the birds and watching them take flight in fluttering clouds of dirty feathers, screeching indignantly at being interrupted in their scavenging of the garbage the waiting tourists flung out for them.

The trip across the Straits was itself exciting to boys like Bob and me. It was about as close as we thought we'd ever come to an ocean voyage. Our car stowed safely in the hold of the ferry, we were free – well, mostly; Mom and Dad were watching us – to roam about the upper deck, going from inside the passenger cabin out onto the deck, where we could hang onto the rail and watch the lower peninsula recede as we approached the docks at St. Ignace.

Our excitement was extended for another hour or so when, soon after we disembarked from the ferry, we stopped again at Castle Rock, just north of St. Ignace. Castle Rock was – and remains – a popular tourist stop in the UP. It is basically an outcropping of rock near the highway that rises nearly 200 feet straight up. An observation platform which crowns the rock can only be reached by climbing a set of rustic stairs that are dug and carved into the hillside. Back in the fifties these steps were pretty crude, if I remember correctly, a series of railroad ties set into the slope and varying intervals. To Bob, already a budding track star, something like this was a competition, and for once I went along with him as we raced to the top of the Rock, leaving Mom and Dad and the littler kids far below us.

The trouble with being twelve or thirteen though is that a beautiful view of natural or man-made things – the forest, the straits, the highway, etc. – fail to engage you for long, so once we'd looked around a bit from the top, we raced back down to the bottom, passing the rest of the family still on their way up. We may have even done the whole thing twice, I can't remember now. We spent some time too in the souvenir shop at the bottom of the rock. Souvenirs which represented specific places back then – Castle Rock, The Mystery Spot, Tahquamenon Falls, the Pictured Rocks, etc. – tended to bore me. I was usually more interested in buying something useful, like a "genuine" (*sure*) Indian tomahawk or headdress, a cowboy hat, or – something that always intrigued me – one of those little brass horses with western saddles and a tiny little gold chain hanging from its bridle. I think I may have gotten to buy one that trip.

Once we got north of St. Ignace however, there wasn't a helluva lot to look at. Endless pine forests and swamps on both sides of the highway as we continued west. Those "infinite" forests and that "upwelling of boredom" Anderson spoke of began to seep in. It was time to get out the comics – *Superman, Captain Marvel,* Mickey Mouse and Black Pete, and – our favorite – *Uncle Scrooge.* We were pretty well immersed in these colorful stories when we began to climb into the Porcupine Mountains. I remember vaguely hearing Dad in the background as I read, exclaiming about the view and "Isn't that beautiful, Daisy?" And there may have been a "Whaddaya think of these mountains, kids?" soon after that, but we weren't really paying attention. Bob was busy with Billy Batson and his super alter ego, Captain Marvel, and I was rolling in the money bin with Uncle Scrooge, and wondering when the Beagle Boys would show up.

Suddenly Dad broke through. *"Bob! Tim!* What the hell are you *doing* back there?!"

Startled out of our comic-induced daze, we both looked up just in time to see Dad jerk his head around to survey us crouched over our comics. Guiltily, we closed the books, keeping a finger in them to mark our place. But it was too late.

"Gee, *Christmas,* Daisy, is this why we just drove almost two hundred *miles?* So these kids can look at *comic books?!"* Dad slowed the car abruptly, shaking his head. Pulling over onto the shoulder of the road, he turned off the engine and just sat there, the back of his neck turning a bright angry pink – a very bad sign. We quietly laid our comic books on the floor, and drew ourselves back into the corners of the seat, hopefully out of his reach. We could always find our places later. But he didn't look at us again. "We might just as well turn around and go home right now," Dad said, shaking his head disgustedly.

By this time Mom had turned around in her seat, "Give me those comics," she ordered. Guiltily we handed them over. "Now you boys sit up straight and, and … well, look out the windows," she finished lamely, trying her best to find a point of interest for us as she looked out the window herself. "Okay," she told Dad. "They're going to pay attention from now on. Why don't we pull of at one of these overlooks so they can see the mountains?"

Huffily conceding, Dad restarted the car with a sigh and drove a little farther up the road to a turnoff and parked the car. Bob and I burst from the car, wanting to get out of range of Dad's anger. We raced out to the edge of the overlook, a cliff really, causing Mom to yell at us not to get so close, "You might fall!" Bob and I glanced at each other. What fun was it if there was no risk? Glumly, we stood safely back away from the cliff, looking off at the rather tame peaks of the Porcupines, probably wondering what was the big deal, anyway. It was just hills and a lot of trees.

I remember thinking of that family trip another time, years later, when watching the movie, *National Lampoon's Vacation.* Remember the scene where Chevy Chase, as Clark Griswold, took his wife and kids out to the rim of the Grand Canyon and stood there, bobbing his head and fidgeting for about five seconds over this natural wonder, then said, "Okay, let's go"? That's kinda how Bob and I felt looking at the Porcupine Mountains.

I think the trip went rapidly downhill after that. I'm pretty sure we camped in the tent one or two nights because I can still remember turning away in my blankets, feeling embarrassed and vaguely excited and guilty, as Mom undressed in the tent's near darkness to put on her nightgown. It rained one of those nights, soaking the old tent and causing a few uncomfortable leaks. Dad kept telling us not to touch the tent roof, because it would cause another leak. Of course once he told us that we had to find out if it was true. It was.

After that we stayed in a motel one night, which I'm pretty sure we all enjoyed more than the tent. But Dad worried about the expense. The next night we'd just gotten our tent erected in a park way up near the top of the UP and dad went to use the park manager's phone to call home and see how things were going at the mill. He learned from Rich that something had broken on the grinder. The part had been ordered, but this "emergency" was enough for Dad. We broke camp immediately, packed everything back up again and Dad drove through the night to get back home again the next day. The Bazzett family vacation was, mercifully, over.

Oddly enough, even though I always remembered that ill-fated family experiment, in the summer of 1971, following my first year of teaching in Monroe, Treve and I decided to take a vacation to the UP. Well, it was probably my idea. Back then Treve usually went along with whatever I suggested. She was "just the wife" then, remember? Jeff was about two and Treve was five or six months pregnant at the time. I can't really say what possessed me to think a car trip to the UP would be fun. Maybe it was just a feeling that, well, I was an adult now, with a job and a family, and, by golly, families went on *vacations* in the summertime. And if you lived in Michigan you went to the Upper Peninsula. Or maybe it was just a case of temporary insanity.

At least by that time there was a bridge across the Straits; no wait for the ferry or any rough passages to weather. We just zipped on across the Big Mack in our trusty blue Beetle, and headed into the north woods. Treve and I both look back at that trip and chuckle a bit ruefully now. We both remember getting barely across the bridge and heading west on Route 2, where the pine barrens and swamps rolled endlessly by on both sides of the road – that "familiar upwelling of boredom" again.

I looked over at Treve and said, "Man, look at all them trees, huh?"

"Yeah," she replied, gazing out the window.

A half hour went by, more trees. "There sure are a lot of trees up here," Treve commented. I shook my head, smiling, if a bit grimly.

Another half hour of emptiness. Feeling silly by now, I said it again, "Lookit all them trees."

Treve looked at me, the tiniest trace of a smile on her lips. Then we both began to laugh uproariously, snorting out between guffaws, "Lookit them trees, huh?" We laughed until we nearly cried, and then both wondered aloud what in the hell we were doing up there in the wilderness when we could have been home relaxing. But we continued gamely on, all the way to Escanaba, where we spent the night and visited with Larry and Joanne Leffel, friends we had known at Central. Larry had gotten a job in the English Department at Bay de Noc Community College. We had a pleasant visit, and then we headed home. Some families just aren't very good at vacations. Our own boring sojourn to the UP seemed to carry on a family tradition.

In all fairness, however, I should tell you that once all of us kids were gone from home and Mom and Dad were retired, they made an annual trip up into the UP, all the way up to Copper Harbor at the tip of the Keweenaw peninsula. They always went in the fall, when all the trees were changing color, and usually stayed at the same place, the King Copper Motel. They loved the vibrant changing colors and the quiet beauty of the UP in the fall. They had already made motel reservations on Beaver Island in September 1989 when Dad became ill. They didn't make it; by the end of October he was gone.

April 15, 2009

Man, almost two weeks gone by and I didn't write anything. I feel so guilty. Lots of reading though. I just finished a terrific book called *The Secret Life of Cowboys* by Tom Groneberg. It's a memoir about this guy who grew up in Chicago but headed west to pursue his dream of becoming a cowboy. So of course a lot of the book is about his attempts at cowboying in Colorado and Montana, some of which are reasonably successful and some not. But here's the passage that really grabbed me, about his being present when his first child was born –

I hold Jennifer's hand the entire night, through the contractions and the fears. And then, after seventeen hours, it is time. I have seen so many cows give birth, witnessed the bloody miracle of a calf's first breath, but when the nurses coax me to look at the crown of my son's head as it pushes into the world, I cannot. Instead I watch Jennifer, her beautiful and weary face. I don't know how to explain why I can't watch the birth, except to say that it is too much.

I get it, Tom. Reading this, I relived that moment when Suzie was born in the Augsburg military hospital. It was the first time I'd had the chance to witness the birth of one of my children, but like Groneberg, I couldn't. I was holding on to Treve's hand and watching her face, and praying with everything that was in me that everything would just be okay. It was a time when we didn't know the sex of the baby in advance. I knew how much Treve wanted a girl this time, but I didn't care at that moment. Girl or boy didn't matter. *Just make it all okay, Lord. I love this woman more than life itself. Please keep her safe and give us a healthy baby.* Over and over I was repeating this prayer. So, yeah, I understand, Tom. It was just too much.

Groneberg is only a few years older than my older son, Jeff, something I was very conscious of as I read his book. It seems somehow odd to me that I am now reading memoirs of people the ages of my children. There was also Brandon Schrand's wonderful memoir, *The Enders Hotel*, about his childhood in rural Idaho. Schrand is no older than my second son, and, like Scott, is a fan of the heavy metal, big hair and headbanger bands of the eighties. And right now I am nearly finished reading a military memoir by a young army veteran who is only around thirty. It's a current bestseller called *The Unforgiving Minute: A Soldier's Education,* by Craig Mullaney.

Reading these memoirs by young people makes me figure I'd better get back on the stick and start writing again. The next generation is gaining on old geezers like me, even in writing.

But instead I keep on with my lazy habits, reading and napping and watching TV. Making popcorn every night to go with *American Idol* or *Dancing with the Stars.* I know these are awful shows, but my wife controls the TV remote, so I just watch whatever is on while I eat my popcorn, then maybe a dish of ice cream. Because of my chronic tinnitus, I can seldom really hear dialogue on TV anymore, but these mindless so-called "talent" shows don't really require good hearing, so I zone out over them or any number of the equally horrible "reality" shows that Treve watches regularly.

But I think maybe I've been eating too much popcorn lately. You know this when you start finding popcorn hulls in your shorts. Or maybe not. At least they're coming through. Remember Beatle George Harrison's first solo album, a mammoth triple-disc thing called *All Things Must Pass?* Like that.

You'd never know to look at us now, old homebodies that we've become, but we were once world travelers. Treve says she can't remember much about those times, but we do have the pictures to prove it. We've been to Amsterdam, Paris, Zurich, Cologne, Munich, Strasbourg, and Vienna. And none of these trips were really all that expensive. If they had been, we couldn't have taken them. But we did.

Our first tourist adventure in Europe was a bus trip to Amsterdam. In fact all of our trips were by bus, arranged by the local service club folks. That first trip may have been one of our least favorite, but it had its moments. The Mercedes buses used for these trips were all very comfortable and quite luxurious, with wide seats and lots of leg and foot room. Usually they had an onboard toilet, but I don't think that was true with that first trip to the Netherlands. The reason I remember this seemingly small point is that there were a bunch of obnoxious young GI's in the back of the bus who got drunk quite early on in the trip and started hollering out to the driver that he needed to stop the bus because, "we hafta piss!"

Needless to say, these guys made at least part of the trip rather unpleasant, but I think a few of the older men on the bus – senior NCO's, I believe – had a little talk with them later on, and they behaved much better after that. Even so, it was a long journey from Augsburg to Amsterdam, and unfortunately it rained a lot too. We had booked the trip to go to the world-famous Tulip Festival, and we were there for it, but the nearly constant rain dampened our fun considerably.

We stayed at a bed-and-breakfast for a couple nights in an Amsterdam suburb and each day we were bused to the Tulip Fest where we trudged about with umbrellas exclaiming over the extensive fields of flowers. There were also indoor greenhouses and other displays to see, so we were able to get in out of the rain part of the time.

Here's what I remember from the trip, besides the drunks on the bus. At the B&B we were served sumptuous breakfasts with bread and cold cuts, bagels and jams, soft-boiled eggs served in egg cups – a first for us.

Our first day at the Fest, I dropped my Kodak Instamatic camera on the ground, breaking it and exposing my film. Fortunately, some friends of ours on the trip, Jerry and Julie Janowich, had an extra camera they lent us. Otherwise we'd have had no photos from that trip at all.

By the second day we were all kind of "flowered-out," but the sun had finally come out, so the bus took us into downtown Amsterdam and left us to wander around for several hours. I think we may have gone to some museums or other regular touristy kinda stuff, but if we did, I have absolutely no memory of that. We did go into a large department store and shop a bit. I bought a pair of small painted wooden shoes as a souvenir and Treve found a small cast-iron frying pan – what my folks used to call a spider – with a bright orange enamel finish on the outside. It matched the orange carpet and the two table lamps with orange shades we had then. Orange was still an "in" color then. We even had an orange telephone while we lived in Germany. We still have the wooden shoes, and we used the fry pan for many years, but I don't think we have it anymore.

And here's a typical American tourist kinda memory. We were happy to discover a McDonald's restaurant right downtown in Amsterdam, where we feasted happily on Big Macs and fries for lunch. But here's my most vivid memory of Amsterdam. After lunch a group of us, perhaps a dozen or so, were wandering around near Canal Street, which is, of course, famous for its red-light district – although I'm not sure we knew that at the time. As we passed by a large plate-glass display window, our whole group glanced in, and then did a rapid double take, or maybe even a whip-lashing triple take. Because the window was filled with a vast display of dildos. No, that's not a misprint. Dildos. Several rows of them, in fact, of all shapes, sizes and colors. And each of them was mounted on a spring affixed to display shelves that must have been moving – or perhaps vibrating – ever so slightly, because this colorful display of dummy dicks was bobbing and weaving, bouncing and waving at us as we all stood transfixed, staring open-mouthed at this garish spectacle. *Boing, boing, boing!*

Yeah, I remember the tulips, the egg cups, the wooden shoes and barges. But mostly I remember all those colorful dancing dildos, bouncing around in that big window, gaily inviting us all in. It was a sight to remember.

Another shorter trip we took was to Zurich, which may be one of the financial capitals of the world. I ain't rich, and don't ever expect to be, so I could be wrong about that. What we remember about that trip are Smurfs. We were missing our two boys after only a day away from them, so when we were shopping in a big department store there, we gravitated to the toy section, where we discovered a varied display of all these little blue creatures of molded rubber, together with little houses and other accessories. We spent the bulk of our disposable cash on a bunch of these little toys to take home for the kids. They were tickled pink with them and played with them for years. Zurich – the city of Smurfs.

Our other memory of that trip to Switzerland is a poke in the eye. The bus had stopped for gas somewhere on the trip home and we all got out to use the facilities and look around at a nearby herd of cattle in a pasture and take some pictures. Treve inadvertently walked into a tree limb which got her directly in the eye. It was a very painful poke, enough so that I took her to the hospital when we got back to Augsburg. She had a scratched cornea and had to wear a cover and a patch over it for a week or so while it healed. So her memories of Switzerland are about as pleasant as a sharp stick in the eye.

Treve also took a solo day trip to Strasbourg with some friends. Her main memory of that trip is how the Moroccan artisans and peddlers there – all of them so black as to be nearly purple – besieged her group so aggressively with their wares of carved ivory and leather. She found it a bit frightening, and was glad when their bus pulled away.

Paris was a mixed bag sort of trip. We saw the Arc de Triomphe, the Eiffel Tower, the Champs Elysees and walked along the Seine. We stayed in a small room at a hostel, with a tiny shower and a not very big bed. We remember the rudeness of waiters at an outdoor café, and how they did their best to ignore us. And I don't think we were being "ugly Americans" either. These guys just seemed to have it in for Americans. But what we both probably remember best was our visit to the world famous *Les Folies Bergeres*.

May 5, 2009

Man, have I been lazy! But all those books waiting on my bookcase shelves and in small piles all over the house – waiting to be read. So I've been busy reading them. The best one recently was *This Stubborn Soil*, a memoir of growing up dirt poor in the sandy hill country of east Texas, by William A. Owens, born 1905, died 1990.

But I should try to finish what I started last month, our trip to Paris more than thirty years ago, and a night at the famous *Les Folies Bergeres*. The Follies were probably about the closest thing Paris had to the showgirl extravaganzas of Las Vegas. Hell, maybe they still are; I don't really know. It's been a long time, but here's what I remember. We had seats in the balcony on the right side of the stage, so we were looking down at the show from up above. Lemme see now, would that be "stage right" or "stage left"? How did old Snagglepuss put it in those Saturday morning cartoons? "Exit stage left."

But no matter.

The thing is when the chorus line came out we were looking down on a long line of about forty tits. (I can't actually remember for sure, but it had to have been an even number.) No *kid*ding! There they were, all lined up across the stage below us. At least that was how they appeared. The truth is I'm pretty sure they were actually wearing some kind of transparent mesh body stockings, but from our vantage point … Well, you get the idea. And they were all jiggling and bouncing away as the girls did their synchronized kicks and other classy choreography. It was all very high class, you understand, tits and all. And I might have long forgotten our night at the Follies, except for what Treve did.

No sooner had the chorus line started into their routine when she reached over and snatched my glasses right off my face. Well, I don't know if I've mentioned this previously, but I am very nearly blind without my glasses, so this was probably just about the most awful thing she could have done to me at that moment. I was shocked and probably more than a little bit angry when she did this, and I let her know it too, demanding in an irritated whisper that she "give me back my *glasses, dammit!*" Which she did, after a few moments, muttering most ungraciously about how I didn't need to watch all these "naked women."

Of course, that's what the Follies are all about – naked women, I mean. Or, perhaps more accurately, "simulated nudity." And I tried, none too delicately, to explain this to her, still whispering, of course. But Treve wasn't having any of it. She all but accused me of bringing her to this *place* under false pretenses. I think I'd probably told her that the Follies was one of the most famous shows – and tourist attractions – in all of Paris. Which was true.

"You never said anything about *naked women* though," she hissed furiously.

"They're not *really* naked," I protested. "And anyway, why the hell do you think it's so *famous?!*" Still whispering, since we were surrounded by other theatergoers who were beginning to shoot unpleasant glances in our direction.

After this Treve lapsed into a stony silence which she pretty much maintained through the rest of the show. I had my glasses back, so I watched. And I'll admit it really was something for an ol' boy from Reed City to see all those tits in one place. But the initial enjoyment was somewhat diluted. Having an angry spouse sitting next to you while you watch something like this, kinda spoils things, ya know?

But the worst part of our evening in Paris was that when we returned to our tiny hotel room that night, she was still mad at me. We were in *Paris* for cripesakes, and there was no sex. You'd think just being in the city would have made it all special, but nope. I'd looked – well, probably *gaped*, actually – at all those other women's tits, so the shop was closed for the night.

We were reminiscing not long ago about all the places we'd been and things we'd seen when we lived in Europe, and Treve said she can barely remember being in Paris, but we did both remember that night at the Follies, and she still insists that I got just what I deserved. Hmm …

The fact is she claims that's really about all she remembers of Paris. I dug through a box of old photos and found a picture of her with the Eiffel Tower in the background. She looked closely at it and then said she can't remember that day at all.

Memories of Paris. Shit. But at least we got there.

One of the books I read in the past few weeks was a novel consisting of interrelated short stories called *Olive Kitteridge*, by Elizabeth Strout. The week after I read it, I learned it had just won the 2009 Pulitzer Prize for fiction. I was not surprised. The title character, an irascible, mostly thoroughly unpleasant old woman in her sixties, and then seventies as the story progressed, moved me in ways that much nicer fictional characters never have. Strout had lessons to teach – about how people are not always what they seem. This was a book I did not want to end. Widowed and lonely and filled with regret at seventy-two, at the close of the book Olive had met another man, a widower who was just as lonely as she.

What young people didn't know, she thought, lying down beside this man, his hand on her shoulder, her arm; oh what young people did not know. They did not know that lumpy, aged, and wrinkled bodies were as needy as their own young, firm ones, that love was not to be tossed away carelessly … because she had not known what one should know: that day after day was unconsciously squandered … It baffled her, the world. She did not want to leave it yet.

As I read this passage I thought of my own "lumpy, aged, and wrinkled" body; was hyperconscious of it, in fact. And I felt a sudden wash of love for the woman lying next to me in bed, reading her own book. And I was thankful beyond words that we still had each other, that we were still together and had this shared history. I thought of friends and acquaintances we've had over the years who have not stayed married; who have separated, divorced and remarried. And I wondered, what happens to that history, to those shared experiences, the memories? Are they like those wedding albums and photos from failed marriages that get packed away on a basement shelf or into an attic closet never to see the light of day again? Or do they get taken out at unexpected, unguarded moments and reexamined?

Hey, *Olive Kitteridge* is very powerful stuff, lemme tell ya. Good fiction matters, and this Strout woman knows what she's about, believe me. Pulitzer Prize? Damn straight, man! Way to go, Elizabeth.

The night before last I finished reading yet another memoir, a slender book, a fast read. It's called *The Film Club*, and was written by a Canadian, David Gilmour. No, not the David Gilmour of Pink Floyd. This is another guy who's been a writer of fiction and a rather famous film critic and TV personality in Canada for some years now. Here's the premise of the book. Gilmour's fifteen year-old son, Jesse, a dreamy and disaffected kid, is doing very poorly in school – hates it, in fact. So Gilmour makes him a startling proposition. He will let Jesse quit school if he agrees to watch at least three films a week with him. Well, Jesse, who is basically a good kid despite some dabbling with drugs and alcohol, jumps at the chance. There are, of course, some ups and downs in this risky educational experiment over the next few years, but a closeness develops between this father and son that I found myself envying as I read. Because they talk not just about films, but about everything. Jesse opens up to his father in a way that almost never happens these days.

They watch all kinds of films together over the next three years, films which open dialogues about the important stuff of life. I'm not gonna get specific about it, but this is one entertaining and thought-provoking read. I kept thinking of my own sons as I read, and I regretted all those extra hours I was putting in at work when my kids were growing up. I know most kids grow to hate school, or at least certain aspects of it, during their teen years. It's such a difficult time anyway, without throwing countless hours of boredom into the mix. Because let's face it, a lot of high school is really boring shit, ain't it?

I would quote something from the book here to give you a better idea of what it's like, but I mailed the book to my son, Jeff, yesterday. That's how important I felt it was. And Jeff has always been a big fan of films. He and his brother, Scott, both had part-time jobs at the Crofton Cinema, a local movie theater, while they were in high school in Maryland. It gave them the opportunity to see literally hundreds of films for free. But Jeff in particular kept this affinity for films. In fact, he celebrated his fortieth birthday recently by going to a screening of the latest celluloid installment of Wolverine, in which Hugh Jackman once again reprises his role as the furry superhero.

These "comic book films" fit nicely with Jeff's other passion – comics. In any case, I think he will like Gilmour's book.

Let me try to give you an example of some of those shared memories of a long marriage, some of that shared history.

One of the ways Treve and I were especially blessed with our two boys was in how close they always were. Jeff was two and a half when Scott was born, and he loved his little brother from the day we brought him home. And from the time Scott could crawl, he attached himself to Jeff, following him around the house and yard wherever he went. There was never any sign of sibling rivalry from either of them as children. They always backed each other up and tried to look after each other. I, on the other hand, had always had a very difficult relationship with my own next-older brother, Bob, which I talked about some in my first book, *Reed City Boy*. So I was always just a little bit amazed at how my own two boys were, from the very beginning, best friends – and still are.

My own early mid-life crisis may have had something to do with their closeness. When I quit teaching and went back into the army, Jeff and Scott were only six and four, respectively. Scott hadn't started school yet and Jeff was in the first grade when I left for Minuteman training in Missouri. Scott went to kindergarten and Jeff to second grade in Monterey, during my year at language school there. It was the beginning of a pattern of moves for them, for all of us, over the next several years. They went to school a year in California. Then they spent part of a year at a school in Belleville while I was TDY to Texas and Maryland and they were living with their Zimmer grandparents. Then they spent the next three years in an American school in Augsburg during my tour in Germany. When kids are constantly uprooted and moved from one place to another, they don't have the opportunity to form lasting friendships. While they did both form some close friendships while we lived in Augsburg, the nature of military life was such that their friends were always moving away when their parents were transferred to new duty stations. And of course after my three year tour was up, we moved again too, back to the States. There was another period then in a Belleville school, followed by a mid-semester move to Maryland. They were constantly starting over in new schools, new neighborhoods, and forced to find new friends each time. So perhaps that explains why Jeff and Scott depended so much on each other – why they became and remained best friends.

Or maybe they just liked each other, huh? That's possible too, I suppose. Why analyze it? Like I said, Treve and I were just always very glad that they did get along so well together. It could have been so much worse. I still remember a horror story Scott told us one day in Maryland when he was about ten and came back from down the block where he'd been playing with a friend who had two older brothers. He seemed a bit shaken when he came home, and when Treve asked him what was wrong, he told her, "I came home because Trip and Billy got in a fight, and then Trip was chasing Billy around the house with a *butcher knife!*" (These are not the boys' real names.) So, yeah, we were reminded once again how glad we were that our sons liked each other.

I remember too an incident in Germany when one of Jeff's school friends began picking on Scott out on the playground one afternoon. Jeff asked him to stop, and when he wouldn't, our peace-loving ten year-old son apparently jumped on this kid and began pounding him. Meanwhile, Scotty ran all the way home and up the stairs to our third-floor apartment to alert us that Jeff was "in a fight" out on the playground, something we were shocked to hear. When I went running to see what was going on, I met Jeff coming home, covered with dirt and grass stains, accompanied by one of his other friends who, wide-eyed with excitement, told us, "It wasn't Jeff's fault! Wayne was picking on Scott, so Jeff *beat him up*! Wayne got a *bloody nose!*"

I was shocked to hear this about our Jeff. I flashed back to a day in Monroe when he'd come in from playing when he was about five or six and told us another kid had called him a name.

"What did he call you?" I asked.

"Some kinda food," Jeff had replied.

"*Food?* What do you mean, *food?*" I asked.

"He called me chicken."

Well nobody was calling him chicken that day in Augsburg. But when I looked to Jeff to get his side of the story, he looked up at me and suddenly burst into tears.

"I *had* to fight Wayne, Dad," he blurted, tears and snot streaming down his dirt-streaked cheeks. "He was hurting Scott. But Wayne's my *friend*! I didn't mean to *hurt* him! Now he won't *like* me anymore!"

There was, I suppose, a confused kind of child's logic there, but I couldn't recognize it at the time. I just felt bad for my son, and proud of him too, for looking after his little brother. I don't remember what I might have responded, but I doubt if there was any wisdom in it. I wasn't much good at wisdom back then, any more than I am now. I hope I at least put my arm around my boy, maybe gave him a hug, told him it would be okay – something comforting. Because that's really all he needed, a little understanding, a little love from his old man.

And it *was* all right, as it turned out. Wayne remained his friend. I don't know how they might have resolved that playground scuffle, but Wayne kept on showing up at our house. He was too valuable a friend for Jeff to lose. He liked GI Joe's and comic books, and knew how to execute a well-formed fart and appreciate someone else's too. Friends like that are hard to replace when you're ten. Or any time in your life for that matter.

May 7, 2009

So of course my sons had other friends, but I think that if you asked either one of them today, who is your *best* friend, they would still name each other. Because they were still very close in the fall of 1988 when Jeff left home to go into the army, a decision that had taken us all completely by surprise. It wasn't that I hadn't talked about the advantages and "joys" (*Ha!*) of military service to my sons. I had. I had even encouraged Jeff to consider a hitch in the military when he was nearly finished with high school, but he – and Scott too – had just laughed whenever I got started on the subject. After high school Jeff had enrolled at Anne Arundel Community College, a local commuter's school, and was doing okay in his classes there. He started dating a girl he met there, and seemed quite serious about it – the girl *and* school. Then one day that first summer he came home and announced that he had enlisted in the army. Treve and I were both absolutely stunned. We'd had no clue that he was even considering going into the service. Suddenly I understood what my own parents must have felt when I had done exactly the same thing twenty-six years before.

Treve was shocked and upset at Jeff's revelation. Her first impulse was to wonder if he could still get out of it. She thought it was some kind of terrible mistake. My reaction was quite different. I was shocked, but I was also secretly pleased and proud at what Jeff had done – and on his own; not because I had badgered him into it, as Treve suspected, and may have even accused me of. But although I was proud of Jeff's decision to enlist, I also began to second-guess myself and wonder if he was really suited for the rigors and terrors of army basic training. I remembered how hard it had been for me, how I had struggled to keep up, and the culture shock I had felt at the hard-core, no-frills, harshly crowded environment of BCT. And to us, his parents, Jeff had always seemed just a bit backward. He had chosen not to take driver's ed in high school, so he didn't even drive. We were never sure if it was simply timidity on Jeff's part or had something to do with his being, like his mother, "directionally challenged," that he was afraid of getting lost. I mean here was a kid who didn't even *drive* yet. How was he gonna survive in the military? But I kept these fears to myself. Jeff had already signed his name on the delayed enlistment contract. He was, after all, nineteen years old, technically an adult, although Treve and I still had some trouble accepting this fact. He was our first *baby*, for cripesakes. How could he be going into the *army*?

But he was. The deed was done. And, at least unconsciously, we all began counting down the days he had left with us before his departure date in November. He continued his summer job working at the Crofton Cinema on into the fall, after his former classmates were going back to college. He also continued to see his girlfriend, and spent more time away from the house. She had a car, and would come and pick him up. Treve worried and fussed over him whenever he was at home, and sometimes at night, thinking about it after she went to bed, she would cry. I would try, ineffectually and clumsily, to comfort her, telling her he would be okay. But she would pull away. She still blamed me, in some obscure way, for his enlistment. And I worried too, silently, feeling, I suppose, that I *was* somehow guilty.

September and October passed all too quickly, and then it was November, and the day of his departure was suddenly upon us. His recruiter would come and pick him up and take him to the AFEES center out near BWI airport, where he would get his assignment orders and then be flown out to his BCT unit, at Fort McClellan in Alabama.

The recruiting sergeant arrived as scheduled at 5:30 in the morning in the pitch-black of what seemed more like the middle of the night. But we were all up, waiting. We knew we wouldn't see Jeff for another two or three months. The longest he'd ever been away from home before this had been a week-long basketball camp he'd attended at St. Mary's College in southern Maryland in the summer between ninth and tenth grade. All Treve and I could think was *our baby is leaving*. I think that perhaps it is at moments like this that we become more purely and simply parents than at any other time. For Treve the grief was almost too much. I was feeling the same grief, and was at the same time wracked with a feeling of overwhelming guilt, deserved or not. I knew we'd get through this, that he would be okay, but it didn't help. When the headlights of Jeff's ride pulled into our drive and illuminated our living room through the slats of the blinds, it was time for him to go. Hurried hugs, pats, kisses, murmured parting words – and then he was gone.

Scott and Suzie went back upstairs to their rooms and closed their doors, thinking their own thoughts. Treve and I went back into the dimly lighted kitchen, tears now trickling down our cheeks. Alone, wrapped in each other's arms, we stood in front of the sink and gave in to our grief, bawling great heaving sobs – tears and snot, great shuddering intakes of breath. We tried to do it quietly. We didn't want to upset the other kids. But it was hard. He was gone.

Our own grief and feeling of a kind of bereavement at Jeff's leaving was so great at the time that I don't think we gave too much thought to how it was affecting Scott. But a few weeks later we found a paper that Scott had written for an English class. Not quite seventeen, he was a senior at Arundel High that fall. It's been over twenty years now, but we still have that paper, creased and torn from many readings. His mother saved it. Scott had entitled it "Destiny Calls." Here it is.

"He'll be back soon."

The words echoed softly in my mind. The haze of the early morning made the things happening around me seem slow and dream-like. The voice seemed to be whispering to me from far away so that I couldn't quite understand what it was saying. But on that cold November morning the only thing I understood was that my brother was leaving. My nineteen year-old brother, who still read and collected comic books, had joined the Army and was going away. My brother, who had been there since the day I was born, wasn't going to be there anymore.

The Army had always been a suggestion from my father, a veteran himself. It was an option that my brother and I had always laughed at or chosen to ignore. In fact, to my father's dismay, the idea of my brother or I joining the Army had become no more than a bad joke. That's the way it was anyway until my brother enlisted. But somehow, as my family sat around the living room together at five in the morning waiting for the recruiter to come take him to the airport, it didn't seem quite so funny.

*An awkward silence fell over the house. I sat silently looking
at my brother. He looked mature and childlike at the same
time. His large hands nervously fidgeted with his small
bag of belongings, and his six and a half foot frame rocked
back and forth as he crouched on the stairs. My brother
and I exchanged nervous glances from across the room as
the ticking of the clock grew louder and louder with each
passing second. Again I heard the distant voice: "He'll be
back soon." This time the voice was more insistent, and
yet the unfamiliar voice was still too quiet to understand.
The message was gone as quickly as it came though, and
there was no time to think about it as my mind was flooded
with more jumbled thoughts. I was quickly brought back to
reality as my father's voice broke the silence to once again
go over the supplies my brother was taking. As the checklist
droned on, it became apparent to me for the first time that
my brother was leaving and how much my life would change
because of it.*

*I swallowed hard against the lump forming in my throat as
I struggled to think of something to say. My mind raced to
find the right words that normally came so easily to me, but
there were none. The voice was beginning to nag at the back
of my mind again when it was sharply cut off by the honking
of a horn outside.*

*An immediate mixture of panic and relief filled the room. All
eyes were focused on my brother as he stood up. The waiting
was finally over, but now he had to leave. The final words
of luck and love briefly passed between hugs and kisses,
and then there was nothing left to do, nothing left to say.
As he turned and started toward the door we followed like a
solemn funeral procession. He opened the door and turned
to face us once more. With a final half-hearted smile he
stepped off the porch and started toward the car.*

*We watched in silence as his silhouette marched into the
headlights of the waiting car. With one last wave, he got
into the car and rode away. A street light flickered above the
street like an ominous sentinel standing tall in the morning
darkness, a halo of light and mist surrounding it as it
watched over the street in its silent vigil, patiently waiting
for the sunrise that never came that day.*

*We stood in silence and watched as the red glow of the
taillights faded to darkness. Then, with a confidence I
hadn't felt in a long time, the words that had haunted me all
morning escaped my lips in my own unfamiliar voice.*

"He'll be back soon."

Brothers. Best friends. *Whew!* Powerful stuff from a sixteen
year-old, huh? Or am I just being a proud papa here? I don't
think so. The first time Treve read this she wept. Me too. And
I just had myself another snuffly old "geezer cry" as I re-typed
Scott's message from our collective past. Hard as it was for us
to read this paper – and for him to write it – twenty-plus years
ago, I am so thankful now that he wrote it. Kids. They can
really surprise you sometimes, ya know?

May 13, 2009

Wow, Wednesday the thirteenth. Isn't there something unlucky about that? Wait, no; that's Friday. Never mind.

Jeff did okay in the army, of course. But I felt so overwhelmed with guilt at his being in the army, and so worried about him, particularly during BCT, that I actually wrote him long, rambling, maybe even a bit crazed letters nearly every day of his basic training. I just didn't want him to feel too alone or cut off from us during what I knew would be a traumatic time. So yeah, every day. He told me later, when it was all over, that it was a bit embarrassing, his getting all that mail every day, sometimes in bunches of two or three letters, when so many of the guys got no mail at all. But he survived BCT and then did fine too in his AIT. He went on to Fort Sam Houston for medic training and then specialized to become a "psych tech." He was posted overseas to Germany where he served a tour at Landstuhl Army Hospital during the first Gulf war. But that's Jeff's story to tell. And I hope he does some day. Maybe it's enough to just say how proud we are of the man – and husband and father – that he has become.

I've been lost in books for the past week or so, which is why I haven't been writing. It's the same old story. So many books. And yet the real problem is that reading becomes less pleasurable when you know you're shirking on the writing side of things. Lately I've been thinking that if I ever finish this damn thing – this cockeyed, half-assed memoir about a lifetime of reading, or *whatever* it is – I'll just call it quits, so I can simply enjoy my reading. I guess "we'll see," as my parents used to always say, when what they really meant was *No*.

Right now I've got a few books going. There's Ralph Beer's *In These Hills* – a wonderful collection of essays about ranch life in Montana. It's from Bison Books at the University of Nebraska, and a beautifully packaged, glossy, large-ish kinda format. I may try to write to Ralph and recommend any later printing of this book be reformatted into a smaller size so it will fit better in the stack of *Reader's Digests* and *Guideposts* next to the toilet. Because the short pieces in the book lend themselves perfectly to commode reading. No disrespect meant, Ralph. I do some of my best reading in that most private of rooms.

And, just as I'd gotten about halfway into that book, I got in the mail my copy of Doug Stanton's brand spanking-new book, *Horse Soldiers* – a tome that's been in the works for over six years now. So naturally I had to start that one right away too. I'm about a hundred pages into it now and finding it just fascinating. Perhaps more on this once I finish reading the book.

My wife is currently reading a book by Gilberta Guth called *The Fighter Pilot's Wife*, a memoir; not to be confused with Anita Shreve's novel, *The Pilot's Wife* (which we both read some years back and also enjoyed the made-for-TV film, which starred one of our very favorite actresses, Christine Lahti, a Detroit-area girl). I read Guth's book last year, and at first I found it to be a bit slow, but as I got into it I began to realize that at least part of the story Guth was telling could reflect Treve's own experiences as a military wife during my second hitch in the army.

The Cold War was still a fact of life during those years, and the Soviet Union was still considered the biggest threat to world peace. This made my work in the army as a Russian linguist that much more interesting and exciting. As part of the military intelligence network that monitored the activity of the "Soves," as we called that shadowy entity operating just across the border in East Germany, I was having the time of my life. But for Treve, the implied threat of the Soviet military being so close by was a grim and sometimes frightening thing to consider. Recently she remembered something from our time in Germany that I had pretty much forgotten.

All spouses of U.S. military personnel – from all branches of service – were required, upon their arrival in Augsburg, to attend a briefing about evacuation preparedness. Treve, who was several months pregnant when she attended the session, still remembers being more than a bit intimidated by the volume of information and detailed instructions she received in printed handouts. While it's true we had been married nearly ten years by this time and she was, at least in theory, "a big girl," she had never really done any traveling by herself, and certainly not alone with the boys. But what she learned at this session, much to her horror, was that in the event of an emergency – i.e. a declaration of war, or an invasion of West Germany by the Soviets or any of their communist allies – she would be expected to have appropriate supplies immediately at hand so that she could pack the boys and said supplies into the car and join a convoy of vehicles heading … well, *some*where, presumably west.

She still remembers the sheer terror she felt as hearing all this, for a number of reasons. One, *I* would not be with her and the boys. She would have to do this on her *own*. Anyone who knows my wife also knows how "directionally challenged" she is, and that she does not like to have to drive anywhere by herself, especially in unfamiliar territory. Well, here we were, suddenly in another *country*, on another *continent*, for cripesakes, and they're telling her she has to be ready to flee at a moment's notice – to become part of a controlled (she *hoped*) column of American refugees in the event of *war!* This was *not* something my six months pregnant highly excitable and nervous wife wanted to hear.

The briefers who ran the session did caution the women that they weren't trying to frighten them – but they *were*, and they *did!* Treve, who was still pretty new to military ways, could think of nothing but that she had not signed up for this kind of crap when she married me.

"He was this college student with nice hair when I met him. He wanted to be an *English* teacher," she always protests to people when she tells this story. "He'd already *been* in the army. He was *safe* from all that, I thought. And then he went back into the army and everything changed!"

And she was right. Things *did* change rapidly. And she had adapted admirably for the first two years, while I was still in training, despite all the moves and shuffling of family here and there, dealing with realtors and movers, packing and moving, changing schools and living with her parents and long separations. She'd weathered that entire period of upheaval well, and even enjoyed parts of it, like living in California. But now they were talking about wartime contingencies and possible invasions and evacuation plans and routes, and she was quietly terrified. Quietly, like most of the other wives, because they were all new and didn't know each other – or anyone, for that matter. Who could they talk to, how could they voice all those unspoken fears?

So the husbands bore the brunt of these fears and terrors. After all, *they* were the bastards who had made the career choices that had put all these women and their children in this fine mess, or "revoltin' development," as Chester A. Reilly used to call such things.

When we talked of these long-ago fears and events again today, I had to admit that I had virtually no memory of any of it. I only remember all the fun I was having at work those early days, learning my trade and trying to be as good at it as I could possibly be. Because successfully completing language school and follow-up training didn't automatically make you a whiz-bang genius – or *fluent* – in the language you had studied. You had to work at your craft for years, and the truth is, in the language game you never master it all. There's always something else to learn – more vocabulary, more nuances of the spoken and written word. I worked with the Russian language for more than twenty-five years and I am here to tell you that I learned something new every single day. Maybe that's why I liked my job so much. It never really got boring. It kept me humble. In fact, as I was reading Doug Stanton's book, *Horse Soldiers*, last night, I felt an instinctive ripple of skepticism whenever he described a Special Forces soldier or CIA operative as being "expert" or "fluent" in Dari or Arabic or Russian. I couldn't help thinking, *No way*. These guys may have gone to school to learn these languages, but none of them were old enough or really experienced enough to merit either of those glib terms. But these are terms that newspapermen and journalists often play fast and loose with, simply because they are too easily impressed that someone can say or understand any words at all in a strange-sounding foreign tongue. Even after twenty-five years in the business, I never felt "fluent" or considered myself an "expert" in Russian. It just doesn't work that way.

But no matter.

So, no, I don't remember Treve's evacuation briefing or her terrified response to it, or how I might have reacted. I was busy at the time. So whom did she turn to in order to allay her fears and incipient terrors? Well, probably to Carol Olivas, who lived across the hall from us with her husband, John, and her two little boys, Anthony and Damien. John was, I think, on his third enlistment by then, so they'd been through the whole drill before, so Carol probably told Treve not to sweat it. Part of the instructions handed out detailed a list of supplies we should keep packed and ready to go at a moment's notice, preferably stored in a closet or under the bed for quick and easy access. I can't remember that we ever complied with this, so I guess we didn't worry about it all for very long.

May 20, 2009

Well, I've shamed myself away from other people's books and back to this, this *thing* I'm trying to write. I'm not really sure exactly what it is anymore. In the interim I've finished reading Ralph Beer's beautiful collection of essays about ranch life in Montana, and also read Doug's *Horse Soldiers* and wrote up a review of it which I posted on Amazon and also on LibraryThing.com, a website I've been having a lot of fun – and wasting a lot of time – with recently. I quite enjoyed *Horse Soldiers*, although it may have run just a teensy bit long for my taste, as I'm not normally much of a history buff. What the hell though. I gave him five stars anyway. What do I know? The book is already zooming up the bestseller charts only two weeks after its release date. Congrats, Doug!

In Beer's book, he refers very obliquely in a few of his essays to his military service, and to his return from southeast Asia in 1974, so I assume he served in Vietnam, and is probably just a few years younger than I am. But he doesn't ever really dwell on that period of his life, so this morning I picked up his novel, *The Blind Corral*, which won the 1986 Spur Award for best western novel. I think it is Beer's only novel, but it sucked me right in immediately. It's that good. I was less than a dozen pages into the story, about a young man returning from that war where he'd been an artillery sergeant, coming back to ranch life in Montana, where he begins training a horse as a kind of rehabilitation therapy. There is a line about the horse – *"He'd fart like a field gun throwing high-explosive rounds ..."* – that made me chuckle, and took me suddenly back nearly thirty years, to Germany.

In our family we call this story "A Romantic Sleigh Ride in the Bavarian Alps with a Typical Bavarian Meal." Because that's how this particular day trip was advertised in a flyer from the service club in Augsburg. Treve and I didn't take the kids many places with us when we traveled in Europe, but this seemed the perfect opportunity, since it was a Saturday trip and we wouldn't have to take the boys out of school. So we arranged for John and Ruth Williams to stay at our place that day with Suzie and the dog.

It was either late November or early December when we

set off on that all-day Saturday jaunt, and it was unseasonably warm, even for southern Germany. Jeff was especially excited about going. At eleven, he had been experiencing the first pangs of puppy love that year, pining quietly over a girl in his sixth-grade class named Romy Wiederle. We knew Romy's parents. Tony Wiederle was an army Chief Warrant Officer who worked out at the operations building with me, and his wife Sharon was very active with the local girl scouts. They had three daughters and Romy was the middle one. (Scott was later similarly interested in the youngest Wiederle girl, Stacy.) With her short hair and bangs, Romy was very cute, with an assertive tomboyish air about her. We knew about Jeff's crush, of course, so we'd asked him if he'd like us to ask Romy's parents if she could go with us on the bus trip to the Alps that Saturday. Of course his answer was in the affirmative, after some embarrassed hemming and hawing. So we arranged to pick up Romy early that morning on our way to the service club where we all boarded a bus, one of those luxurious Mercedes tour coaches that you never seem to find the likes of here in the States.

It was a dark unpromising-looking day as we departed Augsburg, headed south toward the Alps, and it didn't get a whole lot better. For most of the day, a chilling drizzle prevailed, and as we got into the foothills of the mountains north of Fuessen, we drove in and out of an enveloping fog. But the boys seemed contented as we rode the bus, especially Jeff, who got to sit next to Romy, who wasn't quite as tongue-tied as Jeff and managed to keep a conversation going.

Somewhere along the way, the bus pulled into a small village for that advertised meal that was included in the price of the trip. As it turned out, we were not sufficiently Deutsche-ified to enjoy that "typical Bavarian meal." Once all the bus passengers had been seated at tables in the restaurant, a crew of waitresses came hustling out of the kitchen bearing large steaming platters of sausage and sauerkraut which they placed on our tables. As the platter came around, Treve and I each took small helpings and encouraged the kids to do the same. They balked at this strange-looking and –smelling foreign fare, but did each take miniscule portions on their plates. But they wouldn't eat it, couldn't perhaps. Because the

273

sauerkraut was *very* sour, and the sausage – *blood* sausage, or *Blutwurst* – was, to our American palates, all but inedible.

Romy and the boys sniffed and poked at the food. Treve and I took a few polite bites, but even we couldn't bring ourselves to eat much of this strange food.

But it was lunchtime, and we were hungry, so I decided to order something we knew we'd like – French fries. It was one of the few food items I could order in German, so, ever the cosmopolitan traveler and gourmet, I motioned a waitress over and ordered.

"Eine grosse Pommes Frites, bitte," I requested in my best Bavarian. I didn't know how much things cost off the menu here, but I figured I could afford one large order of fries, which would at least take the edge off the kids' appetites.

"Grosse?" the waitress echoed doubtfully.

"Ya. *Grosse!"* I repeated back, holding my hands several inches apart in front of my chest and smiling confidently.

Nodding her head, the waitress hurried off and disappeared into the kitchen.

Meanwhile the other bus passengers were doing their best to consume the "typical Bavarian lunch" provided. Maybe they liked it, or maybe they were just being a bit more adult than we could be about this new culinary experience. That was fine with us. We'd be happy with our French fries. So we waited. And waited. Fifteen or twenty minutes went by, and many of the diners were nearly finished eating when finally our waitress came sailing out of the kitchen. She was carrying an enormous platter with one of the LARGEST orders of large fries we had ever seen. A serving platter was piled high with glistening, steaming hot fries. There must have been three or four pounds of potatoes on that plate.

Proudly placing this huge pig-sized portion of potatoes down on the table before me, the Fraulein smiled smugly and said, "Eine grosse Pommes Frites!"

My mouth gaped open – as did Treve's and the kids'. I was so stunned at this plethora of potatoes that I couldn't speak at first. I closed my mouth, opened it, and closed it again.

"Um … aah … Duh- Danke," I finally got out. "Danke shoen."

"Bitte," replied the girl, bowing – curtsying nearly – and departed our table.

The kids and Treve were all staring open-mouthed at me. Then we all began to laugh at once. It was all just too silly for words. So we dug in and ate. There were far too many fries for us, of course, so after taking some for ourselves, we passed the platter around our table and then over to the adjacent tables too, until they were all finally gone. Everyone around us was smiling and laughing at this fine joke on us. But they didn't mind eating the fries.

My boys still remember this incident. All we have to say to them is the phrase "typical Bavarian lunch," and it all comes back to them – the unappetizing *Blutwurst* and kraut, of course, but especially "eine grosse Pommes Frites."

We made another stop along the way to take pictures of Mad Ludwig's hundred year-old Neuschwanstein Castle near the village of Hohenschwangau. This is the castle that Walt Disney used as a pattern to create his own Sleeping Beauty's castle in Fantasyland. It was still foggy and drizzling rain, so we didn't linger long with our cameras. We didn't travel much further to get to our destination, which was somewhere around the ski resort of Garmisch. I can't remember anymore the name of a village, or if there even was one. Our bus pulled into a farmstead, with a house, barn and other outbuildings and we all disembarked. We were there – the Bavarian Alps. It was time to take our "romantic sleigh ride."

But there was a problem. There wasn't any snow.

But no matter.

We went anyway. The tour people were ready for just such an eventuality. They had "sleighs" that were fitted with automobile tires. Which made them just plain old wagons, actually, with a couple rows of seats for passengers. There were several of these sleighs/wagons – enough to accommodate all the bus passengers, riding in two separate shifts. Treve and the kids and I managed to get on board a wagon in the first bunch to set off along a well-traveled, heavily rutted and muddy trail.

Each wagon was pulled by a powerful-looking team of large shaggy horses, Belgians perhaps, or maybe a larger German breed like the Oberlander. I don't really know that much about horses. They were imposing-looking beasts, in any case, with huge iron-shod hooves that they stamped impatiently as we settled ourselves onto the wagon. And here was another hitch in the plans for our "romantic" ride – at least for poor Jeff. Because Romy wanted to ride up front on the high seat with the man driving the team. The driver had no objections, and quickly and easily swung her up onto the seat beside him. Jeff was crushed. His face fell as he settled sadly into a seat beside his brother, behind Romy and the driver. Treve and I would have been laughing at the way this so-called "romantic sleigh ride" was turning out if we hadn't felt so badly for Jeff.

And things didn't get a whole lot better either. *Funnier*, maybe, but not better. Because we had barely started out up the trail from the farmyard when those enormous draft horses, pulling our weight up that hill, began to fart. And yes, it was just as Ralph Beer described it in his novel – farts "like a field gun throwing high-explosive rounds."

The drover, obviously used to horses and their ways, never batted an eye. But poor Romy, seated beside him directly in the line of fire, flinched back in horror, ambushed by that first sulphury salvo of equine flatulence. Because these were *not* dry odorless farts like the ones we all so often enjoyed as kids following an evening of popcorn, when all it took was to draw your knees gently up to your chest to unleash a salvo of satisfying shots which would ripple the bedclothes with nary a whiff of stink. *Ooh, noo!* These horses were charging the atmosphere for several feet with perhaps one of the most powerfully putrid smells we had ever experienced, the kind of odor that George Carlin once famously said "could knock a buzzard off a shit wagon."

"Oh, pee-*yew*," Romy whimpered softly, fanning the air in front of her face. "Do they *always* do that?"

The driver, who may or may not have understood English, simply nodded, smiling cheerfully back at her, as the horses continued to huff and snort – and yes, fart – their way up the trail, harnesses and tack jingling gaily.

Jeff and Scott, who sat in the seat beneath and behind the driver, were both wrinkling their noses and giggling, as were Treve and I. It was still misting slightly as we rumbled up the hill. When we reached the top of the first ridge, the driver stopped to give the team a chance to blow. One of the horses took that opportunity to download a large batch of fresh road apples, greenish and glistening as they plopped to the ground before Romy's horrified, open-mouthed gaze.

The driver, perhaps noting Romy's discomfort, simply raised his eyebrows briefly, then clicked his tongue and started the team and wagon down the other side of the ridge.

I wish I could provide you with some lovely images of snow-clad mountains and alpine meadows or some such descriptions here, but the truth is I can't remember any of that, and probably neither could Treve or the boys. We remember the horses and the horse shit though. So we have at least *some* memories of that "romantic sleigh ride in the Bavarian Alps." Jeff is forty now, and so is Romy. I wonder if she remembers, wherever she is.

May 21, 2009

Last night I indulged in something shameful. Certainly shameful at least to a dedicated reader and book lover. I watched the finale of *American Idol* on TV. This is not a show I can usually stand for more than a few minutes at a time. For some reason it seems the gold standard on *American Idol* is who can scream the loudest for the longest. Melody and real talent seem secondary. But this year I was immediately taken, as apparently were a million other Americans, by the stage presence and sheer showmanship of Adam Lambert, with his perhaps permanently black-mascaraed eyes and piercing gaze directly into the eye of the camera. And yes, he can scream long and loud with the best of them, but he can also carry a tune and never hits a false note. His take on a Led Zeppelin tune a couple weeks ago was dead-on and absolutely mesmerizing. And I was never even really a Zep fan.

Geeze, this is kind of embarrassing, writing about my watching this usually awful show. But I did, so ... Lambert didn't win last night, even though his talent was very obviously so much larger than that of the winner, Kris Allen. Their musical styles were so radically different that they both shoulda won. Allen's style is more in the laid-back troubadour mode of Jason Mraz, a young singer I appreciate very much.

So why am I writing about this? Because for me the high point of the show last night was the surprise appearance of KISS, whom Lambert introduced by singing a few bars of the group's ballad (a rarity for the heavy metal glam band), "Beth." And then suddenly the curtain lifted on an upper level stage and there they were, in full seventies-era costume and makeup, flanked by tongues of fire, belting out what has become a signature song for them, "Rock and Roll All Night." Again, I feel stupid and embarrassed to say it, but it was unexpectedly AWE-some.

> *"AH*-A-EE WANNA ROCK AND ROLL *ALL*
> *NAH*-A-IGHT,
> AND PARTY *EV*-ER-EE *DAY*-EE! ..."

We immediately phoned our son, Jeff, in Maryland, who is, as I mentioned here earlier a KISS fan since he was eight or nine years old, and still is, although perhaps a bit less rabidly now that he is a father of two little girls. He was already watching, so we agreed to call back later and hung up.

And then Treve and I sat there side-by-side on the couch, heads bobbing – *headbanging?* – in time to the outrageously loud lyrics and music (we'd turned the TV volume *UP*), the same stuff we had listened to with Jeff and Scott thirty-plus years ago as it blasted from our stereo in Monterey and Germany and Maryland. It was fine – and weird – lemme tell ya.

Because I know we were both also remembering even earlier times, before KISS came along in our lives, when our two little boys, five and three, would sit on our overstuffed floral-patterned gold couch in our Monroe living room, rocking together to other tunes, their round heads bouncing off the couch cushions, shiny blonde hair flopping. Back then it was to the bright bubblegum sounds of The Archies' "Sugar Sugar," or to the contagious lyrics of Brit group Vanity Fair's "Hitchin' A Ride" –

"A thumb goes up, a car goes by
It's nearly one am and here am I
Hitchin' a ride ..."

"Thumb" became "sum" in their bright voices as they rocked and bounced in unison, two arms extended, small pink thumbs upraised. I could weep, remembering their sweetness, their innocence.

Our tiny rockers had other rock-and-sing-along favorites. One was Jim Croce's "Bad, Bad LeRoy Brown," but when they sang along with this tune, the "damn" in the line, *"baddest man in the whole damn town"* was sung *sotto voce*, and they would glance guiltily about as they whisper-sang this "bad word." Another favorite of the boys' in those days was one they'd probably just as soon forget now. It was a tune written by Shel Silverstein about a bar-girl, with these lines in the chorus:

"She's the queen of the Silver Dollar,
And she rules this smoky kingdom,
And her scepter is a wine glass,
And a bar-stool is her throne ..."

Which would be fine, except the version of the song I had was on an album called *Barbi Doll*, by Barbi Benton. Remember

Barbi? She was a *Playboy* centerfold and Hugh Hefner's main squeeze for a few years back in the seventies. And a pretty decent C&W singer too. Anyway, when Barbi sang the song, the lyrics became "*I'm* the queen." And that's the way the boys learned the song, so they became – for at least a few short minutes – our two small "queens" rocking and singing along with Barbi.

All these memories, brought back by KISS on *American Idol*.

When we talked later, Jeff, chuckling, once again calling Simmons and Stanley "just a couple of ultra successful semi-retired Jewish businessmen." Maybe so, son, but they put on one hell of a show and can still rock with the best of 'em.

Which was more than I could say about Rod Stewart, who appeared later in the program – another surprise guest. He just couldn't hit the notes anymore, and he was singing a favorite of mine, his now-classic college-boy lament, "Maggie May."

I first heard that song one night in 1971 when I was driving back home to Monroe from Eastern Michigan University in Ypsilanti, where I was taking one of many graduate courses needed to boost me to the next level on the salary scale at the college where I was teaching full-time. I would probably not remember the first time I'd heard this particular tune except for the fact that as I was listening to Rod on my '66 VW's Blaupunkt, head bobbing, boppin' along, the muffler suddenly blew out, making the engine noise so loud that I had to turn the radio nearly all the way up to hear the rest of the song. I remember thinking, *This song is just so* great! That muffler business was a bummer though. A couple days later I took the car into the garage and then went to K-Mart or Bargain City and bought Rod's album, *Every Picture Tells A Story*. It was the first of many Stewart albums to grace my record collection. His career continued unabated into the eighties and even the nineties. My sons even became fans, with his songs like "Da Ya Think I'm Sexy?", "Young Turks", "Some Guys Have All the Luck", "Downtown Train" and others.

Rod Stewart's chart successes have continued into the new millennium despite a bout with thyroid cancer at the end of the nineties, after which he purportedly had to "re-learn" how to sing. I know he's still got it, so I don't know why he sounded so old and sad on *Idol* last night. After all, the guy's not quite as old as I am. Rock on, Rod – *please!*

But no matter, I suppose.

May 22, 2009

Well, I'll be damned. I'm back again. I'm sore as hell this morning after cutting the grass last night after supper. I wonder if there's a particular or officially okay age when you can start hiring some kid to mow your lawn. I don't think I'm quite there yet, but when it hurts to get out of bed the day after, I begin to at least think about it. Fortunately Treve likes to push the mower too, something she never expressed the slightest interest in for the first thirty-six years of our marriage; but when we retired here to Reed City she developed an interest in working outside occasionally, and now she loves to mow grass. Of course we have made the concession of buying a self-propelled mower, which gives our old muscles a little help.

It got up over eighty degrees yesterday, so we waited until after supper, when it was *only* about seventy-five, to mow. There was a breeze, so it wasn't too bad. It's kinda weird to have weather this hot already here in Michigan. The dogs begin to trudge, tongues out, by the time we get halfway around the block when the temperatures rise like this. But they hate to miss their walks no matter what the weather.

But no matter. I mean who cares about lawn mowing, weather or dogs anyway? Well, maybe dogs. Because I know there are a lot of dog lovers out there.

After my shower, I settled in with Ralph Beer's novel last night. I'm more than halfway through with it now, and it just keeps getting better. *The Blind Corral* was first published twenty-some years ago. I picked it up for a penny plus shipping. Sadly it's been out of print for years now. Hell, *more* than sadly! It's a damn *shame*, that's what it is! Good writing like this should *never* go out of print!

In the chapters I read this morning Beer introduced a character named Duncan Carlisle. who is, I am almost certain, a thinly veiled fictional version of James Crumley, a favorite author of mine, who lived in Montana until his death last September. Beer mentioned a few other state authors in his essay collection, and Crumley was one of them. And he was also – in his prime – famous for his drinking and bar crawling in Missoula, so yeah, Carlisle has *got* to be Beer's homage to Crumley.

I first "discovered" Jim Crumley in an Ann Arbor bookstore nearly forty years ago. Or rather I found his first novel on a sale table. *One to Count Cadence*, first published in January 1969, was one of the very first novels about the Vietnam war. And I still think it is one of the best. I had a personal reason for liking the book. The main characters, Slag Krummel and Joe Morning, were both ditty-boppers in the Army Security Agency, just as I had been from 1962 to 1965. For you uninitiated, a ditty-bopper, or dit-chaser, is a manual Morse code intercept operator, MOS (military occupational specialty) 058 (later 05H). I wrote about that hard-drinking carousing life in my second memoir, *Soldier Boy* (2005).

I can still remember my excitement, standing there in that Borders store browsing Crumley's book, when I discovered this – that here was a story about the *ASA*, and it was filled with all the same kinds of nasty stuff my friends and I had gotten into and a lot more besides. Because Crumley's fictional ASA unit deployed from the Philippines on an early clandestine mission into Vietnam. But I'm not gonna tell you the whole story, because – unlike Beer's fine novel – forty years later *One to Count Cadence* is still in print. So if you're curious, go buy it and read it, okay?

I bought two copies of the book that day and sent one to my brother, Rich. I later learned that he liked it so much he went out and bought a half dozen more copies himself and sent them off to some of his old ASA buddies.

Around 1976 the Army Security Agency began to disappear, morphing slowly into something a lot less special called INSCOM, the Intelligence and Security Command. So the guys who served in the old ASA are all getting a little long in the tooth by now, but many of them have read Jim Crumley's book and they pretty much unanimously agree that it is "fucking good stuff," if I may use a popular description among we old ASA-ers.

Crumley never wrote another book about the ASA – never reprised those terrific characters. Instead he began writing literate, character-driven, often violent, *noir*-type mysteries, beginning with *The Wrong Case* in 1975. He wrote several of these over the next thirty years, but never did become a mainstream bestselling author here in the U.S. His books were translated into other languages, however, and he became very popular in France and Japan, so he managed to make a living. And he *needed* to, considering he was married five times and had several children.

There's a little more to this story, so bear with me. In early 2006, a few months after I published my ASA memoir, *Soldier Boy*, I phoned Jim Crumley in Missoula to ask him if he'd like to read my take on the ASA. I got an answering machine, so I left a brief message. A month passed and I figured I might as well write off that idea. Because I had written and phoned other writers I admired and learned that most of them just don't want to be bothered.

Then one night about six weeks after I'd called, the phone rang here. Treve took the call, listened for a moment, then, putting her hand over the receiver, she asked me, "Do you know somebody named Jim Crumley?"

I'm sure my eyes widened as I snatched the phone from her and said hello, and heard this gruff, gravelly voice on the other end, "apologizing" for taking so long to return my call. Yes, he actually *apologized* to me! A guy who'd written nearly a dozen books and was read by people in Europe and Asia. I mean I was shocked and flattered all at the same time. I think we talked nearly a half hour that night. Jim explained he'd been on a book tour in France and had just gotten back the week before. We compared notes on our ASA time then and chatted like old friends, swapping "war stories" and lies like two old army buddies. And before he hung up, he said yeah, he'd like to read my book.

I sent Crumley a book, and I know he read it because he emailed me some of his reactions and told me some more of his own stories, as so many of my other readers had done. We never talked on the phone again, but we did keep in touch by email. I kept urging him to write a memoir of his life, but he intimated that there were just too many skeletons in his closets. Jim Crumley died in September of last year, a victim of too many years of hard living. He will be missed by many. I know *I* already miss him.

June 19, 2009

Geeze, how embarrassing. It's been nearly a month since I checked in here. I have a couple excuses, but not good enough ones to excuse four weeks away. We did go visit our kids in Pennsylvania early this month, but we were only gone for ten days. And it was so wonderful to get back home again that I've been loafing ever since.

Not that we didn't enjoy our visit. One of the most important things that happened – at least as far as I'm concerned – was that our eighteen month-old grandson, Zachary, learned to say "Bram-pa" while we were there. That's *Grandpa* for those of you who don't speak Toddler.

Or I could use the excuse that I've been battling a cough and draining sinuses for the past few weeks. At first we didn't know if I had the flu (Swine flu was much in the news this spring), or just a bad cold. I've finally decided it's really only allergies. It gets worse after I've been outside or working in the yard. That yellow pollen dust is all over everything these days. So I've been trying to stay inside. Treve was doing the lawn mowing up until this week when I had to drive her down to our daughter's place near Detroit. Suzie put her back out and needed help with her little boy, who is just ten months old, but at twenty-five pounds was just a little too much to handle with a bad back. So I've been batch-ing it for four days now while Treve bonds with her daughter and "the boy," as they both call little Adam.

So how come I haven't been writing? The usual answer. So many good books to *read!* And I just got some more in the mail recently and have already read a couple of them. Mary Clearman Blew's *All But the Waltz* is another excellent Montana memoir of five generations of one family's good times and lean, mostly the latter, in Fergus County of that state, with its long history of cattle and cowmen that always fascinates me. I finished it off in just two days. I often feel guilty when ripping through a book at such a pace, because I know how long it takes to write a book like that, but sometimes you just can't help it. The story just pulls you along and you can't wait to see what happens next.

Another new purchase I perused this week with considerable interest is a book a bit off the beaten track called

Elephas Maximus: A Portrait of the Indian Elephant. It's written by Stephen Alter, who grew up in northern India on the slopes of the Himalayas, the son of American missionaries. He documented those years in a delightful memoir called *All the Way to Heaven.* The first chapter in the elephant book caught my attention when Alter described his childhood visits to Corbett Park where he and his two brothers rode on the back of an elephant named Malan Kali, "whom we had rechristened Melancholy because of the sad yet patient look in her eyes." He describes their rides in the howdah on the back of the enormous pachyderm and I was once again reminded of our "romantic sleigh ride in the Bavarian Alps" by the following passage –

> *"We also delighted in the way she farted, pinching our noses and snickering into our fists whenever we heard the sputtering sound, like air escaping from the bladder of a football. Whoever was seated at the back could see the elephant ceremoniously raise her tail and expel huge clods of dung the size of cannonballs."*

I have to confess that I snickered a bit myself upon reading this. Horses, elephants or people, it doesn't matter. It seems small boys – and maybe a few old men – are always tickled by things scatological in nature. Farts are funny, whatever their source. Period.

June 22, 2009

Back again after a weekend of coughing, sneezing and feeling generally miserable. I was talking about the writer James Crumley last month before my long interruption. Jim spent most of his later years in Montana, but he grew up in Texas. I spent a few months in west Texas back in the late summer and early fall of 1977 after leaving Monterey.

If I remember correctly, most of the graduates of DLI who were slated to go into signals intelligence (SIGINT) went on to Goodfellow Air Force Base for several weeks of additional equipment training following their language training in Monterey. Goodfellow, or "Goodbuddy," as it was affectionately known to its denizens and graduates is located outside the city of San Angelo, which is southwest of Abilene, if that helps.

Now San Angelo is a pretty good sized town, but the only thing I knew about it was that Marty Robbins had written and sung a song by that title on his album, *More Gunfighter Ballads and Trail Songs* back in 1960. My brother Bob and I were both big Marty Robbins fans back in high school and used to put both of those Gunfighter Ballads albums on the hi-fi in our room to listen to as we fell asleep. If you remember Marty's monster hit, "El Paso," then you pretty much know the story sung in "San Angelo" too. Except this time the girl's name is Secora instead of Falina, and in the latter song, not only does the singer get blown away, so does the girl – a kind of cowboy *Romeo and Juliet*. If you're a Robbins fan, you probably also remember he did a later tune called "El Paso City." I mean he really milked the success of that first western hit for all it was worth. But hey, I had no problem with that. The guy had to make a living, right? He couldn't live forever on royalties from "A White Sport Coat (and a Pink Carnation)" and "Singin' the Blues."

But no matter.

I got to Goodbuddy in late August of 1977, after a week or so of home leave in Belleville, where Treve and the boys were getting settled in with her folks in Belleville. I felt a little funny about suddenly saddling them with my family, and even offered to pay some rent for them while they lived there. Of course Chet and Wanda wouldn't hear of it. This was their daughter and grandsons, after all, and family help family when they need it. That's just the way it was. I understood this, but still wanted to do something in return, so before I left Belleville, I took Chet with me and went shopping at Sears, where we found a washer and dryer and had it delivered to Zimmers. Strangely, at least to me, they had never had these most essential appliances in their home since I'd known them. Treve tells me her mom had once had a wringer washing machine, but it was gone by the time I joined the family. Wanda worked every day as a beautician, and on weekends she would do their washing at the laundromat in town.

I found out what this was like, because while I was there on leave that August Treve and I took the boys and a couple of enormous bags of dirty clothes to the laundromat on the main street of Belleville. It turned out to be kind of a horror. The first washing machine we tried to use was liberally speckled with some sodden bits of straw and traces of manure, both inside and out, obviously just used by some farmer – or cowboy. So we had to wait for a couple more washers to be freed up. It was hot in the laundromat, and depressing. Most of the people using the machines looked poor and shabby. Of course there may have been a logical explanation – other than outright poverty – for this. Because I know from experience that when I had to do my own laundry I used to wait until pretty much everything was dirty before I'd go to the laundromat. And then I'd wear my shabbiest least-often worn clothes while doing my wash, because of course you want all your good stuff to be clean when you're done. Or maybe the people we saw in the Belleville place really *were* poor folks.

In any case – and I know I'm digressing here – I have always remembered that one day we spent in the downtown laundromat of Belleville, because while we were there we heard over the radio the shocking news that Elvis Presley had just died. It was August 16, 1977. Elvis was forty-two years old. So, you see why I remember that particular wash day.

It was such a depressing and demoralizing experience, just being there in the laundromat with my wife and kids, not to mention the sad news about Elvis, that I decided then and there to go buy Wanda a new washer and dryer. And I did. Although it was a bit more complicated than I'd expected. Because they'd had some problems a few different years when their basement had flooded in the spring. So they were a bit worried about setting up a couple electric appliances down there. But Chet and I put our heads together and came up with a half-assed solution. We couldn't predict spring floods, but we could get the appliances up off the basement floor. Chet scavenged around the place and found some old planks and two-by fours and a couple old joists and we spent an hour or two measuring and sawing and then hammering and nailing it all together to form a platform large enough to hold both washer and dryer that stood about a foot off the basement floor. He even found an old piece of linoleum to cover the framework with and give it more of a "finished" look. The final product may not have looked pretty, but it worked. And by paying for the pair of new appliances, I felt a little better about leaving my family there for the next six months or so. (Because there would be yet another temporary posting for me after the one in Texas.) Wanda wouldn't have to spend her Saturday afternoons or Sundays at that depressing town laundromat anymore, and Treve would do the wash for all of them as long as they stayed there.

When we cleaned out the house several months after Wanda's death (in December of 2001; Chet died in 1984), that same washer and dryer were still there, still sitting on that makeshift platform Chet and I had cobbled together. They still worked, nearly twenty-five years later, and were sold with the house, so I guess you could say it was a gift that kept on giving.

But I was talking about my TDY to Goodfellow. I was there only a couple of months, but I do have a few lasting impressions from that time.

I distinctly remember my arrival at the San Angelo airport. I had flown from Detroit to Dallas-Fort Worth, and then taken a smaller plane to San Angelo from there. It was a smallish airport, so when we disembarked from the aircraft there was no walkway tunnel into the terminal. We came down steps from the plane right onto the tarmac. And the first thing I felt was as I came down the stairs onto the runway was this furnace-like blast of hot air that just kept on blowing as I stepped off the last stair step. My first thought was that the jet engines were still running and I was feeling the back blast from them. But as I walked away from the plane it didn't take me long to realize that what I was feeling was simply the west Texas wind across the runway on a one hundred degree summer day. It was strong and it was *hot!*

It was to be my introduction to – and first personal experience with – the concept of *dry heat.* You know how you're always hearing people from the southwest talk about how their temps in the 90s and even higher don't seem so bad, because "it's a dry heat." Well, as it turned out, they were right. Because for most of my stay at Goodfellow, all the way through late October, the mercury rose regularly into at least the nineties nearly every day. But I got used to it very quickly, believe it or not. *Dry heat* – versus the humid, sticky heat we endured for over twenty years while living between Baltimore and Washington.

Fortunately the barracks we lived in were air conditioned, as were our classrooms and work areas. Texans aren't masochists, after all. Because even *dry* heat like that could bake you to a fine crisp in short order. Uncle Sam obviously didn't want his soldiers and airmen deep fried, so yeah, most of the main buildings on Goodfellow were well cooled with central air.

Technically, I could have brought my family with me to Texas, but I would have had to pay for their housing out of pocket, which we didn't feel was really an option, unless we wanted to run through all our savings in a few months. That and the fact that we would have had to put our kids in school there for just a month or so and then pull them out again. So I went alone and lived in the barracks with the single guys, most of whom were ten to twelve years younger than I.

The Air Force barracks I lived in were quite new, and a vast improvement over any barracks I'd ever seen in the army. If I remember it correctly, my own barracks was a single story cinder block building that consisted of what we called "quads," meaning there were four two-man rooms which surrounded a central latrine and a common room with a big TV and enough seating for about a dozen people. And we had real beds to sleep in, with an innerspring mattress and box springs – not the standard saggy link spring bunks I'd become accustomed to in the army barracks. I had heard about the better living conditions the Air Force enjoyed for many years, but now I believed it. And the administrators pretty much left us alone for most of the time I was there – about nine or ten weeks altogether, I think. We may have had a couple walk-through inspections when we had to GI the latrine and showers and mop and buff a bit, but it was not a big deal. The Air Force seemed to recognize that we were there to go to school for a couple of months and learn something, so they didn't bother to harass us. It was decent of them.

And I got lucky in my roommate too. He was a big jovial kid, maybe twenty or so, named Christian Hoffman. And I think he kinda recognized right away that I was this "older guy" and decided he wouldn't give me any trouble and would try to take his natural inclination to party somewhere else. And he did. On our off time, Chris was off doing his own thing somewhere, so we got along fine. He was an intelligent kid, and I think he already knew some German (hey, his name was *Hoffman*) in addition to the Russian he'd learned at DLI, and he had ambitions to attend a German university once he got overseas. I don't know if he ever did, but I hope so.

I didn't know too many guys in the barracks because the members of my original basic Russian class from DLI had already come and gone at Goodfellow, because I had stayed that extra several months at DLI for intermediate Russian, remember? So I knew the other five guys from my LeFoxe class who arrived at Goodbuddy the same time I did. But Bob Protosevich was the only unmarried guy in our bunch, and he was assigned to a different quad and a different class schedule than mine, so I didn't see too much of him. The other four guys – Squires, Egbert, Davidson and Jenkins – all bought their wives with them, if I remember correctly, so they were living in apartments they found off post. They had no children at the time, so I guess they managed somehow.

So I was kind of on my own, thrust into a barracks setting again, albeit a much nicer one than I'd ever experienced in the military before. I missed Treve and the boys terribly, of course, but I buckled down and did what I had to do. I went to class each day and I studied.

I also got a great tan.

Here's the thing. The Cold War was still very much around in 1977, so there were some pretty large numbers of linguists being processed through those courses at Goodfellow at the time. So many, in fact, that the classes operated on a shift schedule. There was the day shift and the swing shift. I was part of the swing shift, which means that I attended class between four and midnight. This actually turned out to be a pretty cushy schedule, if you want to know the truth. It meant that I didn't have to get up early. No one came around to roust you out in the morning. You slept as late as you wanted to. But I think they stopped serving breakfast by nine, so I usually got up in time to eat, since breakfast – bacon and eggs, pancakes, French toast, that kinda stuff – has always been my favorite meal. And the Air Force food was really very good.

We started class in early September, but it was still ninety-plus degrees out most days. The base swimming pool was still open, so I decided to go check it out. I'd get my swim trunks and towel and show up there around ten or so most mornings. The pool was mostly deserted in the mornings. Some days I'd be the only one there, besides the life guard. Now *there* was a cushy job. I mean *that* guy had *nothing* to do, but he got paid anyway. I'd take a book along, pick out a lounge chair by the pool and lie in the sun and read until I got too hot. Then I'd jump in the pool for a little while to cool off. Then I'd bake for a while again until I needed another dip. And I'd be in and out of the pool like that for a couple hours, or until it was time to go to lunch. I followed this schedule for most of the next two months. The pool was supposed to close for the season after Labor Day, but the weather continued so hot for the whole time I was there that they decided to keep it open. So yeah, I cultivated a great tan that fall. It was the last time in my life that I ever had a tan. And I gotta tell ya, Treve was pretty impressed when I showed up in Belleville again at the end of October with this killer tan. I mean she *liked* it, if ya know what I mean. *Nudge, nudge.*

I mean I was *working* too during those two months. Don't get the wrong idea here. Like I said, I had the evening class schedule Monday through Friday, and there was a lot of material to cover, mostly memorization stuff. We were learning all about the various radios that the Soviet military used for communications – their designators, frequency ranges, characteristics and types of antennae required. We listened to sample radio traffic and learned to identify types of Soviet army units – artillery, rocket troops, and infantry. And to distinguish army from air traffic or missile activity. I mean there was a lot of stuff to cover and we needed to study for tests that were thrown at us every few days. We got some study time during our class hours, but on some afternoons I would go into the operations area to study for an hour or two before classes began too. Because most of what we were learning was classified, we could not take any materials back to our barracks to study. We kept a locker in the classroom areas and there were designated study areas we could use outside of our regular class schedules to prepare for tests. There was a lot to remember, and I always felt driven to excel. I felt I owed it to my family after the way I had uprooted them and carted them around the way I had. So I worked hard at doing the best I could.

But all work and no play … Well, you know the rest. And believe me there was plenty of play going on at Goodbuddy while I was there. Most of the troops were still young and single and there was plenty of hanky-panky going on among all these guys and gals. There were a couple of the women troops who turned up pregnant – obviously a carryover from Monterey. And a few more babies probably got started right there in the hot Texas sun too. I remember one very good-looking young female soldier who was spending way too much time with one of our instructors, an army staff sergeant who was married. And everyone noticed too. There was a divorce that came out of that. And the "new couple" showed up overseas the following year. So yeah, the juices were flowing, the sap was high, and they "were out there havin' fun, in that warm California sun" – or west Texas sun. Or maybe both, in some cases.

But I stayed outa trouble. Besides the pool, I also found my way to the base library. I know I read quite a few books in those two months, but the writer I remember "discovering" in the Goodfellow library was Jon Hassler.

His first novel, *Staggerford*, was brand new in hardcover the summer of 1977, and I found it there in the library that fall. What a find it was. Staggerford was a mythical place in a part of Minnesota that Hassler was to visit and revisit many times over the next thirty years in his fiction. His character of the old maid Catholic school teacher, Agatha McGee, is enduring and special, a person you will never forget if you read Hassler's books. In all, Hassler wrote a dozen novels about his beloved Minnesota, as well as a couple of children's books and several collections of stories and essays. It all started with *Staggerford* and another unforgettable character, a young school teacher called Miles Pruitt. I was so touched and moved by this book that I did something I almost never do. When I was finished reading it, I went back to the beginning and read it again. I had meant to just take a look at the opening pages again, but nope. I read the whole damn thing over again. It's just such a *good* book, ya know? I kept reading Jon Hassler for the next thirty years. *All* of his stuff is good! Was good. Hassler died last year of complications from a rare form of Parkinson's. Another wonderful writer and human being gone.

I always seem to come back around to books. They have always been – still are – so very important in my life. TV and movies used to play a bigger role, back when I could hear well. But I've had tinnitus for over thirty years now, a condition that doesn't ever improve; it just gets worse. It's a high-pitched ringing in the ears which indicates a hearing loss in the upper frequencies. It probably dates back to my days as a ditty-bopper during my first hitch in the army. Morse code signals are often surrounded by other radio noise, some of it man-made (QRM) and some of it natural static and other crap (QRN). All that did a job on my hearing, as did a lot of loud music over the years. So I'm about half deaf now – which ain't all bad, when you come right down to it. But it plays hell with trying to hear dialogue in a film or TV show. So I don't watch much TV or even many movies any more. But I still have books.

Goodfellow was a rather lonely interlude for me, but not all bad. I swam, not only at the base pool, but I visited Chuck and Jake Squires occasionally at their off post apartment and we'd swim at the pool there and cook out on a little hibachi Chuck had. And I went to some kind of a unit picnic once out at Lake Nasworthy outside of town. The GI's called it Lake "Nasty," because it was always kinda cloudy and didn't look all that clean. But folks did swim and go fishing and boating and even water skiing there. It was the only lake around, and offered some relief from the heat.

On Saturdays (or maybe Sundays, I'm not sure anymore) I usually wrote a letter home to the boys while I listened to Casey Kasem's American Top Forty on the radio. We were deep into the days of disco in 1977 and Donna Summer and the Bee Gees were big. Elvis had a posthumous number one hit with "Way Down," and the song I remember hearing the most during that time was "Best of My Love," by The Emotions. Listening to the music and Casey's corny dedication spiels I would think back to the times I'd spent with Treve and the boys in Monterey, listening to Dolly Parton singing "Apple Jack," and Donnie and Marie doing "A, My Name Is Alice," and Cliff Richard singing "Devil Woman" from three albums that always went well with a big Sunday breakfast of bacon and eggs, sometimes with waffles, in our sunny DLI kitchen. And I would ache with missing them.

And on Saturday nights all the guys in the quad who were around would gather in the TV room to watch Saturday Night Live, which was still pretty new and really catching on about that time, and laugh at the "wild and crazy" antics of Belushi, Chase, Ackroyd, Murray, and Gilda and Jane.

Sundays I'd go to Mass and pray that everything would turn out okay for us and that we'd all be together again soon, and that I wouldn't let my family down.

I don't remember ever going into town much at all. I pretty much stuck close to base most of the time. The most vivid memory I have of Goodfellow – and Texas – is one afternoon when I was walking back to the barracks from the Base Exchange and I looked off down the street and farther out across a vast plain – you could see a long way there; it was all so flat – and watching a storm approach from the west. You could see the clouds moving and the lightning flashing before you heard the thunder. And soon I could see a wall of rain approaching fast, and I ducked into a doorway of a nearby building and waited as the storm swept through in a matter of minutes. Then I stepped back out in the street and watched the storm keep going – east. There was a kind of vast emptiness there that I'd never seen before, a whole different perspective on things. It made me feel very small. Texas.

One of the things we had to do while we were at Goodfellow was attend a security briefing. It was, I guess, a kind of last ditch effort to weed out any undesirables from our ranks before we got sent on to our unit assignments.

June 23, 2009

We had this big master sergeant (I don't remember his name, which is probably just as well) who was conducting the briefing and he did his best, with what seemed to be a fairly limited vocabulary, to reduce the event to its simplest terms. Here's a fair rendition of how he put it.

"Mins [that's *men* in old-time army-speak], the army don't want no druggies or *dee*-vi-ates workin' for 'em, so if you've kept anything back about your past, now is the time to fess up, so's you don't get in no wuss trouble later on."

Someone asked him what he meant by deviates, and the sergeant replied he meant any kind of funny stuff having to with sex.

"Lahk if you ever done any funny stuff with another man, for example, faggoty kinda stuff. Y'all know what Ah mean," he added meaningfully, furrowing his brow. "Or if y'all ever participated in any kinda orgy or group sex – the kinda stuff y'all might be blackmailed for." He pronounced the word orgy with a hard "g."

Another question from the crowd: "How would you define 'group sex,' Sergeant?"

"Hell, y'all know what Ah mean. It's any kinda sex involvin' more'n one person."

There was a beat, then a roar of laughter from the assembled troops, followed by hooting and whistling. The sergeant's face turned beet red as he realized his mistake, muttering, "Well, y'all know what I meant."

I could hardly wait to get back home for some 'group sex' with my wife.

I was thinking about this long-ago episode earlier this morning, maybe because my wife is a couple hundred miles away and has been gone for a week. I hope she comes back home again soon.

This morning I've been sampling some essays in a book by Tom McGuane called *Some Horses*. I first read McGuane over thirty years ago when I was still teaching in Monroe and was researching Michigan writers for my course, Modern Michigan

Authors. Tom McGuane had been a Michigan State classmate and pal of Jim Harrison and Dan Gerber back in the late fifties. By the early seventies he'd already had a few novels published. I can't remember anymore which one I used in my class. It was either *The Bushwhacked Piano* or *Ninety-two in the Shade*. The kids in the class like McGuane for his skewed sense of humor and a penchant for the bizarre in his fiction.

It's probably been close to thirty years since I read any of McGuane's stuff, even though he's been busy writing and has probably a dozen or more books to his credit by now. I was reminded of him again a few weeks ago while reading Larry Woiwode's memoir, *A Step from Death*. In it, Woiwode tells a story about Harrison and McGuane coming to a cabin he was renting near the shore of Lake Michigan and asking if they could do some bird hunting. Woiwode, by the way, had a couple bestselling novels back in the sixties and seventies in *What I'm Going to Do, I Think* and *Beyond the Bedroom Wall*. Do you see now how one book can lead to another, and usually *does*?

Well, McGuane relocated to Montana and has lived on a ranch out near Livingston for over forty years now and has worked a bit at becoming a half-decent cowboy during that time. *Some Horses* is his tribute to a number of horses he's owned and loved over the years and to the old-time western style of life in general. There was a particular passage in the piece, "Roping, from A to B," that had me both wincing and laughing out loud. He was telling about a mishap he had in roping a steer and being unable to find the saddle horn to wrap the rope around –

> "... I went to dally and broke my thumb in a few places, tearing the end off it. When I went to the emergency room, the nurse said, 'Miss your dally?' 'Tell the doctor I hate pain,' I said. Nevertheless, he pulled my thumbnail out with a pair of needle-nosed pliers and told me I would have lost it anyway."

See what I mean? *Ouch!* But *hee-hee* too, all in the same thought. I love the way this guy writes. So much so that I wrote him a letter, just to tell him so, and I sent along a copy of my *Reed City Boy*, telling him I thought he might like a close-up and personal look at the town where his pal, Harrison, grew up. Wonder if I'll ever hear back from him.

I think I might have also admitted to him in my letter that the only times I ever sat a horse myself were at those pony rides at the county fair. You know the ones – where they have four or five tired-looking old ponies tied to the ends of poles and they all plod around and around in a circle with little kids on board who've paid a quarter for five or ten minutes of riding. Looking back at those rides, I can see how pathetic they really were, but I grew up watching Gene and Roy at the Saturday matinees and it was my only chance to ride a "real horse." The only other time I can remember being on a horse was when I was eight years old and I went to Patsy Kearns' birthday party on her folks' farm west of town. It was the end of February (Patsy was a leap-year baby, so it was, technically, only her second birthday). I think our whole third-grade class from St. Philip's was there, and Pat Kearns, Patsy's dad, took us all on a sleigh ride back through the woods and fields behind the farm. But first he gave us all a chance to sit up on the back of one of the giant horses that pulled the sleigh. The horse's back was so broad I could barely straddle, and when Mr. Kearns swung me up onto the horse it seemed so frighteningly high off the ground it was all I could do not to piss my pants.

Yup, that pretty much sums up my experience with horsemanship. But I still love to read about horses, the west and the cowboy life. I've got a few more Montana books still waiting in my to-read pile here.

At the tail end of October of 1977 I finally did finish up my training at Goodfellow and flew back to Detroit for a week's leave in Belleville with Treve and the boys. And yes, there was probably some "group sex" that week, conducted very quietly in the dead of night while the kids and her folks were sleeping.

But it was over all too soon. The leave, I mean, not the sex. Well, maybe both, come to think of it. I had one more TDY to get through before my training was over and we could all head to Germany. This time I flew to Baltimore and caught a ride to Fort Meade, where I and the other five LeFoxe guys would undergo another twelve-week course of training, this time to learn more about the specifics of our "targets" – the Soviet groups of forces in Eastern Europe.

June 29, 2009

Treve is finally back from her sojourn at Suzie's. God, how I missed her! Dogs are good company, but they never bicker, and at our age, bickering is an important component of the good life. I'm not quite old enough to remember listening to *The Bickersons* on the radio, but we do love Earl and Opal in *Pickles*.

What do I remember from my Fort Meade TDY? It stretched from early November 1977 until the end of February 1978. I actually made it home twice in that time. The first time was for a long Thanksgiving weekend, which included the night we made Suzie on the bedroom floor of Treve's room. Otherwise, I don't remember much from that stolen weekend. I call it "stolen" because I wasn't really officially authorized to travel that far from post on my military pass. But I risked it, and - well, *Suzie*. The second time was Christmas, of course, a longer leave during which my trip *was* officially sanctioned. Again, I can't remember much, although I know the Zimmer clan was all there for Christmas day, Treve's three brothers and their families. And there was undoubtedly much good food and drinking and smoking – the good life incarnate, with lots of presents for the kids. One in particular that I still remember was a kind of superhero figure called Stretch Armstrong. He stood about a foot tall, as I remember, and was made out of this extremely flexible material. You could pull on his arms and legs and extend his "wingspan" or height to three feet or more. Once you let go of Stretch's limbs they would gradually shrink back to their normal size. Both the boys enjoyed this "elongatable" hero immensely. The reason I remember it though is that they shipped it overseas a couple months later in a box of toys. When they unpacked the box in Augsburg, Stretch was hard as a rock and refused to stretch. Jeff and Scott were extremely disappointed, and put him aside. Much to their great delight, however, after ol' Stretch had "rested" for awhile, he was back to his old tricks. He had just needed to thaw out from his long transatlantic voyage in the freezing hold of a cargo ship.

Of course I kept pretty busy during that four-month stay at Meade. We went to class for several hours every day, learning all about the organization and order-of-battle of the Soviet forces stationed in Germany, Czechoslovakia, Poland and Hungary, and continued to practice our Russian skills as well. With only five of us in class, we had to keep up with our assignments. There's no place to hide in a group that small. One of the things we appreciated was that we weren't required to wear our uniforms to class. We were required, however, to wear a tie, which made for some strange combinations. I often adhered to the letter of that law, but barely. I would wear my favorite flannel shirts and corduroys (it was winter, after all), and simply wear a black military tie with my plaid shirt and a warm fleece jacket. No one complained, and I was happy, if strangely dressed.

Only three of us lived in the barracks: Bob Protosevich, who was single, lived there, of course. Chuck Squires and I lived in a double room, right next door to Bob. Chuck's wife, Jake, had moved back to live with her folks (in Pennsylvania, I think) during this TDY, maybe so they could save some money before heading overseas. In any case, I was grateful for Chuck's company during the week. Because on weekends he would pack his VW Rabbit and head out to join Jake for a couple days. The only company I'd have then would be the nearly life-sized poster of Suzanne Somers (from her *Three's Company* days as "Chrissie") which Chuck had seen fit to decorate his side of the room with. Chrissie didn't say much, but she was always smiling.

The other two guys, Steve Egbert and Joe Jenkins, lived in off-post apartments with their wives.

For some unexplained reason, although Chuck and I were living in the barracks, we were also drawing "separate rats" on our pay, which means we got extra funds to pay for food. This was probably because our families were living elsewhere, but what it meant to us was that we were not issued meal cards for the mess hall across the street from our barracks. Not that this was a hardship, because when we did eat there, all we had to do was show our military ID card at the door and pay some really minimal fee, like a dollar or two. I can't remember exactly how much anymore, but it wasn't much. Even so, we only ate in the mess hall a few times a week. But when we did, we got into the habit of making certain we got our money's worth. Which means we really pigged out. And I mean really, *really* pigged out. We would usually go through the regular serving line and get whatever main entrée looked good, along with a vegetable or two and maybe a salad. Then, after we'd polished that tray of food off, we would go through the line at the grill where we'd get a hamburger or cheeseburger with all the fixings, and maybe a few fries on the side. Of course we would be almost painfully full by this time, but we would press on, and go queue up in the dessert line, where there was always a good selection of cakes, pies and puddings. But we would usually bypass these goodies and go directly to the "build-your-own" ice cream sundae station and put together a really pig-ly portion of ice cream with all kinds of tasty toppings.

I don't know if you've ever seen that Monty Python film – I think it might have been called *The Meaning of Life* – which depicts the sin of gluttony so well. You know, the one where this character eats himself so sick that he tells his waiter/servant to "bring the bucket." Well, that was kind of how Chuck and I would feel as we heaved ourselves out of our chairs at the mess hall and waddled on back to our room in Davis Hall (named for Spec 4 James Davis, the first ASA casualty in Vietnam) where we would lie on our bunks and moan in discomfort, wondering yet again why we'd made such horrible hogs of ourselves. But we knew why, of course. It was that making sure we got our money's worth kinda thing. After all, we'd had to *pay* for that meal.

When we weren't eating in the mess hall, we fixed our own meals in our room. There was a refrigerator in the room and we scrounged around the unit area and found a couple of straight chairs and a small metal table, institutional battleship gray in color, and carried them back to our room. The table even had a drawer in it, where we kept a couple sets of tableware and a few other utensils we "borrowed" from the mess hall. (We put everything back where we'd gotten it before we departed Fort Meade.) I also purchased a small electric-coil corn popper at a nearby store in Odenton. We used it not just for popping corn, but also for cooking soup or various canned delicacies – Spaghetti-O's, ravioli, ramen noodles, etc. We also purchased milk, cereal, pop, bread, peanut butter and jam, cheese and lunch meat and kept it in the fridge or our lockers for packing daily lunches or evening snacks. It was actually one of the nicer rooms the army ever provided for me during my "single" days in a barracks, and Chuck and I were quite comfortable living there. I'd brought along that little TV I bought in Monterey and every day we tried to catch re-runs of *The Andy Griffith Show*, sometimes managing it even twice a day. There was often a kind of unsettling disconnect when we'd see two shows on the same day in which Opie was first thirteen and then suddenly seven again.

But since Chuck had a car, we did get out of the barracks some evenings. I remember going to see the movie *Star Wars* at the Laurel Mall Cinema that winter. I wasn't crazy about the film, but Chuck seemed to like it. Maybe I was just too old to "get it." (Or maybe it really *is* just a lot of juvenile junk, as I thought at the time.) We also drove into D.C. a few times to look around and play tourist. We did climb to the top of the Washington Monument one weekend, if I remember correctly. This was back when you could still climb those narrow circular stairs all the way to the top. There was an elevator too, of course, but that would have presented no challenge. I know my thighs and butt ached for a couple days after that stunt. Maybe I was too old for that too.

Weekends were long and empty. Chuck would be gone, and Protosevich, next door, was kind of a loner and often disappeared on his own expeditions. There was a small branch library appended to a service club next door to our barracks, so I would often head over there and find something to read. One weekend just before Christmas I signed up for a service club bus tour to the brand new White Flint Mall in Montgomery County, just outside D.C. It was probably one of the most lavish and extensive indoor malls I'd ever been in. The military bus dropped us off at the mall entrance by around ten AM, and wouldn't return to pick us up until four PM, so we had plenty of time to shop. I spent a couple hours just walking around and gawking with my mouth hanging open. Many of the stores were way too upscale for my pocketbook, but it was a treat to get out of the barracks and off post, so I spent a few hours making my way around the mall just looking at everything.

Then, since it was a fairly mild day for December, I left the mall proper and headed back up Rockville Pike, looking for a Korvettes department store I'd seen out the bus window on the way down. It was a pretty good walk, as it turned out, probably more than a mile, but I finally found it, and the prices there were more in keeping with my meager means than those at the White Flint shops. I found a nice blouse for Treve in the ladies wear section. Well, it probably wasn't all that nice, but it was affordable. And as it turned out, it was too small for her, and I think she might have ended up giving it to her sister-in-law after Christmas. Ever the music fan, I spent most of my time in the record department, where I discovered a mother lode of Jimmy Buffet stuff, an artist I'd been enjoying for a couple of years by then. Even in the mid-seventies, Buffet already had a pretty vast following, although I'm not sure if the term Parrot-head had been coined yet. One of his most popular party songs back then was (and probably still is today) a charming little ditty called, "Why Don't We Get Drunk and Screw." I didn't look for Christmas presents for the boys because Treve had assured me she was taking care of that. I did bring them both tee-shirts and sweatshirts emblazoned with US Army and Fort Meade. They were both still young enough to think such clothes were cool, thank God.

That bus shopping trip was a rarity for me though. On most weekends I read or took long walks around post, trekking up over the wooded hill opposite Davis Hall and then across the golf course to the main PX where I'd flip listlessly through the magazines and books or peruse the record racks. I found Rick Nelson's latest album, *Intakes*, in the PX. Not many people were buying Rick's stuff anymore, but I still was. Of course, I didn't have a record player in the barracks, so I saved it to take home for Christmas.

I must have read a dozen or more books during those months at Meade, but I can only remember a couple of them. One was C.D.B. Bryan's *Friendly Fire*, a true story about an Iowa farm couple whose son was killed in Vietnam by his own forces' artillery. The book was a bestseller at a time when the U.S. had finally managed to disengage itself from the awful mess that was Vietnam. I found it a morbidly compelling page-turner, as I read of the gut-wrenching agony experienced by these parents who had lost their son. A couple years later the book was made into an award-winning TV film, with comedienne Carol Burnett turning in a sobering and near-heartbreaking performance as the bereft mother.

The other book I remember reading at Meade was James Jones' classic of the Second World War, *From Here to Eternity*. I had seen the movie adaptation, which had rejuvenated the career of Frank Sinatra and earned him an Oscar, but I had never read the book. When I did though, it served to reinforce the serious readers' axiom that the book is always better than the movie. While the film was indeed a great one, the book really was better. I read it in a single weekend and it's a pretty long book.

But there was one event from that winter that I remember better than anything else. It was my birthday.

I was thirty-four years old at the end of January in 1978, so it wasn't exactly a milestone of any sort, and shouldn't have been a particularly memorable birthday. But it was, for a couple of reasons.

I must have mentioned that my birthday was coming that weekend, because the other guys in the class decided I should have a party. I was, after all, the "senior" member, in years, of our LeFoxe class. I'm sure I protested with typical midwestern modesty that there was no need for a party, but the other guys insisted, so I gave in and plans for the party proceeded. My birthday, the 27th, fell conveniently on a Friday that year, so it was decided we would all gather at the Jenkins' apartment that evening for a party of homemade tacos and other treats.

What we were not expecting that night was a rather heavy snowstorm that blew in across Pennsylvania from the Great Lakes. It was snowing pretty heavily by the time Joe Jenkins came to pick up Bob Protosevich and me at the barracks to take us to his and his wife Lou's place in Odenton, or maybe it was in Laurel. I can't remember anymore. Chuck had, I think, left earlier in the day to drive to Pennsylvania to get Jake and bring her back to spend a rare weekend with him at a motel near Fort Meade.

Not long after we got to the Jenkinses, the Egberts and Davidsons arrived, and we sat around and talked with drinks and snacks, waiting for Chuck and Jake to arrive. The snow and wind continued unabated outside. An hour or more passed and the Squireses still hadn't arrived, so we went ahead and began to eat dinner. We were a little concerned about the dismal driving conditions, but we all knew Chuck was a good driver, so we didn't worry too much. Finally, nearly two hours late, Chuck and Jake arrived.

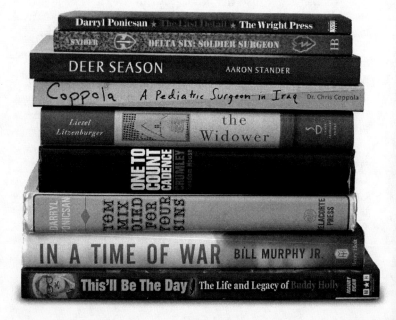

July 29, 2009

I'm finally back, sitting here looking at the blankness of the computer screen below this line. I almost skipped July altogether. It's been a long time and I really don't have any excuse for laying off from this writing thing for so long – except laziness, I suppose. That and the always-there nagging feeling that it's really kinda pointless, writing all this stuff down. The despair that all writers give in to on occasion.

But I'm back, so no matter, I guess.

I should probably get back to finishing that story about my birthday back in 1978, and I will, but first here's some other stuff I've been thinking about this morning. I'm reading this book right now (big surprise, huh? I'm *always* reading *some* book) called *Breaking Smith's Quarter Horse*, by Canadian author Paul St. Pierre, and I'm really enjoying it. It keeps making me chuckle. I'd read another book by St. Pierre years ago, a collection of stories called *Smith and Other Events*, which, of course, featured this same comical cowboy character. I still remember how that book made me laugh too. These are kinda modern-day cowboys and Indians stories Canadian style which I can personally guarantee will make pretty much anyone laugh.

Anyway – and it's funny how just a single reference in a book can take you way back to something out of your own childhood – there was this passage that mentions Smith's wife Norah "carrying out the slop pail" before she went to bed. Because we had a slop pail in our back room in Holdenville when I was a little kid. It was back before the time of under-the-sink garbage disposals. Mom would throw out her potato peelings and any other garbage that accumulated during the day into this old ten-gallon bucket that stood by the screen door in the back room off the kitchen. And my brothers and I had to take turns emptying that bucket every night before we went to bed. It got emptied into a garbage pit we dug somewhere out behind the yard. Once that pit got full, we'd cover it up with dirt and dig another one. In today's politically and environmentally correct world I know this sounds awfully irresponsible, what with all the old cans and jars and other odd bits of junk that ended up buried out back, but all I can offer as an excuse is that it was just a different world back then.

So Smith's wife's slop pail took me back there, and to those icy cold mornings when Mom or Dad would be using the bathroom and so I and my brothers would have to use that slop pail to piddle in, hopping from one foot to another on that cold linoleum floor waiting our turn to pee. I was the youngest of four boys back then, before my sister and little brother were born. I know I wrote about this in my first book, *Reed City Boy*, but I was always a little surprised how many people would bring this particular thing up when they wanted to talk with me about the book. Apparently a lot of people had slop pails back then. Go figure, huh?

So I was thinking about that old slop pail this morning when I went out to the kitchen to get my second cup of coffee. Treve was still sleeping and I had some music on low in the living room – Miles Davis's *Someday My Prince Will Come* album, a personal favorite of mine that Treve can't stand, so I play it while she's asleep or not around. I love the way he just kinda tootles along, Miles, almost absentmindedly it seems.

So Miles was playing softly and I came back into the living room with my coffee and there was Barney, our Tibbie, sprawled out behind the couch, half in and half out of his little round plush dog bed that Treve got on sale at Rite-Aid for five bucks a year or so ago. And Daisy, our other dog – a Michigan Barnyard Dog breed, I call her – she was lying up against the wall under the big picture window right next to my chair, with the bottoms of the vertical blinds all askew around her, some tucked behind her and some lying across her. It drives Treve crazy when she does that, because the blinds end up with dog hair stuck all over them and periodically Treve tries to clean them off, quietly cussing Daisy the whole time. Me, I don't care all that much, I guess 'cause I just love having Daisy around. She turned twelve this month and her muzzle and ears have gone all white and she's got these warts all over her face and body and just the worst dog breath you can imagine, especially when you're trying to enjoy a bowl of cereal or ice cream or something and she's sitting right there beside you and hoping she'll get to lick the bowl when you're done and she gets so anxious about it when she hears your spoon start to scrape the bottom of the bowl that she begins to pant and the smell that comes up out of the depths of her stomach is like death itself. I mean you just have to push her away, it's so awful. But I usually do let her lick the bowl, unless Treve is watching, because she always makes like it grosses her out, but I know that when she thinks I'm not looking she will let Daisy lick her bowl too. In spite of all this I really love Daisy, because she's the first dog I've ever had that's been mostly just *my* dog, and I try not to think about how old she's getting and how she probably won't be around much longer. Our back fence neighbors, the Murniks, have a greyhound. They rescue these former racing dogs and their Lilly is about the third one they've had since we've lived here because greyhounds often have this problem of twisted gut which can suddenly kill them. That's how their last one, Gracie, died, and Jim was just devastated when it happened. He didn't say much, but I could tell he was mourning her.

I remember him saying at the time, "Dogs. No matter how much you love 'em it always ends in grief."

Anyway, I was sitting there in my chair this morning, considering my two dogs. Well, actually Treve always insists that Barney is *her* dog, because it was her idea to get him and she picked him out and all, but try to tell *Barney* that. Because he knows who feeds him every day and who calls him to come take a nap each afternoon. Yeah, it's a little embarrassing to admit, but Barney is my "snuggle buddy." I don't know if you've ever seen a Tibetan Spaniel, but one of the things that makes them so unique and special is that they always look like a puppy, even when they get older. Maybe it's their rounded domed little noggins, but they are just so darn cute that you want to pick 'em up and cuddle 'em, ya know? Treve figured Barney would make a great lap dog, but, strangely, Barney does not like to be held, and will only sit on your lap if you catch him and hold on to him, but after five or ten seconds tops, he's squirming to get down. So that was a bit of a disappointment to Treve, of course, but like I said he does love to cuddle. He'll snug himself up against your side or your back when you lie down and do that really cool and contented dog sigh that always makes you feel that all is right with the world whenever you hear it, along with the warm pressure of his full furry length pressed up alongside you. Jim's right, I suppose. But while a relationship with dogs may always end in grief, while they're here and with you, there's nothing quite like it.

So I was thinking about my dogs this morning and about coyotes too. Why coyotes? I'm not sure, but maybe it was because I'd just been reading about them in this *Smith* book. The opening chapter described the extreme winter cold of the Chilcotin country of British Columbia, the kind of cold that caused the sap in pine trees to explode and the two-foot thick lake ice to thunder and crack, and sometimes killed old animals too.

> *"The previous night an old dog coyote had lain down and tucked his gray nose into his thin tail beside the Russel fence of Smith's Home Place and in the coldest hour, just before the dawn, he had died. Man is supposed to be the only animal who spends his adult life anticipating death, but it would be easy to believe that the old coyote had some sense of the futility of it all when he had lain down in the poor light of a young moon that night.*
>
> *The ravens were now at work upon the coyote's carcass, beginning with the eyes ..."*

Maybe I should have mentioned that St. Pierre's stuff isn't all just chuckles and fun. Sometime he can be pretty profound. Because I wasn't thinking just about coyotes when I read that passage. I thought about my own mortality too, something I do fairly often now that I've reached the Medicare stage of my life. Such thoughts are rarely voiced, I know, but I'm pretty sure everyone thinks about it. When I try to kick-start myself back to writing this stuff, I often think about how long I might have left. I think of my dad, who died at seventy-nine of cancer. And I do the mental calculations. Do I only have fourteen years left then? Then I consider my mom, who is still here at ninety-three, all her faculties intact, and who does a crossword puzzle (or two) nearly every day, plays scrabble regularly with my brother, and never misses *Wheel of Fortune* or *Jeopardy*. So I relax a little, knowing I seem to favor my mother more so than my dad. Maybe I have another twenty or even thirty years left. But even so, I feel this continuous sense of urgency to get my story down. And this feeling can really kind of spoil my pleasure in reading, knowing I am neglecting my writing.

But maybe I've already said this, so no matter.

Coyotes.

Since I moved back here to Reed City – nearly eight years ago now – I have looked for coyotes. I wanted to see a real live coyote, maybe like Jim Harrison's fictional alter ego, Swanson, in his first novel, wanted to see a wolf. That book was called *Wolf: A False Memoir*, and came out nearly forty years ago. Harrison is, of course , perhaps Reed City's most famous son, at least in the literary world, by now having published more than two dozen books, about half of which are fiction, the others poetry and essays. His books have been translated into several languages and have enjoyed world-wide attention. Jim spent several of his formative years here, until he was twelve or thirteen, when his father, who was the county extension agent here, moved the family south to Haslett, near East Lansing. He wrote about his time growing up in Reed City several years back in his *real* memoir, *Off to the Side.*

July 30, 2009

I could say more about Harrison, I suppose, because I really admire the guy, but hell, anyone who is a serious reader already knows who Jim Harrison is, and they either love him or hate him, because Jim's stuff is pretty raw sometimes.

But back to coyotes. When I was a kid there hadn't been any coyotes around here for years. They'd all been hunted down and killed for bounty or pretty much completely chased out of the lower part of Michigan. It was just a fact of life. Coyotes were something you read about or heard talk about in the movies. And yet we were the Reed City Coyotes during our high school years. That scavenging carrion-eating beast was the Reed City High School team mascot, or symbol, as far back as anyone can remember. So probably when that name was picked, there were still coyotes around here. I don't really know, but it seems logical. I guess you could say then that every kid who went to high school here was always at least dimly aware of coyotes. And of course for those of us who grew up in the fifties and sixties there was also the crafty but dim Wile E. Coyote, forever pursuing the Roadrunner, and forever being violently squashed by a falling Acme anvil or blown to smithereens by Acme explosives. I guess if coyotes were really that stupid it's no wonder they had disappeared from the west Michigan landscape by the time I came along.

The truth is coyotes are anything but dumb. They are, I have read, extremely resourceful and endlessly adaptable animals. Which is why they have returned in the last twenty years or so not only to Michigan, but to much of America, both rural and urban areas. Not long ago I remember reading something in the paper about a coyote that walked into a convenience store in Chicago and somehow got trapped in one of the glass-fronted refrigerators there.

My own first awareness that coyotes were back came around fifteen years ago while driving across the state on one of my semi-annual visits home from Maryland. Driving across I-96 toward Lansing I saw a coyote carcass on the shoulder of the road. I was so shocked that I almost stopped to verify that it was indeed a coyote, and not a dog. But I didn't. You know how you fly along those freeways and hate to slow down for anything. But when I did get back home to Reed City, I began asking around and was assured by pretty much everybody who still lived here that yes, the coyotes were back, that there were plenty of them around.

From that time on I watched for coyotes as I traveled home, and while I did see a few more dead coyotes along the highways, I never did see a live one. So when I moved back here to live at the end of 2001 I figured I would see one eventually.

And one day I finally did. It was on a Sunday morning about two years ago. I was walking my dogs along Slosson Avenue around 9:30 in late October. It was one of those beautiful fall mornings, bright sunshine and crisp cool air. There was no one else stirring, a lazy Sunday morning when people would be having breakfast, sleeping in, or getting ready for church. The dogs had been doing their usual doggy stuff, stopping at every tree, stump or bush they could get away with, sniffing and marking. We were right in front of Murniks' house when suddenly the dogs both stopped dead in their tracks, staring intently up the street, not making a sound. Barney backed up a step or two and tucked himself behind my legs, still peering up the street. I looked to see what had spooked them, and there, trotting south across the Slosson and Park intersection, was a coyote. I didn't at first recognize it as a coyote. I thought it was a dog. But if it had been a dog, mine would have been barking or straining at their leashes to go meet it, to investigate. Instead they'd turned quickly quiet, watching this other animal, perhaps sensing the wildness, the other-ness.

The coyote, a reddish-gray in color with a brush tail, trotted jauntily, head up, to the center of the cross street and stopped and looked down the street at us. He considered us briefly, perhaps five or ten seconds, then continued unconcernedly on his way, disappearing behind Duane and Connie Hurst's house on the corner. My dogs then began moving again, heads up this time, no sniffing, watching. When we reached the corner at Stewart Smith's house and turned south down the sidewalk there, I saw the coyote emerge from the grassy swale behind the Hurst place and trot back out into the road, still heading south. My dogs both stopped again, watching this wild one, intent, cautious. Daisy whined softly.

The coyote crossed the street and sniffed briefly around the base of the big maple on Platz's lot, then turned and looked back at us. Breaking into an easy lope, it crossed Todd and headed up the last short block of Park Street and disappeared down the school bus alley behind the elementary school. Daisy and Barney relaxed now and busily investigated the area around the maple where the coyote had trod, but, strangely, neither one of them marked the area; they only sniffed. Then both looked up the empty road where the other animal had headed.

For me it was a rather surreal experience. My first brush with the wildness I had sought ever since moving here. And, so far, my only one. Since I encountered the animal right here in town, I guess I can say it was a Reed City coyote. And the alley it disappeared down is the same one that ran behind the high school when I was a student there. That old building is gone now, torn down in 2005, but the ghosts of generations of Reed City Coyotes still linger there.

Go, Coyotes!

Okay, so I guess I've got some of *that* out of my system – life on the frontier and all that.

I'll try to somehow segue back into where I left off about my thirty-fourth birthday in Maryland. I know I've pretty much lost any momentum or forward motion I might have had in that story, so I'll just tell you what happened. You'll remember that Joe and Lou Jenkins were hosting an informal birthday party for me at their off-post apartment. We'd had dinner already when Chuck and Jake Squires finally arrived late. The biggest surprise though – and my best present of all – was that they brought Treve with them.

I mean you could have knocked me over with a feather I was so flabbergasted to see Treve there that night, some four or five hundred miles from home. It had all been arranged earlier by her and Chuck, who was, obviously, *very* good at keeping a secret, since we roomed together. In any case, I was so happy – overjoyed and *stunned*, actually - to see her there that I nearly wept. I can't remember anymore if we knew yet then that Treve was pregnant, but I don't think we did.

What made her presence there that night even more unlikely was the horrific weather that had been gripping the whole Great Lakes region, the Ohio River Valley and much of the northeast for the past few days. Michigan had not yet even begun to dig out from one of the worst blizzards in the state's history which had swept through the Midwest from the 25th through the 27th of January, extracting a deadly toll. In Michigan alone during that period at least twenty people died because of the storm, mostly from heart attacks or traffic accidents. Various reports later noted that more than a hundred thousand vehicles were stranded or abandoned on Michigan roads and highways, mostly in the southeastern portion of the state, which of course includes Belleville.

All of this explains – certainly in retrospect – why she and the Squireses were so late in getting to the party. Her flight out of Detroit had been delayed for repeated de-icings of the aircraft. She recalls that afternoon and evening as being extremely stressful and that she had doubted seriously whether she would ever get off the ground. Her anxiety had begun even before she left her folks' home though, wondering if she'd even make it to the airport, even though it is less than ten miles from her house. The roads were drifted over and some were completely impassable, but the snowplow miraculously showed up on Martinsville Road that afternoon, refilling the mouth of the Zimmers' driveway, necessitating another quick snow removal just to get on the road with her brother Dick, who took her in his four-wheel drive pickup. Then all the waiting and waiting at the airport and on the runway, wondering if Chuck would still be waiting at the Baltimore airport when she landed, hours late. But he was, and he got her to the party. There were lots of stories about the storm to exchange once we were all gathered. Chuck had even made weekend reservations for us at Abrams Hall, the military guest house on Fort Meade. And I think he and Jake stayed there too, because we spent a good part of that weekend with them, touring D.C. in their yellow VW Rabbit, seeing what we could of the sights there, given the deplorable weather conditions that lingered throughout the weekend.

I'm pretty sure Treve didn't leave until Monday morning, because I can still remember the two of us trekking through drifts and over crusted snow to get to the PX, just a hundred yards or so behind Abrams Hall, where we brunched at a cafeteria eerily empty that winter morning.

In spite of the snow and cold, it was an idyllic interval for Treve and me. Our room at Abrams had a private bath and color TV and we had access to a kitchen just down the hall. The building was, as I recall, mostly empty that weekend, making it seem even more private – perfect even. I was so grateful to Chuck for doing this for us, and I still am today.

I stayed at Abrams Hall again a couple years later, by myself this time. At that time I was about a year away from my ETS (estimated time of separation) date and was trying to cover all bases about where my life would go if I didn't decide to reenlist. A civilian career with the National Security Agency seemed an interesting option to explore, since my three years of experience as a Russian linguist in the army would give me a big advantage over kids just out of college with a Russian major.

August 28, 2009

Almost a month since I opened this file, I know. Mea culpa and all that. But it's not *all* my fault. There are all those good *books* I can blame too, and I've read several since I last wrote anything here. I've become a big fan of Curtis Harnack in the past month or two. I learned about him through a new cyber-acquaintance I met on LibraryThing.com. Dewie Gaul is a retired judge out in Iowa who has kept a record of every book he's read since he was eight years old. And Dewie is over *eighty* now! It's a pretty extensive list of well over four thousand books by now, and he has been busily transcribing this long record of reading from his many notebooks into cross-indexed files online, and also onto his account at LibraryThing. Anyway, being an Iowan, Dewie reads as much about his home state as he can, and he told me about Harnack's beautiful memoir of growing up on a farm there back in the 30s. It's called *We Have All Gone Away*, and it is simply a wonderful story, on a par with Ronald Jager's Michigan farm memoir, *Eighty Acres*. I liked it well enough to write to Harnack, who has lived in New York City for many years now. Since then we have become email friends and have swapped some books and try to stay in touch. I've read four more of his books since that first one, including another marvelous memoir called *The Attic*.

It's become a habit with me now, this communicating with authors whose work I enjoy, and it's a very gratifying thing. I did hear back from Tom McGuane, by the way, after writing him and sending him a couple of my own books. He sent me a postcard from his Montana ranch, thanking me for sending me the "delicious-looking books" and promising to read them immediately after finishing the editing on a new novel he is working on.

Only a week or so after receiving McGuane's postcard I was cleaning out a closet in our basement bedroom/family room (in preparation for a visit from my younger son's family) and found an old newspaper my mom had given me a couple years ago. It was an *Osceola County Herald* from 1949. Mom had saved it because there was a piece at the bottom of the front page about Dad, the new owner of the Kent Elevator, which he had just purchased from Ray Kent. What caught my attention this time, however, was another article at the top of the same page. It was about the local county farm agent, Win Harrison, who would soon be relinquishing his post in Reed City to move to the Lansing area. There was a photo of Harrison with the piece and I was immediately struck by the family resemblance to his son, the author Jim Harrison. I decided to send the newspaper to Jim, but since his address and other contact information is a closely protected secret, carefully guarded by his personal secretary up in the Traverse City area, I sent it off to Tom McGuane, along with a note asking he give it to Jim. They have been close friends ever since their college days at Michigan State. I also sent an email off to Jim's secretary telling her about it. She was pleased, and told me that Jim was at that time in Nebraska and McGuane in Iceland, but she was sure the connection would be made eventually.

All these connections. We really *are* all connected, you know, regardless of how widely separated we might be by years or geography. The longer I live, the more I believe this.

Yesterday I drove to Big Rapids to pick up some medicine for my mom, who's recently been having some pain in a hip, bothersome enough that she actually went to the doctor, something she rarely does despite her ninety-three years. Every time she does show up at the doctor's office they have to go dig her records out of the archives or else start all over again with a new medical history. They're never impolite enough to *say* so, but I suspect the girls in the office are always surprised that Mom's still here.

Anyway, I went to get some free samples of some new topical ointment that might alleviate Mom's pain. But anytime I drive through Big Rapids and past Ferris State's campus I get just a little bit nostalgic. Well, maybe *more* than a little bit, if I'm gonna be truthful here. I mean I met the love of my life at Ferris over forty-two years ago so it's an important place to me. Oddly, Treve doesn't share this nostalgia, and, if she's with me on any of these trips, she often gets a bit impatient with me for wanting to go drive by St. Paul's campus parish where we met, or the Alumni building where she attended cosmetology classes, or Helen Gillespie Ferris Hall where she lived. She just wants to get our errands run and get back home again. Maybe it's got something to do with her needing to pee more often these days. But hell, that's only because she's always drinking so much *water*. Got to stay *hydrated*, don'cha know.

There's one other place I try to drive by every now and then too, and that's the bowling alley on the old highway just south of campus, the one that used to be the Casa Nova Lanes, with its lounge and restaurant, back in our student days. We went there the night we met, and a few other times after that. Well, yesterday, much to my horror, when I drove by that hallowed landmark I saw heavy equipment and piles of brick parked and strewn about the building. Our Casa Nova is being demolished. To make way for a bank building. *Kee-rist!* Is nothing sacred? And aren't there already at least a half dozen banks in Big Rapids? And wasn't there just this huge financial meltdown in our country (and in the world at large)? What the hell do we need another bank building for? Couldn't people just drive an extra block or two to one of the *old* banks in town?

No.

Yes.

Yes.

We *don't*.

Apparently they can't, no.

Shit.

I was so upset at seeing the old Casa Nova half gone that I immediately proceeded up the street, turned onto campus and drove hurriedly down Damascus Drive to St. Paul's to make sure *it* was still there on the river. It was, thank goodness, but on the way down the hill I noted that several of the old married housing buildings along the street had been recently wiped out and work was already underway on some new "more modern" apartment buildings for students.

From there I drove over to the student union, or Rankin Center, as it's now called, and fed a couple of quarters into a parking meter outside the college bookstore (which is now a Barnes & Noble, fercripesake). It's move-in week for all the college students, classes begin next week, so things were pretty crowded everywhere I looked, with exhausted-looking parents and excited-looking kids carrying furniture and computers and televisions and boxes of stuff into dorms all around us. Inside the bookstore there were long lines at every register, so I knew I wasn't going to buy anything but went in anyway, just to browse through the books and do a bit of people-watching.

After taking note of a couple interesting books I found, *Fighting in the Jim Crow Army* and *The Professor and the Housekeeper*, I watched the people milling about in the store.

A tired-looking man in carpenter jeans and a red tee-shirt stood dispiritedly nearby and asked his wife and daughter who were in line at a cash register, "Do you need my money ... or anything?"

The two women barely seemed to notice him, the wife casually displaying a credit card in one hand while she fingered a rack of FSU sweatshirts next to her, the daughter, holding hundreds of dollars worth of textbooks in her arms and checking out a couple of male students in the next line, her face colored with the excitement of everything around her.

"Okay, then I'm just gonna ..." he trailed off, and headed out into the lobby looking for a place to sit down.

I know he wanted to sit down, because I remember being in his shoes at least three different times, when I took my kids off to college years before. Today they are 40, 37 and 31, so it's been a while, but I remember – mostly the tiredness, but also a vague sense that time had somehow gotten away from me, that my kids couldn't *possibly* be old enough to be going to *college*. Now, all of them, parents, older, maybe beginning already to feel that vague sense of unease themselves. Well, good. Let 'em. I've been there. Now it's their turn. I hope I'm through with carrying furniture and other large heavy objects. And then driving away, leaving my children behind.

They're not children anymore, of course. Now they come to visit us on occasion, and it is cause for much upheaval here at the old homestead – a flurry of cleaning, cooking, baking and other preparations.

November 24, 2009

Geeze, how em*bar*rassing. *Again!* It's been nearly *three months* since I've opened this file. But here I am back again, for better or for worse. Which makes a great segue into why I guess I kicked myself in the ass and finally got back to work on this particular day.

Today is our anniversary. Yup, forty-two years ago today Treve and I tied the knot, reciting those traditional lines which included the "for better or for worse," richer, poorer, sickness, health, etc. And we've pretty much been through all that stuff except the "richer" part. Well, maybe even that, considering how, as time went by, we gradually got a little less poor. Although I will tell you that having a few kids will keep you pretty poor. Things are a little easier now for us, financially. It's just us and the dogs now and we've been reasonably healthy most of the time, despite our advancing age. (*Ooh*, Treve's not gonna like *that* crack.)

Our dogs are getting up there now though. I think I mentioned earlier about how our bigger dog Daisy, who is twelve now, had a really bad case of garbage breath and warts all over her face and body. Well, in the past couple of months she's developed a kind of oinky wheeze that worried us, like her nose is plugged up, or something. So we finally took her to see our vet, Dr. Barbara Todd, who suggested it might be just a seasonal allergy. We also mentioned Daisy's horrible breath, so Barb opened the dog's mouth and looked at her teeth, which were, admittedly pretty yellow, almost to the point of being *orange*. She reached into Daisy's mouth and with just a fingernail, popped something out, which landed on the exam table with an alarmingly loud clunk.

Holy crap, I thought. *It's a tooth!*

But no, it was just a huge chunk of plaque or tartar, or whatever you call that hardened crud that forms on poorly tended teeth. I was embarrassed, and I think so was Treve, that we'd paid so little attention to poor Daisy's teeth. The vet then pointed out how red and inflamed Daisy's gums were, probably infected.

So we didn't find out exactly why Daisy was oinking and

wheezing, but we left with some antibiotics and ointment and an appointment to bring her back in the following week to have her teeth cleaned – a first for our old dear, I am ashamed to say.

When a dog gets its teeth cleaned, it's done under a general anesthetic. So I asked Barb to please take some of the warts off Daisy's muzzle and lips while she was under. So she did, and even threw in a couple extra "wartectomies" while she was at it, removing one from above her right eye and a big one from the top of a hind foot. When I went to pick Daisy up that afternoon I was a bit shocked at how she looked, as she'd had part of her muzzle and the one back foot shaved for the surgery. Her mottled black and pink skin was showing through then, and her fresh wounds – small craters actually – had been painted over with some kind of brown solution. She looked like a car wreck survivor, one who'd been thrown through the windshield. But she wagged her tail when she saw me. It didn't matter what I'd subjected her to. She still loved me. And, as we were to find out over the next few days, her death-like breath was gone. She smelled better. It hadn't been just old age. It was neglect on our part. Mea culpa, Daisy.

And then, that same week, our little Barney started slowing down noticeably. He wouldn't – or couldn't – jump up onto the bed or couch anymore. Coming up stairs became a very slow and careful operation, and he lagged behind on our twice-daily walks around the block. This was all very un-Barney-like for our nine year-old Tibbie. I was afraid he might have blown out his ACL, like Daisy had back when she was just two – that it was his knee, or perhaps a hip that was paining him. But when Murniks came for dinner one night, Jim suggested it might be something in the dog's back, since Tibetan Spaniels do fall into that category of long-backed dogs.

So back to the vet, this time with Barney. Uncharacteristically quiet and submissive, Barney stood quivering all over on the metal table while Barbara examined him, carefully feeling with both hands, starting at his head and neck and working her way slowly down his spine. When she reached his lumbar region, Barney let out a pathetic yelp – a definite canine *OUCH!* The Murniks had been right. It was his back. Dr. Todd said he'd probably strained it somehow and it was inflamed and sore. So she gave him a steroid shot directly into the affected area and sent us home with a week's worth of Rimadyl tabs. Barney seemed himself again within twenty-four hours. But I'm still keeping the baby gate up at the top of the stairs for a while, to keep him here on the main floor.

I say *I'm* doing this, because Treve left shortly after Barney's vet trip. Last Friday I drove her to the Grand Rapids airport and she flew out to Pennsylvania to spend Thanksgiving with Scott's family. (Isn't this kinda where I came in?) So yeah, it *is* our anniversary, but I'm here and Treve is several hundred miles away – again. But we're okay, mostly. We talked on the phone this morning and I sang her my own unique version of Happy Anniversary. She is just loving being with her two older grandsons, Nick and Zach, who are four (almost five) and two, so it's a tradeoff. And she'll be back in about ten days.

So what have I been doing? Why haven't I visited this file, this kind-of-a-book or whatever you want to call it in so long? Well, the usual, I suppose: just being "retired," which means you can do whatever you damn well please, which is often simply nothing. But mostly I've been reading other people's books, and buying and swapping even more books, at such a rate that I often despair of ever having the time to read all the books I'd like to, even though these days I read an average of one or two books a week – sometimes more, sometimes less, depending on the length of the books and what other stuff I have to do that week.

My main problem with reading all the time is feeling like I'm getting rewarded without having earned it. Which means I feel like I should be working at least part of the time. And these days for me "working" means writing. So what the hell. Here I am back at work.

Back in September, in an attempt to get started writing again, I printed out the two hundred-plus pages I had so far, and Treve started reading it. And right away she noticed a couple of errors. She pointed out that Jeff was only four months old when he rolled off the changing stand, not a year old. She also said she *never* had an episiotomy. She should know, so, okay, I was wrong. She said if I wanted to write about gruesome stuff, why didn't I write about some of the bloody accidents the kids had over the years.

So here's one. When we were living in Augsburg and Suzie was just beginning to walk – she was just ten months old – Treve left me to watch her one afternoon while she went to do someone's hair down the block. I was sitting sprawled on the couch with my feet stretched out in front of me and Suzie was toddling around the living room of our third floor apartment. I was probably (of *course*) reading, and not paying very close attention to her, because, as she tottered across the room towards some toys, she tripped over my outstretched feet and went down hard, her head hitting the sharp corner of the coffee table. Her reaction was immediate, a loud wail, and by the time I looked up from my book she had already begun to get to her feet and, to my horror, her whole face was covered with blood, flowing freely from a nasty gash in her right eyebrow, dripping off her chin and onto the front of her little bib overalls.

Horrified and feeling nearly sick, I picked up my screaming child and took her into the bathroom and blotted the blood from her face with a damp washcloth, but the cut continued to bleed, so I held a folded dish towel tightly against it. I can't remember anymore what happened between there and the army hospital emergency room, but somehow I got Treve back home and all three of us were there, Suzie still hollering. Treve was simply beside herself with worry. And when the doctor told us he needed to sew it up and I helped him get Suzie strapped onto a "papoose board," arms pinioned at her sides, and she began to scream even louder, Treve just had to leave the room. She couldn't handle it.

The doctor, apologetic, said that he could probably just put some butterfly bandages on the cut, but that would probably leave a scar, and since this was a girl, well … So I sat with Suzie, holding onto her and trying ineffectually to comfort and soothe her, but she continued to wail piteously while the doctor quickly put several tiny stitches in her eyebrow. Treve cried quietly in the next room. It was one of those moments – or hours, as it seemed at the time – which you'd just as soon forget, but never can. All part of being a parent, I suppose.

In any case, the doctor did such a skillful job that there is no visible scar from this traumatic day – only our own emotional ones. Suzie, of course, doesn't remember any of this.

All of our kids had various scrapes like this. Scott, when he was only about two, fell down a neighbor's stairs in Monroe and hit the edge of a marble windowsill, necessitating stitches in his forehead. I was home sick in bed with the flu that night, doctoring myself with a potent prescription of elixir terpin hydrate with codeine, so Treve and the neighbors endured that ER visit. Jeff once fell on the playground in Augsburg, gouging open a knee and filling it with dirt and gravel, which had to be picked painstakingly out with a probe and tweezers at yet another ER. And a few years later, when he was in junior high in Maryland, he broke an ankle in a basketball game. No ER that time, just a trip to our family doctor in Crofton where an X-ray was taken and a plaster cast applied.

And while we're talking about traumatic events and injuries I might as well include our dog, Daisy, in the mix. When she was not quite two, she had an epileptic seizure. It didn't last very long, and she seemed okay after a little while. We called our vet and were told to just keep an eye on her. A month or two later, on a Sunday night, it happened again, only that time it didn't pass. She was having what we later learned was a cluster seizure, meaning one after another after another. Watching anyone, human or animal, have an epileptic fit is not easy. It's not pretty. It is, in fact, frightening as hell. Daisy's eyes went blank; she didn't know we were there. Her limbs went stiff, her toes spread and her back arched as she spasmed and seized. She vomited and lost control of her bladder. We panicked. While I held Daisy, trying to talk her back to herself, Treve fumbled through the yellow pages, looking for a veterinary ER. She found one finally in Annapolis, about a half hour's drive from our home in Odenton. When she described to the on-duty vet what was happening, he told her to get the dog into the ER as soon as possible; that she could die. We had to get directions to the clinic over the phone, then bundled Daisy, wrapped in towels, into the back seat of the car with Treve. I tore full-speed down route 32 towards Annapolis in the dark. I'd never been to this particular animal clinic before, but somehow I found it, and, amazingly, it only took us twenty minutes. Where the hell was a cop when you needed one, I kept thinking. Immediately upon our arrival, some vet techs took Daisy in and gave her a shot of Valium to bring down her racing heartbeat and spiking temperature. We had to leave her overnight. We were utterly wrung out with fear and worry. She was, after all, our "baby." She has been on daily doses of Phenobarbital ever since that night.

It wasn't too long after that that Daisy blew out her ACL, her anterior crucial ligament, while romping in the yard. One minute she was fine and the next she was crying and dragging one leg. The ligament just popped. It's the same injury often suffered by professional athletes, and, if I remember correctly, I think President Clinton tore an ACL back when he was still in office. I'm not sure how a person's ACL is repaired, but for Daisy it involved replacing it with a length of high-test fishing line, or at least that's how it was explained to me. And very expensive fishing line, as it turned out. That surgery set us back over a thousand dollars – this for a five-dollar pound puppy, keep in mind. But, like I said, "our baby."

November 25, 2009

People have often asked me what's the hardest part about writing. My usual answer is, simply, writing. Because it's easy to daydream about writing a book, seeing it in your mind, a pyramid display of your book with your name on the cover, on a table in the front of a large bookstore with perhaps a line of eager fans wound around the block outside, waiting to get in to meet the "famous author." Kinda like the recent Sarah Palin phenomenon, with the release of her autobiography, *Going Rogue*, which has supposedly, in less than a week, already sold over 700,000 copies from an initial printing of over two million. Well, more power to her, I suppose, although I'm with syndicated columnist Kathleen Parker, who, when asked if she would read Palin's book, commented, "Sure. Right after I finally finish reading *Ulysses*." (And I'm pretty sure, since Palin has rarely ever put together a coherent complete sentence during her various interviews, that she hired a ghost writer do the actual writing.) Of course for people like me – and maybe you too, if you have aspirations to write – it just ain't that easy. The physical act of planting your ass in a chair in front of a PC or at a table with a tablet and pen and beginning to type or write is, I think, the very hardest part of writing. It requires discipline and dedication.

Which I probably don't really have. Case in point, exhibit A: my recent nearly three-month absence from writing. Although that's not strictly true. Because I do write at least *some*thing nearly every day, even if it's only a few lines, in a daily journal I keep on a table by my chair in the living room, the chair where I settle with a satisfied sigh each morning with my first cup of coffee, dogs sitting at my feet, eyes pleading, watching me hopefully – *Cookie? Walk?*

And they usually win. I mean who could resist those cocked heads and soft brown eyes. So I dole out treats while I sip my coffee. And then, weather permitting, we walk around the block: west on Todd, north on Sears, east on Slosson, south on Park, and back up Todd and home. If it's wet out I have to stop in the garage and towel off muddy feet, legs and bellies before letting the dogs back in the house where they sit patiently in

327

the kitchen while I take off my shoes and put on my slippers, quietly hoping for maybe just one more coming-in cookie.

I'm telling you all this just to illustrate that even if you do have even a little bit of discipline about writing that sometimes the hardest damn part is just getting *started*. Last night I finished reading a book called, interestingly, *My Father Is a Book*, a memoir-cum-biography by Janna Malamud Smith about growing up with her famous father, the writer Bernard Malamud. Malamud, Philip Roth and Saul Bellow were considered three of the most important contemporary writers of the middle of the twentieth century; I started reading them all back in college. In her memoir, Smith writes at length of the tremendous discipline and solid work ethic her father cultivated, how he insisted on working at his craft every morning for at least four or five hours, usually between eight and one.

> *"Intensely competitive in spite of himself, acutely aware of his contemporaries, and always weighing and sizing his own talent, he liked to retell to dinner guests a story Philip Roth had told him probably in the early 1970s: On days when Roth pulled himself out of bed with difficulty, lingered over breakfast and newspaper, and tried to push himself reluctantly, late morning, to his desk, he would goad himself on, 'Malamud,' he'd growl, 'has already been working for three hours.'"*

Reading this late last night, I felt a little better about my own sloppy work habits, just knowing that even Philip Roth had trouble getting started some days. But I know, of course, that I'll never be a Malamud or Roth. First of all, I'm not Jewish, with that long ethnic history of suffering and striving. I'm white-bread shanty-Irish cradle-Catholic, and probably with a lazy streak to boot. But I will keep plugging away. I almost added "trying to make a living," but then laughed to myself. No way, Bazzett. Be glad you have a decent federal pension and can afford to write for your own amusement. And can keep buying books by *real* writers that you enjoy, like Roth and Malamud.

And here I should probably make a confession. Book collecting can become like an addiction, particularly if you frequent websites like Amazon, where, when you go looking for a particular book, you are oh so helpfully directed towards *other* books that you might like – and usually do. But while you can find so much – practically *any*thing – online, there is still no experience, if you are a booklover, quite like browsing in a real sure-enough bricks-and-mortar bookstore. A good well-provisioned bookstore is a kind of heaven on earth where time can stand still as you graze up one aisle and down another.

I spent about an hour and a half in such a place the morning I dropped Treve off at the airport in Grand Rapids. From Gerald R. Ford International it is only perhaps a couple miles down 28th Street and then left on Radcliffe over to 29th, where Bargain Books has occupied a corner lot for over twenty years now. It's not bricks-and-mortar, but more of a large steel pole-barn of a building, the former site of a Wicks Lumber. Inside this cavernous warehouse area is a booklover's paradise. Rows and rows of books of all categories, genres and descriptions – and all marked down to bargain basement prices. Yes. Paradise. And time did seem to pause during my time there, even though I tried to hurry. Book browsing does not lend itself to hurrying, I know, but I had a couple of elderly dogs waiting for me at home, which was still an hour and a half away. Older dogs, older bladders. So I tried to hurry that Friday morning, and did leave by noon.

I came away with (don't tell Treve, okay?) ten books, and only spent about fifty bucks. One of those books was the Malamud memoir/biography. Another was a collection of essays by poet Donald Hall called *Life Work*. I dipped into this book this morning during my morning *toilette*, as it were. Ah, what the hell. I read it on the *can*, okay? Doesn't everybody do some of their best reading there? Otherwise how to explain why all those stacks of *Readers Digests* and *Guideposts* end up there.

Hall's early chapter talks of his forbears – great grandparents and grandparents, many of whom were farmers in the stony unforgiving soil of New England. He notes –

> *"Every man outside the city was a farmer … every family kept a cow, and keeping a cow fresh meant a heifer every year or two and meant borrowing or hiring the services of*

a bull; it meant haying in summer. And every family kept
chickens for eggs. And every family grew a huge garden and
canned vegetables and fruits, the woodstove burning red in
hottest summer with kettles of blueberries or tomatoes; and
the root cellar filled with apples, potatoes, squash, beets,
carrots and cabbages."

Here in west central Michigan where I grew up, nearly
everyone my age and older knows exactly what Hall is talking
about. While the land may be a bit flatter than the hillsides and
foothills of New Hampshire and Massachusetts, the rocks,
clay and sand that comprised our soil was just as unforgiving.
My parents were probably the last generation that truly
understood Hall's words. My dad grew up mostly on a tenant
farm near Wayland, south of Grand Rapids, and knew what
hard work was. He couldn't get away from there fast enough,
once he'd finished high school – an accomplishment in itself in
those days. My mom too spent part of her girlhood on a family
farm west of Oakley, the village where she lived later. She was
lucky too, in that her dad, my grandfather Whalen, was a rural
mail carrier and so stayed employed during the worst years
of the Depression, and was able to send his only daughter to
college.

Mom and Dad may have escaped that hardscrabble rural
existence, but they never forgot it, and the Depression years
taught them further habits of thrift and making do with what
they had. So although my brothers, sister and I never had
to farm for a living, we all have some memories of keeping
a garden and working on the small hobby farm my Bazzett
grandparents kept near our home in Reed City in the fifties
and early sixties. Cows, chickens, haying and gardens –
we experienced, at least on a small scale, all of it. I can still
remember the long hot days of hoeing, weeding, planting and
picking in the fields around our house on West Church, and
how much I hated it – all of it. My drill sergeants in the army
a few years later might have called it "good training," which
is undoubtedly what my father thought too. And I suppose, in
grudging hindsight, they were right.

I wrote about these things in my first memoir, *Reed City*
Boy, a book that, much to my amazement, continues to sell,

if not in great numbers at least steadily, five years later. Back in August I was invited to be a guest speaker at the fiftieth reunion of Reed City High School's class of '59. *Reed City Boy* has made me at least locally famous in a small way, so I get these invitations from time to time and have found that I enjoy attending these reunions, partly because, as my wife says, I'm a bit of a ham and enjoy "performing," but mostly because I always run into people I know at these gatherings, some of whom I haven't seen in forty or fifty years. I never really prepare anything for these appearances, aside from maybe bookmarking a passage or two in one or more of my books to read. Mostly though, I just wing it, talking a bit about my own high school years and what I've done since, then reading a bit and taking questions. So far it's been a lot of fun and people seem to enjoy my stories.

It's not surprising that I know so many people at these reunions. Reed City is, after all, a pretty small town, but it's more than that. The Bazzett family was pretty well represented at RCHS for quite a few years. We had graduates there in '55 (Dick, aka Rich), '58 (Bill), '60 (Bob), '62 (me), '69 (Mary) and '71 (John, aka Chris). And you usually tend to remember who your siblings' friends were. It was also pretty common for the guys to marry girls who were a year or two – or three or four – behind them in school, so there are also those connections.

At this summer's gathering I had an interesting conversation with Eunice Evans, whom I remembered as Eunice Stieg, who graduated in 1961. She was one of those "older women" I admired from afar back in high school. Maybe you've heard that old rhyme, "Guys don't make passes/ At girls who wear glasses." Well Eunice wore glasses, but if I'd had some guts – and maybe a little more self-confidence – I'd certainly have made a pass. I mean she was *cute*. But alas, I didn't really know her.

So I was little surprised when Eunice came up to me that August evening at the Spring Valley Golf Course clubhouse and started telling me about how she'd read *Reed City Boy* and how it had triggered memories of her own childhood years, and how she'd envied kids like me – the "town kids." She told me about how *back*ward and, well, how *country*, she'd always felt in high school. How she'd always had to get right on the bus when school was out and go back home – back to the farm – when all the "popular" kids, the "cool" town kids, got to walk downtown to Mike's place for a soda and to congregate and hang out and listen to the juke box there, or maybe, if they owned or had access to cars, would drive up to LeBaron's Diner on the north end of town for the same reasons. And how the same kids all got to go to the home football and basketball games. She told me how *long* she had to spend on that darned school bus (yes, "darned" – she married a local preacher's son) every day going to and from school, while kids like me were still rolled up in our warm beds or having a leisurely hot breakfast, and then hanging out with friends when school was dismissed.

"We used to be so happy when we found out the Keelean kids weren't coming to school," Eunice said. "Because they lived out at the farthest end of the bus route, near Strawberry Lake, and picking them up and taking them home added another half hour or more to our time on the bus."

"And I used to so envy families like yours that would stop at our roadside produce stand to buy sweet corn and other stuff in the summer, because I knew you were headed for your cottages out on the lake where you got to play and swim every day. My brothers and I were lucky if we got to go swimming two or three times in a summer. We had all these chores to do on the farm. And we hardly ever got to go into town."

I think my mouth might have dropped right open as all this poured out of Eunice. And she wasn't complaining, mind you. She was just telling me how it was being a farm kid back in those long ago fifties and sixties. Back when going to town on Saturday night was a big deal for all the farmers in the surrounding area, when they'd come in to do their shopping and bring their corn and oats to grind for cattle feed at the elevator and buy seed and fertilizer and other supplies. Reed City was still full of thriving stores and businesses and the movie changed at the Reed Theater two or three times a week. As one of the town kids, although I certainly never considered myself "cool," I took all that stuff for granted growing up. Eunice couldn't. She may have lived only six or seven miles from town, but it might as well have been a hundred; it all seemed that unreachable to her.

I do remember stopping at the Stieg's produce stand for fresh sweet corn on summer days (and yes, on our way to our Indian Lake cottage) – and probably seeing Eunice there – freckles, glasses and overalls. Across the road from her place on that abrupt bend in the Cedar Road was Forest Finkbeiner's farm. He owned pasture on both sides of the road and I can remember often having to stop our car there in the road while Forest herded his cows back across to the barn for milking time. That enormous barn blew down in a bad windstorm one summer and I can still remember my shock and surprise seeing the structure completely flattened the next time we drove through, and wondering if any of those cows had been killed. I mentioned this to Eunice and she may have told me that she was somehow related to the Finkbeiners, but I could be wrong. The truth is many of the families around Reed City have been here for so long that they all seem to be related to each other, either by blood or marriage. I remember my high school friend, Keith Eichenberg, chanting a local kind of limerick that went, "Haists, Faists and Jesus Christ/And all the rest are Finkbeiners." Or Stiegs. Or Eichenbergs. You get the idea. You have to be careful what you say about folks around here. You're probably talking with their cousin.

November 26, 2009

It's about 5:30 here, already dark outside and it's been drizzling rain or dropping a mix of snow and sleet pretty much all day, and it is Thanksgiving. I'm alone here and feeling, I don't know what. Alone, I guess. My brother Bill is up for the weekend from Chicago, so he, Mom, Chris and I went to the Lutheran church today for Thanksgiving dinner. At 93, Mom has finally given up the kitchen. No more cooking or baking anymore. Chris does that now, such as it is, for both of them. And with Treve in Pennsylvania, we – my two brothers, Mom and I – found ourselves cook-less on a day known for its national gluttony. So we took advantage of the complimentary meal put on by a number of very good ladies from St. Paul's today. And it was good. It wasn't home cooking, but it wasn't "institutional" food either. It was fine. I experienced a new taste treat from the dessert table, a chocolate pecan pie that was simply delicious. I meant to inquire about who made it and trying to get a recipe, but forgot. When your belly is that full, much of your blood rushes there to help in digestion, hampering the flow of blood to the brain and slowing thought processes and memory. Oh, well. We all had plenty to eat without completely glutting ourselves and then came back to Mom's place and sat and visited for a couple hours, until we all began to yawn and run out of things to talk about. So I came home and let the dogs out, fed them, let them out and back in again. Then I looked out the window at the rain hitting the puddles for a little while, feeling perhaps just a bit blue, missing Treve.

I've been trying to read, off and on, for the past few days a truly awful book. It's called *The Autobiography of W.N. Ferris*, and is, of course, written by the founder of the college where Treve and I met – back when I still thought her given name was Terri. Woodbridge Nathan Ferris himself died about eighty years ago, and this absolutely undistinguished piece of prose must have languished in a drawer or file cabinet for at least that long, until it was finally published by the university in 1995. The fact is the writing is wooden and terrible and the book has very little to recommend it. Someone gave me the book recently though, so, since old Woody was instrumental, at least in a distantly tangential way, in putting Treve and me together over forty-two years ago, I thought I ought to give it a chance. But I put it aside tonight to read something else.

My brother Bill brought along a couple books for me, which he gave me to bring home, but he also gave me this curious old yellowing newspaper he'd found somewhere. I didn't think to ask him how he happened to bring a supplement from the *Chicago Tribune* that was already over eighteen years old. Maybe he was cleaning out a closet or a desk drawer, I don't know. Anyway, the top of the supplement says "The 1991 *Chicago Tribune* Literary Awards," and it's all about that year's winners for the Heartland book awards and the Nelson Algren awards for best short stories.

I asked Bill, "What's with the old newspaper?"

"Oh, it's got a story in it that mentions DLI, so I thought you might be interested," he replied, in his mild characteristic murmur. Bill is so soft-spoken he is often hard to understand, so I had to ask him to repeat his answer. He refers to this sometime communication problem as his "Midwestern mush-mouth."

In fact, Bill and I had just been laughing and joking about a book we'd both recently read. It's called *Deaf Sentence*, by the British novelist, David Lodge. Early on in the book, which deals with, among other things, problems associated with encroaching deafness in people as they age, Lodge's protagonist, Desmond Bates, replicates a typical conversation between him and his wife, Fred (short for Winifred) – or at least the way it seemed to him minus his hearing aid –

"Fred: Murr murr murr.
Me: What?
Fred: Murr murr murr.
Me: (playing for time) Uh huh.
Fred: Murr murr murr.
Me: (making a guess at the content of the message) All right.
Fred: (surprised) What?
Me: What did you say?
Fred: Why did you say 'All right' if you didn't hear what I said?
Me: Let me get my hearing aid.
Fred: No, don't bother. It's not important."

Bill and I could both appreciate both the humor and the frustration represented in this exchange, since we are both afflicted with some high frequency hearing loss, and have both had identical conversations with our wives at various times.

"It's that story about Fort Ord," he told me, further clarifying the DLI remark.

He was right. I *was* interested. So I brought the paper home with me and, after taking care of the dogs, I reheated the last of the coffee from this morning and sat down to read "Leaving Fort Ord," by Patricia Stevens, which was the first runner-up for the Algren award that year, 1991. I didn't read the winning story, but Stevens' story, set on Fort Ord in the summer of '69, immediately grabbed me. It was narrated by Shelley, the wife of David, a young army Captain who was leaving for Vietnam in two days. She is feeling a kind of inexpressible anger at his imminent departure – at him, at the army, and at her own situation as an army wife, left at home with a small child. At a party with three other couples she also feels drawn to Richard, an unattached young officer whom she has become close to – and feels guilty for feeling this way. Her husband is, of course, about to go off to war. He won't articulate his feelings, but seems angry and distant, bottled up. Richard, on the other hand, also bound for Vietnam, has privately confided to her how frightened he is. It is, in short a complex and tension charged scenario, rendered in an extremely sensitive and skillful fashion. It is a beautiful and in many ways heartbreaking story.

Maybe because I am missing Treve tonight, I was drawn into the story, because there is a scene where David, Shelley and their four year-old daughter, Rachel, drive to the beach at Carmel for a picnic. I could immediately picture that sparkling white sand, where Treve and I had spent a few lovely and lazy afternoons, the boys playing with their pails and shovels and romping in the surf, and coming home afterward, back to our DLI apartment, tired, sunburned, and often filled with a lazy sexual tension that always played out pleasurably after the boys had been put to bed.

David and Shelley quarrel on their last days together, ostensibly because she wants to leave Fort Ord while he's in

Vietnam and go back to school in Iowa City. He wants her to stay where she is and wait for him. Her plans to make a more independent life for herself in his absence seem vaguely threatening to him. They finally reach a kind of truce, making love the night before he is to leave, after which he weeps, something she had never seen him do before.

"I was whispering to him, 'It'll be okay, it'll be okay.'

When he stopped crying, he lifted his head onto the pillow next to mine and, staring up to the ceiling, he said, 'I can't lose you while I'm gone.' ..."

Reading this passage, I wept. I was remembering that rough spot we had back in '92 when I had moved out of the house. It was springtime. I had been gone a couple of weeks when Treve phoned me and asked if I would come for Easter dinner. "For Suzie," she explained. And I understood. Suzie was fourteen, and going through enough hell just for being at that difficult age. Our separation had not helped things.

So I came to dinner that Easter Sunday. Suzie acted like she didn't care, and left the house soon after the meal, slamming the door behind her. Treve just sat miserably, looking down into her lap. Then, leaving the dishes on the table, she took me by the hand and led me upstairs to our bedroom. We didn't talk. We made love, or something like it. She wept, as did I. There were things going on in our life we couldn't seem to discuss. We simply could not speak. Our bodies could, but we still couldn't. I got dressed and left.

Sometimes communication is just too hard, to the point where it becomes impossible. And when something dark and unknowable is looming in your life, no matter how badly you want to connect, instead you do the opposite. You pull away. You lash out. You fight. And the pain of an impending separation is often just too great to contemplate.

During those five years that we spent with the army in the seventies and eighties, Treve and I were separated many times, often for weeks and even months at a time. And every time I had to leave, there was always that emotional distancing on both our parts, which began a day or two before the actual departure. I got so I learned to expect it, and steeled myself against it. I'm not sure if Treve ever got used to it, but I know she felt it too.

So I guess this long, gray, empty day, with the rain and sleet and snow – and the strangeness of the holiday – got to me today. David and Shelley's story was familiar – the anger, the fear, the not knowing what would happen. Would they have a future? Could they keep on loving each other? I remembered all of it. I understood. So, those tears – making me feel just a bit foolish at this stage of my life. Because here we still are, and we still look to the future, Treve and I. We still love each other, in our old folks kind of way, with all the usual bickering that goes along with it; even with the *"Murr murr murr"… "What?"*

Maybe she'll call later.

November 29, 2009

Raining. It's 10:30 and I've been up for four hours already and figured I've put off doing this long enough. It wasn't raining earlier, fortunately for the dogs. I took them on a long leisurely stroll just after nine, around a couple of blocks with countless long pauses for sniffing and peeing. I'm kinda like them, I suppose, with all the cyber sniffing and peeing I've been doing for the past hour, sitting here checking my email, looking to see if I have any new comments posted on my LibraryThing (LT) account, checking the headlines online, and so on. Any such activity will do, as long as it delays finally opening up this file again and staring at the whiteness of this empty page.

But now I've begun. Which means I've gotten past the hardest part.

I was pleased to find an email this morning from Joyce Dyer, a new cyber acquaintance. Joyce is an English professor at Hiram College in Ohio. I learned of her a few days ago when I got a notice on my LT account that I had "snagged" a free copy of her 2003 memoir, *Gum-Dipped*, which is about her growing up years in rubber-town, USA – Akron. I took a look at the book on Amazon and it sounds fascinating, so of course my reaction was/is, *Oh boy, another memoir to read – and a free one at that!* Then I looked up the author online, and found her webpage at the college, so emailed her that I was going to be reading her book, a complimentary copy from her publisher, The University of Akron Press. Joyce writes back that she thinks maybe I'm getting her new book, *Goosetown*, instead. She may be right. We'll have to wait and see. There will probably be more to come here later, on whichever book I receive, once I've had time to read it. We have also agreed to perhaps swap a couple of books soon.

Book-swapping with other authors is, I have found, grand fun. I have already amassed a pretty sizeable collection of personalized books from other writers. Molly Gloss's novel, *The Hearts of Horses*, for example, is a personal favorite of mine and a real prize. Molly is about my age and lives out in Oregon and has probably been writing for twenty years or more, but *Hearts* hit it big on the Amazon charts a year or so ago and she's been enjoying some much deserved popularity recently.

My most recent swap was with a young man who is at least forty years younger than I. Michael Anthony's memoir of his time serving as an army reserve operating room technician in the Iraq war has been making a splash this year, both sales wise and critically. *Mass Casualties: A Young Medic's True Story of Death, Deception, and Dishonor in Iraq* (a rather unwieldy subtitle, I know, but subtitles in general have been getting really out of hand lately) boasts a half dozen pages of blurbs and endorsements from more than two dozen other writers and various experts on war and foreign policy. Not too shabby for a first book by a kid still in college. Oh, and yes, it is an excellent book, although it wasn't quite what I had expected. ...

It's much later and I have piddled away most of the day, pacing about the house ruminating on what I might write, and then giving up and fixing myself a pig-sized portion brunch of bacon, eggs, toast and juice. After that more dithering about until I got tired and took a nap with the dogs, Barney tucked warm up against my back. When we awoke around 3:30 the rain had stopped, so, after I fed the dogs, we took another walk. Checked my email and found a note from Curtis Harnack. So I called him and we talked of books and authors. I read him an Updike poem I'd found in *Good Poems*, a fat Penguin edition put together by Garrison Keillor from poetry he'd been reading for many years on his five-minute radio spot, *Writer's Almanac*. It was one of the books my brother Bill had just given me. I think he left his bookmark at the Updike poem on purpose. It's called "Hoeing" a boring activity much hated by most farm boys of the past hundred years and more, and begins –

> *"I sometimes fear the younger generation will be deprived of the pleasures of hoeing ..."*

and ends –

> *"Ignorant the wise boy who has never performed this simple, stupid, and useful wonder."*

Upon hearing the poem, Curtis, an aged Iowa farm boy who has lived for decades in New York City, laughed as hard as I had, despite a recent painful bout with a kidney stone.

Another interruption, but a welcome one. Treve called, and we talked of nothing for more than a half hour, mostly just to hear each other's voices. At least that is true for me, and I'm fairly certain for her too. Often, after one of these daily phone conversations I can't even remember what she said. Tonight, however, I seemed more acutely aware of the sound of her voice, a beloved sound, and a corollary to her absence of more than a week now. And I know why.

Just yesterday morning I finished reading a memoir that moved me to my very core. It is about love, and about loss. Anne Roiphe is a writer I remember reading in college, but hardly at all since those days. Her first big success was a fanciful, virulently feminist novel called *Up the Sandbox!*, which came out back around 1970. It was a bestseller at the time, and later became a film, starring Barbra Streisand. I think I may have read her next novel, *Long Division*, but then kind of lost track of Roiphe's work. She kept on writing, but never achieved the popular success of *Sandbox* again. The book I just finished, *Epilogue*, is an achingly real and brutally honest journal she kept following the sudden death from a heart attack of her husband of thirty-nine years. Keep in mind that this is a very strong, professional and independent woman, but she was totally unprepared for the waves of despair, sadness and even suicidal thoughts that washed over her for months after suffering this tragic loss. She found herself totally unmoored, despite her best efforts to cope, and to understand what was happening to her.

Perhaps the passage that hit me the hardest was what Roiphe said about touch. It was so chillingly *there*, so *true*, that I could have wept.

> *"Touch. I took it for granted. He took my arm when we were walking in the street. He took my hand in the movies. He lay his head in my lap while reading the Sunday paper. He rubbed my shoulders when I was stiff. He wrapped his legs around mine while he slept. In the shower we soaped one another. In the kitchen we leaned into each other. And then, not as often as we did a decade ago, we did all those things that although most private are usual among human adults. We lay afterwards body to body, my head on his chest, his arms around me, breathing softly together: even the night before he died.*

> *And now I think I may never know another man so well …*
> *We know that babies if they are not held in human arms do*
> *not thrive … the human infant must be rocked and touched*
> *and wiped and soothed by another's smell, flesh against*
> *flesh. I think perhaps at the other end of life this might be*
> *true also …"*

Treve will be back home in a week. I know that. But even
so, reading the above passage gave me a chill. And I thought of
all the people who do not have someone coming home, all the
women – and men – who have lost someone forever. It's almost
too much to contemplate. Too sad.

Epilogue is a beautiful book, an exceedingly *brave* book. But
it will not be an easy one to recommend.

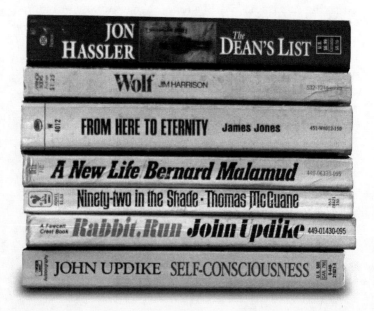

December 3, 2009

More books, more reading. And last night I had to watch *GLEE* on television, a new show this season which has become a favorite for both of us. The music is terrific and it has an interesting storyline too, a kind of tragicomedy. It probably won't last. It seems like every time we find a show we can both enjoy, it gets canceled after just one season or two. The last one was *American Dreams,* a Dick Clark production, I think, about a typical Catholic family in sixties Philadelphia, the birthplace of *American Bandstand,* which played a prominent role in the story. The show was very believable, and tied in important events of the mid-sixties – things like race riots and the Vietnam war – as well as the usual coming-of-age angst that we all went through in our teens. It only lasted three seasons and left a plot-line hanging most unsatisfactorily when it went off the air. *Loved* that show. I wonder if anyone else remembers it.

Thinking about it made me remember, back when the kids were little, how we'd all watch *Little House on the Prairie* or *The Waltons* together every week. With popcorn, of course. Family stuff. Seems like a lifetime ago now. (*BIG sigh.*)

I finished reading Donald Hall's *Life Work* a couple of days ago, composed of essays he wrote back in the early nineties which comprised a kind of journal of a year, much like what I'm attempting here. During that year he was diagnosed with liver cancer, which rather knocked him off his pins, and caused him to deviate some from the pieces he'd been concentrating on, about his parents and grandparents and family history. Instead his writing began to reflect his thoughts on his own mortality, and he particularly worries about what would become of Jane Kenyon, his wife, who was also a poet of some repute, if he should die. The edition I was reading was printed in 2003, ten years after the book's original publication. In a preface to the new edition, Hall comments –

> *"In the ten years since this book was published, my life and my work have changed utterly. I finished it, after a cancer operation, convinced that I wouldn't live long. If forebodings were accurate, they were radically misdirected. At the end of Life Work, I wrote, 'Today if I begin a thought about 1995*

*I do not finish the thought.' These words will forever spew
irony's acid. In 1995, it was my wife Jane Kenyon who died,
at forty-seven."*

Hall documented his twenty-three year-marriage,
including his wife's struggle with manic depression and her
final illness and death in a moving memoir which I read
earlier this year called *The Best Day the Worst Day: Life With
Jane Kenyon.*

Hall, at one point in *Life Work*, equates work, or at least
his own work, with contentment, and illustrates this by
remembering a conversation he once had with the Indian
novelist, Gurcharan Das, who defined contentment as
"absorbedness." And Hall was quick to agree, noting that
contentment "is work so engrossing that you do not know that
you are working ... total loss of identity, hours that pass like
seconds or without any notion of time elapsing ..."

How many of us have been lucky enough in our lives to
equate our work – what we did, or *do*, for a living - with that
kind of contentment, that *absorbedness?*

As I read these words I found myself nodding in
agreement, smiling in recognition. Because *I* have felt those
things – contentment, *absorbedness*, and that feeling of no
time having elapsed – while doing some of my own writing
in the past five years. Not *all* of it, mind you, but *some* of it.
Because writing is also sometimes a brutal struggle to get
things right, and can consist of getting up and pacing around
the house, turning words, phrases, sentences over and over in
my mind, sometimes saying them out loud, checking them for
genuineness, for how they sound. But every now and then, the
words just come easily and quickly and you know they're right,
and those are the times when you lose track of time, when you
look up finally and find that an hour or more has gone by, and
it seems like only minutes. *Absorbedness.*

And I am almost embarrassed to tell you that my other job,
my former day job, was like that too, much of the time. Because
I number myself among those fortunate few who loved his
work. Like Don Hall, I never really thought of it as a *career.*
Perhaps it is my middle-class background showing, but I just
never thought of what I did for nearly twenty-six years, first

with the army and then with the National Security Agency, as a *career*. Each day I went to *work*. And it *was* work, make no mistake. Because I returned home at the end of each day exhausted, both physically and mentally. But I felt good about what I'd done that day, and usually looked forward to going back the next day.

December 12, 2009

Treve has been home for a week now. The house seems more like a home with her here again. Last Saturday, when I went to pick her up in Grand Rapids, it snowed for much of the day. I hate traveling in that kind of weather, so I was a bit nervous about making the drive, which is a round trip of about a hundred and fifty miles. And I also worry about leaving the dogs in the house alone for too long. At twelve and a half, I'm not always sure how long Daisy's bladder will hold out. And, to be perfectly honest, I just hate being away from them for too long. Some would call it silly to be that attached to a couple of animals, I know, but there it is. I just love them. Perhaps too much, but again, there it is.

My dilemma at leaving them was made a bit more worrisome in that I wanted to also attend a reading and talk at Great Lakes Book & Supply in Big Rapids that day. A friend of ours, Ben Busch was reading from an essay he'd published in the latest issue of the *Michigan Quarterly Review* called "Growth Rings." He had stopped by the house a week before to give me a copy of the magazine, which is more like a book, actually, in its sleek glossy binding. It was a special issue called "Bookishness: The New Fate of Reading in the Digital Age."

It was certainly an intriguing subtitle, and one that engaged me immediately. Because there is no question that reading and books, and the publishing industry itself is in a sad state of decline these days. The major publishing houses seem to be run by accountants who are interested only in that "bottom line" – i.e. *will this book turn a major profit?* And Benjamin Busch is a casualty of this kind of thinking; or at least he is so far. An extremely talented writer, Ben published another essay earlier this year in *Harper's Magazine* called "Bearing Arms: The Serious Boy at War." Both of these essays are absorbing and painstakingly crafted, and touch on Ben's boyhood in upstate New York as well as his combat experiences as a Marine officer in the current Iraq war. There are also frequent references to his late parents, who would both have easily related to the theme of "bookishness," since his mother was a librarian and his father, Frederick Busch, was a very respected writer of more than two dozen books and an English professor at

Colgate for over thirty-five years. Oddly, Ben himself professes to not be much of a reader, and said at his talk that day in Big Rapids that when he does read, he tends to read very slowly, which helps him to better remember what he has read. His writing too, he admitted, is a slow, circular and sometimes painful process. The results, however, at least to my mind, are stunningly effective. And yet Ben has been unable thus far to find a publisher for a book of autobiographical essays he has completed, so he is peddling the pieces separately to various magazines. There's that "bottom line" mentality of the major publishers I was just talking about. What a pity for serious readers – *and* writers, of course.

In any case, I made it to Ben's talk – a bit late, as I didn't want to have to leave the dogs alone for *too* long. He drew a very respectable crowd at the bookstore that blustery snowy day, more than twenty booklovers, many of whom appeared to be fans of his father, judging by the questions they had. I'm one of them, a Fred Busch fan, I mean. I discovered Fred's books back in the eighties sometime and have read at least a dozen of his books. The novel, *Girls*, is perhaps his best known and most successful – a chilling mystery that probes and delineates the depths of deceit and depravity that humans are capable of.

I also – obviously – made it safely to the airport and back later that day. We drove through heavy snow for most of the trip home, but arrived home safely by around six-thirty. The dogs were overjoyed to see Treve again, and there were no signs of weak bladder indiscretions, so I suppose I needn't have worried. Except I'm the worrier in the family, as Treve will tell anyone. It's my job.

I was starting to talk about my twenty-one-year job with NSA when last I was writing here. Most of what I did there is probably still classified, but those years were, for me, exciting and always interesting. That contentment – that *absorbedness* – was a constant factor. I can certainly tell you that. It is, I suppose, a bit strange to realize that in all the years I worked at the Agency, my wife and children never set foot in my place of work, and know almost nothing about how I managed to make a living. On occasion, when we would drive by the main gates of the Agency campus, I would point out the buildings and tell the kids, "Well, there it is, kids, the money factory. That's where the money comes from that buys your clothes and food and keeps a roof over our heads." And everyone seemed satisfied with that. No one ever expressed any particular interest in what Dad did there. I guess they knew I was a Russian linguist, but never speculated much beyond that. Which was, I suppose, for the best, since I couldn't really tell them anything. I do remember that, in our initial security briefing, when I began work at NSA, we new hires were told that, if asked where we worked, we should only tell people that we worked for the Department of Defense. And for a while I did just that, but most times when I gave this answer I would get a response like, "Oh, so you work at NSA then." So after a while I just said I was at NSA. And most people knew enough not to question you any further. It was common knowledge that if you lived near Fort Meade and said you were with DoD, that you were with NSA, which was, after all, one of the largest employers in the area at a time when twenty or thirty thousand people worked there or at its many field sites around the globe. None of this is a secret. James Bamford's books, *The Puzzle Palace, Body of Secrets* and *The Shadow Factory* have supplied the reading public with a pretty good look at NSA and what it does. And now there's a brand new book on NSA called *The Secret Sentry*, by Matthew Aid. So if you want to know what I did for those nearly twenty-six years as a Russian linguist, read those books and you'll probably get at least an inkling, okay? It was fascinating stuff every day – *absorbing*.

I was discharged from the army that second time in February of 1981 in Augsburg. Or perhaps I should say I was separated, or processed out there. My actual discharge didn't come until April. I took two months of unused leave – terminal leave – when we departed Augsburg that winter. Our destination was Belleville, Treve's parents' place on Martinsville Road, since we were, upon my discharge, for all practical purposes, homeless. But nearly a year before that I had flown back to Maryland and spent two or three days in interviews and testing at NSA, having submitted an early application for employment there. NSA could not, of course, offer me a job while I was still on active duty with the army, so

I simply had to believe – to have faith – that a job offer would be forthcoming as soon as I was free of that encumbrance. It would be, however, a time of worry and uncertainty for us, wondering for the next two months whether there would indeed be a job offer made. Because of this, I found myself in no position to dicker over important things like salary when the offer was finally made, just a few days after my final discharge in mid-April of 1981.

All of these things, although several weeks in the future, were already weighing heavily on my mind when we boarded a flight for home at the Munich airport in February. In New York our landing was delayed due to a snowstorm and we circled in a holding pattern for nearly an hour, with periodic musings by the pilot over the PA system as to whether he might have to find an alternate airfield – Boston, perhaps. Another thing for me to worry about. We finally did land in New York, but we discovered, once we were on the ground, that all the planes there had been grounded due to the storm, so we were stuck in the terminal with a duffel bag and several pieces of luggage and three overly tired and hungry kids. The airline did issue us meal vouchers to use in the airport, so that helped some, but not much. There were other complications.

While we were going through customs, juggling luggage and bags, I somehow managed to split the whole seat out of the corduroy trousers I was wearing. This might have been a real breaking point for me, but Treve calmed me down, and actually found a small sewing kit in her purse. She had the three kids form a kind of barrier around us with the bags and crouched behind me busily sewing my pants back together while other passengers milled around us.

"There. All fixed!" she exclaimed proudly, standing up and redepositing her little leather sewing case into her purse. And so it seemed, as I breathed a sigh of relief over another minor problem solved. But not long after that, when I took the boys to the bathroom, and then went to go myself, I found that she had somehow managed to sew the seat of my pants securely to my underwear. Not a huge problem, actually, but still frustrating, after what had already been a very long day.

Finally, after a couple hours of waiting in the terminal, the kids trying to nap on top of our luggage or across our laps, the airline announced that no flights would be departing that night (it was already one or two in the morning), and we were issued a voucher for a hotel room.

December 13, 2009

By the time we got ourselves checked into the hotel airport and the kids put to bed it was nearly three AM and our flight was scheduled to leave at eight AM, so I asked the hotel desk for a six o-clock wakeup call and Treve and I simply flopped, totally exhausted, for a few hours. I don't think I slept at all. I kept watching the clock, scared to death we'd oversleep. In point of fact, *I* wasn't flying out with Treve and the kids. I had to catch a bus to Bayonne, New Jersey, to go pick up our car from the military ocean terminal there. We had shipped it from Bremerhaven a few weeks earlier, and I had all the appropriate paperwork in hand to claim it. Or at least I *hoped* I did.

In 1981 we still had that '75 AMC Hornet Wagon we had bought new just a few months before I reenlisted in the army. It had been a source of problems for us off and on for the last year or so we lived in Augsburg. But these problems had forced me to improvise solutions. I will say that. A rear tire had gone flat one night while Treve was at the bowling alley. I was at home with the children at the time. The husband of one of Treve's bowling friends came into the alley and told her about the flat, and then was nice enough to change the tire for her. But when we tried to order another inflation bottle for our space saver spare at the PX Garage, we learned it was simply not available. I didn't feel we could afford to be without a spare for the next year, so we simply ended up buying another tire and had to haul it around in the back of the car, since it wouldn't fit in the spare well.

Another recurring problem we had with the wagon was a defective distributor cap. Whenever the weather got damp – which was often – the car was extremely difficult to start. It would crank and crank to no avail, and sometimes it would wear the battery down to almost nothing. Other times it might finally start, but with something of a loud bang under the hood. Now I'm one of those guys that know almost nothing about that stuff under the front lid of a car, but that year I learned a few things, out of necessity. When I'd pop the hood following one of these scary little explosions, I'd find that the distributor cap had blown off. Usually, once I'd reseated it and fastened the clamps, the car would start right up and run okay for a while. Until the next time we had to start it in the rain or damp foggy weather. After several of these episodes, however, those little metal clamps that held the cap on rusted through and broke off. These tiny metal pieces were also unavailable at the local garage, so I improvised fasteners with long wire twisters. We kept running the car that way for the rest of our tour in Augsburg. I always kept a supply of long twisters in the glove box. We later found out that the distributor cap had a hairline crack in it, which apparently allowed moisture inside creating a vapor lock or something. I really didn't understand it; still don't.

But my biggest challenge with the wagon came one day when we were all in the car – Treve, all three kids, and even the dog – coming back from Sheridan Kaserne where we'd gone to get our mail. It was only a few miles from our Cramerton apartment, but about halfway home, something suddenly went *kaflooey* (that's a very technical, mechanical term, by the way; I believe it comes from the French for *Aw, shit!*) underneath the car and the engine got loud as a Sherman tank and we could hear something scraping the pavement under the car. My heart sinking, I pulled to the side of the road, shut off the roaring engine and got out to look underneath. Down on my hands and knees, I discovered that our exhaust pipe had broken off right behind the engine manifold and was lying on the ground. The muffler and tailpipe were still fastened, but wouldn't be for long if I didn't do something right away. And here is the first part of a solution devised on the spot that I am still proud of today. Well, first of all, think I stood up and scratched my head and probably swore a few times and looked up and down the street hoping someone might stop and help me out somehow. But no one did, although cars were going by the whole time at a rapid clip, some people peering out at us as they went by. I decided it was up to me – the husband, the dad, the staff sergeant – to figure out how to solve this knotty problem. And, after studying the situation a bit more and thinking hard, I did.

"Jeff," I said to my eleven year-old, "hand me Heidi's leash, will ya?"

"Whaddaya want the leash for, Dad?" he inquired, understandably enough. "Are we gonna walk home?"

"No. We aren't gonna walk home!" I replied irritably. "Just gimme the leash, okay?"

So he handed me the dog leash, a shiny metal six-foot chain with a red leather loop on the end. Reaching under the car, I slipped the leash loop around the front end of the exhaust pipe, then pulled the chain out and fed it up through the window of the car's back door and handed the end to Jeff. Then I instructed him to make sure the door was firmly closed and locked, then turn his back to the door and put the chain over his shoulder and hold on tight with both hands. I pulled up the slack in the chain, lifting the tailpipe a few inches off the ground.

"Got a good hold?" I asked Jeff.

"Yeah, but it's heavy, Dad!"

"That's okay," I said. "You can do it. We'll be home in just a few minutes. Hang on now, okay?" I said as I hurried around the car and got behind the wheel and started the engine. It roared – and I mean *ROARED* – to life, and I quickly swung back into traffic and sprinted for home, just a mile or so away.

"Hurry, Dad. It's *heavy!*" Jeff whined.

"Tim, you're going too *fast!*" Treve breathed, holding Suzie tightly on her lap with one arm and white-knuckling the armrest with her other hand.

And I probably was, but we got there safely, pulling into our parking place at Cramerton just as Jeff finally lost his grip on the leash, dropping the exhaust pipe onto the concrete with a loud *crump!*

The second part of this problem was a bit more mechanically complex. Because when I called the PX Garage, as usual, they didn't have the parts needed to fix the car, and told me they would have to send to the Netherlands, or maybe it was Belgium, to get the parts, and it would probably be around three or four weeks. This was unacceptable, of course, but I was used to this kind of crap by now. I went back downstairs and peered under the car again, studying the problem. And figured out a quick fix.

I came back upstairs and poked around in our kitchen wastebasket and found an empty Campbell's tomato soup can.

I rinsed it out, peeled off the label and removed the other end of the can with a can opener. Then I borrowed a pair of tin snips from a downstairs neighbor and carefully snipped open the can along one side. I took this modified tin can downstairs and crawled under the car and tried wrapping it around the exhaust pipe. So far so good. Then tried wrapping it around the stub of pipe still projecting off the back of the engine. Again, a good fit. Then I squirmed under the car a bit further and hoisted the dragging pipe up even with the manifold stub and joined the two pieces, wrapping the opened can around the juncture where they met. By God, it was a perfect fit, i.e. a perfect fit. Now I just needed something to hold it in place. I thought about it a moment. A wire coat hanger probably wouldn't hold very well. I opened up the hood to look down through the engine compartment at the problem. As I raised the hood I happened to glance down at the radiator and there was my solution. A *hose clamp!* Maybe two would be better. So I measured the diameter of the pipe, the soup can and wrote them down, then walked over the PX and found a couple hose clamps, walked home, got my screw driver, put the whole jerry-rigged mess together and tightened down the clamps around the can-joint, and *Voila!* I had fixed the problem. I started up the engine and the roar was gone! My *God*, I had *mechanicked!* I had actually *fixed* my *car!*

I know this might seem like a small matter to most folks, but ya gotta understand I'm the kind of guy who usually has trouble just trying to figure out how to open the hood on a car. And I had *fixed* something, all by *myself!* I can't tell you how many times I've probably told this story to people over the past twenty-some years, and yet when I told Treve just now what I was writing about, she claims to have no memory of this momentous event at all.

In any case, it was this same car that I picked up at the Bayonne terminal that frigid February morning after I had gotten Treve and the kids and all of our luggage onto a much-delayed flight to Detroit. And I soon learned that my troubles with the Hornet were not quite behind me. After processing my paperwork at the port office, I sat in a waiting room while the port drivers went to find my car in the vast parking lot. After nearly an hour of waiting, a man finally came in and got me, explaining that they'd had to jump start the car, which wasn't that unusual, but he also complained that even with the charger, the car was "a bitch" to get started. But there it was parked outside the door, chugging away, if a bit unevenly, even to my amateur ear. The lot attendant said it might be a good idea to let it warm up for a little while before I got on the road, so I did. Then, filling up at the port gas station, I left the yard and got onto the Jersey Turnpike, heading west for home. It was probably nearly eleven o'clock or so by this time and traffic was pretty heavy.

I had only gone a few miles down the highway when I noticed some steam – could it be *smoke?* – coming off the front of the car. It was white, then a bit darker, and then I saw *flames* licking out from under the hood! *Holy crap! Now what?!* I remember thinking, as I braked quickly and pulled off the side of the turnpike, traffic whizzing by me as I killed the engine. When I popped the hood, flames shot up from the engine and then, quickly, seemed to sputter and die. I scooped some dirty snow from the shoulder of the road in my hands and dumped it onto the smoldering whatchimacallit in the engine compartment. The fire was out. As I remember it, I think it was some kind of papery hose that came off the air cleaner and carburetor and then connected back to the engine that had caught fire. As soon as it had cooled down, I reached in and pulled off most of the remaining scorched and ruined remnants and threw them by the side of the road. Then I closed the hood, got back in the car, and, praying silently, turned the key. And it started *up*, praise God. I drove rather slowly to the next exit and found a service station where I popped the hood and explained what had happened to a mechanic. Or I *think* he was a mechanic. He may have just been a pump jockey. He looked at the scorched area and pulled off another small piece of the hose still clinging to the metal, and told me he didn't think it was anything essential and I should be okay now. I guess he was right, because I drove the car all the way home to Michigan without any further problems.

After a couple of days with almost no sleep, it was a real struggle to stay awake that day and evening as I crossed New Jersey, Pennsylvania and Ohio, aimed for Michigan and Belleville, where my family was waiting. There was heavy wet snow falling for most of the trip, and I can still remember after night fell, how I kept myself awake by rolling down my window and reaching around onto the windshield to get a handful of snow to rub across my face. My AM radio picked up only a few stations as I crawled though the mountains in Pennsylvania in that blizzard. But I can still remember one particular piece of music from the car radio that night. It was Earl Klugh's new (at the time) album called *Late Night Guitar*. I had never heard of Klugh at the time, but the DJ was just letting the whole album play, and Klugh's softly haunting solo guitar renditions of "Smoke Gets in Your Eyes," "Laura," and especially the beautiful "Jamaica Farewell" somehow helped me relax a bit and got me through those snowy mountains and into Ohio. I later bought the album, and it is one of the few vinyl records I still own. And I just looked online and found that it is still available, nearly thirty years later, on CD. I guess someone else must have liked it too.

Treve's own particular memory of finally arriving home at her parents that February is one of trying to put an overtired Suzie, who was two and a half at the time, to bed in her own childhood bedroom. Suzie, exhausted, disoriented and cranky, refused to go down, crying, "I don't *want* to sleep here. I want my *own* bed in *Augs*burg, *Ger*many. And I want my *daddy!*"

And I believe that Suzie really *did* say it just that way. Because Suzie never did speak in short words or phrases, and never spoke baby talk either. From the time she began talking, she spoke in complete sentences, sometimes even compound complex sentences.

All this *stuff* I remember. What am I gonna *do* with it? I'm gonna write it down, that's what. Maybe no one will care, but these little bits and pieces of me – of my life – will still be here, at least for a while, once I'm gone.

I just finished reading another terrific memoir the other day. It's called *The Duke of Deception: Memories of My Father*, by Geoffrey Wolff.

It's the only thing I've read of Wolff's, although he has written several other books. This one has been around for thirty years already, but is still in print, and *should* be. What a strange and chaotic life Wolff had as a child, living with his father from the time he was twelve – a father who was the ultimate con man who worked the system to live. Wolff went from living high to living in near squalor. But somehow he survived, as did his younger brother, Toby. Both Geoffrey and Tobias Wolff are respected and admired writers now. You probably might know the younger Wolff's work from the movie version of his memoir, *This Boy's Life*, which starred Leonardo DiCaprio and Robert De Niro as his abusive stepfather.

I highly recommend both the books, but here's a very small point I noticed in Geoffrey Wolf's book. He mentioned that during one of his many moves as a child, when he first arrived in Florida with his mother and little brother, that Christmas "Rudolph the Red-Nosed Reindeer" was a brand new song and was being played ad nauseam everywhere he went. I found this interesting, since I'd always thought of "Rudolph" as one of those songs that has just *always* been around. But then the next morning, as I turned on my CD player, loaded now with Christmas discs, the first two songs I heard were "Jingle Bell Rock" by Bobby Helms, and Brenda Lee's "Rockin' around the Christmas Tree." It occurred to me suddenly that *I* can remember when both of *those* songs were brand new and being played to death, in the same way Wolff remembered Gene Autry's "Rudolph" and its first Christmas of 1949. The Helms song debuted in 1957 and Brenda Lee's song the following year. Geoffrey Wolff was twelve when Rudolph came out. I was thirteen and fourteen when *my* two songs first appeared. Now all those songs are Christmas staples, of course. Books. They trigger these connections, these commonalities. Am I alone in making these connections when I read? I wonder.

December 23, 2009

Probably not. I think everyone makes these mental connections. They just never bother to remark on them, or write them down the way I seem to be doing here. The thing is, everything really *is* connected, whether we realize it or not. An interesting example of this is going on right now, right in our own back yard, *literally*. Let me explain.

Sunday night, our back fence neighbors, Jim and Mary Murnik, got company for the Christmas holidays. Jim's son, Michael, arrived with his wife, three little kids, and two dogs. Michael is a medical doctor – a family practitioner – who lives and practices in Blue Hill, Maine. You may remember that I began this opus, or whatever you wanna call it, talking about the writers Doris Grumbach and Roger Angell. Well, Grumbach lives right in the Blue Hill area, and Angell also summers in Maine, and has ever since he was a kid, and so did his famous stepfather, E.B. White, who was, among other things, the *Charlotte's Web* guy.

I walked around the block on Monday morning to meet Michael and his family. I walked *around* because the snow in the back yard is kinda deep and I would have had to shovel out the back fence gate just to get it open. And too, much of the snow-filled back yard is now a minefield of dog doo that we haven't been able to find and scoop since winter arrived to stay early this month.

The younger Murniks proved to be a delightful group. Their girls are seven, six and two, and the littlest one, Emmy, climbed right up in my lap where I was seated at the kitchen table and told me all about a "bonk" she had on her head, from walking under the table, and also pointed out a nearly invisible "ow-ie" on her small bare foot, which her mother obligingly acknowledged and even got her a tiny Band-Aid to cover it with. Kids love Band-aids, you know.

Michael, of course, knew all about our Doris Grumbach "connection," since his dad, Jim, has also been a Grumbach fan ever since I introduced him to her work. And Jim himself has a Maine connection too, as a graduate of Colby College, in Waterville, Maine, *waay* back in the Dark Ages sometime. (Just kidding, Jim.) In fact, he has told me that one of his classmates at Colby was the writer, Annie Proulx. Jim also told me, a year or two ago, about meeting Proulx at a conference of some kind in Chicago. He reminded her at the time that they had been classmates, but, much to his chagrin, she claimed not to remember him at all. Jim still festers over this, grumbling that the classes were pretty small. How could she *not* remember him?

Michael knew about Angell's Maine connection too, and one-upped me by telling how he and his wife had met writer Michael Chabon at a local beach last summer, and had him autograph one of his books they had.

And if I want to carry this Maine writer connection even further, I'll bring up Fred Busch again. Monday night Ben Busch and his family came for the evening, to sample some of Treve's pierogies and other seasonal treats, and to visit for a few hours. Ben brought along another essay he'd written, which I read later that evening, after they had left. In this as yet unpublished piece, Ben writes of spending summer vacations as a child with his family at a beach house in Cutler, Maine. I found it on a map, farther up the coast from Blue Hill, only about twenty or thirty miles from the Canadian border.

See? It's all con*nec*ted. *We* are all connected. Ol' Buddha knew what he was talking about.

It's nearly noon. Daisy and Barney sat and looked at me with their sad eyes until they shamed me into taking them for a walk around the block, even though it's still barely twenty degrees outside. But while I was walking I was still "writing" – internally, the way I always am. Thinking about Christmas – this one and Christmases past. This one had promised to be rather low-key, but now we've been invited to the Murniks for Christmas eve dinner, as well as to celebrate the eighth birthday of Silas, the oldest of the three granddaughters. So we won't be by ourselves for Christmas. Treve was dreading that, I know. She has been in a frenzy of cooking and baking for the past few days now, nearly wearing herself out. I keep wondering, and asking her, for what? It's just us this year. But I should have known that this turmoil of traditional activity is simply to keep her busy, to stave off the awful loneliness she feels so strongly – missing our kids and grandkids during this special time of year. So I'm trying to just shut up and let her do her thing, trying to understand. Because I don't think that a man – even if he's a father and grandfather – feels this disconnection and loneliness quite as strongly as a woman does. I'm not sure why this is. Maybe simply because we've fulfilled our biological imperative to reproduce and, for us, that's enough. We're just happy that our mates didn't bite off our heads once we'd done our job, like the praying mantis female does – or so I've heard. I do miss my kids and the little ones, but not nearly as *pain*fully so as Treve does.

When you're young you never really think much about what it might be like to be sixty-five and retired. And in love with an elderly woman. Well, I've found I like it. And I am. No regrets. No particular complaints. Treve still isn't quite sure how she feels about it all, but for me it's okay. Into my old brain here pops the title line from Don McLean's beautiful ballad, "And I love you so ..." as rendered by Perry Como on one of his last albums.

I guess I'm writing all this down because, as the same song says later: "The book of life is brief/And once a page is read/All but love is dead/That is my belief ..." But perhaps the most hope-filled and life-affirming line from the song for me is: "And you love me too ..."

Yes, I miss my children. But I know they all have their own lives now. And we – Treve and I – are so very blessed to still have each other. That is the thought that sustains me this Christmas, and always.

And I keep on reading, of course; so many books. Currently I'm taking my time perusing my way through several books. The first, and perhaps most enjoyable right now, is a delightful novel by Marina Lewycka called *A Short History of Tractors in Ukrainian*. Another, a short memoir from the Vietnam war called *Last Night I Dreamed of Peace: The Diary of Dang Thuy Tram*, I'm only a couple dozen pages into. The diarist was a young woman Vietcong doctor who was killed at the age of twenty-seven by American troops. This particular book was recommended to me by Richard Snider, who served in Vietnam with the U.S. Army when he was a very young doctor himself. (Rick wrote about his own war in a memoir called *Delta Six:*

Soldier Surgeon.) I can already tell the Vietcong diary will be a very sad read. There are always two sides to every war, after all. And no one really wins.

I'm also slowly sampling pieces from David Barber's recently self-published collection of his newspaper columns from the past twenty years or so, *Stone Checkers and Wheelbarrow Rides*. Dave, like me, was a Reed City boy. His father, Don, was a city mailman here for many years. Dave is now a newspaper editor in Manistee. Marc Sheehan's second collection of poems, *Vengeful Hymns*, has been part of my bedside stack now for a couple of months. Marc is a public relations man at Ferris State. And only this morning I read a few more pages from David Michaelis's bestselling *Schulz and Peanuts: A Biography*, a physically enormous and exhaustively researched examination of the life and work of the late cartoonist-philosopher from Minnesota.

Yes, so *many* books ...

So maybe that's enough writing for today. After all, it *is* nearly Christmas.

December 30, 2009

And now Christmas has come and gone, and we survived our child-less holiday. It helped, I think, that we spent a couple hours on Christmas Eve afternoon at the Murnik house, helping to celebrate their granddaughter's eighth birthday, an occasion complete with cake and ice cream, presents, pointy party hats and those things you blow into that roll out into a kind of paper erection. The three little girls all had presents to open, although technically it was only Silas's birthday. (Yes, her name is *Silas*, as in *Marner*.) This is a girl who will obviously be going places and will make her mark in life, because the presents she got (and had actually *asked* for) included a small chemistry set and a genuine sure-enough adult-type *metal* detector, the same kind you see being used by beachcombers along the coast. This latter gift was the most popular of all, as the three girls took turns using it after their dad had put it together and installed batteries. It was beeping at hidden coins and at the watches on our wrists. But the beeping the girls seemed to enjoy most was when they got close to Grandpa Jim, when the detector picked up on his brand new titanium knee. Jim seemed to enjoy this too, grinning and waggling his bushy eyebrows at the small prospectors.

We went home for a few hours after the birthday party and even worked in a short nap before returning for a Christmas Eve dinner of prime rib and all the trimmings. A confirmed carnivore, Treve was in heaven, since prime rib is her favorite meal. And Jim, who was once (in addition to being a one-time college English teacher) a restaurateur in his home state of Massachusetts, cooked everything to lip-smacking perfection, as usual.

When we left the Murniks that time, around eight-thirty in the evening, we discovered it had been sleeting, and our entire car, parked in the street out front, was encased in ice. It took about ten minutes of scraping and warming the car up before we could drive back home around the block. And once I got the car safely into the garage I was disinclined to get it back out again that night, although Treve had had her heart set on going to midnight Mass. I didn't exactly talk her out of it. I simply refused to go, which caused a minor rift in our merry Christmas that night.

The next morning it was still raining and the streets were glazed and rutted with ice and frozen slush, and when we left for ten o'clock mass it began to pour down rain even harder. There were only three cars in the church parking lot when we arrived, but more people straggled in until we had a group of forty for Christmas morning Mass, if you counted the priest and the server, young Eric Chase, who volunteered to help out of the small crowd. On the way into the church, Treve had "confessed" to Father Loc that she'd been mad at me for not getting her to midnight Mass, and he unofficially "forgave" her, so she was in a much better frame of mind for the rest of the day, which included a holiday dinner of ham and pierogies, with green bean casserole and rolls. And later we packed up a "dinner-to-go" of all the same stuff and took it down to Mom and Chris at the end of the block. Mom had not wanted to come out in the ice and snow, which was probably a very good idea, since she gets around with a walker now and this was definitely not walker weather.

At various times during the day, we talked on the telephone with all three of our kids and a couple of the grandchildren too. Scott and Suzie both emailed us some Christmas Eve and Day photos of their families' festivities, and we'd received a beautiful card from Jeff and Megan with photos of their two little girls. So we *did* have at least some electronic, voice and visual connections with our kids and their kids for the holiday. Then throughout the late afternoon and evening we read. Treve's first choice that day was the double holiday issue of *People* magazine which I'd picked up over at Rite-Aid for her on Christmas Eve day, in a last-ditch desperate effort to "surprise" her with *some*thing – *anything* – for Christmas. Because it's hard to get really excited about Christmas without kids around, and the presents we had wrapped were just things we had bought for ourselves – in Treve's case, mostly clothes she had bought at Kohl's or Penney's during her visit to Scott's family out in Pennsylvania; and for me it was mostly books I had picked up here and there, or ordered from Amazon over the past couple of weeks. So we were in no particular hurry to open our presents on Christmas day. Treve did seem to enjoy that *People* though, which caught my eye, I should perhaps guiltily admit, with its front cover of Taylor Swift and back cover of Jennifer

Anniston, a couple of my current favorite show-biz girls. But Treve likes 'em too, and we both ponder the deep mystery of why can't poor beautiful Jen find herself a good man. We also wonder how much longer Taylor can keep on being the sweet girl-next-door type that she still is despite all this sudden success. How long, in other words, before she turns into the usual "celebrity slut"? So far so good, with Taylor though. We still love her music and her videos and what still seems to be a kind of wide-eyed innocence that has charmed most of America.

Anyway, Treve sat and read that whole magazine, cover to cover. I was taking my time finishing up Marina Lewycka's beautiful novel about a family of Ukrainian immigrants in England, *A Short History of Tractors in Ukrainian*. Wise and beautifully written, I was savoring this book, which I am sure was at least partly autobiographical, since Lewycka herself was born in a refugee camp after the war before her family moved to England. And here's another one of those odd connections I'm always finding as I read. Lewycka is now a part-time English and writing teacher at Sheffield Hallam University in Sheffield, England. As it turns out, I know someone who lives in Sheffield. John O'Hara of the once semi-famous rock band, John O'Hara and the Playboys lives there. O'Hara and his band were featured prominently in my second memoir, *Soldier Boy*, as one of the most popular touring bands in western Europe back in the mid-sixties. I knew John only slightly at the time, but somehow managed to find him through the magic of the internet some forty years later and sent him a copy of my book, which he circulated among the other Playboys, all in their sixties now. John still performs occasionally, but is mostly, like me, retired. And here's the clincher of coincidences and connections. John doesn't have a computer, so when we correspond by email he goes over to a computer lab or room at Sheffield U and uses their equipment. It's like that six-degrees-of-separation thing again, Marina Lewycka and Sheffield and John O'Hara. I know it doesn't seem like that big a deal, but I'm always so amazed and delighted to make these connections. Maybe I'm just weird that way.

Another book I sampled on Christmas morning before Mass was a book I've had around for a while, but I recalled a particular essay in it that seemed holiday-appropriate. The book was Fred Busch's *A Dangerous Profession: A Book About the Writing Life*. I had read and thoroughly savored the book in its entirety when I first got it over a year ago, and each time I take it down from the shelf, I touch the cover with a kind of reverence, because Busch was such a gifted, if underappreciated, writer, and I still mourn his untimely passing. The essay in question is called "The Floating Christmas Tree," and recounts the first Christmas he and his then-new wife, Judy, spent together in a tiny apartment on Morton Street in Greenwich Village, when he was still a struggling, undiscovered and unpublished writer. Nevertheless, he kept hammering away at his craft, and it made me laugh when he told of how he did his writing in the bathroom after Judy had gone to bed.

> *"I had a portable typewriter, given me by my parents when I left for college. I sat on the edge of our enormous bathtub, rested the typewriter on top of the closed toilet, and, while Judy slept, I wrote. In those days I needed little sleep – I was twenty-two – and I was going to be a writer, I was a writer, I was going to get them to admit I was a writer, and I sat in that awkward position and wrote my awkward prose ..."*

Perhaps one of the best things about Fred Busch's prose is that, while he always took his craft seriously, he did not hesitate to poke fun at himself occasionally. When he writes of that first Christmas he and Judy shared, this self-effacing sense of humor immediately becomes evident. I'm pretty sure Fred wouldn't mind if I shared it with you.

> *"For our first Christmas, we gave each other a single paperback copy of* The Family of Man. *I don't apologize for our sentimentality: We loved each other taxingly, hopefully, stupidly, and dearly. We had no money for a Christmas tree because in the city anything that's vegetable and not dead costs more than a human life. I had stashed three dollars away though, and at 11:45 on Christmas Eve of 1963, I stole out to Seventh Avenue, where a man who sold trees for far too much sold me the runt of his litter (it came, at most, to my waist). Judy cut paper chains for it and I spent until 2:00 A.M. trying to fashion a stand from wood given and tools lent ... I failed to build the stand, as I have failed to build*

nearly everything from 1963 to the present, so I strung wire and cord from each corner of the room, and I suspended the tree, using a bumbled bowline around its tip, in the center of my inept web. It was an artifice built of failure and affection, the best I could do. The tree floated and swayed, and the paper chains rustled, and Judy laughed, and it was a most excellent Christmas because we were what we had dreamed to be – in love, and undefeated in New York ..."

In copying this out just now, I am laughing, and then maybe crying just a little bit, because it is simply perfect – *beautiful*. And the best part about it is that Fred wrote it all down, so now his sons and his grandkids will know about that Christmas before they were born, and will perhaps laugh and cry themselves when they read it again each Christmas for years to come.

One of the presents I unwrapped Christmas night was a bulky brown bubble mailer I'd received in the mail a week before. It was a book swap I'd arranged with an Ohio writer named Joyce Dyer. A few weeks before I had read one of her memoirs, *Gum-Dipped*, a bittersweet remembrance of her father, who worked most of his life for Firestone in Akron. I enjoyed it so much I wrote to Joyce at Hiram College, where she is an English professor, and proposed the swap. I sent her my "complete works," and she sent me her other two memoirs and a few other things. It was such a fat, rich-looking bundle when it arrived in the mail that Treve decided I should save it until Christmas to open. So I did, and the books inside were worth the wait.

I ended up reading Joyce's memoirs out of sequence, which was okay, since all three books are complete in and of themselves. *Gum-Dipped* was published a few years ago. *Goosetown* is her newest book, just published by the University of Akron Press this month, and is an attempt to look back at the first five years of her life, when her parents and grandparents, as well as numerous aunts, uncles and cousins, all lived in an old German inner-city neighborhood of Akron. It was called Goosetown because many of those early immigrants kept geese in their yards back in the late nineteenth century. The book ends up being more an examination of her Haberkost grandparents' lives and those of other relatives in the tight-knit community. Dyer digs up many family memories which are not necessarily pleasant ones, but she believes firmly in the importance of telling, as she puts it, "The truth, the whole truth, and nothing but the bloody truth, please." This makes for a very moving and at times heartrending book.

But when it comes to heartrending – and heart*breaking* – both *Goosetown* and *Gum-Dipped* pale in comparison to Dyer's earlier memoir (1996) about her mother's years-long ordeal with dementia, entitled *In a Tangled Wood: An Alzheimer's Journey*. In it, Dyer takes you inside the Alzheimer's unit where her mother was a resident for the last few years of her life. It is not an easy book to read. Although I have had some first-hand experience with Alzheimer's patients during my time as a volunteer "friendly visitor" with both a hospice (Hospice of the Chesapeake) and the county Commission on Aging in Maryland, and then here in Michigan at a local nursing home, I was not quite prepared for the vivid and brutally honest and unflinching looks at the daily life in an Alzheimer's ward. The tales of incontinence and adult diapers, playing in and flinging feces, struggles with the simplest tasks, like getting dressed and undressed and keeping clean are bad enough. But when words fail, when language itself slips away, and when mothers no longer recognize daughters, the pain felt is nearly overwhelming. All of these indignities and losses are tellingly told here in Dyer's "whole bloody truth" credo. It is indeed a heartbreaking tale to read, of course, but Dyer explains towards the end, at least partly, why she wrote it. After her mother died, her friends encouraged her to get away, to take a vacation. But she can't, and explains –

> *"They are kind, but they do not understand. Alzheimer's disease is not about recovery, either for the patient or for the family members who watch.*
>
> *My dear friends have not been where I have been.*
>
> *Alzheimer's disease has changed me forever. The Florida sun or a Bahamas breeze will not help me forget any of this.*
>
> *And why would the daughter of a woman who forgot everything find comfort in forgetfulness?*
>
> *I want to remember every moment I had with my mother, including every second of the last nine years …*
>
> *I don't want to forget a single thing."*

Joyce Dyer's mother died nearly fifteen years ago, but I am sure she still misses her. I thought about this two days ago when I noticed that Treve seemed rather blue. I asked her what was wrong, and she reminded me that it was just eight years ago on December 28th that her mom died.

As the youngest child and only girl (after three boys) in her family, Treve and her mom were always exceptionally close. That was always apparent to me, from the first time I saw them together, back in the spring of 1967, when Wanda made a weekend visit to Ferris to see her only daughter. Even Treve will tell you that her mom was concerned about protecting her little girl's virtue in that college town full of predatory men. That was why she always encouraged Treve to wear a girdle, a formidable rubber contraption of an undergarment that was about as close to a chastity belt as the twentieth century had to offer.

Well, I guess it must have worked, because her virtue was still intact when we married that fall.

December 31, 2009

When I retired in the fall of 2001, Treve was ready and anxious to make the move from Maryland to Michigan. After twenty-five years of living on first one coast, then overseas, and then on the other coast, she would finally be reasonably close to her mom again, only a few hours drive away. We had already purchased our home here in Reed City. In fact we had bought the house at the end of 1999, in anticipation of my taking a buyout and an early retirement in the spring of 2000. Unfortunately, shortly after we purchased our retirement home here, the "early out" I had been planning fell through. The Agency withdrew its offer of the buyout, at least for a while. Treve and I were understandably disappointed, but sometimes things work out in spite of your best-laid plans.

We had bought the house from Lorraine Brenner, who was a family friend of many years, and also the mother-in-law of my longtime childhood friend, Keith Eichenberg. As it turned out, the new condo she had planned to move into on the south end of town was behind schedule in its construction, and she still needed a place to live, so we simply worked out a deal allowing her to stay in the house until her new place was ready. We closed on the house in December of 1999. Lorraine moved into her new place the following May. In July we moved our daughter, Suzie, to Reed City to live in our house while she finished her last year of college at Ferris. It would be Suzie's third college in four years. She has started out at another FSU, Frostburg State in western Maryland, then transferred to University of Maryland Baltimore County (UMBC) and then dropped out for a while to work. She was ready for a change and another stab at higher education and we needed a tenant, so, like I said, things worked out for everyone concerned. A kind of value-added feature, at least for Treve and me, was that Suzie did finally graduate, and from the same college where we had met back in 1967. And she graduated with honors. It was the first year Ferris offered a liberal arts degree, and I think Suzie was the very first English major to graduate from FSU.

But no matter, I suppose. (Except we're pretty proud of Suzie, and still grateful to Ferris for a number of things in our lives, obviously.)

By the fall of 2001, however, NSA gave me another crack at the early out – *with* incentive – and I jumped on it. My biggest fear was that we would have trouble selling our house in Odenton. Real estate prices were still high everywhere at that time, but the house we had been living in for the past seventeen years was not in a particularly good neighborhood. It was a community of duplexes, which had always been advertised as "starter homes." And they *were* for most people, but we stayed and stayed, saving our money and then doubling up on mortgage payments for a few years. By doing this, we had managed to pay off our mortgage the year before I retired. The house was ours, free and clear. We had kept the place well maintained and even made some major improvements along the way – new roof, windows, doors, furnace and central air, to name a few. Unfortunately, the rest of the neighborhood – all those "starter homes" – had not followed suit. Most of the original owners and even subsequent ones had moved out and many of the houses had been bought up by real estate speculators and – dare I say it? – okay, I will – slumlords. Lots of rentals, and lots of houses going rapidly to hell, so to speak. Walking the dogs had become distinctly unpleasant those last few years when I saw garbage, junk cars in the street and back yards, and some distinctly unpleasant types hanging about on the street corners. There had even been some drug raids on houses on various nearby blocks in the past few years.

As it turned out, I needn't have worried. Like everywhere else in the country then, real estate prices were still sky high. Our house was only on the market nine days and it sold, and there wasn't even any haggling over price. We got the asking price. I was shocked. *Happily* shocked, but still … shocked.

Here's another interesting coincidence. We had our first meeting with our realtors on September 11th. Yes, it was *the* infamous day – 9/11. And it did affect our plans for a while.

I should probably tell you something of what I remember from that day. I was at work by six-thirty or so that morning, as usual. It had been my habit for the past several years to try to get to work between six and seven in the morning. My office at NSA offered a flex-time kind of schedule that allowed us to start work anytime between six and nine o'clock, as long as we put in our eight hours. In fact, I often worked a nine- or ten-hour day, taking overtime or "comp" (compensation) time, whichever was authorized. By doing this, I either picked up some extra money (overtime), or compiled extra vacation hours (comp time), allowing me to stockpile my regular vacation hours. The truth is I never minded working extra hours, because, as I've already told you, the work was always interesting enough that I would become so absorbed in what I was doing that the time would simply fly by. Sometimes I would look up from my computer and realize I had skipped lunch. There's that "absorbedness" I talked about.

In any case, I had been at work a few hours already and was deep into it that fateful morning when I looked up and noticed that the people who usually worked at the desks near me weren't there. Our office was a long open floor plan divided up by fabric covered partitions which enclosed small cubicles of three or four desks. My three cube-mates were conspicuously missing. Curious, I stood up to look around. The partitions were only about six feet high, so, since I am (or *was*) nearly six foot five, I never had any trouble looking around the length of the whole office by simply gazing over the tops of the dividers. I immediately noticed a group of my office mates clustered around the open door of the branch office. The office was also unnaturally quiet for that time of morning, but I could hear a TV announcer's voice coming out of the office door where the people were grouped. I knew that each branch office was equipped with a television, usually tuned to CNN, but people seldom paid much attention to it. This was an unusual anomaly. I think it was around nine o'clock when I walked over to the office door to see what was going on, because everyone there was very quiet. The first hijacked plane had already crashed into one of the towers. A few minutes after I joined the crowd clustered in the branch office we watched in utter disbelief and horror as a second airliner hit the other tower. Even the CNN announcers seemed confused at first, but I'm pretty sure I don't need to walk anyone back through the horror of that day. I'm sure everyone remembers the endless loops of that video film which replayed nearly nonstop for days afterward. The planes, the two towers, the smoke and fire – the *horror*. And then, less than half an hour later, the word about the other plane which hit the Pentagon, and reports of another plane headed back toward Washington.

I'm not going to try to reconstruct it all here. That's been done to death in the past several years. What I will say is that there was a growing sense of fear and uneasiness that began to spread through the employees at NSA that morning, not just in my office, but throughout the multi-building campus spread across the edge of Fort Meade. We had just watched – and continued to watch – the broad daylight attack on the twin towers of the Trade Center in New York and the ensuing devastation there. Then we saw live coverage of the Pentagon burning from a third attack. Another hijacked airliner was heading back in our direction, target unknown.

I worked on the sixth floor of an eleven-story building connected to another multi-story building. Our two towers were connected to another complex of lower buildings. Yes, I said our "two towers"! Because I'm pretty sure I wasn't the only one among those thousands of employees that morning who was nervously wondering about the destination of that fourth rogue-piloted airliner. Hell, let's call it what it *was*. I was *scared*! I don't know if that's cowardice or just plain common sense. Our complex of buildings and twin towers was placed smack in the middle of acres of surrounding parking lots just off the Baltimore-Washington Parkway. I felt that morning like I was standing in the center of a giant bull's-eye.

Rumors were already circulating that the Director would soon be issuing a general evacuation order. The rumors were enough for me. I walked quickly back to my desk, shut down my computer, locked up my files and desk, grabbed my jacket, and headed for the elevator, walking at a brisk pace. There were plenty of others doing the same thing. I was just going through the security gate on the ground floor when I heard the announcement to evacuate come over the public address system. I was barely ahead of the crowd for what was supposed to be, ideally, a "staged" evacuation of all except essential personnel. I quietly thanked God that I was not considered "essential" that day, and, emerging from the building, I sprinted for my car, probably a half mile away in the massive spread of paved parking lots.

Just by heading out those few minutes early I got the jump on the mass employee exodus that followed. I made it out to Route 32 in a reasonable amount of time and was already heading into Odenton by the time the rest of NSA's thousands of workers erupted out of the buildings and into their cars to form a massive and impenetrable gridlock of traffic that lasted for hours. So much for that carefully "staged" evacuation.

When I arrived home, Treve had the TV on in the kitchen. I hadn't had time to phone, so she was surprised to see me, but she got up and hugged me hard.

"God, I'm so glad you're *home*," she said.

I don't think I even replied. I may have still been in a kind of shock. We both turned back to the TV and continued to watch the horror of that awful morning unfold. At first we stood, still holding each other. We needed to hold onto each other. Human contact was so very necessary right then. Finally, I suppose, we let go and sat down. It was going to be a long day.

I remember walking our two dogs later that morning. It was a beautiful sunny day. I could hear birds singing. Daisy and Barney were doing their usual sniff and pee stuff. The neighborhood seemed unnaturally quiet. Of course it should have been. People were at work, after all. But it seemed *too* quiet. Then I noticed – *realized* – that there were no planes in the sky. We lived less than a half hour from BWI airport, so, ordinarily, there were *always* planes. And you could hear them. But we had lived there long enough that the sounds of planes overhead was just part of the normal sounds, like birds and cars, kids playing. But that morning – *quiet.* An *eerie, unnatural* quiet. *Surreal. Frightening.*

It wasn't until well after noon that Treve and I remembered we were supposed to meet with the realtors about our house at four-thirty that afternoon.

"Do you think they'll come?" I remember Treve asking. Which seemed like a perfectly logical question. Our whole world had, after all, just changed forever. Would a realtor actually keep an appointment made a few days earlier after all that had just transpired?

She did. The realtor, I mean. Betsy Oliver and her son-in-law showed up on time at four-thirty that day, 9/11/2001. We remember it because, as Treve just reminded me, we had to sign our names and the date, probably a dozen times or more on the paperwork that authorized Betsy's agency to help us sell our house. But here's what else we both remember. Because of what had just occurred – in New York City, Washington, and yes, sadly, in a desolate field in Pennsylvania – I instructed the realtors to just hold onto our paperwork for the time being; *not* to put the house on the market yet; to wait until I found out what was happening at work.

Which was a good thing. Because my incentivized early out was pulled out from under me once again after that day. And I understood. We all went back to work after that day with a renewed sense of purpose. I still wanted to retire, but I knew things had changed, so I kept my mouth shut and waited.

Everything changed quickly at NSA. New physical security measures were put in place throughout the campus. Fort Meade, where the National Security Agency is located, had always been what is known as an "open post," which means main roads ran through the post and there were no obstacles to entering or exiting the post. Almost overnight all this changed. Fort Meade became a "closed post." Security check points were established at all the entrance roads onto post. Reinforced concrete barriers cropped up all over post. Army trucks mounted with machine guns and soldiers armed with rifles and sidearms were stationed at these checkpoints to beef up the regular force of MP's who checked badges and identification. The once peaceful NSA campus became a heavily guarded and armed camp. Employees had to show their badges and id's as they negotiated a gauntlet of new security check points and barriers to get to work each day. These new measures provided a sense of comfort, but were, nevertheless, a grim reminder of the new order of things post-9/11.

About a month after the attacks I managed to wangle some vacation time. I had accrued nearly three weeks of comp time over the past several months and I decided to take it. Treve and I headed back to Michigan to spend some time in our "retirement home," wondering when that would finally happen. We spent a few days en route visiting her mom in Belleville and then continued on to Reed City, where we took up residence with our two dogs, joining Suzie and her dog. Early October in Michigan can often be beautiful, and that year it was. We had only been here a few days, however, when I got a call from my branch chief back at work. She informed me that the early out window had been reinstated, and if I still wanted to retire, I needed to get my paperwork in as soon as possible. So we cut our vacation short and hurried back to Maryland. I got my retirement papers filled out and turned in as quickly as I could and began attending retirement seminars provided by the Agency.

In the meantime we also put our house in Odenton on the market and I began to sweat again over that. What if it didn't sell? How could we possibly maintain two houses on a retirement check? But it sold. No hitches. I retired on 15 November. We closed on our house sale the end of that month.

I can still remember leaving our Odenton home of seventeen years that morning of December 1st. All of our stuff had left by moving van a few days earlier. Our car was fully packed; our two dogs in the back seat.

As I pulled out of the drive I said to Treve, "Well, we're leaving. Wanna tell the house good-bye?"

Treve looked at the house, grimaced, and said, "G'bye house. Good *rid*dance." She too had watched the neighborhood go to hell. I think she meant it.

Perhaps I should note here, before going on to other things, that in the ensuing years our old neighborhood in Odenton has made something of a turnaround. There are signs of gentrification, or suburban renewal, or whatever you wanna call it now when we go back to visit. A few years ago, before the real estate bubble burst, a house like we'd lived in had risen in price by another hundred grand since we had sold ours. Treve heard this and tried to do a little second-guessing, wondering if maybe we should have stuck around longer. "Think about that extra money we could have had," is what she says.

I think about it, but only for a moment. I have no regrets. I'm glad we got out when we did. And I'm also glad for the people who still live there that the neighborhood has begun to rejuvenate itself. I suppose I could have worked a couple more years and ended up a little bit richer. But I'm one of those lucky, rare people, I guess. I'm pretty happy with what I have.

Today is New Year's Eve 2009. In fact we're only about an hour away from the New Year 2010 as I write this. Which is unusual, since I normally only write in the morning. But today I didn't start until nearly nine at night.

And I've been working my way toward telling about another New Year's Eve eight years ago. It was the day we buried Treve's mom.

Because those regular visits Treve had so eagerly anticipated with her Mom once we'd retired back here to Michigan were never to be, sadly.

When we moved to Reed City in December 2001 it was already obvious that Wanda was ill. We just didn't know how sick she really was. She was noticeably thinner. She was always a tiny woman, at barely five feet tall, but she had shrunk even more that winter, and was having trouble eating and keeping food down. Just a couple weeks after we'd set up housekeeping in Reed City, we traveled back downstate to see Treve's mom and to take her to see a doctor. Then she saw a surgeon. There was a blockage of some sort in Wanda's esophagus that needed to be repaired. The surgeon, a nice young woman, assured us all – Wanda, Treve and I, and Treve's two brothers and their wives – that she could fix the problem.

It was around Christmas time when Wanda had the surgery. I know that, because Treve and I attended a special midnight mass in the hospital cafeteria. It was a full house too. You never think about all the people who are in hospitals at a time like Christmas, but we found out that year that there are plenty. And all those family members who are there, standing by, sitting vigil, or whatever you may want to call it. And all the doctors and nurses and other staff that have to work, even on Christmas. A lot of those people were there, attending mass that night. St. Joseph's Hospital in Ypsilanti is an enormous complex, but we got to know it pretty well those last several days of Wanda's life. After mass that Christmas Eve we sat with Wanda and visited. We gave her a few little presents.

I remember bringing her a cheap little AM/FM transistor radio so she could listen to WJR, the AM radio station she had listened to in her kitchen every day for the last several years of her life. After macular degeneration had robbed her of most of her sight and she could no longer enjoy television. She listened to all the news and talk shows, and all the Detroit sporting events on the radio. This eighty-something year-old woman knew the names of most of the Tigers, Lions and Red Wings. That's how much and how faithfully she listened. I can't remember if that little green plastic radio could even pick up AM signals in that huge glass, concrete and steel hospital building, but Wanda was touched by the gesture anyway. Her operation had been deemed a success. She was beginning to eat a little and keep it down.

We left Ypsilanti and returned home on Christmas Day, leaving Treve's brothers and wives there to sit with Wanda in the hospital and monitor her recovery. But sometimes things just don't go according to plan. A couple days after Christmas we got a call from Bob. He told Treve if she wanted to see Mom again she'd better come quickly.

On our previous trip downstate for Wanda's hospitalization and surgery, we'd been involved in a minor fender-bender on an icy road in Ypsilanti. Our car was in the shop for repairs when Bob called, so I borrowed my mother's car and we headed south again in a heavy snowstorm. When we arrived at St. Joseph's that day Wanda was in the ICU. Her heart and lungs had begun to fail. She couldn't seem to catch her breath. I think she was on oxygen and probably a morphine drip too, but she was still struggling. I can still remember how she kept raising her arms above her head, her eyes wide in distress, probably instinctively trying to just somehow pull more air into her rapidly failing lungs. I can't remember any more if someone told us she was dying, or if we just knew. Bob, or Helen, his wife, asked the nurses if they couldn't do something to ease Wanda's obvious distress, and I think the morphine drip was increased, and she seemed to quiet down a bit.

Why am I trying to remember all this, to get it all down? I'm not sure. I don't know. Maybe because it was all so intense, and because Wanda had been so close to Treve, who is still the most important person in my whole life. And because I know that Treve still feels her mom's absence so acutely; still feels cheated out of those years she expected to spend more time with her once we'd retired back here to Michigan. They were as close as any mother and daughter I've ever known, and that closeness was nearly over.

I remember Helen and I holding Wanda's hands there in the ICU and singing softly to her.

> *"Gonna take a sentimental journey*
> *Gonna set my heart at ease*
> *Gonna make a sentimental journey*
> *To renew old memories …"*

I don't think we knew any more of the lyrics, but we faked it the best we could. It had always been "their song" – Wanda's and Chet's.

Wanda died later that night, the 28th of December, surrounded by her family. Her breathing just became shallower and shallower, then the breaths came farther and farther apart, until, finally, she simply stopped breathing.

It was the first time I had ever actually seen anyone die. My mother has told me about the day she sat alone by Dad's bedside in a Grand Rapids hospital a little over twenty years ago. Dad was in a coma. His doctor had already told Mom that he probably would not wake up. With a look of wonder in her eyes, she described how his breathing had become shallower, and then slower, until it simply ceased altogether.

"So I just sat with him for a little while," Mom said. "It was the first time I'd ever been there when someone died, had actually *seen* it."

There is something so "awe-full" in watching someone you love die that it's hard to describe. Maybe it's simply the bearing witness to what awaits us all, to that transition, that crossing of the void, to the "unknowable." It is, in the end, indescribable. But I felt like should try, here. Wanda Rose Bartuzel Zimmer mattered.

Her funeral at St. Anthony's Catholic Church in Belleville was held three days later. After the service, we all returned to Wanda's house – Bob and Helen, Dick and Lillian, Treve and

I. It was New Year's Eve. We had a late supper provided by friends and neighbors. Treve and her brothers were still up talking when I went to bed upstairs around eleven o'clock. I think it was sometime after midnight when I was awakened by some loud noises. When I reached to turn on a light, nothing happened. No light. No electricity. I pulled on my clothes and groped my way downstairs where Treve and the others were still up and were all peering at something out the dining room window.

There had been a sleet storm that afternoon and evening. Everything outside was coated in ice and the moon was reflecting brightly off the snow. What we saw out the back window of the house, just beyond the circular driveway that came around the house, was an SUV lying on its side on top of some bushes. Beyond it lay a power pole which had been snapped off by the impact of the vehicle. Wires lay across the driveway. The wheels of the car will still turning. The teenage driver had been unable to stop as he came down the ice-covered Fret Road, which dead-ends into Martinsville right where the Zimmer house was located. Somehow he had managed to miss two enormous old maple trees, but hit the power pole and brought it down.

January 4, 2010

I remember that Bob, Dick and I all grabbed our coats and made our way gingerly outside around the back of the house across the icy lawn until we reached the upended vehicle. The somewhat dazed driver had by then managed to unbuckle himself and climb up to the passenger side and push open the door and was lifting himself out.

Bob went into his DNR Park Manager mode and went over and helped the young man down from the high side of the car and then I think he may have even ordered him, just like you see in all those cop shows, to "step away from the vehicle!" But then when he saw how befuddled the poor kid seemed to be, he took him by the arm and led him over to the stump of a giant old maple that had blown down a few years before and eased him down onto it. Treve and Helen and Lillian were inside peering out the dining room window at all this.

I mean, it was a strange night. New Year's Eve, which we had nearly forgotten about what with the funeral home, the church and cemetery and everything. And now this poor kid (who, fortunately for him, was *not* drunk) wrecking his car in the back yard and knocking out the power to the house on one of the most bitterly cold nights of the winter. But only *half* the power was out for some reason. One circuit still worked. So, once the police and fire department arrived – yeah, two or three fire trucks and a couple cars each from the county sheriff's office and the state police all showed up with lights flashing within twenty minutes or so, and then a couple trucks from the power company not long after them – and the confused, but luckily uninjured young driver had been taken away, Dick and Bob put their heads together down in the dark basement with a couple of big flashlights and a few tools and figured out how to reroute the furnace circuit to the one circuit that was still working, so they got the heat back on in probably less than an hour. But, yeah, a *very* strange night. And the last New Year's Eve that any of the Zimmers would ever spend in their childhood home. It was sold a little over a year later.

I was thinking about all this on New Year's Eve, just a few nights ago, and I think so was Treve, missing her mom, as she does every year around this time. She has declined to read Joyce Dyer's book about her mother's death from Alzheimer's.

"It just sounds too sad," she said, when I told her about it. "I just don't think I want to read that kind of stuff. Not right now anyway."

And I understand.

Well, it's a new year and I'm still reading, of course. Over the weekend Treve and I were both completely blown away by reading a new novel I'd just gotten in the mail last week. It's called *Season of Water and Ice*, by Donald Lystra., and was one of the picks for Michigan Notable Books for 2010. It is a coming of age story of teenage love and heartbreak set in northern Michigan fifty years ago. I mean it's really much more than just that. It is simply a *beautiful* book. I'm not gonna say more, because I don't want to spoil it for anyone. Suffice it to say that the teen characters of Danny and Amber will steal your hearts. I'd never heard of Don Lystra, but when I saw his book listed in the newspaper a couple weeks ago, I wrote him (through his website) and boldly proposed a book swap. He wrote back right away and graciously accepted. I wrote him just yesterday and told him that, after reading his stunning debut novel, I'm afraid he got the short end of the stick on our swap. But maybe he'll like my simple little stories. I hope so. Don's bio at his website and on his book jacket says he was an engineer for most of his life. He's nearly as old as I am, which makes me even more awed at the talent displayed in this book. Okay, maybe he's an engineer, but to me he is a *Writer*. It has all the ingredients of a national bestseller, except for one thing. Its publisher is a university press. I have nothing against university presses, and Northern Illinois's Switchgrass Books has created a beautiful package for Don's story. But typically these presses have little or no budget for promotion, so a lot of wonderful books often just sink and die. Two fine Michigan memoirs by Anne-Marie Oomen come to mind. Both *Pulling Down the Barn* and *House of Fields* were published by Wayne State University Press and should by all rights be a lot better known than they are.

But no matter, I suppose. Don Lystra's book is a pure gem of fiction writing and I will do all I can to promote it myself, as I have already done with Oomen's books.

Last night I began reading another swap book, and I can tell already that it's a prize. I met John Smolens in Paradise – Michigan, that is – in late August of 2004. We sat next to each other at a row of long tables in "the authors' tent" at the Wild Blueberry Festival in Paradise, up in the Upper Peninsula. The tent was sponsored by Safe Harbor Books, a lovely little independent bookstore in Cedarville and it may have been the first and only time they did it. John was one of the better known "literary" writers at the event, and was also the main reason I'd agreed to participate. I had just read his novel, *Cold*, not too long before and was very impressed with his ability to set a scene and tell a story. I was really looking forward to meeting this guy, so it was icing on the cake when the organizers happened to seat him right next to me at the table. I only had one book at the time, so I *gave* him a copy of *Reed City Boy*, but *bought* a signed copy of his at-the-time newest book, *Fire Point*, which turned out to be as good as *Cold*. John's genre of choice – and he is a master at it – is the suspense novel, or the thriller. To this popular form he brings a literary finesse seldom found in such books.

This time, in exchange for a *Soldier Boy*, I got an earlier novel of his which I hadn't read, *The Invisible World*. Another suspense-thriller, this book differs from the other two novels in its setting, which is the Boston area, where Smolens grew up and went to college. The other two books are set in northern Michigan. *Cold*, a deep winter *chiller*-thriller, is set in the U.P. near Marquette, where Smolens is currently an English professor at Northern Michigan University.

Early this morning, as I continued to read my newly acquired if several-years-old Smolens book, I was struck by his attention to detail in describing a bar three of the characters "adjourned to" after leaving a newspaper office. It's a real place, I learned, called the Cask'n Flagon, located on Brookline Avenue.

> *"Five minutes later we were walking toward Fenway Park. The bar was on the corner, just across the street from the left field foul pole ... The backside of the Green Monster loomed above us ..."*

Reading this, I chuckled, and thought at once of Joe Rindini, a lifelong rabid Red Sox fan, who will seize any opportunity to sing the praises of his beloved Sox. Rindini would probably like this book, I thought to myself; he would recognize all these streets and places. I wondered idly if he'd ever been to the Cask'n Flagon.

For those of you who read my second memoir, *Soldier Boy*, Joe's name will probably ring a bell. He was the bass guitar player with The Panics, the GI cover band I ran with in Germany in the sixties, back when we were all far from home, being as nasty as we could get away with, and sowing our wild oats. An Italian kid from Massachusetts, Rindini was a natural fit with my long-time army roomie from Yonkers, Joe Capozzi, who started the band and played lead guitar.

Perhaps one of the best things to come out of my writing that book was a Panics reunion that happened a year or so ago in Las Vegas. I wasn't there myself. Treve and I had made our Vegas trip the previous year. She had always wanted to see Vegas, and I went along mostly to see Joe Capozzi, who is now retired there. We were both pretty happy that we went – Treve because she got to gamble a little and see a show or two, and I because I got to spend some time with Joe, whom I hadn't seen in over forty years. We stayed at Harrah's, right in the middle of the strip, across from the Mirage. Joe and his wife, Barbara, spent a little time with us nearly every day, showing us the sights around town, and also entertaining us in their beautiful home in the Vegas suburbs.

January 9, 2010

Yet another sizeable gap in this haphazard narrative of my life and my worst vice, books. And I'm back mainly because Treve has left the house for a few hours, gone to the local CURVES to learn all over again in yet another class how to stay slim and svelte. And I'd better not say more than that if I value my life and typing fingers.

Truth be told, I didn't much like Las Vegas. Too noisy, too showy, just plain too *much* in every way. My small town sensibilities just couldn't get comfortable there. I enjoyed the time I spent with Joe and Barbara more than any of the rest of it, although Treve and I did damn near laugh ourselves sick one night when we went to see *Menopause the Musical*, along with Joe and Barb at a small dinner-theater venue. Joe and I were part of a distinct male minority in the audience. But you didn't have to be female to get most of the humor in the show. You just had to be married and of a certain age. It was absolutely *hilarious*.

If I remember correctly, I think we went to Vegas around the end of April, because that was supposed to be a more temperate time of year. Alas, it was in the high nineties nearly every day that week, and even broke into the triple digits a couple of days. I'm sure of that, because one afternoon I accompanied Joe to rehearsal of his start-up band. It was held in the garage of one of the guys, Frank. We kept the garage door open, but it didn't help. The heat just stood there like a solid wall. Joe and Frank and this other guy didn't seem to notice it nearly as much as I did. I guess when you live in a place like that your body gets acclimated after a time. Frank kindly noticed my heat-induced distress, and sat me next to a refrigerator well stocked with bottled water. We were there for a couple hours and I think I drank at least three bottles of water and kept reaching in for a colder one to roll across my forehead. But I did enjoy hearing Joe and his pals play and sing. It had been more than forty years since Joe left the Panics, but he'd never stopped practicing and learning new stuff – had always "kept his hand in." And, as a kind of postscript, he now does have a band that performs at the smaller clubs around Vegas, after going through a few false starts trying to find the right lead singer.

The other Panics – Rindini, Mike Chesley, Gene "Mooch" Hedgepeth and Chris Musser – all *did* get to Vegas for that reunion several months after our trip out. Some of the wives were there too, and the guys got to noodle about a bit on instruments while there. From all the emails I've gotten since then, they must have had a wonderful time, because they are planning another get-together at Joe R's place in Massachusetts near Cape Cod later this year. All those "old guys" together again, trading lies and stories and just enjoying each other's company again, simply and easily picking up where they left off forty-plus years ago – proof positive of my long-time theory that there is no friend quite like an "old army buddy."

Here's another perhaps odd – to *most* people – highlight of my Vegas trip. After we'd been there a few days I began to suffer from book-withdrawal. The constant casino noise and smoke was making me just a little crazy, I think, so we ventured out into the scorching heat of the strip one morning and found our way down the street to an enclosed mall. I was able to find a small Borders book store, where I hung out and browsed for an hour or two while Treve went to look at clothes. I say *small* Borders, because it was – a kind of pocket-sized store in comparison to the usual Borders behemoths. I mused to myself at the time that Vegas probably just barely tolerated bookstores. After all, they didn't want visitors to their town holed up in a hotel room *reading*, of all things. But I did. The book I settled on was a soldier's memoir of his Afghanistan tour. Johnny Rico's *Blood Makes the Grass Grow Green* was not like anything I had expected. True, its setting is a real and still ongoing war in a faraway land, but this was one of the most flat-out funny reads I had come across in years. Think *Catch-22* in the modern-day army. Rico's well-developed sense of irony and his skewed sense of humor come across on nearly every page. Maybe I would have been more prepared for it had I known that he had even borrowed his *name* from a Heinlein science fiction novel. But while I *have* read *Stranger in a Strange Land*, I had never read *Starship Troopers*, so Rico's heady blend of horror and humor came as a delightful surprise to me and a welcome relief from all the crowds, smoke and mirrors – and did I mention the constant *noise?* - of Vegas.

A couple years down the road, I still try to recommend Rico's book to appropriate audiences. I have to be careful though, because not everyone finds masturbation as a way to fight boredom funny. Maybe it's significant that he enjoyed my *Soldier Boy* nearly as much as I liked his book. I kept in touch with Johnny, who lives in England, for a couple of years, but then his email changed and we lost touch. Where are you, Johnny Rico? Write me.

I think I have amassed a few shelves full of military memoirs in the past few years. I'm not quite sure exactly why I'm so drawn to these books, but it's probably because I can usually relate strongly to them, whether they are from the first World War, the Afghan or Iraq wars, or anything in between. Military life has a kind of sameness that has not changed a lot in the past hundred years, and a well-written military autobiography is always a joy to read.

The one I'm reading right now is a bit of an anomaly – or maybe not. It's different mainly, I suppose, because I had to go to the UK site of Amazon to get it. I keep thinking of Rico's book as I make my way through this one. But there are definite differences. Rico was an enlisted man in the US Army. This author, Patrick Hennessey, was an officer in the British army who did tours in both Iraq and Afghanistan. He is Oxford educated and followed university with training at Sandhurst, which is, I think, the English equivalent of West Point. But the irony and the humor I found in Rico's book are also reflected here. Both guys *get* the insanity and absurdity that often permeates the military life, whether it's during peace or wartime. Hennessey's book is called *The Junior Officers' Reading Club*, named for all the hours of boredom that are part of any military tour, which in the case of Hennessey and his friends were often filled by books, by reading. I'm about a third of the way into the book right now, but I keep chuckling as I read, sometimes ramping up to an outright guffaw, as when in his description of a feared and yet revered Color Sergeant (Brit equivalent of a Drill Sergeant) at Sandhurst he notes:

> "*Hanging on every word of this man whom we had feared and hated in equal measure but now worshipped and envied, his professionalism his experience, his implied hardness and*

*the fact that he would come grinning into work after a leave
weekend with impressive bar-brawl scars, growling at us
that we'd better not piss him off that day because he loved
his wife and if we annoyed him he'd have to beat her up
because he wasn't allowed to beat us."*

A few months ago I read an interesting memoir by an American officer who served in the current Iraq war, Nathaniel Fick. But his book, *One Bullet Away*, didn't make me laugh the way Hennessey's does. He doesn't really get into the grittier, nastier parts of being a soldier – or about all the nasty stuff one might *think* about. Now I realize that war memoirs aren't necessarily *supposed* to be amusing; probably shouldn't *be* funny. And yet the best ones are. Maybe it's because a little comic relief is necessary if the writer expects his readers to get through a story of what is essentially an extremely grim business. And almost everyone who has ever served in the army, or *any* branch of service, will tell you that a good sense of humor is absolutely essential to surviving the absurdity that characterizes military life.

If it seems to you that this journal/memoir is beginning to be more about books than it is about me, then you're probably right. With nearly a year of entries here, maybe I'm simply running out of stories to tell. But I know that's not entirely true, because often I'll wake up at three or four in the morning to go take a pee, and in the short time it takes me to empty my bladder (or *mostly* empty it; you know how it is with old men and prostates), I will formulate whole brilliant passages in my head to put down here. Alas, by morning they are gone. Perhaps I should keep a notebook in the bathroom. Or not.

Treve's home. Time for lunch. In the meantime, get ready for the end of this thing, this *book* (?) I'm trying to write. It's coming. And maybe, from your yawning standpoint, not a day or a moment too soon.

January 10, 2010

Today is one of those blindingly bright midwinter days so typical to Michigan, the kind I remember from my childhood, with the temperature hovering around the twenty degree mark, even though it's nearly noon. We've been stuck in this sub-freezing mode for a week or more now and the extreme cold has somehow caused our extra refrigerator out in the garage to malfunction. Translation: the top freezer compartment has stopped working. And it stays just warm enough in the garage for the food in that freezer to begin to thaw. Some of the stuff Treve had cached in there had already spoiled and had to be thrown out, but a few things seemed salvageable. So, last night when we got back from five PM Mass followed by a pasta dinner put on in the church basement by the Knights of Columbus, we decided to take action, belated thought it might be. I found a large plastic storage bin, about the same size as an old Coleman cooler we have, down in the basement. It was jammed full of a tangled collection of old coat hangers that Treve had put there after she got in an order of some kind of "designer" hangers from one of those TV shopping channels. (I can't really argue successfully against her ordering crap like that. She always comes back at me with, "Well, you keep ordering all those *books!*" See? How can I argue?) So anyway, I pulled out the tangle of old wire, plastic, and wooden hangers and piled them on the floor temporarily. Then I found the container's snap-on lid and took the whole thing out into the cold garage where we unloaded the contents of the faulty freezer into the container. Then we snapped on the lid and set our makeshift freezer on a small table on the back porch where the thermometer was then reading about nine degrees. Problem solved – for now. Although I worried a bit about this attracting critters (how about a *coyote* on our back slab, Lord?), it was not a problem. This morning, upon checking the contents of the container, I found everything secure and, once again, frozen rock hard.

All of this reminded me of a long-ago fiasco involving ice cream. In our very first apartment, the one in Mount Pleasant I've already told you about – yeah, the same one with the sway-backed bed and all that sweaty sex – our refrigerator, which was situated underneath the kitchen sink, was so small that its freezer compartment was only big enough to accommodate one ice cube tray and one half gallon of ice cream. Of course, since our weekly grocery budget was only five or six dollars a week, we could never really stock up on things anyway. It was pretty much a hand-to-mouth kind of existence back then, and I sometimes supplemented our food supply by bringing home those little individual boxes of cereal I'd filch from the serving line in the food commons where I worked in the dish room and mopped floors after meals. I could usually stuff four or more of them into the front pockets of my army field jacket. The full-time "lunch ladies" who worked the serving lines there would often save me a couple pieces of pie or cake too, surreptitiously slipping the baked goods into my hands and saying, "Here, Hon. You take this home for you and that pretty new wife of yours. There's plenty here to go around."

And there was indeed. I used to be simply appalled at how much food was wasted in those college cafeterias. Working in "the pit" where the students would bring back their trays and dishes after they'd finished eating, I was witness to this waste. This was back when smoking was still permitted pretty much everywhere, and often a soggy cigarette butt would crown some uneaten mashed potatoes or be stuck smack in the middle of a half-eaten square of cake or slice of pie. Not only did this disgust me, it also made me kind of angry, since I was often *hungry* while doing my crap-job of scraping garbage and stacking plates for all these spoiled, overfed, over-privileged little shits. In fact, if I were hungry enough, I would, after a quick guilty look around, sometimes grab up an undisturbed piece of returned cake and cram the whole thing in my mouth and gobble it down as quickly as possible. I was pretty much cured of this commando-style of sneaky snacking one day when our supervisor poked her hair-netted head into the dish room just as I had stripped the paper wrap off and stuck a whole square of Neapolitan ice cream into my mouth.

"Everything okay in here?" she asked. "Need anything?"

"*Mmff,*" I responded brightly, mouth pressed firmly shut, smiling around my frozen contraband and shaking my head. Then I involuntarily swallowed, and the whole damn square of ice cream went down, fairly frosting my voice box and freezing my esophagus. "Everything's just *fine*," I rasped hoarsely.

Being an ice cream enthusiast can get you in trouble.

Which brings me back to that other ice cream fiasco I started to tell you about. The Bazzetts are no different from most northern Michiganders in their love of ice cream, I suppose. (Ain't it strange that people who live in one of the country's coldest states are all so nuts about ice cream?) When there's a sale on ice cream, we always try to take advantage. I can still remember Mom buying several boxes of ice cream at a time and stowing them in the enormous chest freezer we had in our basement when we lived on Church Street.

Well, I already told you about that little fridge with its tiny freezer compartment in our first apartment, but I still hadn't reconciled myself to that kind of limited cold storage at that early stage of our marriage. So one day or our first winter together I took advantage of an ice cream sale at Kroger's and brought back *three* half gallons. I knew I *shouldn't* have, but it was just such a *bar*gain.

"*Tim*, what are you gonna *do* with all that *ice* cream?" Treve asked me, quite sensibly. "You *know* we've only got room for *one!*"

But I was ready for her. "We'll put two on the back porch shelf," I responded smugly. "It's only twenty degrees out. It'll stay frozen."

And it did, for a couple of days, while we were still working on that first half gallon. But then one day while I was attending classes and Treve was at work, the sun came out and the temperature spiked into the high thirties. When I arrived home that afternoon to change clothes to go to work over in the food commons across the street, I found two soggy, nearly empty cartons drooping off the porch shelf and a large puddle of ice cream running across the floor, the chocolate mixing sadly with the vanilla. Well, I guess ice cream can't really be sad, but I know *I* sure was.

I scream, you scream, we all scream for ice cream.

Remember that old childhood rhyme? Me too. And I also remember making homemade ice cream back when I was a kid.

Or *helping* to make it, at least. Because as number four, I always had to compete with my three older brothers for the privilege of turning the crank on that old manual ice cream maker. I don't remember the ingredients anymore (if I ever knew them), but I think I remember packing snow and rock salt into the outer chamber of the bucket, then fitting the cover snugly back on and turning that crank – and turning and turning and turning it – until the ice cream in the inner cylinder solidified. It only made a couple of quarts, I think, which made for rather meager portions all around (in our family of six, then seven, then eight), but once it was ready, there was nothing like it. When we acquired an electric ice cream maker in later years, I know it used the same ingredients, and the process was pretty much the same, but something always seemed to be missing. It must have been the winter-cold sweat equity – all that cranking that Rich, Bill, Bob and I always fought over.

You know what? A sundae sounds good right now.

January 16, 2010

A year ago I asked myself if I could write a book in a month. Nope, obviously not. So I decided to see what I could do in a year. Today then, for better or for worse, marks the end of this thing, this opus, as I have been calling it in my (other) daily journal, or sometimes, more affectionately, Opie. An opus, after all, is an artistic work or composition – literary or musical. But what I've been working on here is probably more of an opuscule, something more minor. Sometimes it felt more like a pustule, i.e. an annoying boil or pimple that I felt periodically compelled to examine and probe, to squeeze it and pop it onto the mirror of my mind to see what came out. Shades of adolescence and all that awful acne, huh?

I did finish reading young Mr. Hennessey's book about his service with the Grenadier Guards and his combat tours in Iraq and Afghanistan. The final fifty pages or so were something of a slog, and seemed a bit redundant. Many of those last pages could have been summed up by a couple of very telling and pertinent passages Hennessey wrote about preparing for re-entry into the real world after his multiple baptisms of fire in the patrols and daily defensive battles fought in the deserts and dry wadis of southeastern Afghanistan.

> *"I suddenly know that I hate this and love it at the same time because I can already feel both how glad I will be when it is over and how much I will miss it. How difficult to convey to anyone that matters something which they will never understand, and how little anything else will ever matter."*

And a bit later, when he tries to describe the intense frustration and guilt and the distance he felt both geographically and emotionally between him and his girlfriend following a transoceanic phone call, he says –

> *"I'm not sure if this disjoint is a symptom of what we will all have to deal with when we finally get back, the wall that's been quietly built between those of us who are here and have lived these things and everybody else, no matter how close to us they previously were … Part of me, part of everyone I suspect, wants to shout down the phone that we're sorry, that we love you and the only reason we pretend we don't*

know what you're going through is that to acknowledge it would be to acknowledge our own crippling longings. ..."

I bought Hennessey's book because I was curious to know how the British military experience in the current wars compares to all those American war memoirs I have been reading for the past few years. What I think I have learned is that the crucible of combat is universal, that the bonding, the initial sense of adventure and exhilaration, followed by the fear, horror, pain, and inevitable loss of innocence happened to all of these guys. I learned over and over, in every story, that war sucks, and yet it continues to hold a kind of magnetic attraction for young men who want to know that ultimate test of what it means to be a man; who want to know if they can pass that test, if they will measure up. I also learned that the long-distance misunderstandings and the "crippling longings" Hennessey speaks of so eloquently are another kind of universal experience of boys-become-men so far from home. And I learned that I have nothing but the utmost respect for every one of these young men grown too soon old beyond their years.

Last night I sat mesmerized for close to four hours as I watched the first few episodes of an HBO miniseries about the Iraq war called *Generation Kill.* The show is based on the book of the same name by Evan Wright, who was a reporter for *Rolling Stone,* embedded with a Marine Corps Reconnaissance unit in the early days of the US invasion of Iraq. The dialogue is prolifically laced with the casual obscenity and dark humor that characterizes military life, with running rants by various characters that make you laugh out loud. And suddenly you would be brought up short by sudden glimpses of dead mutilated bodies strewn haphazardly along the invasion route, or the frightening reality of an ambush and firefight in rubble-strewn city blocks of the same Nasiriyah where soldier Jessica Lynch was captured, crippled and finally freed in the early days of the war.

We got the DVD boxed set of *Generation Kill* on loan from Ben Busch, who was not only an active participant in the invasion of Iraq while on active duty as a Marine officer, but also acted in the miniseries several years later, playing a staff officer with the recce unit. I have had Wright's book here for nearly a year now, but have read only about half of it.

I discovered long ago that if I have a choice between reading a biography or an *auto*biography (a memoir), I will always choose the latter. That first-person point of view always wins out over what might be a more objective account of a life. I want to get inside the head of the book's subject, something only a memoir will allow. So when I put down Wright's book, I picked up Nathaniel Fick's book instead, and read it straight through. Fick was the platoon commander who played a central part in Wright's book. Is this getting confusing? I hope not. Fick's *One Bullet Away* gives that first-person viewpoint to much of the same story that Wright tells in *Generation Kill*.

So because I had read half of Wright and all of Fick, I already had a good sense of the story being told in the film, giving it all a kind of strange déjà vu air as I watched it.

I had the TV volume cranked way up as I watched the film – I didn't want to miss any of the dialogue. It was just too good, too true, too genuine GI in its nature. In its profanity, irreverence and nastiness. I could remember it, all of it, from my own long ago days as a young soldier. Treve soon tired of it though, maybe because of the nastiness, but maybe just because it was too loud. My creeping deafness is a frequent source of strife whenever we try to watch TV together, which isn't very often anymore. So she wandered off to talk on the phone with Rita Sobecki, a friend going all the way back to her Catholic grade school days. For once then, I was the master of the remote control. So I watched and listened in a kind of horrified fascination. I learned.

Watching TV is not how I planned to end this book about books and their importance in my life. But Ben had lent us the film nearly a week ago and I really did want to see it. And it *is* a film based on a *book*, so …

The truth, of course, is that I am still reading. I have a good start on two more memoirs already – two very different kinds of stories, I suspect. One is Willie Morris's story of his Mississippi boyhood and later life in Texas and New York, *North Toward Home*. The other is yet another Iraq war memoir, Clint Van Winkle's *Soft Spots*.

I might have more to say of these two books and others, but real life continues to intrude on my reading. The past week has been a mixture of these – annoying and welcome. After discussing, bickering and arguing for a couple of days about its necessity, we finally made a trip to Big Rapids and bought a small chest freezer to put in our basement – to replace the old, bought-used refrigerator-freezer in the garage that we were sure had finally given up the ghost and expired. Of course on the very day that our new freezer was delivered we discovered that the old unit had kicked back on and seemed to be working again. It figures.

And then, just a couple of days ago, our daughter made an overnight visit from downstate with her husband, Jeff, and little boy, Adam, who is not quite a year and a half old. He's been walking for a few months now, but this was the first time we'd seen him "toddle," so we very much enjoyed witnessing this small miracle all over again. Adam's mother, Suzie, was our own last toddler, over thirty years ago. They departed yesterday afternoon, after a quick side visit down the street to see my mom. So now the house is quiet – and neat and uncluttered – once again. And it's okay, really. As I'm pretty sure I have already said here at least once, I love my life the way it is now. And I love the "nuclear" family I have left – Treve and the dogs. I love all my children, but they have lives of their own now, which is as it should be. I pray for them and their families every day – to Whomever might be listening (and I've thought long and hard about that capital "W"). I worry about them on occasion, because I am by nature a worrier, I suppose. But I try to let go. For now it's enough for me that Treve is still here, that we still love each other. And I will keep on loving my dogs and enjoying their company as long as they're around. I don't want to think about a time when they won't be.

I know there are still stories I haven't told, but I don't know if I will ever write another book. I will probably, out of habit, keep on with my daily journal. And, as long my eyes hold out, I will keep on reading. Perhaps I will be one of the last of a rapidly disappearing breed – a booklover.

But no matter.

Be well, and please, *read*.

Afterword, or – maybe – *Final*word

Today, January 27th, is my birthday. I am sixty-six. One more six at either end and I'd be that digital devil himself.

But no matter.

How strange it feels to be suddenly so old. Only it hasn't happened all that suddenly, of course. But I feel it so acutely today, as if I've come to the end of something. That something, I suspect, is this *book*, this *al*batross, this *mill*stone, which has weighed me down for so long, for much longer that the mere year reflected in the preceding pages.

Last night I printed up a bibliography I had painstakingly compiled over the past few days of everything I could think of that I had mentioned or quoted in the text, or had simply read with*out* referencing here, during those long silent blank spots this past year. I assigned an asterisk to each book or piece I had actually *read* this year, and I was somewhat shocked – *astounded*, actually – to find that I had marked well over a *hundred* books.

How is it possible, I wondered, to read that many books – and to also *write* a book at the same time – in just *one* year? While I admit, and can see, in retrospect, that all that reading may have been a kind of bibliophilistic *over*kill, it's probably not really all that unusual for me. As I have explained in my earlier books, reading has always been, as far back as I can remember, as natural and essential a part of life to me as eating or breathing. And *this* book will act, I hope, as a lasting testament to that truth, to that literate *queerness* in my makeup.

Reading, writing, authors and books – all these things, objects and people alike, are, for me, tangled together in a gloriously hopeless kind of Gordian knot which I'm not sure I have either the skill or the will to loosen. As I have also commented before, both here and in previous works, I am a firmly committed adherent to that Buddhist belief that every thing, every person and every action are somehow connected.

Here then, as an example of this, are just a few of the strands I've managed to separate out of that tangled knot, a few of those connections I always seem to find.

Starting at the top, Dan Aadland's memoir about his family ranch in Montana, *Sketches from the Ranch*, is only one of many books about the American West, both contemporary and historical accounts. Some listed here are Mary Clearman Blew's books, along with those of Bill Kittredge, Annick Smith, William Owens, Thomas Savage, Elmer Kelton, Louis L'Amour, Fred Haefele, Ralph Beer and Tom McGuane. My fascination with the West and cowboys goes back, of course, to the early fifties when I would sit for hours in the cool Saturday matinee darkness of the Reed Theater while Roy, Gene, Rex or Johnny Mack Brown worked their white-hat, six-gun, horseback magic.

Another boy obviously lassoed early by the masculine mystique and not-so-esoteric attractions of the cowboy life was young Tom Groneberg, raised and schooled in the Chicago area (as was, a generation earlier, Annick Smith). After college, Tom followed his dream west to find work on ranches in Colorado and Montana, finally taking his impressionable young bride with him. He wrote about their life together in two books, both noted here. Once I'd read the first, *The Secret Life of Cowboys*, then I naturally had to read the second, *One Good Horse*. Then I found out that Tom's wife, Jennifer, was also a writer, so ... You *see* how these things naturally follow, how they are all connected? And Treve and I were both so floored by Jen's book – by its sweetness and honesty – that we passed it along to our daughter, Suzie, who later raved about it back to us, wondering, "Who *is* this, this ... well, this *mom*, who writes so beautifully and movingly about her children and her life in Montana?"

I couldn't pry Jen's *Road Map to Holland* back from Suzie, so I ended up writing to Tom and Jen and arranged a mutually satisfying book swap (one of many such deals with other writers) and am now the proud owner of a complete and signed set of Groneberg books.

You will notice several books listed here by Curtis Harnack. Besides being an accomplished writer, Curtis was also the President of the Yaddo artists' colony for many years, so he has many interesting stories to tell about other writers too. His late wife, Hortense Calisher, was also a writer, and I've sampled her work here as well.

A few other "cyber" author friends I've made in the past year or two are Joyce Dyer (Ohio), John Smolens and Don Lystra (Michigan), Neal Bowers (Iowa), Ruth Doan MacDougall (New Hampshire), John Dalton (Missouri), and Ted Judson (Wyoming).

From Canada I have "met" Paul St. Pierre in British Columbia, Rod McGillis in Alberta, and even had an answering letter once from Farley Mowat, author of that classic Canadian memoir, *Never Cry Wolf*.

And from England I've met Harry Shukman and Geoffrey Elliott, both Emeritus Fellows from Oxford, who have, separately, each written a few learned and scholarly books, and also co-authored a little book I very much admired called *Secret Classrooms*, about their national service time as students at the Joint Services School of Languages (JSSL). The JSSL (now defunct, as is national service, or the draft) was the British equivalent of our Defense Language Institute, in Monterey, which I have written a little about in this book. And Leslie Woodhead, another JSSL alumnus, wrote his own recollections, with the somewhat tongue-in-cheek title, *My Life as a Spy*. He went on to become a much-honored documentary filmmaker. All three of these "old soldier" Brits are recipients of the Order of the British Empire. Woodhead's most recent film success, *How the Beatles Rocked the Kremlin*, played on our own PBS this past fall. I enjoyed it immensely.

That film led me to a fat book, a novel, called, simply, *Beatles*, which was first published in Norwegian over twenty-five years ago and was recently voted one of the most popular books in Norway. Last year it was finally translated into English. I bought it, read it, and *loved* it! I was unable to contact the book's author, Lars Saabye Christensen, but I did exchange a few emails with its translator, Don Bartlett, in England. Have you ever considered how much a book's success in another language is dependent on the skill of its translator? Think about it, okay? Bartlett thanked me for my interest in his – and Christensen's – work, and pointed me toward another Norwegian novel he'd recently translated, which sounded simply *scrump*tious and is still on my "to read" list, a document which continues to grow exponentially.

I have met so many writers in the past few years, online through email, by phone, or even sometimes by exchanging real letters – what our kids call "snail mail." I value all those contacts – whether in-person, electronic or handwritten – with people like Donald Hall, Sam Hynes, Darryl Ponicsan, the late Jim Crumley, Michael Dirda, Doug Stanton, Chuck Pfarrer, Ed Hannibal, Tom McGuane, the Gronebergs, and others. And I treasure all those value-added swap books I've received from many of them.

Writing is a solitary, lonely task, and hard work, which demands a kind of discipline and dedication that is rare in the human animal. Writers can be a closed and clannish community, I suppose, but they all have one thing in common, something I have found out in all these contacts I have made. They crave recognition. They want their work to be affirmed and noticed.

Yesterday UPS delivered to my door the last book completed by John Updike just before his death one year ago this week. It is a collection of short stories published posthumously that bears the sad and perhaps telling title, *My Father's Tears*. In a writing career that spanned over fifty years, John Updike published more than *sixty* books! I am simply in *awe* of the work ethic and dedication to his craft represented by such a staggering output. His final book bears a dedication that touched me. It is to his grandchildren, who are all named. There are fourteen of them. I wonder if perhaps he hoped one or more of them would follow in his footsteps, would become writers.

Some years ago there was a popular country song I liked very much by Lee Ann Womack. In it she sang of a hope for her daughters – a simple hope that their lives would be rich and full, filled with love and happiness. It was called "I Hope You Dance."

I have the same hopes of happiness for my grandchildren. I hope that what I have written here in these pages illustrates adequately how books and reading have made my life rich beyond measure. If I could write a song to my grandkids, it would be called "I Hope You Read."

Tim Bazzett
Reed City, Michigan
January 27-30, 2010

A Selected Bibliography

After some careful thought and no little soul-searching, I decided a bibliography was important for a book like this – a book which will probably appeal mostly to book nerds like me, if indeed it appeals to anyone at all. Because I'm the sort of reader who reads *all* of a book, including introductions and afterwords or epilogues, epigraphs, publication information, author notes, and – *especially* – a bibliography. So here it is.

*Aadland, Dan. *Sketches from the Ranch: A Montana Memoir*. Lincoln, NE: Bison Books, 2008

Aid, Matthew. *The Secret Sentry: The Untold History of the National Security Agency*. New York: Bloomsbury Press, 2009

*Alter, Stephen. *All the Way to Heaven: An American Boyhood in the Himalayas*. New York: Henry Holt & Company, 1998

*Alter, Stephen. *Elephant Maximus: A Portrait of the Indian Elephant*. New York: Harcourt, 2004

*Andersen, M.J. *Portable Prairie: Confessions of an Unsettled Midwesterner*. New York: St. Martin's Griffin, 2006

*Angell, Roger. *Let Me Finish*. New York: A Harvest Book (Harcourt, Inc.), 2007

*Anthony, Michael. *Mass Casualties: A Young Medic's True Story of Death, Deception, and Dishonor in Iraq*. Avon, MA: Adams Media, 2009

*Argula, Anne. *Krapp's Last Cassette*. New York: Ballantine Books, 2009

*Armstrong, Karen. *The Spiral Staircase: My Climb Out of Darkness*. New York: Anchor Books, 2005

Bamford, James. *Body of Secrets: Anatomy of the Ultra-Secret National Security Agency*. New York: Anchor Books, 2002

Bamford, James. *The Puzzle Palace: Inside the National Security Agency, America's Most Secret Intelligence Organization*. New York: Penguin Books, 1983

Bamford, James. *Shadow Factory: The NSA from 9/11 to the Eavesdropping on America*. New York: Anchor Books, 2009

Bannerman, Helen. *The Story of Little Black Sambo*. New York: Harper Collins, 1923

Barber, David L. *Stone Checkers and Wheelbarrow Rides*. Manistee, MI: David Barber, 2009

*Barker, Pat. *Regeneration*. New York: Penguin Books, 2008

Bazzett, Timothy James. *Love, War & Polio: The Life and Times of Young Bill Porteous*. Reed City, MI: Rathole Books, 2007

Bazzett, Timothy James. *Pinhead: A Love Story.* Reed City, MI: Rathole Books, 2006

Bazzett, Timothy James. *Reed City Boy.* Reed City, MI: Rathole Books, 2004

Bazzett, Timothy James. *Soldier Boy: At Play in the ASA.* Reed City, MI: Rathole Books, 2005

Beecher, John. *Hear the Wind Blow! Poems of Protest & Prophecy.* New York: International Publishers, 1968

*Beer, Ralph. *The Blind Corral.* New York: Penguin Books, 1987

*Beer, Ralph. *In These Hills.* Lincoln: University of Nebraska Press, 2003

*Bell, Margaret, and Mary Clearman Blew, Editor. *When Montana and I Were Young: A Frontier Childhood.* Lincoln, NE: Bison Books, 2003

*Blew, Mary Clearman. *All But the Waltz.* Norman, OK: University of Oklahoma Press, 2001

*Blew, Mary Clearman. *Balsamroot: A Memoir.* Norman, OK: University of Oklahoma Press, 2001

*Botsford, Gardner. *A Life of Privilege, Mostly.* New York: St. Martin's Press, 2003

Bourjaily, Vance. *Brill among the Ruins.* New York: Dial Press, 1970

*Bowers, Neal. *Cats Rule: The Bookstore Cat's Guide to the Care & Training of Humans.* Charleston, SC: BookSurge Publishing, 2009

*Bowers, Neal. *Loose Ends.* New York: Random House, 2001

*Bowers, Neal. *Out of the South.* Baton Rouge, LA: Louisiana State University Press, 2002

*Bowers, Neal. *Words for the Taking: The Hunt for a Plagiarist.* Carbondale, IL: Southern Illinois University Press, 2007

*Broyard, Anatole. *Kafka Was the Rage: A Greenwich Village Memoir.* New York: Vintage Books, 1997

Bryan, C.D.B. *Friendly Fire.* New York: Bantam Books, 1977

Burgess, Anthony. *A Clockwork Orange.* New York: Ballantine Books, 1971

*Busch, Benjamin. "Bearing Arms: The Serious Boy at War." *Harper's Magazine*, February 2009

*Busch, Benjamin. "Dying in the Snow" (unpublished essay, 2009)

*Busch, Benjamin. "Growth Rings," *Michigan Quarterly Review*, Fall 2009, pp. 556-576

*Busch, Benjamin. "Houses Without Cellars" (unpublished essay, 2009)

*Busch, Frederick. *A Dangerous Profession: A Book About the Writing Life.* New York: Broadway Books, 1999

Busch, Frederick. *Girls.* New York: Ballantine Books, 1998

*Busch, Frederick. *Rescue Missions: Stories.* New York: W.W. Norton & Co., 2007

*Calisher, Hortense. *Textures of Life*. New York: Little, Brown & Company, 1963

*Cavolina, Mary Jane Frances. *Still Catholic After All These Years*. New York: Main Street Books, 1993

*Child, Julia, and Alex Prud'Homme. *My Life in France*. New York: Anchor Books, 2009

*Christensen, Lars Saabye (translated by Don Bartlett). *Beatles*. London: Arcadia Books, 2009

*Clark, Robert. *Love Among the Ruins*. New York: Vintage Books, 2002

Clavell, James. *Shogun*. New York: Dell Books, 1976

*Cohen, Richard M. *Blindsided: Lifting a Life Above Illness: A Reluctant Memoir*. New York: Harper, 2005

*Coppola, Chris. *Coppola: A Pediatric Surgeon in Iraq*. Chicago: NTI Upstream, 2010

*Cornwell, John. *Seminary Boy: A Memoir*. New York: Image, 2007

Crumley, James. *One to Count Cadence*. New York: Random House, 1969

Crumley, James. *The Wrong Case*. New York: Bantam Books, 1978

*Crystal, Billy. *700 Sundays*. New York: Grand Central Publishing, 2006

*Daly, Maureen. *Seventeenth Summer*. New York: Simon Pulse, 1985

Dean, Maury. *Rock 'N' Roll Gold Rush*. New York: Algora Publishing, 2003

Dean, Maury. *The Rock Revolution*. Detroit, MI: Edmore Books, 1967

Dean, Maury. *This'll Be the Day: The Life and Legacy of Buddy Holly*. New York: Maxwell Hunter Publishing, 2009

*Dickerson, Debra. *An American Story*. New York: Pantheon, 2000

Dirda, Michael. *An Open Book: Coming of Age in the Heartland*. New York: W.W. Norton & Co., 2003

*Dyer, Joyce. *Goosetown: Reconstructing an Akron Neighborhood*. Akron, OH: The University of Akron Press, 2009

*Dyer, Joyce. *Gum-Dipped: A Daughter Remembers Rubber Town*. Akron, OH: The University of Akron Press, 2003

*Dyer, Joyce. *In a Tangled Wood: An Alzheimer's Journey*. Dallas, TX: Southern Methodist University Press, 1996

*Elliott, Geoffrey. *From Siberia with Love: A Story of Exile, Revolution and Cigarettes*. London: Methuen Publishing, Ltd., 2006

Elliott, Geoffrey, and Harold Shukman. *Secret Classrooms: An Untold Story of the Cold War*. London: St. Ermin's Press, 2003

*Ferris, Woodbridge N. *The Autobiography of W.N. Ferris*. Big Rapids, MI: Ferris State University, 1995

*Fick, Nathaniel. *One Bullet Away: The Making of a Marine Officer*. New York: Mariner Books, 2006

*Fleischman, Sid. *The Abracadabra Kid: A Writer's Life*. New York: Harper Trophy, 1998

*Gilmour, David. *The Film Club: A Memoir*. New York: Twelve, 2008

*Gilmour, David. *How Boys See Girls*. Toronto: Random House of Canada, 1992

Goldman, William. *Marathon Man*. New York: Dell, 1975

*Goolrick, Robert. *The End of the World as We Know It: Scenes from a Life*. Chapel Hill, NC: Algonquin Books, 2008

*Groneberg, Jennifer Graf. *Road Map to Holland: How I Found My Way Through My Son's First Two Years With Down Syndrome*. New York: NAL Trade, 2008

*Groneberg, Tom. *One Good Horse*. New York: Scribner, 2006

*Groneberg, Tom. *The Secret Life of Cowboys*. New York: Scribner, 2003

*Grumbach, Doris. *Coming Into the End Zone: A Memoir*. New York: W.W. Norton & Company, 1993

*Grumbach, Doris. *Extra Innings: A Memoir*. New York: W.W. Norton & Company, 1995

*Grumbach, Doris. *Life in a Day*. New York: Beacon Press, 1997

*Grumbach, Doris. *The Pleasure of their Company*. New York: Beacon Press, 2001

*Guth, Gilberta. *The Fighter Pilot's Wife*. Novato, CA: Call Sign Press, 2005

*Haefele, Fred. *Rebuilding the Indian: A Memoir*. Lincoln, NE: Bison Books, 2005

*Hall, Donald. *The Best Day the Worst Day: Life with Jane Kenyon*. New York: Mariner Books, 2006

*Hall, Donald. *Life Work*. Boston: Beacon Press, reprint, 2003

*Hall, Donald. *Unpacking the Boxes: A Memoir of a Life in Poetry*. New York: Houghton Mifflin Harcourt (HMH), 2008

*Hall, Donald. *White Apples and the Taste of Stone: Selected Poems 1946-2006*. New York: Mariner Books, 2007

*Hall, Meredith. *Without a Map: A Memoir*. New York: Beacon Press, 2008

*Hampl, Patricia. *The Florist's Daughter*. New York: Mariner Books, 2009

Hannibal, Edward. *Chocolate Days, Popsicle Weeks*. New York: Signet, 1970

*Harnack, Curtis. *The Attic: A Memoir*. Ames, IA: Iowa State University Press, 1993

*Harnack, Curtis. *Persian Lions, Persian Lambs: An American's Odyssey in Iran*. Bloomington, IN: Backinprint.com, 2007

*Harnack, Curtis. *Limits of the Land*. New York: Doubleday, 1979

*Harnack, Curtis. *Under My Wings Everything Prospers*. New York: Doubleday, 1977

*Harnack, Curtis. *We Have All Gone Away*. Ames, IA: Iowa State University Press, 1988

*Harp, Grady, with Stephen Freedman. *War Songs: Metaphors in Clay and Poetry from the Vietnam Experience*. Los Angeles: Lizard/Harp, Inc., 1995

Harrison, Jim. *Off to the Side: A Memoir*. New York: Atlantic Monthly Press, 2002

Harrison, Jim. *Wolf: A False Memoir*. New York: Simon & Schuster, 1971

Hassler, Jon. *Staggerford*. New York: Scribner, 1977

*Hennessey, Patrick. *The Junior Officers' Reading Club: Killing Time and Fighting Wars*. London: Allen Lane, 2009

Hynes, Samuel. *Flights of Passage: Recollections of a World War II Aviator*. New York: Penguin Books, 2003

Hynes, Samuel. *The Growing Seasons: An American Boyhood Before the War*. New York: Penguin Books, 2004

Irving, John. *The Water Method Man*. New York: Avon, 1973

Jager, Ronald. *Eighty Acres: Elegy for a Family Farm*. Boston: Beacon Press, 1992

*Johnson, Joyce. *Minor Characters: A Beat Memoir*. New York: Penguin Books, 1999

Jones, James. *From Here to Eternity*. New York: Signet, 1964

*Jordan, Pat. *A Nice Tuesday*. Lincoln, NE: Bison Books, 2005

*Judson, Theodore. *Tom Wedderburn's Life*. Baltimore, MD: AmErica House, 2002

Keillor, Garrison. *Good Poems, Selected and Introduced by G.K.* New York: Penguin Books, 2003

*Kelton, Elmer. *Sandhills Boy: The Winding Trail of a Texas Writer*. New York: Forge Books, 2007

Kittredge, William. *Hole in the Sky: A Memoir*. New York: Vintage Books, 1993

Klise, Thomas S. *The Last Western*. Niles, IL: Argus Communications, 1974

*L'Amour, Louis. *The Education of a Wandering Man*. New York: Bantam Books, 1990

*Lewycka, Marina. *A Short History of Tractors in Ukrainian*. New York: Penguin Books, 2006

*Lisicky, Paul. *Famous Builder*. Minneapolis: Graywolf Press, 2002

*Lodge, David. *Deaf Sentence*. New York: Penguin Books, 2008

*Lystra, Donald. *Season of Water and Ice*. Dekalb: IL: Switchgrass Books, Northern Illinois University Press, 2009

*Martin, Steve. *Born Standing Up: A Comic's Life*. New York: Scribner, 2007

*Martin, Steve. *Shopgirl*. New York: Hyperion, 2006

*Maxwell, William. *They Came Like Swallows*. New York: Vintage Books, 1997

*McCrum, Robert. *My Year Off: Recovering Life After a Stroke*. New York: Broadway Books, 1999

*McGillis, Roderick. *He Was Some Kind of a Man: Masculinities in the B Western*. Waterloo, Ontario: Wilfrid Laurier University Press, 2009

McGuane, Thomas. *The Bushwhacked Piano*. New York: Warner Books, 1971

McGuane, Thomas. *Ninety-two in the Shade*. New York: Bantam Books, 1974

*McGuane, Thomas. *Some Horses*. New York: Vintage Books, 2000

*Mendelsohn, Jane. *I Was Amelia Earhart*. New York: Vintage Books, 1997

Michaelis, David. *Schulz and Peanuts: A Biography*. New York: Harper Perennial, 2008

*Morton, Brian. *Starting Out in the Evening*. New York: Harvest Books, 2007

*Mullaney, Craig. *The Unforgiving Minute: A Soldier's Education*. New York: The Penguin Press, 2009

*Nelson, Sara. *So Many Books, So Little Time: A Year of Passionate Reading*. New York: Berkley Trade, 2004

*Nguyen, Bich Minh. *Stealing Buddha's Dinner: A Memoir*. New York: Viking, 2007

Nichols, John. *The Sterile Cuckoo*. New York: Avon, 1969

Obama, Barack. *Dreams from My Father: A Story of Race and Inheritance*. New York: Three Rivers Press, 2004

*O'Brien, James M. *Making a Priest in the 'Fifties: Memoir of a Nervous Seminarian*. Bloomington, IN: iUniverse, Inc., 2006

Oomen, Anne-Marie. *House of Fields: Memories of a Rural Education*. Detroit: Wayne State University Press, 2006

Oomen, Anne-Marie. *Pulling Down the Barn: Memories of a Rural Childhood*. Detroit: Wayne State University Press, 2004

*Owens, William A. *A Season of Weathering*. New York: Scribner, 1973

*Owens, William A. *This Stubborn Soil*. Guilford, CT: The Lyons Press, 1999

*Pancake, Ann. *Strange as This Weather Has Been*. Berkeley, CA: Shoemaker and Hoard, 2007

Pfarrer, Chuck. *Killing Che*. New York: Random House, 2008

Piercy, Marge. *Gone to Soldiers*. New York: Fawcett, 1988

*Piercy, Marge. *Sleeping with Cats*. New York: Harper Perennial, 2002

Piercy, Marge. *Small Changes*. New York: Fawcett Crest Books, 1973

*Ponicsan, Darryl. *An Unmarried Man*. New York: Dell Books, 1984

Ponicsan, Darryl. *Cinderella Liberty*. New York: Bantam Books, 1974

Ponicsan, Darryl. *The Last Detail*. New York: Signet, 1970

Ponicsan, Darryl. *Tom Mix Died for Your Sins*. New York: Delacorte Press, 1975

Price, Reynolds. *A Long and Happy Life*. New York: Avon, 1969

Price, Reynolds. *A Whole New Life: An Illness and a Healing*. New York: Plume, 1995

*Richards, Susan. *Chosen by a Horse*. New York: Mariner Books, 2007

Rico, Johnny. *Blood Makes the Grass Grow Green: A Year in the Desert with Team America*. New York: Presidio Press, 2007

*Robison, John Elder. *Look Me in the Eye: My Life with Asperger's*. New York: Three Rivers Press, 2008

*Rochlin, Fred. *Old Man in a Baseball Cap: A Memoir of World War II*. New York: Harper, 2000

*Roesch, Mattox. *Sometimes We're Always Real Same-Same*. Columbia, MO: Unbridled Books, 2009

*Roiphe, Anne. *Epilogue: A Memoir*. New York: Harper Collins, 2008

Roiphe, Anne. *Long Division*. New York: Simon and Schuster, 1972

Roiphe, Anne. *Up the Sandbox*. New York: Simon and Schuster, 1970

*Salinger, Margaret A. *Dream Catcher: A Memoir*. New York: Washington Square Press, 2001

*Savage, Thomas. *The Power of the Dog*. Boston: Back Bay Books, 2001

*Schrand, Brandon. *The Enders Hotel*. Lincoln, NE: Bison Books, 2008

*Schwartz, Lynn Sharon. *Ruined by Reading: A Life in Books*. New York: Beacon Press, 1997

Seton, Ernest Thompson. *The Biography of a Grizzly*. New York: Grosset & Dunlap, 1930

Seton, Ernest Thompson. *Wild Animals I Have Known*. New York: Bantam Books, 1946

*Shaffer, Mary Ann, and Annie Barrows. *The Guernsey Literary and Potato Peel Pie Society*. New York: Dial Press, 2009

*Sheehan, Marc J. *Greatest Hits*. Kalamazoo, MI: New Issues Poetry Press, Western Michigan University, 1998

Sheehan, Marc J. *Vengeful Hymns*. Ashland, OH: Ashland Poetry Press, Ashland University, 2009

Sholokhov, Mikhail. *And Quiet Flows the Don*. New York: Vintage Books, 1966

Shreve, Anita. *The Pilot's Wife*. New York: Back Bay Books, 1999

*Shreve, Susan Richards. *Warm Springs: Traces of a Childhood at FDR's Polio Haven*. New York: Mariner Books, 2008

*Small, David. *Stitches: A Memoir*. New York: W.W. Norton & Company, 2009

Smith, Annick. *Homestead*. Minneapolis: Milkweed Editions, 1995

*Smith, Bill, and Larry Ten Harmsel. *Fred Meijer: Stories of his Life*. Grand Rapids, MI: Wm. B. Eerdmans Publishing Company, 2009

*Smith, Janna Malamud. *My Father Is a Book: A Memoir of Bernard Malamud*. New York: Mariner Books, 2007

Smolens, John. *Cold*. New York: Three Rivers Press, 2003

Smolens, John. *Fire Point: A Novel of Suspense*. New York: Shaye Areheart Books, 2004.

*Smolens, John. *The Invisible World*. New York: Shaye Areheart Books, 2002

*Snider, Richard L. *Delta Six, Soldier Surgeon*. Frederick, MD: Heritage Books, Inc., 2003

Stanton, Doug. *In Harm's Way: The Sinking of the USS Indianapolis and the Extraordinary Story of its Survivors*. New York: Henry Holt, 2001

*Stanton, Doug. *Horse Soldiers: The Extraordinary Story of a Band of US Soldiers Who Rode to Victory in Afghanistan*. New York: Scribner, 2009

*Stevens, Patricia. "Leaving Fort Ord," *Chicago Tribune* (Section 14, Books/ Algren), Sunday, September 15, 1991, pp. 9 and 20-22.

*St. Pierre, Paul. *Breaking Smith's Quarter Horse*. Vancouver, BC: Douglas & McIntyre, 1984

St. Pierre, Paul. *Smith and Other Events*. Vancouver, BC: Douglas & McIntyre, 1985

Strong, Jonathan. *Tike and Five Stories*. New York: Avon, 1970

*Strout, Elizabeth. *Abide with Me*. New York: Random House, 2007

*Strout, Elizabeth. *Olive Kitteridge*. New York: Random House, 2008

Tauber, Peter. *The Sunshine Soldiers*. New York: Ballantine Books, 1972

Terhune, Albert Payson. *Treve*. New York: Grosset & Dunlap, 1924

Tram, Dang Thuy. *Last Night I Dreamed of Peace: The Diary of Dang Thuy Tram* (translated by Andrew X. Pham). New York: Three Rivers Press, 2007

*Turnipseed, Joel. *Baghdad Express: A Gulf War Memoir*. New York: Penguin Books, 2003

Updike, John. *My Father's Tears and Other Stories*. New York: Alfred A. Knopf, 2009

Updike, John. *Rabbit Redux*. New York: Fawcett-Crest, 1971

Updike, John. *Rabbit, Run*. New York: Fawcett-Crest, 1966

*Van Winkle, Clint. *Soft Spots: A Marine's Memoir of Combat and Post Traumatic Stress Disorder*. New York: St. Martin's Press, 2009

Vonnegut, Kurt. *Slaughterhouse-Five*. New York: Dell, 1976

*Watson, Larry. *Orchard*. New York: Random House, 2004

White, T.H. *The Once and Future King*. New York: Dell, 1960

*Williams, John. *Butcher's Crossing*. New York: NYRB Classics, 2007

*Williams, John. *Stoner*. New York: NYRB Classics, 2006

Woiwode, Larry. *Beyond the Bedroom Wall*. New York: Avon, 1976

*Woiwode, Larry. *A Step from Death: A Memoir*. Berkley, CA: Counterpoint, 2009

Woiwode, Larry. *What I'm Going to Do, I Think*. New York: Ballantine, 1973

*Woiwode, Larry. *What I Think I Did: A Season of Survival in Two Acts*. New York: Basic Books, 2001

*Wolff, Geoffrey. *The Duke of Deception: Memories of My Father*. New York: Vintage, 1990

Wolff, Tobias. *This Boy's Life*. New York: Grove Press, 2000

Woodhead, Leslie. *My Life as a Spy*. London: Pan Books, 2006

Wright, Evan. *Generation Kill: Devil Dogs, Iceman, Captain America, and the New Face of American War*. New York: Berkley Caliber, 2008

Acknowledgements

First of all I am once again indebted and most grateful to my son, Scott, who designs my books, and continues to coordinate so seamlessly all the various steps that go into printing and publishing a book. Without him there would be no RatholeBooks, and I probably wouldn't be an author.

I also thank my daughter, Susan, for writing such a personal and thoughtful introduction to *Booklover*, a task my mother fulfilled so well for my second book, *Soldier Boy*. Now there are three generations of writers involved.

And thanks yet again to my mother, Daisy, for her careful and meticulous proof-reading, a role she has filled free of charge for all five of my books now.

Thanks too go out to other family members, readers, and friends too numerous to mention for their continuing encouragement and support.

A special thanks to Ben Busch, who took time out of his harried and hectic schedules as writer, actor and filmmaker to provide the professional photos seen both on the covers and inside the book. (Thank you, Tracy and girls, for loaning Ben to me for those few hours.)

And to all the writers mentioned, quoted and cited in *Booklover* - and many who are not - I offer my sincere thanks for your example and for your art, and, in some cases (you know who you are), for your friendship.

Finally, as always, my love and gratitude to Treve: wife, friend and lover these many years, and now my companion in this wonderful country called Retirement. As the song so succinctly puts it, "My life would suck without you."

About the Author

A Michigan native, Tim Bazzett holds degrees from Ferris State, Central Michigan and Eastern Michigan Universities. He has been a guest on WTCM talk radio, Interlochen Public Radio and WCMU-TV. His essays and book reviews have appeared in several west Michigan papers, including *The Grand Rapids Press*, *Traverse City Record-Eagle* and *The Pioneer Group* newspapers. Bazzett lives with his wife in Reed City. *Booklover* is his fifth book.